MODERNISM AND THE THEATER OF CENSORSHIP

Modernism and the Theater of Censorship

ADAM PARKES

New York   Oxford
OXFORD UNIVERSITY PRESS
1996

Oxford University Press

Oxford New York
Athens Auckland Bangkok Bombay
Calcutta Cape Town Dar es Salaam Delhi
Florence Hong Kong Istanbul Karachi
Kuala Lampur Madras Madrid Melbourne
Mexico City Nairobi Paris Singapore
Taipei Tokyo Toronto

and associated companies in
Berlin Ibadan

Published by Oxford University Press, Inc.,
198 Madison Avenue, New York, New York 10016

Oxford is a registered trademark of Oxford University Press

Library of Congress Cataloging-in-Publication Data

Parkes, Adam, 1966–
Modernism and the theater of censorship / Adam Parkes.
p. cm.
Includes bibliographical references (p.   ) and index.
ISBN 0–19–509702–5 (acid-free paper)
1. English fiction—20th century—History and criticism.
2. Fiction—Censorship—Great Britain—History—20th century.
3. Trials (Obscenity)—Great Britain—History—20th century.
4. Modernism (Literature)—Great Britain. I. Title.
PR888.C4P37 1995
823'.91209—dc20   94–48939

1 2 3 4 5 6 7 8 9

Printed in the United States of America
on acid-free paper

For Kris

Preface

In Evelyn Waugh's second novel, *Vile Bodies,* Adam Fenwick-Symes confesses to a Customs officer that he has some books in his suitcase:

> One by one he took the books out and piled them on the counter. A copy of Dante's *Purgatorio* excited his especial disgust.
> "French, eh?" he said. "I guessed as much, and pretty dirty, too, I shouldn't wonder. Now just you wait while I look up these here *books*"—how he said it!—"in my list. Particularly against books the Home Secretary is. If we can't stamp out literature in the country, we can at least stop its being brought in from outside. That's what he said the other day in Parliament. I says 'Hear, hear. . . .' Hullo, hullo, what's this, may I ask?"

The Customs officer pounces on Adam's autobiography. A dictionary and some books on architecture and history are allowed through, but a book on economics "comes under Subversive Propaganda," and the *Purgatorio* (which "doesn't look right") is held "pending inquiries." As for the memoirs: "that's just downright dirt, and we burns that straight away, see."[1]

The first three decades of the twentieth century are remarkable for the regularity with which works of modern literature were censored. In Britain and in the United States, novels by D. H. Lawrence, James Joyce, and Radclyffe Hall were the objects of celebrated obscenity trials. It is clear in Adam Fenwick-Symes's encounter with British Customs that by 1930, when *Vile Bodies* was published, the censorship of modern literature had become commonplace, even a joke. Waugh's satire outlines several features of the culture of censorship within which Anglo-American modernism evolved in the early twentieth century. There is suspicion of writing about sex; such writing is associated with France and, as the official's confusion about Dante's origins indicates, with the Continent as a whole. As the Customs officer reveals, and as the trials testify, the British government, like its American counterpart, expended considerable energy in its efforts to keep obscenity out of the country. Moreover, the official's error about the *Purgatorio* ("French, eh?") suggests that censors are philistines, a common view implicitly tested out in this book. Waugh identifies this philistinism with the office of British Home Secretary, occupied from 1924 to 1929 by Sir William Joynson-Hicks, the infamous "Jix," who once boasted: "Since January 1, 1923, there have been 73 prosecutions in this country in connexion with the importation and sale of various indecencies."[2] Joynson-Hicks also featured in popular cartoons such as Beresford Egan's 1928 parody of the Radclyffe Hall case in *The Sink of Solitude* (Figure 1), and David Low's "Jix, the Self-Appointed Chucker-out," published in the *Evening Standard* on 26 February 1929 (Figure 2). In Low's cartoon, Joynson-Hicks, dressed in policeman's uniform, expels from "The Literary Hyde Park" a phalanx of controversial authors, each "accompanied by his literary inspiration": Shakespeare, George Bernard Shaw, H. G. Wells, Arnold Bennett, Aldous Huxley, James Joyce, D. H. Lawrence, and "a 'frank' woman novelist," probably Norah C. James, whose *Sleeveless Errand* was banned a few days after the cartoon appeared. Jix's operation is watched from the clouds by the guardian angels of nineteenth-century British fiction: Charles Dickens and Jane Austen.

In matters of censorship, Joynson-Hicks was a man of action, but he was also a man of words. In 1929 he put his case in a pamphlet (*Do We Need a Censor?*) published by T. S. Eliot's firm, Faber and Faber, in the *Criterion Miscellany*. Answering the charge that he had tried to "establish a dictatorship in the realm of literature and morals," Joynson-Hicks argued that public opinion demanded the enforcement of laws against indecency.[3] To the amusement of E. M. Forster, this piece was preceded in the Faber series by D. H. Lawrence's famous essay "Pornography and Obscenity," which attacked "the grey Guardian of British Morals" and his subservience to public opinion.[4] This odd slice of literary history complicates the picture drawn by Low's cartoon (which Lawrence is known to have seen). First, it disabuses us of the misleading notion that censors are necessarily unthinking philistines; whatever one thinks of Joynson-Hicks's arguments, he was able to mount a defense of his position, and Eliot's firm was prepared to publish it. Second, there was clearly a dialogue between censor and censored in the modernist period. The *Evening Standard* cartoon draws attention to this dialogue in its depiction of Lawrence, the only author not accompanied by a literary inspiration, arguing vociferously with the censorious figure at the gate.

This book shows that in the years between the outbreak of the Great War in 1914 and the appearance of *Vile Bodies* in 1930, the development of literary modernism was shaped in significant ways by an ongoing dialogue with a culture of censorship. Situating certain modern works in the context of censorship, I suggest that important aspects of modernism may be appreciated fully only when the extent of its engagement with this culture is recognized. It is my contention that, especially in their responses to contemporary sexual discourse, such novelists as Lawrence, Joyce, and Woolf anticipated and subverted the moral, political, and aesthetic premises on which the culture of censorship was operating. In the introduction I set the stage for my study of modernism with a

Figure 1. Beresford Egan, "St. Stephen," in *The Sink of Solitude* (London: Hermes Press, 1928).

(LEFT TO RIGHT)
A "FRANK" WOMAN NOVELIST, SHAKESPERE, SHAW, WELLS, BENNETT, ALDOUS HUXLEY,
D. H. LAWRENCE, JAMES JOYCE... EACH IS ACCOMPANIED BY HIS LITERARY INSPIRATION.
(AT BACK) DICKENS AND JANE AUSTEN

Figure 2. David Low, "Jix, The Self-Appointed Chucker-out," *Evening Standard*, 26 February 1929; reproduced by permission of Solo Syndication and Literary Agency/Evening Standard. Centre for the Study of Cartoons & Caricatures, University of Kent

discussion of the Oscar Wilde scandal of 1895, a case that illustrates many features of the literary landscape explored in the rest of the book. Focusing in the four chapters that follow on the trials of Lawrence's *The Rainbow* (1915), Joyce's *Ulysses* (1921), and Hall's *The Well of Loneliness* (1928), and on the suppression of Lawrence's last novel, *Lady Chatterley's Lover* (1928), I argue that modern authors often dramatized issues of sexuality, literary expression, and censorship that surfaced in contemporary responses to their work. In this way, modern novelists exploited what I call the "theater of censorship"—the social space in which texts and authors became subject to public censure and legal action—so that the culture of censorship itself was implicitly put on trial.

My concern with the ways in which acts of censorship shaped modernist texts written in the years 1914 to 1928 has dictated certain inclusions and exclusions. The later trials of *Ulysses* (1933, 1934) and *Lady Chatterley's Lover* (1959, 1960) fall outside these historical parameters; they are discussed when relevant, but they are not essential components of my narrative. Similarly, while the suppression of Norah James's *Sleeveless Errand* in 1929 created some public interest, this novel did not bear on the evolution of modernism in the way that *The Well of Loneliness* did, and so does not warrant the kind of attention I give to Hall's book. The same principles, however, demand substantial treatment of Virginia Woolf. Woolf attended the Hall trial in November 1928, and while none of her works attracted the attention of official censors, her art was informed by censorship in crucial ways. Most important, her fictional biography of Vita Sackville-West, *Orlando,* published at the time of the *Well of Loneliness* scandal, dramatizes sexual issues that preoccupied Hall's censors. Reading *Orlando* in the light of Woolf's response to the Hall controversy, I explore these connections in the final chapter.

Attacks on modernism have not ceased, though the accusations of more recent years are somewhat different from those heard in the modernist period itself. Condemned by their contemporaries in courts of law, certain modernists are now considered by some critics as guilty of reinscribing reactionary notions of gender and sexuality. No doubt such views are sharpened by previous claims that Joyce and Lawrence, for example, expressed sexual themes more freely than an earlier censorious culture tolerated. Lingering misgivings about the influence these writers have in contemporary culture highlight the way in which our reading of modernism continues to be conditioned by the theater of censorship. It is part of my defense of modernism that the relation of modern aesthetics to public discourse is more complicated than some antimodernist readers allow. In this book I argue that rather than testifying to the presence of unacceptable moral and political positions, the objections of latter-day as well as earlier readers often register the strange, disorienting effects of artistic innovation. We have not left the theater of censorship; on the contrary, it is still very much with us.

While writing this book I have benefited from the advice and encouragement of many friends and teachers, who have guided me in my attempts to piece together the various components of my narrative and have helped me to appreciate its implications for literary modernism in particular and modern culture in general. From beginning to end I have had the very great fortune of being able to turn to James Longenbach, who kept me on course when I began to stray and enabled me to follow paths I had not known were there. Early and later versions of each chapter profited immensely from the invaluable commentaries of Bette London, Daniel Albright, and Stewart Weaver. I am grateful to Philip Landon, Ralph Locke, and John Paul Riquelme for comments on different aspects of the work, and to Maria DiBattista for helping me to identify the "'frank' woman novelist" in the Low cartoon. The role of general reader has been played admirably by my parents, David and Margaret Parkes, whose interest in the project as it evolved constantly reminded me of the significant place such readers occupy in the audience to which the book is addressed. I would also like to thank my editor at Oxford University Press, Elizabeth Maguire, and her assistant, Elda Rotor, for steering me through the final stages.

A Charlotte W. Newcombe Doctoral Dissertation Fellowship in 1992–1993 enabled me to make considerable headway in this project; research time at the University of Georgia allowed me to complete it. The unflagging efforts of the interlibrary loan staff at the University of Rochester, the University of Georgia, and Trinity University, San Antonio, have helped me to seek out countless reviews and essays from obscure sources. I am indebted to my research assistants, Lisa Boyd and Lisa Kozlowski, who caught numerous errors before it was too late.

Above all, I want to record my largest debt, to my wife, Kristin Boudreau, without whom nothing would have been possible.

Athens, Ga.   A.P.
January 1995

Acknowledgments

Material from Radclyffe Hall's correspondence reprinted by permission of Harry Ransom Humanies Research Center, The University of Texas at Austin, and The Estate of Radclyffe Hall. All rights reserved.

The Well of Loneliness by Radclyffe Hall reprinted by permission of The Estate of Radclyffe Hall. All rights reserved.

Virginia Woolf, Modern novels (Joyce), holograph notebook, n.d., reprinted by permission of The Society of Authors as the literary representatives of the Estate of Virginia Woolf and Henry W. and Albert A. Berg Collection, The New York Public Library, and Astor, Lenox and Tilden Foundations.

E. M. Forster's letter of 31 August 1928 to Arnold Bennett reprinted by permission of The Provost and Scholars of King's College, Cambridge, and Henry W. and Albert A. Berg Collection, The New York Public Library, and Astor, Lenox and Tilden Foundations.

Quotes from *Personae* by Ezra Pound are used by permission of New Directions Publishing Corp. Copyright © 1926, 1935, 1971 by Ezra Pound.

"Lesbianism, History, and Censorship: *The Well of Loneliness* and the 'Suppressed Randiness' of Virginia Woolf's *Orlando*" first published by *Twentieth Century Literature.*

Radclyffe Hall's letter of 14 November 1928 to Gerard Hopkins reprinted by permission of The Estate of Radclyffe Hall and Henry W. and Albert A. Berg Collection, The New York Public Library, and Astor, Lenox and Tilden Foundations.

Contents

Introduction: The Trials of Modernism

At a brief trial in November 1915, the British authorities invoked the 1857 Obscene Publications Act to suppress D. H. Lawrence's novel *The Rainbow,* and in so doing made it virtually impossible for Lawrence to publish fiction in Britain until the Great War ended in 1918.[1] Six years later, a New York court fined the editors of the *Little Review,* Margaret Anderson and Jane Heap, for printing "Nausicaa," the thirteenth episode of James Joyce's *Ulysses.* This novel remained banned in the United States until 1933. It was also banned in Britain, where the censorship of "obscene" modern literature reached its well-known climax in 1928 with the trial of Radclyffe Hall's polemical lesbian novel, *The Well of Loneliness,* and the suppression of Lawrence's last novel, *Lady Chatterley's Lover.*

These events were not the only instances of censorship in the early twentieth century. Censorship was common in Britain during the Great War, when the Defence of the Realm Act (1914) was used to suppress anything that deviated from the views presented in wartime propaganda. But censorship plagued modern authors before and after the war as well. The entire careers of Lawrence and Joyce evolved in the context of censorship. From Joyce's early skirmishes over the publication of *Dubliners* (1914) to the appearance of *Ulysses* (1922), and from the efforts of the British libraries to prevent circulation of Lawrence's *Sons and Lovers* (1913) to the seizure of his paintings (1929), both writers were so beset by the pressure of censorship that they could rarely ignore it. The same was true for some authors whose works were not subject to legal proceedings. E. M. Forster never published his homosexual romance, *Maurice* (1914), because he was certain it would be suppressed; like a number of Forster's stories dealing with homosexual love, *Maurice* only appeared posthumously.[2]

Why was the reception of modernism so often marked by censorship? What was the perceived connection between modernism and obscenity that caused the trials to take place? The topic most clearly at stake in modern obscenity trials was the representation of sex and sexuality in published fiction. Explicitly or implicitly, judges and lawyers often invoked the so-called Hicklin rule, established in Britain in 1868, which defined as obscene works tending "to deprave and corrupt those whose minds are open to such immoral influences and into whose hands a publication of this sort may fall"; it was usually sexual immorality that the courts had in mind. In this sense, the decisions of U.S. and British courts (in 1959 and 1960, respectively) to allow the publication of *Lady Chatterley's Lover* would seem to signify a shift from repression to freedom. Such a view of the *Lady Chatterley* trials is quite commonplace, and it has been perpetuated by many people directly involved in the trials. During the well-documented 1960 trial at the Old Bailey in London, dozens of witnesses testified to the literary merit of Lawrence's novel and urged the court to reject the puritanical morality that had produced the philistine verdicts of the past, so that a work of art could be recognized for what it was.[3] Recent history appeared to offer several examples of such philistinism. When Sir Chartres Biron banned *The Well of Loneliness* in 1928, for instance, he pronounced literary merit irrelevant to the question of obscenity. "A book may be a fine piece of literature and yet obscene," he declared. "Art and obscenity are not dissociated at all."[4] And in 1929 Judge Frederick Mead made an identical ruling when suppressing thirteen of Lawrence's paintings, which had been on show at the Warren Gallery in London. "It is utterly immaterial whether they are works of art," said Mead. "That is a collateral question which I have not to decide. The most splendidly painted picture in the universe might be obscene."[5] As David Saunders has noted, the British Obscene Publications Act of 1959 allowed the matter of artistic merit to enter legal calculations for the first time, obliging the courts to consider allegations of indecency in relation to "the work as a whole."[6] Philistinism, it seemed, had been put to rest.

Following this line of reasoning, several observers have remarked on the ironic frequency with which pre-1959 censorship created unprecedented publicity for both offender and offense, publicity that reversed the results censorship was supposed to produce. The trial of *The Well of Loneliness,* for example, has often been described as generating a previously nonexistent curiosity about lesbianism that virtually installed the novel as a lesbian bible for the next forty years.[7] In our haste to congratulate ourselves on our progress, however, we have sometimes been too quick to interpret the apparent irony of such publicity as confirming the inevitable failure of attempts to prevent the free expression of human sexuality, and as therefore vindicating our own, implicitly enlightened, perspective on earlier events. In so doing, we have neglected to ask how accurately such a view represents the early-twentieth-century trials of modernism, or how useful it is for constructing a narrative about those events.

It is undeniable that the trials of *The Rainbow, Ulysses,* and *The Well of Loneliness* created wide publicity both for the texts themselves and for the various forms of pornography they were taken to represent. Yet it is by no means clear that this effect was counterproductive in the ways that opponents of censorship have sometimes assumed. It is also unclear whether, in their apparent haste to stamp out whatever they considered immoral, the judges and lawyers who participated in the trials were utterly oblivious to artistic considerations. Indeed, a glance at the Hall trial suggests quite the opposite. When Judge Biron pronounced literary merit irrelevant to a ruling on obscenity, he was responding to an attempt by the defense to use its array of learned witnesses to argue that the merits of Hall's novel eliminated the possibility of obscenity. With this end in view, the counsel for the defense began his cross-examination of the first witness, Desmond MacCarthy, by asking him whether he considered *The Well* obscene. It was at this juncture that Biron intervened to declare that only he could decide this question. In fact, the Hall trial, like other obscenity trials, betrayed a marked concern for issues of literary interpretation, which bore, quite inevitably, on matters of legal reasoning. Moreover, this concern was inextricable from the matter explicitly at hand: sexual indecency. Paradoxically, Judge Biron affirmed the relevance of aesthetic issues in the very act of denying it.

The intersection of aesthetic questions with the moral and political concerns informing legal discourse was a salient feature of censorship trials in the early twentieth century. In prosecuting *The Rainbow, Ulysses,* and *The Well,* the authorities produced them as public spectacles, visible sites for staging debates about morality, politics, art, and the relations among those categories. Igniting controversy about the representation of sex and sexuality—controversy that raged in the popular press as well as in courts of law—these texts ultimately served as pretexts for wider arguments about the moral, social responsibilities of the artist and the interpretative prerogatives of the critic. The scandalized reception of these works inevitably raised fundamental questions about the relation between the social and the aesthetic components of literary interpretation: In what way is literary meaning separable from matters of form and style? How is an aesthetic response to literature different from a moral or a political response?

These questions have been taken up by Dominick LaCapra and Hans Robert Jauss in their readings of the 1857 trial of *Madame Bovary,* an important precursor in the history of censorship and Anglo-American modernism. LaCapra argues that Flaubert's novel was prosecuted (unsuccessfully, it turned out) not only because the behavior of its heroine transgressed the church and family morality of nineteenth-century France, but also because the new formal structures of free indirect discourse and impersonal narration denied the possibility of a stable narrative position from which the heroine could be judged. In these ways, LaCapra urges, *Madame Bovary* was "ideologically criminal," for it questioned the moral and structural premises on which the trial was founded. In LaCapra's account, the threat posed by *Madame Bovary* to legally sanctioned moral and political positions was exaggerated by its place in the history of the French novel. Poised on the threshold between conventional realism and modernism, this work could not be dismissed as an experimental aberration; unlike Flaubert's last work, *Bouvard et Pécuchet* (1881), *Madame Bovary* easily insinuated itself into a hitherto familiar genre.[8] Jauss puts a similar emphasis on the ways in which Flaubert's aesthetic innovations provoked its early readers. Comparing *Madame Bovary* with another novel published in

1857, Ernest Feydeau's best-seller *Fanny*, Jauss contends that the two works elicited different responses because they employed different formal structures. Both works rejected romanticism, and they shared a similar content, but whereas *Madame Bovary* conveyed that content by the unfamiliar method of impersonal narration, *Fanny* offered it "in the inviting tone of a confessional novel." That *Madame Bovary* went to trial, Jauss suggests, shows how a "new aesthetic form can have . . . the greatest conceivable impact on a moral question."[9]

There are further reasons for considering the *Madame Bovary* trial in relation to modern Anglo-American censorship. First, there is evidence that the prosecution of Flaubert's novel, and the suppression of Baudelaire's *Les Fleurs du Mal* later the same year, galvanized the British Parliament into passing Lord Campbell's Obscene Publications Act (1857), under which Lawrence, Hall, and others were censored in the twentieth century.[10] In fact, Anglo-American culture frequently associated obscene experimental art with French decadence and sexual immorality. This association was strongly reinforced in the early nineteenth century, when the American authorities banned the importation of obscene pictures; like the British authorities, who followed suit in 1853, Americans regarded Paris as the major source of artistic contamination. Recounting the woes of Henry Vizetelly, Edward de Grazia suggests that the English taboo on literary discussions of sex was "an inflamed aspect of English Francophobia." Vizetelly was tried in 1888 for publishing Zola's novels, one of which, *La Terre,* was condemned in court by the Solicitor General, Sir Edward Clarke, as "a novel full of bestial obscenity, without a spark of literary genius or the expression of an elevated thought."[11] Persisting in publishing not only Zola but also such works as *Madame Bovary,* Vizetelly was tried again in 1889, and this time went to prison. French literature continued to be regarded as the yardstick, if not the source, of literary pollution in the early twentieth century; Zola in particular was often cited as its most pernicious exemplar. As we shall see, attention was diverted from France by the Great War, during which Germany was naturally seen as the fount of Continental depravity. When the war ended, however, France resumed its place in Anglo-American eyes as the primary site of cultural degeneracy.

Moreover, the perceived connection between France, obscenity, and the avant-garde was crucial in determining public responses to the most scandalous figure of late-nineteenth-century British literature: Oscar Wilde. Like Flaubert, Wilde stood on the threshold between nineteenth-century literary conventions and modernism; he was experimental, yet his innovations were intelligible only in relation to traditional notions of form and style. The most celebrated aspect of the Wilde controversy was his imprisonment in 1895 for committing seven acts of "gross indecency" with other men, but this most spectacular of literary trials also illustrates many features of the obscenity trials that took place in the first decades of the next century. Since the sexual aspect of the Wilde scandal was deeply intertwined with his aesthetic practice, his trials helped to establish the terms within which transgressive works of literature were read in Britain, and in the United States, in the early twentieth century. The spectacular nature of Wilde's trials is especially significant here. Writing at the moment when the nineteenth century was yielding to the modern era, and when sexuality (or, to be more specific, homosexuality) was first being defined as a mode of "being," Wilde occupied a highly visible crossroads in art and in sexual politics. Wilde is still read in these terms: whether through persistence or reincarnation, as a gay writer Wilde has become a central figure in the rereading of transgressive literature currently being undertaken in gay and lesbian studies. Thus, in the context of the late twentieth as in the context of the late nineteenth century, Wilde is a useful test case for the relation of avant-garde art to radical sexual politics, illustrating quite graphically the very tangible consequences that attend on certain aesthetic procedures in particular places at particular times. It is with Wilde that the history of Anglo-American modernism and censorship comes into being.

The best place to start tracing that history is not 1895 but 1892, when Wilde became a focal point for the influence of French culture, and the aura of sexual deviance with which it was endowed by the Victorian imagination, on British literature. Wilde was already associated in many minds with the Decadent circles of fin-de-siècle Paris, but in 1892 his French connection became abundantly clear when the British authorities invoked the ban on dramatic representations of biblical characters and refused to license his French play, *Salome*. In the late nineteenth century the Salome theme had fascinated a number of French artists, including Baudelaire, Mallarmé, Flaubert, and Gustave Moreau. Moreau's paintings *Salome Dancing Before Herod* and *The Apparition* (both 1876) inspired Huysmans in *A Rebours* (1884), a novel that Wilde and other Decadents revered.[12] Arguing that the Frenchness of *Salome*, particularly the fact that it was written in French, should have protected it from censorship, one critic has recently contended that the examiner of plays, Edward Pigott, censored Wilde's play merely to demonstrate his usefulness to Parliament at a time when his office was under close scrutiny.[13] But Pigott's private correspondence suggests that the pornographic and blasphemous aspects of *Salome* were inseparable from its French elements. Emphasizing the incestuous passions of Herod for his stepdaughter, and those of Herodias for John the Baptist, Pigott concluded: "The piece is written in French—half Biblical, half pornographic—by Oscar Wilde himself. Imagine the average British public's reception of it."[14] Pigott seems to have been particularly apprehensive, if also slightly amused, at the prospect of the reception that such a play was likely to encounter in Britain. Wilde pointed out that other biblical dramas were prohibited, including Racine's dramatic poem *Athalie*, Saint-Saëns's opera *Samson et Dalila*, and Massenet's *Hérodiade*, which premiered in 1881. But it may have been no accident that, like Wilde's play, these works were French as well.[15]

The Maud Allan trial of 1918 underlined the significance of *Salome* as a defining point in the intersection of censorious public discourses with the aesthetic practices of Continental Decadence and Anglo-American modernism. Taking place in the last year of the Great War, this trial was not explicitly concerned with Decadence but with sexual immorality and deviance. A brief synopsis of the trial, however, will make the connection between them manifestly clear. The case came about when Allan, an actress in a production of Wilde's *Salome,* issued a libel suit against a member of Parliament, Noel Pemberton Billing, who had attacked the play in his magazine, *Vigilante.* "[T]his exhibition as given by these people directly ministers to sexual perverts, Sodomites, and Lesbians," Pemberton Billing exclaimed in court. "They have chosen, at a moment when our very national existence is at stake, to select the most depraved of the many depraved works of a man who suffered the extreme penalty at the hands of the law for the practising of this unnatural vice, or one form of it."[16] A trial in the first year of the war had already revived memories of Wilde as a symbol for the diseased, degenerate art that many Britons believed the war was sent to cleanse: in an ultimately unresolved court case of 1914, Wilde's executor, Robert Ross, had sued Wilde's lover, Lord Alfred Douglas, for libel. As in the Maud Allan trial, the central issue was the crime for which Wilde went to prison. Samuel Hynes notes that in debating not only Douglas's relationship with Wilde but also Ross's deviance, the 1914 trial marked "the beginning of a wartime renewal of feelings that had surrounded the Wilde case in the Nineties—hatred and fear of sexual deviance, and a felt need to suppress the art and ideas about art that were associated with it." As Hynes grimly observes: "Henceforth the higher morality of war would be invoked as justification for the persecution of homosexuality and the censorship of art."[17] When Pemberton Billing condemned *Salome* in 1918, he invoked the higher morality of war quite explicitly, indicating that homosexuality was seen as a sign not only of Decadence but also of wartime dissent and subversion. The Maud Allan trial suggested that the censorious and homophobic feelings exposed by the Ross–Douglas trial continued unabated throughout the war, a perpetual reminder that history had transformed Wilde into something both more and less than the actual person Oscar Wilde: a cipher for homosexuality and, at the same time, for deviant, Decadent art.[18]

That process of transformation occurred most spectacularly in Wilde's own trials in 1895. Strictly speaking, those hearings were not censorship trials: Wilde was condemned for "acts of gross indecency" under section 11 of the 1885 Criminal Law Amendment Act (known as the Labouchere Amendment). Literary matters, however, were never far removed from the central concern of this case; in court and in newspaper reports of the trials, the sexual was repeatedly linked to the textual. A text was the occasion of the first trial. On 28 February 1895, Wilde had arrived at the Albemarle club in London to find a card left, ten days earlier, by the Marquess of Queensberry, the father of Lord Alfred Douglas. On the back of the card Queensberry had written: "For Oscar Wilde Posing as a Somdomite [sic]."[19] Wilde sued Queensberry for criminal libel, and the trial began at the Old Bailey on 3 April, with Sir Edward Clarke (former tormentor of Henry Vizetelly) acting as prosecutor. Since the defense, led by Edward Carson, had to prove not that Wilde had committed specific acts but that he had "pos[ed] as a sodomite," Wilde's writings were as relevant as his actions; as a result, courtroom proceedings often focused on literary affairs, which at one point acquired a French flavor. Clarke and Carson spent considerable time addressing the aesthetic tendencies adduced, as proof of Queensberry's charge, in the plea of justification. Of particular concern were Wilde's "immoral and obscene" novel, *The Picture of Dorian Gray* (1890), and a magazine entitled *The Chameleon*, in which Wilde had published "certain immoral maxims . . . under the title of 'Phrases and Philosophies for the Use of the Young.'" Queensberry's plea alleged that *Dorian Gray* "was designed and intended" by Wilde, and "understood" by its readers, "to describe the relations intimacies and passions of certain persons of sodomitical and unnatural habits tastes and practices."[20] It may seem odd that a novel in which the only clearly specified romantic relationship, that between Dorian and Sibyl Vane, is heterosexual should be characterized in this way, but this reading of *Dorian Gray* was not unusual. When the novel first appeared in *Lippincott's Monthly Magazine* in July 1890, reviews linked it with the Cleveland Street affair of 1889–1890, which had led to the first widely publicized prosecution under the Labouchere Amendment.[21] In a letter published in the *Scots Observer* on 12 July 1890, Wilde replied to one such attack on his book by defending the "atmosphere of moral corruption" that surrounds Dorian as deliberately "vague and indeterminate" (*LOW*, p. 266). Yet it was precisely this vagueness and indeterminacy that troubled Wilde's contemporaries. *Dorian Gray* did not divulge specific sexual acts, but it posed as if it did. Obscurity implied obscenity, a suspicion revived by the appearance in November 1895 of Thomas Hardy's novel *Jude the Obscure*, or "Jude the Obscene," as it was called in the *Pall Mall Gazette*.[22] In the case of Wilde's novel, the obscenity was faintly French as well, as Edward Carson intimated by cross-examining him on Huysmans's *A Rebours*, the Decadent novel read enthusiastically by Dorian Gray.[23]

Similar anxieties about atmosphere informed Wilde's involvement with *The Chameleon*, which was intended, as Queensberry's plea claimed, "for circulation amongst students of the University of Oxford" (*TOW*, p. 327). Queensberry's attorney, Carson, was less concerned with Wilde's actual contribution to the magazine than with "The Priest and the Acolyte," a "blasphemous" story published anonymously but probably written by the editor, J. F. Bloxam, and two poems by Lord Alfred Douglas, "In Praise of Shame" and "Two Loves." The problem with Wilde, Queensberry's plea maintained, was that, as "a man of letters and a dramatist of prominence and notoriety," he "exercised considerable influence over young men" (*TOW*, p. 327). Carson implied that this influence had contributed to an atmosphere in which it was possible for another man (in this case an undergraduate at Exeter College, Oxford) to write "The Priest and the Acolyte." No matter that Wilde, as Sir Edward Clarke pointed out, objected to the story so strongly that he had asked Bloxam to withdraw the copies and suppress the magazine; he was guilty by association. By 5 April, when Clarke withdrew from the prosecution, sufficient evidence of this kind had accumulated to justify Queensberry's words, "For Oscar Wilde Posing as a Somdomite." Unfortunately for Wilde, there was now enough evidence to find him guilty of gross indecency as well. It took two further trials to convict him: a third trial (20–25 May) became necessary when the jury at the second hearing (26 April–1 May) failed to agree on a verdict. But the third trial ended at the Old Bailey with Wilde's conviction and imprisonment for two years with hard labor.

Literary matters continued to feature in the second and third trials, but their status underwent some significant changes. Seeing at the end of the first trial that Wilde was in danger, Sir Edward Clarke had asked that the verdict of "Not Guilty" be limited to reference "to that part of the particulars connected with the publication of *The Picture of Dorian Gray* and the publication of *The Chameleon*" (*TOW*, p. 147). In effect, Clarke had been trying to use an admission of literary obscenity to protect Wilde from the more damaging allegations made in Queensberry's plea of justification. But when, following the refusal of this request, Queensberry was acquitted and Wilde arrested, Clarke's tactics altered. At the second trial it was in Wilde's interest to play down literary affairs because they had been used in the first trial to show that he displayed certain tendencies. In his opening speech for the defense, Clarke argued that Carson should not have cross-examined Wilde at the previous hearing on works written by others. Clarke then tried to divorce the present case from the disturbing atmosphere of literature by telling the jury: "The question of the literature is, therefore, an entirely different question from that which you have now to determine" (*TOW*, pp. 196–97).[24] But as soon as Charles Gill began to cross-examine Wilde it was clear that this prosecutor knew, as Carson had known, that the question of literature could be turned to his advantage. Gill's first question was about *The Chameleon* and, pointing out that the magazine had printed the second poem immediately before "The Priest and the Acolyte," he read out passages from Douglas's contributions, "In Praise of Shame" and "Two Loves." Unsurprisingly (though ironically, considering Clarke's attempts to defuse the literary evidence), it was here that Wilde shone. Called on to explain Douglas's phrase, "the Love that dare not speak its name," Wilde famously described it as "beautiful," "fine," and "the noblest form of affection." It was both deeply "spiritual" and "intellectual"; it was "such a great affection of an elder for a younger man as there was between David and Jonathan, such as Plato made the very basis of his philosophy, and such as you find in the sonnets of Michelangelo and Shakespeare" (*TOW*, p. 201). Enthusiastic applause greeted this speech, which (it is sometimes speculated) may have contributed to the jury's inability to agree on a verdict. It may also explain why the prosecution gave less prominence to literary questions in the third trial; discussion of Wilde's writings now tended to be limited to the letters for which he had been blackmailed by Alfred Wood, one of the young men with whom he was found guilty of committing acts of gross indecency.

It was not just in court that Wilde's crime was related to his status as a man of letters; journalistic accounts of the trials insistently linked his sexual offenses to Decadence and literary obscenity. On 6 April (the day after his arrest), the *National Observer* denounced Wilde as an "obscene impostor," and praised Queensberry "for destroying the High Priest of the Decadents" (*TOW*, p. 156). The *Daily Telegraph* interpreted the verdict of the third trial as a stern rebuke to "some of the artistic tendencies of the time": "The grave of contemptuous oblivion may rest on his foolish ostentation, his empty paradoxes, his insufferable posturing, his incurable vanity." Nevertheless, a few words of warning were thought advisable:

> when we remember that he enjoyed a certain popularity among some sections of society and, above all, when we reflect that what was smiled at as insolent braggadocio was the cover, for, or at all events ended in, flagrant immorality, it is well, perhaps that the lesson of his life should not be passed over without some insistence on the terrible warning of his fate. Young men at the universities, silly women who lend an ear to any chatter which is petulant and vivacious, novelists who have sought to imitate the style of paradox and unreality, poets who have lisped the language of nerveless and effeminate libertinage—these are the persons who should ponder with themselves the doctrine and the career of the man who has now to undergo the righteous sentence of the law. (*TOW*, pp. 17–18)

With Wilde behind bars, young men at the universities and silly women were deemed a little safer. As Ed Cohen has shown, one of the most startling aspects of such accounts is that they never specify the sexual offenses for which Wilde was tried and convicted:[25] complaints about empty paradoxes, or, as the *Evening News* put it, "intellectual debauchery" (*TOW*, p. 18), operated as the cover for such flagrant immorality. In its references to *The Picture of Dorian Gray,* Queensberry's plea of justification made it clear that the Wilde scandal concerned not only specific sexual practices but also obscene aesthetic tendencies. At the end of the first trial, Sir Edward Clarke had tried to use charges of literary obscenity to protect Wilde; press accounts sheltered their readers by using references to literary obscenity to censor the unspeakable crimes for which Wilde was convicted.

Indirectly, Wilde's conviction brought about the censorship of his plays as well. On 6 April *An Ideal Husband* was withdrawn from the Haymarket Theatre in London, and Wilde's name was deleted from advertisements for *The Importance of Being Earnest,* which was running at St. James's Theatre. The public uproar in London after the collapse of the second trial forced *Earnest* to close down altogether on 8 May. Thus, the life span of Wilde's most famous play was virtually identical to that of the scandal: the play had opened on 14 February, just four days before Queensberry left his card at the Albemarle. In a sense it was fitting that the fate of this particular play should have been linked so closely to that of its author, since Wilde himself broke down the barriers between art and life. Wilde told André Gide that he had put his talent into his works but had saved his genius for his life, implying that we should judge his life as his supreme artistic achievement, his greatest theatrical performance.[26] To treat Wilde's life as a drama is to recognize an element of censorship in his 1895 conviction; his trials were, in this additional sense, obscenity trials. If art and life were now indistinguishable, as Wilde suggested they were, it is not easy to tell how far his trials expressed exclusively moral outrage, and how far that outrage articulated aesthetic objections. Indeed, the decorum that Wilde violated is best understood not only in moral and social but also in aesthetic terms. The very notion of decorum implies a certain aesthetic sensibility, and part of the problem with Wilde was that his innovations offended it. As contemporary laments about his "foolish ostentation" and "insufferable posturing" suggest, Wilde's trials dramatized this tension between the social and the aesthetic realms. Such responses underlined another point as well: Wilde exemplified how one kind of trial (an artistic experiment, for instance) may intersect with, and even provoke, a trial in what might have been considered an entirely different realm of human affairs (the realm, in this case, of criminal law). While Wilde's trials expressed a tension between the social and the aesthetic, that tension was essential to Wilde's art. By treating experiments in art and experiments in social life as synonymous, Wilde fostered the conditions that made his trials possible. It was a short step from living life as a drama to having to defend that life in a court of law, and in this sense a jury was just one of the many audiences Wilde sought out during his lifelong performance before British society. By a cruel irony, Wilde was, as the *National Observer* observed, an obscene impostor.[27]

Perhaps the most potentially scandalous or obscene implications of Wilde's experimentalism were those resulting from the relationship he sought with his audience, that is, with the upper- and upper-middle-class society that condemned him in court. As Regenia Gagnier has argued, *The Importance of Being Earnest* may have appealed particularly strongly to London audiences in 1895 because the play's characters looked and behaved just like themselves. Wilde provided upper- and upper-middle-class spectators with mirrors that allowed them to gaze upon, and consume, their own immaculately attired image.[28] As W. H. Auden noted, though, Wilde's trials illuminated *Earnest* in ways that perhaps escaped its first audiences. After the revelations of the trials, Auden lamented, it was difficult to ignore Wilde's homosexuality when reading the play: now one always knows what Algernon means when he says he is going Bunburying.[29] Auden's disappointed tone registered his regret at what he considered a loss of artistic suggestiveness resulting from the revelations of Wilde's biography. While it is quite plausible to interpret Bunburying differently, Auden's reading has irresistible implications for Wilde's audience.[30] If spectators recognized themselves on stage, then Bunburying must have seemed quite a normal form of conduct. In this sense, what Wilde says to Douglas in *De Profundis* might apply to the audience of *Earnest,* or to any of Wilde's audiences: "You see that I have to write your life to you, and you have to realise it."[31] The last phrase is crucial: to realize the life an author has written for one is to enact and embody it, and also to become conscious of it, to become self-conscious. To give an audience characters who closely resemble themselves is not only to disturb the boundaries between art and life, between stage and auditorium; it is also to push to the limits their unconsciousness of the ways in which their mirror images conform to, or transgress, accepted codes of behavior. If Bunburying meant what Auden thought, to what extent did Wilde's contemporaries realize it? What Wilde called the vague and indeterminate atmosphere of moral corruption in *The Picture of Dorian Gray* was taken in court as evidence of immoral tendencies associated with certain unspecifiable acts; the public uproar that forced the closure of *Earnest,* and the even hastier withdrawal of the now ironically titled *An Ideal Husband,* suggested that these works were equally capable of inducing such uneasiness. By generating a relationship of theatrical exchange, Wilde seems to accuse his audience of complicity in the very crime for which he was convicted. Read in this way, *Earnest* undercuts the authority of Wilde's judges, charging them, in effect, with hypocrisy.

Wilde's life and work lend themselves to such interpretation because it was at the end of the nineteenth century that homosexuality, and the entire concept of sexuality as the index of one's being, was first defined in scientific terms. In Wilde this conceptual transition seems directly related to new uncertainties about the function of art. In *The History of Sexuality,* Michel Foucault observes that the birth of homosexuality as a psychological, psychiatric, and medical category occurred as late as 1870, when Carl Westphal published his *Archiv für Neurologie.* A major conceptual shift began, writes Foucault, when homosexuality "was transposed from the practice of sodomy onto a kind of interior androgyny, a hermaphroditism of the soul. The sodomite had been a temporary aberration; the homosexual was now a species." Describing that species, Foucault writes:

> The nineteenth-century homosexual became a personage, a past, a case history, and a childhood, in addition to being a type of life, a life form, and a morphology, with an indiscreet anatomy and possibly a mysterious physiology. Nothing that went into his total composition was unaffected by his sexuality. It was everywhere present in him: at the root of all his actions because it was their insidious and indefinitely active principle; written immodestly on his face and body because it was a secret that always gave itself away. It was consubstantial with him, less as a habitual sin than as a singular nature.[32]

The shift described by Foucault found expression in the Labouchere Amendment, which criminalized not just sodomy but all acts of gross indecency committed between men.[33] Taking place under the auspices of this legislation, the trials of 1895 prosecuted Wilde as the representative of homosexuality; embodying, as Foucault puts it, "a certain quality of sexual sensibility, a certain way of inverting the masculine and the feminine in oneself," Wilde apparently helped to shape perceptions of this new species. Most crucially, Wilde's example highlights the artistic dimension of that shaping process; the sensibility that Foucault calls sexual is also aesthetic.[34] When Max Nordau attacked Wilde in his popular work *Degeneration* (1892), he characterized what he considered Wilde's artistic failings in terms borrowed from fin-de-siècle sexology. In fact, when in a letter of 1896 Wilde pleaded his case with the Home Secretary, he pointed out that Nordau had devoted several pages to diagnosing him in these terms.[35] Nordau's "scientific criticism" drew explicitly on the work of the Italian criminologist Cesare Lombroso, who claimed in *The Man of Genius* (1891) that artists were particularly prone to insanity or "degeneration." Closely allied with criminality, moral insanity, and homosexuality, degeneration often revealed itself in people given to "a continuous flow of epigrams, plays upon words, and assonances—puns, in short, such as are praised in society as evidences of wit." Lombroso added: "it is no wonder that they should abound in lunatic asylums, being, as they are, the very negative of truth and logic."[36] It is startling how neatly Wilde fits this profile. The close fit was not lost on Nordau, who attacked Wilde and other artists, including Wagner and Baudelaire, with a vigor that even Lombroso thought excessive.[37] Wilde's art betrayed all the signs of the homosexuality, or "inversion," that Nordau numbered among the most pernicious forms of fin-de-siècle degeneration. Wilde's inversion was, in Foucault's words, "written immodestly on his face and body because it was a secret that always gave itself away." It was also written, equally immodestly, on the surface of his works and conversation. In Wilde, body and text formed one seamless surface of disease and perversion that demanded, Nordau thought, a new, scientific, critical attention.

Wilde was symptomatic of, and even exacerbated, a late-nineteenth-century crisis of masculinity. Treating the social world as a stage and identity as a mask, Wilde located gender and sexuality on a theatrical terrain which, he implied, was always unstable. If, with the advent of homosexuality as a psychological, psychiatric, medical category, his inner nature was "written immodestly on his face and body," was it not possible to rewrite that nature simply by redressing it? Nordau observed in Wilde an acute susceptibility to hysteria, a condition that characterized the alarming instability of fin-de-siècle masculinity and femininity because, always revealing itself in external symptoms, it threatened to reduce identity to something theatrical. Hysteria suggested that a change of costume or of expression might be enough to effect sexual transformation. To Nordau, this menace was summed up in Wilde, a writer prone to a "hysterical craving to be noticed, to occupy the attention of the world with himself, to get talked about."[38] To the authors of *Studies in Hysteria* (1895), Sigmund Freud and Josef Breuer, whose model of transference also implied the possibility of theatrical exchange, hysteria was primarily a female malady; the name of the disease derives from the Greek word for womb (ὑστέρα). But Nordau did not observe hysteria "exclusively, or even preponderantly, among females." Instead, it was "quite as often, perhaps oftener, found among males."[39] Nordau saw in Wilde the archetypal fin-de-siècle male hysteric, whose sexual deviance was inextricable from a sense of drama, a sense of costume and style.

Jauss, as I have noted, writes that "a new aesthetic form . . . can have the greatest conceivable impact on a moral question." Wilde's example emphasizes that such a formulation is especially apposite when the aesthetic form is also a new sexual form. The challenge to nineteenth-century masculinity signaled by the new Wildean "aesthetics of existence" implied a moral or ethical crisis. The nature of this crisis is suggested by another work of fin-de-siècle sexology, and a victim of censorship, Havelock Ellis's *Sexual Inversion* (1897). "The dramatic and artistic aptitudes of inverts," Ellis wrote, "are . . . partly due to the circumstances of the invert's life, which render him necessarily an actor,—and in some few cases lead him into a love of deception comparable with that of a hysterical woman."[40] Hysteria, inversion, drama, deception: these terms, which critics such as Nordau used to characterize Wilde's art, suggested uncertainty, untrustworthiness, calculated deceit. Wilde, the master of what

Lombroso described as "a continuous flow of epigrams, plays upon words, and assonances—puns, in short," not only threw British masculinity into doubt; he rendered utterly unreliable the very language in which gender and sexuality were defined, and with it the moral categories that masculinity was supposed to guarantee. The deceptiveness of Wilde's smooth tongue lay in its manifest differences from the fragmented speech usually associated with hysteria, for the glossy surfaces of his art concealed a well of potentially subversive effects or, in Lombroso's terms, an underlying "insanity."[41] Puns in particular exceed and disrupt the certainties of single, fixed meanings. Yoking together apparently incongruous contexts, their "duplicitous operations," as Christopher Craft puts it, open in language "a counterhegemonic or revisionary space, a plastic site in which received meanings . . . may be perversely turned, strangely combined, or even emptied out."[42] Nowhere was the subversion of old certainties more complete than in Wilde's most celebrated play on words, his pun on "earnest."

In the nineteenth century, "earnestness" denoted the moral integrity and fidelity to truth at the heart of the British ideal of manhood. In *The Importance of Being Earnest,* however, this term is cut loose from its cultural moorings and becomes a floating signifier, a word that attaches itself by pure chance to a character signally lacking the attributes it was meant to imply. By the last scene, when Jack Worthing discovers from the army lists that his name "naturally is Ernest," the play has already made it impossible for us to believe that this coincidence reflects a deep organic truth about his moral fiber. Rather, the effortlessness with which Jack moves from this discovery to his closing declaration, "I've now realised for the first time in my life the vital Importance of Being Earnest" (*CW,* p. 384), demonstrates how easily a key cultural term can turn itself into a figure of speech. *The Importance of Being Earnest* suggests that the harder we try to anchor "earnestness" in received categories, the more slippery and elusive it becomes. Released into a field of linguistic play, Wilde's "earnestness" resists such cultural determination. Signifying a verbal facility motivated only by language, "earnestness" is emptied of the moral integrity, the sincerity, that British culture had invested in it.

At the same time, Wilde's "earnestness" strangely combines the word's nineteenth-century aura of "manliness" with sexual deviance. Craft notes that "earnest" plays on "Urning," a term of "gay self-reference" coined in the 1860s and exploited by the Uranian poet John Gambril Nicholson in *Love in Earnest,* a book of homosexual verse published in 1892.[43] In this context, the subtitle of Craft's own essay, "Desire and Termination in *The Importance of Being Earnest,*" intimates the way in which gay desire thwarted or redirected the reproductive energies associated with earnest British gentlemen in nineteenth-century sexual discourse. Diverting active male desire from its proper destination, gay desire was nonreproductive. In Wilde's hands, "earnestness" becomes a figure of speech that enables effects at odds with the cultural meanings it was supposed to imply.

Locating "earnestness" at the level of verbal play, Wilde turns the term against the late Victorian discourses of production and reproduction with which it was commonly associated. The only form of production in Wilde's drama is linguistic: words are generated not by the desire to convey meaning or truth, but by other words. As *The Importance of Being Earnest* makes very clear, precious little energy is required of Wilde's characters during their wordplay; quite spontaneously they produce sentences as perfect as if they had labored over them all night, an effect that "astonished" W. B. Yeats when he encountered it in Wilde's own conversation.[44] In this way, *Earnest* undermines the cornerstone of British discourses of production, the Protestant work ethic. As Lionel Trilling has observed, nineteenth-century Britain regarded the work ethic as a guarantee of a gentleman's sincerity, and to realize its power we only need recall how "incomprehensible" ill-directed labor seems to Joseph Conrad's Marlow in *Heart of Darkness* (1899). In contrast to the visible evidence of wasted energy, Kurtz merits hearty approval in Marlow's eyes because he is a good capitalist, and Marlow's own commitment to work apparently ensures the authenticity of his search for meaning and truth.[45] Leaving words to do their own work, however, Wilde's dandies conspicuously abandon the work ethic for a world of play. Recruiting their female counterparts into their verbal swordplay, Wilde's male characters render the masculine space reserved for work indistinguishable from the world of leisure and a supposedly feminine domesticity. The world of work is not only demasculinized, it is rendered unproductive and nonreproductive: the dissolution of sexual boundaries negates even the possibility of reproduction. When Wilde pronounced work the curse of the drinking classes, he not only exposed the class system underlying the British work ethic but turned the idea of work into one more occasion for intellectual posturing and witty repartee.[46] A Wildean dandy is the antithesis of Conrad's Marlow. For Marlow, wasted labor is always cause for concern, but for Wilde work itself is a waste—a waste of time that could be spent perhaps less profitably, but certainly more pleasurably, in pursuit of leisure.[47]

Banishing work, and suggesting that sexual desire may be terminal, Wilde's assault on the ideal of earnestness doubly bears out Theodor Adorno's contention that art represents a critique of society because "it gives the lie to the notion that production for production's sake is necessary, by opting for a mode of praxis beyond labour."[48] Uprooting the poles of sexual difference, Wilde's pun on "earnest" implies that not all romances end in reproduction; it posits a very different kind of repetition, the repetition of play. Hans-Georg Gadamer has defined the "to-and-fro movement" of play as the event of art proper. "The movement of playing," Gadamer writes, "has no goal that brings it to an end; rather, it renews itself in constant repetition."[49] This formulation nicely describes Wilde's punning because it suggests endlessness without implying the absence of all limits. A pun has a to-and-fro movement and has no particular end in sight, but it does not transcend the context (or contexts) from which it emerges. In *The Importance of Being Earnest*, "earnest" leads a double life: it is something as trivial as a name that has accidentally attached itself to a transparently inappropriate object, but it also implies deviant, terminal desires. While "earnestness" flickers between these two poles, however, its power largely derives from the fact that Wilde is undermining the word's cultural inheritance. The reduction of "earnestness" into something trivial and its re-cruitment as a means of subversion only make sense in relation to its nineteenth-century function as the sign of a British cultural ideal; it is from conflict with this ideal that "earnestness" takes its force in Wilde's play. Wilde's wordplay points to possibilities beyond the meanings of inherited cul-ture by working against and within that culture.

Wilde's wordplay is representative of his aesthetic practice as a whole, and as such it indicates the broad scope of his art's implications. While the subver-siveness of his art is incomprehensible except in relation to old certainties, it is through playful repetition that Wilde erodes those certainties; by punning on "earnest," he brings into being a new sexual aesthetics. Translating aesthetic procedures into social practice, Wilde perfectly realizes the potential impact of experimental art on supposedly fixed cultural forms. Wildean theatricality sug-gests that by locating artistic performance in social space, it is possible to surmount and exceed the limits imposed in art and in politics by censorious public discourses. It is in this sense that Wilde, hovering ominously in the background throughout the censorship trials of the early twentieth century, helps to define what I am calling the theater of censorship.

Suggesting not only drama but also a fixed place and social institution, the theater is a useful image for describing the social space in which texts and authors become the objects of official censorship. Indicating a realm that is at once social and aesthetic, the theater denotes the scene of literary encounters with the moral and political discourses of public life. Evoking the often con-straining yet sometimes enabling effects of social and aesthetic conventions, the theater functions as a locus of tension and conflict. My use of the theater is analogous to the figure David Marshall has traced through eighteenth- and nineteenth-century explorations of the relations between identity and society. In Marshall's account, the theater is a site for representing, creating, and re-sponding to uncertainties about selfhood and social knowledge in diverse texts.[50] Understood in this way, the theater evokes the "set of shifting, contra-dictory energies" that Joseph Litvak describes as the theatricality of nineteenth-century English fiction. Arguing, however, that "theater" implies a "circum-spection" resisted by "theatricality," Litvak oddly implies that "theater" has less value as a critical term.[51] This critic underestimates the extent to which the energies denoted by theatricality gather much of their force from the constrain-ing effects of a particular social space, a particular historical context. As Wilde so powerfully demonstrates, theatricality may be most arresting, and discon-certing, when the coercive effects of form and convention, of theater, are most keenly felt. It is at the point where the experimental impulses of modern litera-ture intersect with form and convention that its disruptive and transformative potential emerges most visibly and dramatically.

Wilde's case also draws attention to a point at the heart of the transforma-tive impact of censored experimental works in the early twentieth century: the tensions generated by these works characteristically centered on questions of sexuality and gender. Raising such questions at the end of the nineteenth cen-tury, Wilde set the stage for debates about the construction of subjectivity and sexuality that would surround modernism not only in the first decades but also in the last decades of the twentieth century. His aesthetic practice indicates possibilities for cultural transformation startlingly analogous to those explored by Judith Butler in her recent challenge to the terms in which these debates have been conducted in contemporary gay and feminist theory. In many ways, Wilde embodies the performative self as defined by Butler: a *"stylized repetition of acts"* that "constitute the illusion of an abiding gendered self." This self, Butler contends, "is a performative accomplishment compelled by social sanction and taboo." Moreover, if identity is always subject to forces of social construction, the repetition of acts on which it depends (and in which, as Gadamer says, play constantly renews itself) may create a small space for freedom: "the possibilities of gender transformation are to be found in the arbitrary relation between such acts, in the possibility of a different sort of repeating, in the breaking or subversive repetition of that style." Thus, if traditional concepts of gender and sexual identity are "regulatory fictions" (a term Butler adapts from Foucault), repetition may offer a means of deregulating and rewriting them. In this way, Butler suggests the possibility of rescuing identity from the essentializing, psychological models to which texts and authors were subjected by censorious public discourses at the turn of the century, and in which, she argues, they have been reinterred by certain trends in feminism.[52]

As both Wilde and Butler have suggested, to understand the self theatrically is to accept its necessary construction in terms of certain historical and cultural conventions, and to create possibilities for disrupting and transforming those conventions. The idea of subversive repetition is crucial to theatricality because while, like any performance, the performance of gender and sexual identity rehearses a script, the script must be interpreted. Butler writes: "Just as a script may be enacted in various ways, and just as the play requires both text and interpretation, so the gendered body acts its part in a culturally restricted corporeal space and enacts interpretations within the confines of already existing directives."[53] Without underestimating the "confines of already existing directives," it is possible to understand the interpretative aspect of performance as a form of rewriting, of making visible what had previously been invisible or censored.

Such a model of theatricality is highly suggestive for a reading of Lawrence, Joyce, Hall, and Woolf that situates their texts in the theater of censorship— that situates them, that is, "within the confines of already existing directives" embodied in historically determined public discourses of gender, sexuality, and the body. Performing the cultural scripts for gender and sexual identity, such works as *The Rainbow, Lady Chatterley's Lover, Ulysses,* and Virginia Woolf's *Orlando* (which, though not censored, appeared provocatively at the time of the Hall trial) intimate different ways of interpreting those scripts, and ultimately of rewriting the culture whose directives they express. Read in the context of Anglo-American culture during and after the Great War, the formal and stylistic innovations of these works may be seen to engage such issues as hysteria and sexual deviance in ways that challenge dominant cultural paradigms. Experimental modernism follows Wilde in subverting socially sanctioned concepts of sexuality and gender and an entire system of reproductive discourses, and in suggesting what had been unspeakable, unrepresentable, unthinkable, or obscene. Most strikingly, modernism insinuates possibilities for expressing deviant and nonreproductive configurations of gender and sexuality, possibilities that coalesce most obscenely in lesbianism. The obscenity of lesbianism was sufficient to warrant its exclusion from the 1885 Labouchere Amendment: it is often said that Queen Victoria refused to sign a version of the bill that included lesbianism because she refused to believe it existed; for Radclyffe Hall, the suppression of *The Well of Loneliness* merely confirmed her own legal nonexistence. But while Hall's direct attempt to terminate the lesbian's enforced silence and invisibility resulted only in an unsuccessful court battle, Woolf's *Orlando* shows how the theatrical strategies of an experimental modern narrative can imply the possibility of illicit lesbian desires and quietly undermine censorious legal and sexological discourses. Where public discourses block the route, modernism takes another path, which, though indirect and sometimes barely perceptible, disturbs discursive conventions more radically than a more direct or polemical approach. Locating obscenity at the level of formal and stylistic experiment, modernism dramatizes crucial questions relating to literary censorship, suggesting subversions and transformations that even Wilde might not have imagined.

Read in this way, modernism demands a transformation of the critical narratives in which it has been inscribed, or incarcerated, by certain members of our own postmodern culture. For in a sense, modernism is still on trial. It has become salutary in some quarters to divide modernist authors along gender lines, in terms of "sex war," as Sandra Gilbert and Susan Gubar have done in *No Man's Land*. Such a view does not represent the entire panoply of current readings of modernism: thanks to the efforts of a number of scholars to examine modernism more carefully in its historical context, it has become possible to begin redressing certain imbalances. For instance, Alex Zwerdling's important book *Virginia Woolf and the Real World* (1986) has made it less easy than it once was to accept an ahistorical portrait of Woolf as the "matron saint of contemporary feminism." In a sentence that might be adapted to describe the other writers whom I consider here, Zwerdling writes that in seeing Woolf as an "infallible precursor," ahistorical feminism "plays down the importance of her divided motives and turns her into a more consistently militant, self-righteous polemical writer than she was."[54] The importance of Woolf's divided motives is amply demonstrated by Zwerdling's historical approach to her work. It is precisely this kind of attention that I want to give to Joyce, Lawrence, and a work of Woolf's that receives surprisingly little attention in Zwerdling's account, *Orlando*. While such a project means invoking the time-honored concept of modernist ambiguity, this ambiguity is always functional: it signifies the point at which modernist texts engage the "real world," and thus the ways in which such apparently different authors as Joyce, Lawrence, and Woolf belong in one critical narrative. Experimental modernism, that is, enables an attempt like mine to challenge and rewrite certain critical narratives about the sexual politics of modernism. In fact, I see this attempt as just one of the many ways in which modernist texts, generating theatrical relationships with their audiences, encourage their readers to reactivate some crucial questions of critical interpretation, and so to intervene in cultural history. For modernism challenges us to put our own readerly responsibilities to the test. Modernism puts *us* on trial.

1

"All goals become graves": *The Rainbow* and Wartime Censorship

Following a hearing at London's Bow Street Magistrates Court on 13 November 1915, D. H. Lawrence's novel *The Rainbow,* published on 30 September, was suppressed under the 1857 Obscene Publications Act. This hearing gave the first official sanction to the view that Lawrence's writings allowed unchecked expression of unhealthy sexual themes, which posed a threat to public morals and public decency. In the language of the Hicklin rule, *The Rainbow* tended to "deprave and corrupt." Declaring it "advisable in the public interest that a statement be made," Herbert Muskett, speaking for the prosecution, pronounced the following:

> To him personally it was a matter for the most profound regret that it should have been necessary for the protection of public morals and public decency in literary productions to bring this disgusting, detestable and pernicious work under the notice of the Court. Although there might not be an obscene word to be found in the book, it was in fact a mass of obscenity of thought, idea, and action, wrapped up in language which in some quarters might be considered artistic and intellectual. It was difficult to understand how Messrs Methuen could have lent their great name to the publication of this bawdy volume.

The judge, Sir John Dickinson, agreed that *The Rainbow* was "disgusting" and "utter filth." Adding that it was "appalling to think of the harm that such a book might have done," Dickinson ordered that 1, 011 copies of the novel, seized from Algernon Methuen's premises on 3 and 5 November, be destroyed. Methuen was instructed to pay costs of £10 10s.[1]

Censorship troubles were not new to Lawrence. As I noted earlier, *Sons and Lovers* (1913) had been banned from English public libraries, and, since Methuen had already rejected two previous versions of *The Rainbow,* Lawrence was aware that this novel might prove controversial as well. In August 1914 Methuen claimed that the manuscript, then called *The Wedding Ring,* "could not be published in its then form"; as Mark Kinkead-Weekes has observed, the publisher seemed to imply obscenity.[2] In July 1915 Lawrence was asked again to cut or alter a number of passages that Methuen considered indecent.

Lawrence's response to such objections indicated little reluctance to provoke his contemporaries:

> I have cut out, as I said I would, all the *phrases* objected to. The passages and paragraphs marked I cannot alter. There is nothing offensive in them, beyond the very substance they contain, and that is no more offensive than that of all the rest of the novel. The libraries won't object to the book any less, or approve of it any more, if these passages are cut out. And I cant cut them out, because they are living parts of an organic whole. Those who object, will object to the book altogether. These bits won't affect them particularly.[3]

This passage suggests that for Lawrence literary obscenity represented a point of convergence for moral and aesthetic questions, questions of equal importance for his designs on the audience. Refusing to comply fully with Methuen's wishes, Lawrence implied that if any part of the novel offended its readers, it was crucial to his artistic intentions; he intimated that for the novel to succeed as an organic whole it had to transgress certain moral codes. As is clear in his letters of 1913 to 1915, Lawrence considered his attempt to refashion the English novel inseparable from an attempt to reform English society and the "public morals and public decency" upheld at the 1915 trial. "I do write," Lawrence wrote, "because I want folk—English folk—to alter, and have more sense."[4]

The need for more sense was demonstrated, in Lawrence's eyes, by the outbreak of the Great War in August 1914. Declaring the war "colossal idiocy," Lawrence began "[o]ut of sheer rage" to write "A Study of Thomas Hardy" (*L2*, p. 212). This essay is both a work of literary criticism and a philosophical inquiry into the nature of being. "Hardy" is also an extended meditation on human laws, which Lawrence finds "clumsy and mechanical" in comparison with the "very, very delicate and subtle beings" who make them. Laws, Lawrence argues, deal only with existing conditions, the symptoms of the sickness of modern life, rather than with the sickness itself. "No wonder there is a war," he wrote. "No wonder there is a great waste and squandering of life."[5] In "With the Guns," a back-page article published in the *Manchester Guardian* on 18 August 1914, Lawrence also characterized modern warfare as mechanical.[6] In Lawrence's eyes, laws and wars were equally guilty of obstructing the individual's search for self-realization and for what he called, in the Hardy essay, "Consummate Marriage" (*STH*, p. 127). "There is no need to break laws," Lawrence explained. "The only need is to be a law unto oneself" (*STH*, p. 38). Once a man has submitted to his own law, he should "seek out the law of the female, with which to join himself as a complement." In attaining this "two-in-one" state, man and woman obey the "Law of the Holy Spirit" (*STH*, p. 127). And unlike laws and warfare, which involve striving toward particular fixed goals, this state is a process of "seeking" and "becoming." In a later attack on evolution and Christianity, Lawrence used a compelling image to skewer all modes of thought that pursue predetermined objectives: "All goals become graves."[7] It is an image that resonates with special force when read back into the context of the Great War.

A philosophy upholding the pursuit of self-realization and consummate marriage as the individual's most pressing responsibility was hardly in tune with the public morality of a nation at war. Indeed, Lawrence's conception of law was in direct competition with the legal system that enforced wartime morality. *The Rainbow,* a novel full of images of legality and transgression, suggests this competition in a description of Mr. Harby, the headmaster of St. Philip's School, that links "an abnegation of his personal self" with "an application of a system of laws, for the purpose of achieving a certain calculable result, the imparting of certain knowledge" (*R,* p. 356). Like "A Study of Thomas Hardy," *The Rainbow* challenges received notions of law in a manner expressing sheer rage at the Great War, at the system of laws it keeps in place, at its attempt to achieve a certain calculable result. Lawrence later denied that the war had influenced the composition of *The Rainbow:* "I don't think the war had much to do with it—I don't think the war altered it, from its pre-war statement. I only clarified a little, in revision." The "results in one's soul of the war," Lawrence wrote, were contained in *Women in Love* (1920), which was "purely destructive, not like the *Rainbow,* destructive-consummating."[8] Yet a review of the revisions Lawrence made to *The Rainbow* during the first year of hostilities indicates that the war had a lot to do with it. Lawrence rewrote the stackyard scene in "First Love," and added the first three chapters (which describe the first generation of Brangwens), "The Cathedral," the beach scene in "The Bitterness of Ecstasy," and the lesbian episode in "Shame," which was singled out as particularly offensive at the 1915 trial. Lawrence's revisions not only clarified but in crucial ways modified his prewar statement. Binding the novel's exploration of sexuality and self-fulfillment to the destructive theme of warfare, they invited a contemplation on contemporary history that corresponded in many particulars with what Lawrence proposed in the essay on Hardy. Most important, the revisions implied that the energies devoted to waging the Great War should be directed toward what Lawrence called, in the contemporaneous *Twilight in Italy* (1916), "the strange, terrible sex-war."[9]

Lawrence did not think that the war had much to do with the suppression of his novel either. On 16 December 1915 (one month after the trial), he claimed that legal action had been initiated by the National Purity League (*L2,* p. 477). And in a 1920 letter to the publisher Martin Secker, he implied once again that impiety had been the main cause for complaint: "The scene to which exception was *particularly* taken was the one where Anna dances naked, when she is with child" (*L3,* p. 459). This scene, which occurs in chapter 6 ("Anna Victrix"), has blasphemous implications because it imitates, and explicitly alludes to, the biblical scene in which David dances before the Ark (2 Samuel 6:14–23). While there is no evidence to support the first of Lawrence's claims, there is (as we shall see) possible corroboration for the second, and both claims point to an important aspect of the *Rainbow* scandal that is also related to the war. Lawrence was clearly aware that his novel committed offenses against Christian morality; in wartime Britain, as Kingsley Widmer observes, such offenses were often associated with antipatriotism.[10] Like his reinterpretation of law, Lawrence's understanding of blasphemy conflicted with official and other public views of the time. Calling in "Hardy" for a two-in-one reconciliation of body and spirit, Lawrence defined blasphemy as a denial either of "marriage in the spirit" or of "marriage in the body" (*STH*, p. 88). In a series of essays called "The Crown" (1915), Lawrence developed the dualistic philosophy of "Hardy"; "the fight of opposites which is holy" was now explicitly contrasted with "our blasphemy of the war" (*RDP*, p. 262).[11] Where *The Rainbow* expresses its author's rage against this blasphemy, and dramatizes the higher morality of self-realization and consummate marriage, it also commits offenses against conventional morality. It is in such highly ritualized scenes as the lesbian episode in "Shame" and Anna's dancing in "Anna Victrix" that the competition between opposed moralities may be felt most keenly. The theatricality of those scenes requires the audience to respond to Lawrence's assault on conventional expectation. Within its self-consciously theatrical frame, Anna's dancing highlights Lawrence's subversion of socially and biblically sanctioned sexual roles, which wartime readers found so problematic. Ironically, when Lawrence revised the novel he toned down the more obviously blasphemous aspects of this scene, probably because (as Charles Ross surmises) it was too likely to provoke censorship.[12] Even in revised form the scene may have been provocative enough to arouse censure. And other revisions, while not always explicitly blasphemous, consistently fueled Lawrence's counter-argument that impiety lay as much in a denial of the body as in a denial of the spirit, and that the Great War was the inevitable outcome of the application of a system of laws that suppressed the body. *The Rainbow* emerged from revision as the novel that would be read at the trial as immoral, decadent, and, because it might now be interpreted as a tacit commentary on the war, antiwar.

Lawrence's challenge to received wartime views of the relation between law and religion is signaled quite pointedly in the image of the rainbow, which supplies the title and appears at several key moments in the novel. As a biblical symbol for the Covenant, it suggests a binding agreement, a closure, associated not only with religious but also with legal discourse. Yet in addition to reminding us of the biblical promise of divine justice after the flood, the rainbow suggests openness to future experience. While tacitly acknowledging the power of inherited culture, the image implies the possibility of resisting closure of various kinds: legal, moral, and narrative. In this sense, Lawrence's novel draws on nineteenth-century uncertainties about the meaning of this image and the divine justice it was taken to represent; as George P. Landow has argued, the rainbow's status as a continually reappearing natural phenomenon began to threaten its significance as a "divinely instituted covenant-sign."[13] Lawrence's novel exploits such collisions of sacred with secular meaning in order to suggest that life, rather than aiming at specific goals, is an ongoing process. Indeed, the narrative structure of this novel might be read as an elaborate play on the word "process." As well as its legal and narrative connotations, "process" (deriving from the similarly ambiguous French noun *procès*) embraces the following contradictory meanings: "A continuous and regular action or succession of actions, taking place or carried on in a definite manner, and leading to the accomplishment of some result; a continuous operation or series of operations" (*Oxford English Dictionary*). Lawrence's use of the rainbow image has similar effects. While giving events an overarching structure, the rainbow provides a space for the freedom of play, the space briefly discovered by the young Anna Brangwen and later entered by her daughter Ursula. In his Brangwen saga, Lawrence attempted to introduce a new, vital morality by rewriting the "regulatory fictions" (to use Judith Butler's phrase) of the law and the English novel, particularly those fictions that enforced received notions of sexuality and gender. *The Rainbow* demanded the legal attention it received in November 1915. The trial represented a rejection of the Lawrencean program for national and novelistic reform, but it read the novel as, on Lawrence's terms, it had to be read.

Reception and Trial

Weeks before the case went to court, the *Rainbow* controversy began when several members of the British press accused Lawrence's novel of sexual immorality. The first attack was made in the *Daily News* (5 October 1915) by Robert Lynd, who described the novel as "a monotonous wilderness of phallicism."[14] Thereafter most reviewers wrote in a similar vein. In the *Manchester Guardian* (28 October), the suffragist Helena Maria Swanwick characterized the novel as "morbid or downright insane." Her concluding reference to "Anna dancing to God" was probably the source of Lawrence's later claim that this scene had been found particularly offensive (*LCH*, p. 99); though there is no direct evidence, it is possible that the same objection was raised in court. *The Rainbow* was also condemned in two reviews read out in court by the prosecutor, Herbert Muskett. Ironically, the authors of these pieces, James Douglas and Clement Shorter, had signed a petition in 1912 calling the King's attention to "the grave injury inflicted on the art of the drama, and the obstacles placed in the way of its further development, by the present administration of the functions of the Censorship of Plays under the Department of your Majesty's Lord Chamberlain."[15] The petition—whose numerous signatures included those of Arnold Bennett, Joseph Conrad, Henry James, H. G. Wells, W. B. Yeats, and another of Lawrence's detractors in 1915, John Galsworthy—was a protest against the legal mechanism that had been used in 1892 to ban Oscar Wilde's biblical drama, *Salome,* and numerous other works, including Shelley's *The Cenci* (also in 1892) and three plays by George Bernard Shaw: *Mrs. Warren's Profession* (1893), considered amoral because of its representation of prostitution, *The Shewing-up of Blanco Posnet* (1909), which was blasphemous, and the original version of *Press Cuttings* (1909).[16] But such prewar allegiances failed to soften the attacks on Lawrence's novel by Douglas and Shorter. In the *Star* (22 October), Douglas pronounced *The Rainbow* a decadent work whose characters "are not human beings" but "maladies of the mind, growths upon the brain, diseases more horrible than the good honest diseases known to the pathologist." Douglas blasted Lawrence's "morbidly perverted ingenuity of style" as a deliberate attempt to put "the achievement of mastery in the use of words" in the service of "ignoble ends" (*LCH*, p. 93). In the *Sphere* (23 October), Shorter reinforced the apprehension of Lawrence as an author of "decadent tendencies" by suggesting that he outdid even the most depraved of French authors: "Zola's novels are child's food compared with the strong meat contained in an English story that I have just read—*The Rainbow.*" "The whole book," Shorter wrote, "is an orgie of sexiness" (*LCH*, p. 96).

Helena Swanwick's reference to Anna's dancing in "Anna Victrix" implied impiety; the same theme dominated the review by James Douglas. Douglas likened *The Rainbow* to "a savage rite," and urged readers to let out an "astonished laugh at the rigid pose of it all—at the hard, stiff, pontifical worship of the gross." Lawrence, he declared, had betrayed the "sacred trust" of genius; shirking the artist's "duty of reverence" and "the elementary obligation of restraint and selective conscience," Lawrence had "take[n] the name of art in vain" (*LCH*, pp. 93, 94). In addition to offering such "high, old-fashioned sanctities," Douglas issued a warning that reads uncannily like a response to some of Lawrence's statements in the then unpublished "Study of Thomas Hardy": "The artist is not his own law-giver" (*LCH*, p. 94). Tellingly, Douglas emphasized Lawrence's violation of these "sanctities" by fastening onto his use of the rainbow image. "The rainbow," Douglas pleaded, "is the symbol of strange beauty, of transfigured reality, of dreams that transcend the lower nature. It is the romance of God that springs out of earth into heaven." Lawrence was dangerous because, "possess[ing] the heavenly gift of glamour," he perverted traditional religious symbolism and thus rivaled the Creator: "He can lift the rainbow out of the sunlight and set its arch over the pit from whose murky brink every healthy foot ought to shrink in fear and abhorrence" (*LCH*, p. 95). In challenging the sacred meanings of the universe, Lawrence was a false law-giver, a "sensualist who destroys the godlike mind" (*LCH*, p. 94).

That the prosecution saw fit to read out Douglas's review in court indicates a felt need to protect the public from such a threat to British law and morality. The same review unwittingly reveals a connection between this need and deep-seated wartime anxieties about the place of sex and sexuality in fiction. Like Noel Pemberton Billing at the Maud Allan trial of 1918, Douglas explicitly invoked the war to justify censorship: "A thing like *The Rainbow*, " he wrote, "has no right to exist in the wind of war" (*LCH*, p. 94). His concluding remarks clarified the link between religion and wartime patriotism: "The young men who are dying for liberty are moral beings. They are the living repudiation of such impious denials of life as *The Rainbow*. The life they lay down is a lofty thing. It is not the thing that creeps and crawls in this novel" (*LCH*, p. 95). Implicitly, the ignoble ends to which Lawrence had put his mastery in the use of words were quite at odds with the righteous cause of war; in subverting the war effort, Lawrence was helping to send British soldiers to their graves. These arguments must have influenced Judge Dickinson, whose son had been killed in France shortly before the trial.[17]

Clement Shorter's review also tapped anxieties generated by the war. Denouncing Lawrence's depiction of lesbianism in chapter 12 ("Shame") as unfit "for family fiction," Shorter implied that *The Rainbow* threatened family values, the public morality and public decency that the prosecution upheld in court (*LCH,* p. 96). The war highlighted the importance of those values: they were the preconditions at home for a successful war effort abroad. "Shame" insinuated that women could not be trusted to follow such standards once their patriotic husbands and suitors had left for the trenches. On the day of the trial, Lord Derby threatened compulsory recruitment because an insufficient number of unmarried men had volunteered to fight;[18] by raising the specter of lesbianism, Lawrence seemed to suggest that men should attend to domestic affairs instead.

When Methuen's representatives confessed in court that two members of the firm had read the novel without realizing that lesbianism was the subject of chapter 12, Judge Dickinson established a consensus that "shame" meant lesbianism: "They could not have read it very intelligently," he said, "looking at the name of the chapter—'Shame.'" Although the publisher's oversight seemed nearly as amazing then as it does now, it is interesting that Shorter, Muskett, and Dickinson agreed on this interpretation, since lesbianism (as I noted earlier) was not legally recognized in early-twentieth-century Britain. "Shame" was generally taken to mean homosexuality, a particularly risqué subject in the wake of the Wilde trials. By using the term to refer to lesbianism, Dickinson tacitly acknowledged a legally nonexistent sexual category, but he subsumed it within the public discourse surrounding male homosexuality, a discourse that continued to thrive in Britain. As the Ross–Douglas case showed in 1914, Wilde's ghost and the specter of prewar Decadence were still fresh in the memory when the Great War began. Wilde remained an adequate symbol for sexual deviance and for the art with which it was associated: to evoke him was to articulate, as nearly as possible, the nature of the threat posed in the wind of war by the publication of Lawrence's impious, decadent novel.

Such decadence was the object of a larger wartime campaign in Britain against the corruption of modern art, a campaign implicitly allied with the war against Germany. During the war, as Samuel Hynes has observed, many British cultural critics regarded modernism as symptomatic of a "wave of diseased degeneracy" under which the arts had become submerged, and which the war was sent to cleanse. Further, the "war against Modernism" was informed by suspicions that modernism was Germanic and therefore anti-British.[19] Two weeks after the *Rainbow* trial, Jean Finot wrote in *The Athenæum* that German culture, "inspirée par le militarisme et la dynastie dégénérée des Hohenzollern," was inherently opposed to the intellectual alliance of England, France, and Italy. Finot claimed that if they defeated Germany, the last three nations would create a new Renaissance from the ruins of the war.[20] Writing from a similar perspective in the October 1915 issue of the *English Review,* Marian Cox contended that music, dominated in the nineteenth century by German composers, was dangerously allied to the warlike spirit of the German people. For Cox, music was doubly alarming because, in addition to "electrifying [man] with sound and fury, with creativeness and destruction," it filled women with a "sense of rapturous surrender," releasing them from "the cages and censorships of woman's existence" in civilized countries.[21] Germanic influence seemed to foster opposition to the British war effort and, by unraveling censorships essential to civilized conduct, to undermine accepted sexual roles. It was on account of such unraveling that the reviewer Robert Lynd attacked Lawrence: "The characters in *The Rainbow*," Lynd wrote, "are as lacking in the inhibitions of ordinary civilized life as savages" (*LCH*, p. 91).

Published in the same issue of the *English Review* as Cox's essay, Lawrence's story "England, My England" challenged the grounds on which the war was fought. At a time when photographs of British war dead were prohibited, the story violated wartime protocol by portraying the death and mutilation of the hero, Evelyn Daughtry, at the hands of German infantrymen. The tale also suggests a fracture in relations between the home front and the front line, for Daughtry is urged to join the army by his wife, who wills his destruction. Once he has enlisted, Daughtry by no means toes the official line: "She tried to tell him he was one of the saviours of mankind. . . . But he knew it was all cant. . . . As for the saviour of mankind: well, a German was as much mankind as an Englishman."[22] Daughtry not only refutes British propaganda but subverts the premises of the official view by suggesting that Germans, rather than degenerate, are cut from the same cloth as Englishmen. In fact, when Lawrence revised "England, My England" in 1921, he accentuated the bond between the Germans and the English by describing the "primeval" Saxon roots from which the spirit of the English countryside emanates.[23]

While "England, My England" explored wartime anxieties about the influence of Germanic "degeneracy" in British culture, *The Rainbow* became the focus for the public expression of those anxieties, as we see in two more reviews of the novel, both published one week after the trial. Though noting the excessive fervor of the reviews by Douglas and Shorter, and suggesting that censorship in this case was inappropriate, J. C. Squire wrote in *The New Statesman*: "It is a dull and monotonous book which broods gloomily over the physical reactions of sex in a way so persistent that one wonders whether the author is under the spell of German psychologists, and so tedious that a perusal of it might send Casanova himself into a monastery, if he did not go to sleep before his revulsion against sex was complete. I think it a bad novel: and it contains opinions unpalatable to me and tendencies that I personally believe to be unhealthy" (*LCH*, p. 106). In *The Athenæum*, G. W. de Tunzelmann repeated Squire's accusation of unhealthy, implicitly German proclivities to account for Lawrence's glorification of unrestrained sexual intercourse and for his tendency "to stimulate the perfectly legitimate sexual impulses and appetites into morbid excesses." The following excerpt indicates, moreover, that the war against German culture was a spiritual as well as a temporal affair:

> This is but one of the many futile attempts to reconcile the facts of existence with the materialistic pseudophilosophy which has proved such a powerful instrument for the debasement of the German nation. And many of the humiliating weaknesses

which have so hampered our action against Germany may be traced to the too great readiness which has been shown in accepting this same pseudophilosophy at the hands of those whom we are at last united in recognizing as our foes—in things spiritual as well as in things temporal.[24]

This commentator, who established his British credentials by disguising his German name, implied that *The Rainbow* betrayed its spiritually misguided, Germanic source in its concern with sexual being.[25] This preoccupation supposedly stemmed from a whole tradition of German "materialistic pseudophilosophy," but perhaps most of all from the new, primarily German, sexology, which explained human nature in terms of sexual pathology. Literature promoting such interests would threaten the integrity of British culture just when it needed defending; the duty of the critic was to identify and condemn such art.

Ironically, such diagnoses replicated the "symptomatic" reading practiced by one of the most influential of materialistic German pseudophilosophers, Max Nordau. As we have seen, Nordau had applied Lombrosian criminology to art and literature in order to attack nineteenth-century Decadence. Dedicating his popular work *Degeneration* (1892) to Lombroso, Nordau declared: "Degenerates are not always criminals, prostitutes, anarchists, and pronounced lunatics; they are often authors and artists."[26] Nordau asserted that by reading a work of art as a body of symptoms, it was possible to diagnose the disease, the degeneration, of its creator. Considering the enormous popularity of the 1895 English edition of *Degeneration* in prewar Britain, it is not surprising to find Nordau's brand of "scientific criticism" reproduced in 1915 in British literary reviews also written for popular audiences.[27] Even so, such correspondences are quite revealing. Denouncing Lawrence's style as morbid and perverted, his characters as maladies of the mind, such critics as James Douglas and Helena Swanwick sounded like disciples of Nordau. These similarities provoke some interesting questions. If Lawrence's critics employed strategies deriving from German culture, then what cultural differences were expressed by the Great War? Was the war fought, as Lawrence implied in "England, My England," between two very similar nations? Was the war fought because of that similarity? In the first installment of "The Crown," published in *The Signature* on 4 October 1915, Lawrence suggested that in contrast to the holy "fight of opposites," the "blasphemy of the war" was a "fight of like things" (*RDP*, p. 262).[28] As for *The Rainbow*, it contained nothing (apart from its dedication to Lawrence's sister-in-law, Else) that marked it as innately Germanic, just as there was nothing by which Nordau's scientific criticism might have been so identified. The charge of German influence and sources was made simply because it was considered patriotic in wartime Britain.

Nordau's scientific criticism was notable for another interpretative strategy adopted in hostile reviews of *The Rainbow* and in the trial itself: the treatment of the novel in isolation from the author. In Nordau, this separation occurs in order that a text may be treated as a sick body, independent of the author, before being consulted as an index of the author's mental health. The text is isolated from the author during the first step of this process because it must be studied with supposedly scientific objectivity—an objectivity unlikely to be upheld by the author, who is a less impartial, as well as a less competent, reader of signs than the critic. Having disconnected author from text, the scientific critic is free to diagnose any symptoms of degeneration found in a text and then to read them back into the mind of the author who created them.

Legal and journalistic interpretations of *The Rainbow* depended on a similar strategy of reading. One of the peculiarities of the case was that legally Lawrence had no connection with the novel at all; he merely happened to be the author, "who had no right to appear in the matter," as Methuen learned from Inspector Draper of Scotland Yard.[29] In effect, Lawrence was, as he said four days after the trial, "condemned entirely without hearing" (*L2,* p. 441). He never received official notification of the legal action against his novel; even Methuen did not communicate with him. He learned of the case only on 5 November, when the novelist W. L. George noticed that the book had been withdrawn from the publisher's advertisement.[30] Lawrence's knowledge of the *Rainbow* affair always remained hazy. The legal detachment of author from novel was merely confirmed in the House of Commons on 1 December, when Sir John Simon replied on behalf of the Home Office to Philip Morrell's question about authorial rights: "The Statute requires notice to be served on the occupier of the house where the books which had been seized were found. They are not required to serve any notice on the author, and they would not have any knowledge whether he had or had not an interest in the sale of the book or where he was to be found. The magistrate had before him the most direct evidence possible, namely, the book itself. . . ." Morrell's appeal that the court action jeopardized Lawrence's livelihood weighed lightly in these circumstances; Simon's only suggestion was that "it will be possible, if the author thinks he has been wrongly treated, for another copy to be seized by arrangement, in order that he might defend the book."[31]

The treatment of *The Rainbow* as an entity independent of its author is important, not simply as a quirk of British legal conventions, but because it established the critical assumptions on which the trial read the novel. By severing the novel from its author, it was possible for contemporary readers to practice strategies of reading uncannily close to those deployed in the scientific criticism of Max Nordau, and thus to diagnose the more disturbing aspects of the novel as signs of the author's degeneracy. In this way, art that failed to conform to aesthetic, as well as social or moral, conventions could be dismissed as symptomatic of the psychological disorders of a few overeducated, overrefined individuals. It was not even necessary to convict the author in court; it was sufficient merely to alert the public to the health hazard represented by the work. To condemn the work was the best course one could take because, as Simon said, it was the most direct evidence possible. As in Nordau's criticism, the author's presence in court would have done nothing to facilitate the progress of the trial, and even might have been an unwelcome distraction.

The trial's detachment of Lawrence from his novel is doubly significant because in attempting to explain why the trial took place, one might be tempted to read through the proceedings, as Emile Delavenay has done, and find not a case of literary obscenity but an attempt to silence an opponent of the war. Lawrence did oppose the war, and in October 1915 he tried to organize antiwar meetings. But leaving aside the fact that the evidence for Delavenay's case is only circumstantial, we should recognize that, as Paul Delany argues, Lawrence simply was not important enough as a public figure to be the target of a carefully orchestrated official campaign.[32] That is not to say that Lawrence's views on the war had no bearing on the *Rainbow* crisis. But the challenge posed by *The Rainbow* to the war effort seems to have been the result of the implications of the novel itself, not of Lawrence's minor political activism.

This distinction has crucial implications for a reading of Lawrence's novel, for it is clear that in effect, if not by design, the trial made an example, or a spectacle, of the author. It was largely as a result of the suppression of *The Rainbow* that Lawrence became enshrined, as he later put it, as a "lurid sexuality specialist."[33] Yet Lawrence himself was expressly denied a role in court. He became a spectacle in his own absence; he became a spectacle *of* absence. This process was possible precisely because the court treated the text as the most direct evidence. In other words, the novel was made to perform in its author's stead; the theatricality of the situation was displaced from author onto text.

It is not hard to see how this interpretative maneuver facilitated a guilty verdict at the 1915 trial, especially as there was little or no argument in court. Methuen's representatives cooperated with the prosecution in the hope of a light sentence, which was what they received. At the same time, the trial enforced a model of reading that pointed to the contingent nature of its own procedures. While the exclusion of the author perhaps ensured the smooth progress of the trial, it also provided a theoretical basis for an openness of interpretation at odds with the closure implied by censorship. In this sense, the critical strategies adopted at the *Rainbow* trial only underlined a general rule of all trials, which are essentially matters of contest and performance: trials involve the reenactment and renegotiation of general procedures in specific, determinate contexts. The legal process always aspires to the accomplishment of some result, but each new action offers to modify it. The court's exclusion of Lawrence begged the question because it preempted, so as to preclude, the possibility of a different performance that would contest this particular script. The court's claim to objectivity, the linchpin of its interpretative authority, rested on the exclusion of a potential adversary, whose own claim to authority would indicate the partiality of judicial interpretation. The very act of exclusion betrays the possibility of contest. By the same token, it is by no means clear how the author himself could have avoided partiality. A more lively courtroom debate might have highlighted the ways in which the performance of the text invited interpretations beyond the scope of judicial or authorial control. But the liability of the text to activate a contest for interpretative authority was implied by the authorless model of reading that the trial itself put in place. That such a contest did not take place in November 1915 did not preclude its activation in other contexts.

Such contestation implies potential ambivalence and uncertainty in aesthetic as well as moral judgment, qualities captured in a rare sympathetic review of *The Rainbow* by Catherine Carswell (a review that cost the author her job). Carswell's grappling with the dissolving effects of Lawrencean form and style suggested appreciation but also unease. She praised Lawrence's characterization, some of which, she claimed, "must take rank with the best work done by great novelists in any age," but she was not entirely well disposed toward the new style. She objected in particular to "a distressing tendency to the repetition of certain words and a curiously vicious rhythm into which he constantly falls in the more emotional passages." Carswell's ambivalence about Lawrence's new aesthetic affected her sense of his moral intentions as well. She read his style as describing the present age; she found in the novel a "conviction that the modern heart is in a disastrous muddle where love between the sexes is concerned," an "impassioned declaration" that the "modern world, according to Mr. Lawrence, is mad and sick and sad because it knows not how to love" (*LCH*, pp. 100–101). Carswell did not refute Lawrence's diagnosis, but she seemed to half regret that he did not offer a cure. More receptive than most reviewers to Lawrence's aesthetic innovations, Carswell found in *The Rainbow* a message that she could not condemn. At the same time, she could not entirely endorse it.

The incompletions of Carswell's judgment tell us something about the way in which the novel complicates the question of moral, as well as interpretative, authority. At one level Carswell recognized this dynamic by acknowledging that while Lawrence's message, as she interpreted it, "will be strongly offensive to most readers," *The Rainbow* itself adopts a markedly moral tone in defying contemporary morality (*LCH*, p. 101). But to say that a book adopts a moral tone is not to describe its entire range. It is hard to imagine how any reconstruction of the authorial message, of Lawrencean sense, could do full justice to the text, since to articulate it would be to fix it in ways that the text itself does not necessarily reward. The trial worked on the assumption that the message was fixed, but in banishing the figure of the author it adopted critical procedures implying greater interpretative openness than it wanted to concede. It is just such a crisis of interpretation that is created by the savage rites of *The Rainbow*.

Lawrence's Wartime Aesthetic

The performative and combative structures of trials played a crucial role in shaping Lawrence's wartime project. While the authorities suppressed *The Rainbow*, Lawrence considered British society itself on trial: on trial for sending soldiers to their graves, but also for perpetuating the clumsy and mechanical system of laws that had made war inevitable. The war, "purely destructive," as Lawrence said of *Women in Love*, diverted men and women from the pursuit of self-fulfillment in consummate marriage; Lawrence's task in his "destructive-consummating" novel *The Rainbow* was to direct his reader's attention to these deeper concerns. He recognized, however, that his attempt to reform at one stroke both the English novel and English society created certain rhetorical problems. In Lawrence's terms, to jettison the pursuit of moral reform would be to sell oneself short as an experimental artist. Yet to persist in that pursuit was to present a public persona, to engage in dialogue with other personae. It was to locate oneself in social space, where Lawrencean sense itself could be contested; it was to become theatrical. In this sense, Lawrence's work invited the legal scrutiny it received in November 1915.

Lawrence's need to establish a theatrical, conflictual relationship with his audience was implicit in his famous statement of intent, which he sent to Edward Garnett on 5 June 1914. In this letter, so often (and rightly) celebrated as a manifesto for the new "allotropic" novel, Lawrence hinted at the underlying moral dimension of his aesthetic: "that which is physic—non-human, in humanity, is more interesting to me than the old-fashioned human element—which causes one to conceive a character in a certain moral scheme and make him consistent. The certain moral scheme is what I object to. In Turguenev, and in Tolstoi, and in Dostoievski, the moral scheme into which all the characters fit—and it is nearly the same scheme—is, whatever the extraordinariness of the characters themselves, dull, old, dead" (*L2*, pp. 182–83). Lawrence objected not to the existence of moral schemes in general but to the predetermination of novels according to a "certain . . . dull, old, dead" scheme. He wanted a new scheme, and he thought he had found it in the allotropic novel, in which "the old stable ego of the character" would give way to "another ego, according to whose action the individual is unrecognisable, and passes through, as it were, allotropic states" (*L2*, p. 183). Henceforth the novel would deal not with the accidentals of external form but with "the same single radically-unchanged element," the carbon, the essence of form. As Diane Bonds has shown, Lawrence seems to build, like other novelists, on yet another "principle of selfsameness," but the carbon metaphor destabilizes such principles by installing "a relational and differential model of the self." Carbon is not a "pure single element," as Lawrence put it, but something occurring only in its allotropes. As Bonds argues, "it is known inferentially and indirectly, by means of its differential or differentiating relations with that which it is not."[34] The metaphor not only shapes Lawrence's theory of the self; it conditions the dynamic morality, the new sense, toward which his novel would lead.

The success of Lawrence's project depended on his ability to persuade the reading public to adopt that morality. Such dependence on an audience becomes even more apparent when, later in the same letter, Lawrence expresses a desire to find a reception. This desire surfaces as he attempts to instruct the resistant Garnett in the value of innovative art: "You must not say my novel is shaky—It is not perfect, because I am not expert in what I want to do. But it is the real thing, say what you like. And I shall get my reception, if not now, then before long. Again I say, don't look for the development of the novel to follow the lines of certain characters: the characters fall into the form of some other rhythmic form, like when one draws a fiddle-bow across a fine tray delicately sanded, the sand takes lines unknown" (*L2*, pp. 183–84). Wrestling with Garnett, Lawrence could see that his new aesthetic would not find the audience he desired without a struggle. The difficulty was compounded by his intuition that objections such as Garnett's were moral as well as aesthetic, that Garnett was reluctant to accept his reconception of novelistic character because to do so would be to surrender the certain moral scheme usually found in novels.[35] If Lawrence was to get his reception, he would have to reform English morality as well as English reading habits. At the same time, the very purpose of writing was to engage in such a struggle.

Lawrence hoped to win his reception, and reform England, by writing "the real thing," a novel that would do away with the rind, the dead shells of convention, and probe new depths. As we see in another letter to Garnett expressing both the desire for a reception and the conviction of the moral reformer, Lawrence consciously embarked on this project in 1913 in *The Insurrection of Miss Houghton,* the novel that later became *The Lost Girl:*

> I have done 100 pages of a novel. I think you will hate it, but I think, when it is re-written, it might find a good public among the Meredithy public. It is quite different in manner from my other stuff—far less visualised. It is what I *can* write just now, and write with pleasure, so write it I must, however you may grumble. And it is good too. I think, do you know, I have inside me a sort of answer to the *want* of today: to the real deep want of the English people, not to just what they fancy they want. And gradually, I shall get my hold on them. And this novel is perhaps not such good art, but it is what they want, need, more or less. (*L1,* p. 511)

Casting about for allies, Lawrence encouraged Henry Savage to give up his own mediocre efforts at writing and take up arms as an editor: "I think you ought to remain among books, but rather as a soldier of literature than a writer" (*L2,* p. 169). In another letter to Savage, Lawrence reiterated the same message and emphasized the moral and social dimension of this reforming process, though not without self-mocking irony: "I *should* like to see a few decent men enlist themselves just as fighters, to bring down this old régime of dirty, dead ideas and make a living revolution. But you would rather write 'Carber's Cruise,' and I would rather write dull stories, instead of taking up a gun and a bayonet and ramming holes in the bundled enemy" (*L2,* pp. 179–80). Acknowledging his own unreadiness to bear arms, Lawrence was identifying himself in a crucial way with the audience he sought to reform: he, too, needed to be remade. It was in departing from what he considered the sensational realism of *Sons and Lovers* that he hoped to refashion himself.

At the outset Lawrence seemed to be losing this personal struggle. When in March 1913 he abandoned *The Insurrection of Miss Houghton* and began *The Sisters,* the novel from which *The Rainbow* and *Women in Love* emerged, he was baffled by the gradual changes in his technique. In the letter expressing his desire to make English folk "have more sense," he wrote of *The Sisters:* "Damn its eyes, there I am at page 145, and I've no notion what it's about . . . it's like a novel in a foreign language I don't know very well—I can only just make out what it is about" (*L1,* p. 544). In a letter to Garnett announcing his break with "the hard, violent style full of sensation and presentation" of *Sons and Lovers,* Lawrence wrote of the new novel, now called *The Wedding Ring:* "It is *very* different from *Sons and Lovers:* written in another language almost." As Charles Ross has pointed out, Lawrence's bafflement indicates that the break with *Sons and Lovers* was not as clean as he claimed.[36] Unable as yet to fully articulate his intentions, Lawrence could only repudiate his earlier style. He found himself forced to admit to Garnett: "I shall be sorry if you don't like it, but am prepared" (*L2,* p. 132). Lawrence was not sure that he would get his reception, even from an admirer. And if the novel was barely comprehensible to its author, it was hard to see how it was to make English people have more sense.

Lawrence also felt that he was perpetually in danger of losing the battle with his audience. To remake his readers it was necessary to establish a social dialogue, but the reading public seemed intent on exploiting that dialogue to reduce him to their own terms. In their world of false artifice and dead convention, Lawrence saw himself being treated merely as an entertainer. He registered this apprehension in a letter of 1908 by caricaturing himself as a prospective court jester: "I am learning quite diligently to play the fool consistently, so that at last I may hire myself out as a jester" (*L1,* p. 53). Latent in this figure is a fear of public exposure, a fear Lawrence hinted at again in 1909 when referring to the forthcoming publication of some of his poems in the *English Review:* "I feel rather daft when I think of appearing, if only in so trivial a way, before the public" (*L1,* p. 139). Lawrence continued to experience this anxiety, worrying in a letter to Garnett that the publication of his second novel, *The Trespasser* (1912), might betray his "naked self" to an audience he characterized as "a parcel of fools" (*L1,* p. 353).

Lawrence worried that such apprehension indicated that the reading public was beyond redemption. All too often readers seemed to cast authors in the most undignified roles, turning them into figures of fun or even ridicule. It was on these grounds that Lawrence objected to being called a genius. He experienced this humiliation at the hands of the general reading public, but also at the hands of those who were supposedly leading the way in the appreciation of modern literature: "The Hueffer-Pound faction seems inclined to lead me round a little as one of their show-dogs" (*L2,* pp. 132–33). Lawrence felt that in treating a reforming artist as a show dog, the patrons of the avant-garde, like the general public, diminished him into something as empty and futile as themselves. In Lawrence's eyes, this diminution was a betrayal of literature. The relationship he sought with his audience threatened to undermine the possibility of reforming the world through art.

This threat gave point to the urge to overcome the obstacles of the modern world, the world of sensation and presentation to which Lawrence consigned the style of *Sons and Lovers,* a world full of such dull, old, dead ideas as traditional novelistic character. Any change in such a world, if conceived on its present terms, would necessarily be superficial, ephemeral. Real change, "the real thing," would bring about a rejection of dead forms, the shells and husks of modern life, and a new Lawrencean sense would take hold. It was not immediately apparent to Lawrence in what that sense actually might consist. He trusted, however, that in the process of searching for a true self he would discover the foundation for new life.

Prewar Lawrence perhaps hoped that by writing "the real thing" he might remake the reading public, and so release himself from the trivial role into which it had compelled him. The outbreak of the Great War sharpened his antagonism toward the public considerably. As we have seen, Lawrence described his attempt to start writing "A Study of Thomas Hardy" as an expression of that antagonism. In this essay Lawrence develops his own concepts of law and sexual love, concepts that rival the received ideas and values of modern British culture. Similarly, Lawrence sets his argument about blasphemy, about the relation of body to spirit, in opposition to common public views. Since "Hardy" was not published in Lawrence's lifetime, one might be tempted to regard it as a work of the private imagination, or, as Lawrence himself put it, as "a sort of Confessions of my Heart" (*L2*, p. 235).[37] Yet the arguments of this piece inform "The Crown," the first three parts of which appeared serially in *The Signature* in October–November 1915, and *Twilight in Italy*, a series of travel writings that Lawrence revised into book form during the same autumn. The "Study of Thomas Hardy" provided a platform from which Lawrence launched his ideas into the public arena. And these ideas are couched in ways that repeatedly draw attention to the censorious wartime context in which they were formulated.

According to "Hardy," the war was essentially an expression of the sickness of modern life. This sickness was the result of a breach between the law of the Father, which was also the law of the flesh, and the love of Christ, which demanded "the crucifixion of the body and the resurrection of the spirit" (*STH*, p. 79). It was also a sexual division: the law of Christ was male, while the law of the Father was "the great Law of the Womb, the primeval Female principle," which Hardy treated as "a criminal tendency, to be stamped out" (*STH*, p. 95). Lawrence saw this breach as dividing European history into two epochs: life before the Renaissance had been ruled by the law of the Father, but after the Renaissance (a perfect union of spirit and flesh, male and female) "the New Law" of Christ had gradually taken hold. Now love "suppressed the contact, and achieved an abstraction" (*STH*, p. 126). The war was the natural outcome of the male, flesh-censoring epoch, which bids us die. Calling for a reconciliation of law and love, of body and spirit, Lawrence acknowledged that each epoch was guilty of repression, of a blasphemous denial of the Holy Spirit: "But in some men, in some small men, like bishops, the denial of marriage in the body is positive and blasphemous, a sin against the Holy Ghost. And in some men, like Prussian army officers, the denial of marriage in the spirit is an equal blasphemy. But which of the two is a greater sinner, working better for the destruction of his fellow man, that is for the One God to judge" (*STH*, p. 88).[38] What would have troubled Lawrence's contemporaries was the hesitation about distinguishing morally between the two blasphemies or between the two types of men who commit them: spirit-denying Prussian officers and flesh-denying bishops. Such "fair play," as Lawrence called it, was not generally acceptable in wartime Britain.

This reluctance to judge informs both "The Crown" and *Twilight in Italy*. "The Crown" describes the struggle between the lion (associated with darkness, the flesh, the Father) and the unicorn (light, the mind, the Son). Each is "kept in stable equilibrium by the opposition of the other" (*RDP*, p. 253). They are fighting for the crown (the "Absolute," also figured as an iris and a rainbow), which is a function of their struggle; the crown would disappear along with both combatants "if either of them really won in the fight which is their sole reason for existing" (*RDP*, p. 254). Thus it is impossible to come down on one side or the other. The Great War was a "blasphemy" because, as we have seen, it was a fight between close relations, a sign that the lion and the unicorn had gone mad. Lawrence made a similar point in the Italian essays, characterizing Britain and Germany as representative of the northern mechanical spirit, as opposed to pagan, sensuous Italy. Developing this opposition during his journey through Italy, Lawrence becomes a kind of symptomatic reader, who interprets each monument of Italian civilization as a form of cultural dictation, an index of its maker's spiritual condition. Images of Christ dramatize the cultures that produced them. The Christ of one crucifix is "a peasant of the foot of the Alps," a "hot welter of physical sensation," a "flow of sensuous experience" (*TI*, pp. 5–6). Another, in a valley near St. Jakob, is "the most startlingly sensational" he has seen: "a mass of torture, an unthinkable shame," with a "criminal look of misery and hatred" (*TI*, pp. 16–17). The Christ most truly expressing "the desire to convey a religious truth, not a sensational experience," is, in conventional terms, the most blasphemous: "the fallen Christ, armless, who had tumbled down and lay in an unnatural posture, the naked, ancient wooden sculpture of the body on the naked, living rock" (*TI*, p. 18). To post-Renaissance eyes, Lawrence's treatment of these figures looks blasphemous because he focuses on the outer surface of the body, rather than on its symbolic content. This is Lawrence's point: the modern world has neutralized the flesh by applying the "law of the average," by which flesh and spirit cancel each other out (*TI*, pp. 42, 36). But seeing that Italian iconography has rendered the body of Christ a performative construct that plays a different role for each culture, Lawrence advocates a new role under "the Absolute of the Holy Ghost." In this role, the body of Christ retains its performative fluidity, for, like the carbon metaphor, the "Absolute" is a dynamic, relational term, which Lawrence uses here to describe the marriage of the "two Infinites" of body and spirit. And this absolute, Lawrence writes, "we may call Truth or Justice or Right" (*TI*, p. 95).[39]

In many ways, *Twilight in Italy* is a lament for the loss of the opportunity to achieve this justice. Northern Europe wallows in its confusion of medieval self with modern selflessness. The result is "horrible, a chaos beyond chaos, an unthinkable hell" (*TI*, p. 51). Modern Italy, meanwhile, actively pursues "the perfect mechanizing of human life" that has issued from the north (*TI*, p. 215). In each case, metaphysical sickness reveals itself in political developments. Arguments with the publisher, George Duckworth, about the title of this work indicated both the connection in Lawrence's mind between the metaphysical and the political and the publisher's eagerness to avoid advertising the "political implications" for fear of scandal (*L2*, p. 484). Lawrence's letters during the first year of hostilities chart his deep engagement with these worldly affairs. In early 1915 he talked constantly of social revolution, of the need to do away with democracy, which was founded on the misguided Christian ethic of "self-death and social love" (*TI*, p. 175), and to find "a Ruler: a Kaiser" (*L2*, p. 364). Later in the year he gave up on Britain altogether and started thinking of the American market. On 6 November 1915, the day after the second seizure of copies of *The Rainbow*, he announced: "I will try to change my public" (*L2*, p. 429). The suppression of *The Rainbow* only hardened Lawrence's new resolve. On 17 November, four days after the trial, he wrote: "I think there is no future for England: only a decline and fall. That is the dreadful and unbearable part of it: to have been born into a decadent era, a decline of life, a collapsing civilisation" (*L2*, p. 441). In effect, Lawrence leveled at the British public the very charge that readers and censors brought against him: decadence. As for contemporary readers of *The Rainbow*, their decadence was for Lawrence a manifestation of underlying spiritual sickness, a sign of a large cultural blasphemy; it was an outrage against justice.

Particularly symptomatic of wartime decadence, in Lawrence's view, was the way in which the war dramatized the folly of public life. The British public seemed to treat the war as cheap entertainment. After the shelling of Scarborough in December 1914, Lawrence wrote to Amy Lowell: "England is getting real thrills out of the war, at last. . . . I tell you the whole country is thrilled to the marrow, and enjoys it like hot punch" (*L2*, pp. 243–44). It was under these conditions that Britain became the debased, soulless country that Lawrence later recalled in the "Nightmare" chapter of *Kangaroo* (1923). Perhaps thinking of the reception of *The Rainbow*, he wrote: "It was in 1915 the old world ended. . . . The integrity of London collapsed, and the genuine debasement began, the unspeakable baseness of the press and the public voice, the reign of that bloated ignominy, *John Bull*."[40] In *Kangaroo*, Lawrence remembered an England reduced to a hollow shell by the sensationalistic frenzy, the "vast mob-spirit," of "the ghastly masses" in a depraved, degenerate era (*K*, p. 236). This spectacle led Lawrence to pronounce: "We all lost the war: perhaps Germany least" (*K*, p. 246).

Lawrence's sense of his own role in this deranged drama underwent some fluctuation. While the war was in progress he felt reduced to a disapproving, reluctant onlooker. "The social being I am," he told Cynthia Asquith, "has become a spectator at a knockabout dangerous farce" (*L2*, p. 601). In *Kangaroo*, however, Lawrence imagined himself as the center of a humiliating spectacle, onto which a soulless nation projected its own depravity. The novel recalls the occasion on which its author was examined by army medical officers in Cornwall in 1916. When the smirking officer inspects the anus and genitals of the autobiographical hero, Richard Lovat Somers, Lawrence depicts the scene as an "operette" in a place "full of an indescribable tone of jeering, gibing shamelessness" (*K*, p. 280). Somers feels that he has been violated, demeaned as the victim of a degrading ritual, reduced to a collection of body parts or inanimate matter. To be the center of such a spectacle is merely to be reduced to a false center, to have one's selfhood denied or emptied out. Paul Delany has argued that the doctor humiliates Somers "to show him that even the secret recesses of his body are at the disposal of the authorities."[41] Adapting the terms of the essay on Hardy, we might also say that the doctor's mockery represents a suppression of the body under "the New Law," a regime that led to the war and that the war was fought to preserve.

The roles of degraded spectacle and grudging spectator may seem diametrically opposed, but for Lawrence the point was essentially the same: public life in wartime Britain was hostile to artistic innovator and moral reformer alike. As a result, Lawrence felt increasingly isolated and marginalized. That sense of marginalization was heightened by the *Rainbow* trial, where the only role allowed him was that of absent author. After the trial Lawrence expressed his marginal status in a number of epithets: "anti-social," "outlaw," "brigand," "spectator," "the enemy of mankind" (*L2*, pp. 540, 542, 601, 648). On 19 February 1916 he wrote to Bertrand Russell: "One must be an outlaw these days, not a teacher or preacher. One must retire out of the herd and then fire bombs into it. . . . One can still write bombs" (*L2*, pp. 546–47). Thus, Lawrence appropriated the role of outlaw to dramatize his quarrel with the mechanical habits of mind that caused the Great War and led to the censorship of his novel. To the author whom it diagnosed as decadent and immoral, British culture was merely following the laws of abstraction to their logical, degenerate conclusion.

Lawrence's understanding of his relationship with the British public as theatrical and antagonistic, as an ongoing trial, was sharpened by his experience of the war and by the suppression of *The Rainbow*, but it was not entirely new. Intriguingly, Lawrence revealed his apprehension of the relations between the individual and society in two letters, both written before the war, concerning his reading of fictional trials. The first letter (28 April 1911) was written to Lawrence's one-time fiancée, Louie Burrows, after he had read the trial scene in Stendhal's novel *The Red and the Black* (1830). Writing that he felt "so much like Julien Sorel," Lawrence added: "I feel myself a 'Black and Red' myself— black coal bubbling red into fire" (*L1*, pp. 262–63). Lawrence identifies himself with Stendhal's hero, the carbon in the burning coal, contaminated by the hands that mistreat it, just as the hero is destroyed by the society that inflicts on him its rough justice.

The second letter (11? November 1912), a response to Edward Garnett's play *The Trial of Jeanne D'Arc* (1911), also anticipates the carbon metaphor elaborated in 1914. The link is not as direct as in the description of Julien Sorel, but the letter raises similar questions of identity, especially sexual identity. As in the letter about Stendhal, Lawrence articulates his desire to delve into the inner essence beneath the external form of character, a desire that Garnett's play frustrated. Noting that *The Trial of Jeanne D'Arc* is "a play about the people who judge Joan, rather than about herself," Lawrence writes:

It seems to me queer you prefer to present men chiefly—as if you cared for women not so much for what they were themselves as for what their men saw in them. So that after all in your work women seem not to have an existence, save they are the projections of the men. That is, they seem almost entirely sexual answers to or discords with the men. No, I *don't* think you have a high opinion of women. They have got each an internal *form*, an internal self which remains firm and individual whatever love they may be subject to. It's the *positivity* of women you seem to deny—make them sort of instrumental. There is in women such a big sufficiency unto themselves, more than in men.—You really study the conflict and struggles of men over women: the women themselves are inactive and merely subject. That seems queer.—And I consider the *Jeanne D'Arc* play is an awfully good study of the conflicting feelings of men over the almost passive Maid.—I believe you're a curious monk, a man born to "gloss" the drama of men and women with queer penetrating notes on the men, rather than to do the drama. (*L1*, pp. 469–70)

For Lawrence, Joan should be in Garnett's play what Julien Sorel is in *The Red and the Black,* the embodiment of authenticity at the center of a world of false outward manifestations, but he finds that there is no center. There are moments in the play when Joan could be said to occupy center stage, yet one of the most striking is the scene in which she is tortured, when she is reduced to a spectacle of humiliation like Richard Somers in *Kangaroo.* Otherwise, as Lawrence observes, Joan is marginalized, just as he was in wartime Britain. She is an absent center, as Lawrence believed he was in the *Rainbow* trial when he said, "I was condemned entirely without hearing." In this sense, Garnett's play provided a script that the trial of *The Rainbow* would follow. Lawrence's role in life mimicked Joan's in drama.

Like the carbon metaphor, Lawrence's comments on *The Trial of Jeanne D'Arc* suggest that what he considers the real essence of being is dynamic and inherently unstable; it has the potential to override conventional constraints. In the light of his remarks on *The Red and the Black,* Lawrence's interpretation of Garnett's play implies that a female character is just as likely to provide a center of authenticity as a male character. Women, he argues, have positivity, an internal form and an internal self, which challenges the image of passivity to which they have too often been made to conform in English literature. Especially revealing in Lawrence's commentary is the implicit desire to identify with such characters. In this sense, his attempt to break down the old stable ego of the character involves a related endeavor to destabilize the ego of the reader. Garnett's gloss on Lawrence's reading of the play is apposite here: Lawrence, he said, "blends his own identity with mine, and generally weaves E. G. with the sex web of D. H. L.'s predilections."[42] In other words, Lawrence's effort to recreate the inner world is inextricable from, even constructed by, the outer world. The attempt to remake the inner being inevitably depends on the social negotiations of identities that encounter, modify, and blend with each other. Ultimately, Lawrence's reading practice implies that the old stable ego of the author may be broken down as well, that authorship may be turned into a performance that transgresses previously accepted barriers.

The possibility of reconceiving identity raised questions about sexual relations that informed Lawrence's developing aesthetic. He read Garnett's play as exemplifying what Eve Kosofsky Sedgwick has called "homosocial discourse," in which men establish bonds with each other through the exchange of a female body.[43] Lawrence seemed disquieted by this discourse, yet in the lines she appended to his letter, Frieda Weekley (as Frieda Lawrence was then called) described his desire to get at a woman's inner being as an urge to commit violence. She suggested that this violence, the only means by which men could sympathize with heroines, perpetuated a male bonding that excluded women. Weekley liked "the elusiveness of Jeanne" in Garnett's drama, but, she wrote: "L[awrence] always wants to treat women like the chicken we had the other day, take its guts out and pluck its feathers sitting over a pail—I am just wildly arguing with L and he is so stupid, I think, in *seeing* things, that cannot be seen with eyes, or touched, or smelt or heard. . . . Don't you men all love her better because she was sacrificed! Why are *all* heroines really Gretchens? You dont *like* the triumphant female, it's too much for you!" (*L1*, pp. 470–71). Weekley understood Lawrence's desire to delve into the core and extract the essence of female being as a fantasy of disembowelment; as disembowelment in the chicken's case was presumably followed by consumption, the threat of cannibalism was implicit. Although Weekley was addressing Garnett, this letter was arguing with all men and with Lawrence, whose violence masked a sentimental preference for a female martyr over a woman who might turn the tables on him.

Lawrence seems to have accepted some of Weekley's criticism, for included among his "Italian Studies" in the *English Review* of September 1913 was an essay on "The Theatre," in which he admitted his susceptibility to such sentimentality. Writing of the leading lady in an Italian theater carnival, Lawrence posed the very question that Weekley had asked in November 1912: "I wonder why the Gretchen, Dame aux Camélias, Desdemona lady is the beloved of all male audiences, and the appreciated of all female, in all countries, for all time. I am young, and I am inexperienced. Yet I have seen at least a hundred of these pale, tear-stained ladies, white-garbed, with their hair down their backs. I loathe them on principle. And yet my bones melt and my heart goes big and loving, each new time I hear her voice, with its faint clang of tears."[44] When in the autumn of 1915 Lawrence revised this essay for inclusion in *Twilight in Italy,* he expanded this section and wrote:

> Why are the women so bad at playing this part in real life, this Gretchen–Ophelia role? Why are they so unwilling to go mad and die for our sakes? They do it regularly on stage.
> But perhaps, after all, we write the plays. . . . (*TI*, p. 83)

Tacitly, then, Lawrence confessed his own complicity in homosocial discourse.

Far from apologizing for the violence Weekley had detected in his designs on women, however, Lawrence came to see a particular form of violent conflict as essential to human relations. Lawrence viewed the relations between the sexes as a kind of trial, a trial by combat, and it is here that his conception of sexual relations continues to prove most problematic for feminist critics. When he revised "The Theatre" in the autumn of 1915, he added a discussion of the "strange, terrible sex-war" between the men and women of the Italian village:

> They come together mostly in anger and in violence of destructive passion.There is no comradeship between men and women, none whatsoever, but rather a condition of battle, reserve, hostility. . . .
>
>   . . . There is no real courting, no happiness of being together, only the roused excitement which is based on a fundamental hostility. There is very little flirting, and what there is is of the subtle, cruel kind, like a sex duel. . . .
>
>   In marriage, husband and wife wage the subtle, satisfying war of sex upon each other. It gives a profound satisfaction, a profound intimacy. But it destroys all joy, all unanimity in action. (*TI*, pp. 73–74)

Lawrence's narrator finds that between these villagers "there is no spiritual love"; the "Absolute of the Holy Ghost," or "Justice," has been thwarted because the body has repressed the spirit. Consequently, the sex war in this village represents another form of modern inauthenticity, another symptom of a decadent age. And the lack of equilibrium between flesh and spirit issues in unbalanced sexual relations. The women "are too strong for the men. . . . The woman in her maternity is the law-giver, the supreme authority" (*TI*, p. 75). Yet *Twilight in Italy* finally implies that despite the inauthenticity of this particular manifestation, the war of sex is no less fundamental than events in northern Europe; the suppression of the spirit by the flesh may have dire consequences, but the spirit's suppression of the flesh, as in the war, is equally catastrophic. Traveling through the mountains on his way to the Ticino valley, the narrator writes: "It was a sort of grief that this continent all beneath was so unreal, false, non-existent in its activity. . . . The kingdoms of the world had no significance: what could one do but wander about?" (*TI*, p. 199). What is so unreal and false about those kingdoms is "the perfect mechanizing of human life" they have achieved. For Lawrence, the tragedy of Italy lies in the destruction of its pagan, sensuous life by northern European Christianity, whose work ethic, an expression of "social love," has facilitated the mechanizing process. Italy has joined the quest for "a new goal, a new idea, the Infinite reached through the omission of self" (*TI*, p. 93). This quest dramatizes the love of cold abstraction embodied in a repressive system of laws and clearly visible in the Great War. In this light, the inauthenticity of the sex war between Italian men and women may be seen as a corruption of a previously more vital conflict, a symptom of the larger corruption that had infected every aspect of modern Italian life.

While Lawrence's emphasis on sexual relations may have alarmed his contemporaries by implying the relative insignificance of the Great War, his conception of sexual relations has fanned the flames of another trial or sex war: the continuing critical controversy about the sexual politics of modernism. Following Simone de Beauvoir and Kate Millett, several feminists have attacked Lawrence's work as oppressive to women.[45] Sandra Gilbert and Susan Gubar, for example, have linked the "sadistic fervor" of Lawrencean sex war with wartime anxieties that they consider typical of male modernists.[46] Lawrence's disapproval of the feminist movement of his own time is no secret; he expressly rejected the suffragist demand, "Votes for women, chastity for men." Viewed in its historical context, however, Lawrence's manifest antifeminism looks more complicated than is sometimes allowed.

As the feminist historian Susan Kent has shown, suffragists themselves employed the concept of sex war. Their objective was to redefine a model of sexual relations inherited by the twentieth century from Victorian culture: the ideology of separate spheres. By emphasizing conflict, suffragists hoped to draw attention to widespread male violence against women, a phenomenon not acknowledged by those who clung to separate-spheres ideology. Suffragists also looked to the sex war model as a means of justifying their efforts to combat actual violence and to resist the general cultural perception of women as sexual objects. As a result, antisuffragists often accused feminists of fomenting sex war.[47]

Lawrence had no quarrel with the suffragist desire to change the sexual status quo, but he defined the aims of sex war very differently. To Lawrence the suffragist movement simply was not radical enough. The demand for votes was just another attempt, as he put it in the Hardy essay, "to make more laws"; what Britain needed was "a parliament of men and women for the careful and gradual unmaking of laws" (*STH,* p. 14). In other words, suffragists adhered to the same mechanical habits of mind, the same narrow pursuit of goals, as the system that oppressed them. Similarly, the suffragist call for chastity for men was another symptom of the problem it set out to cure; it sought to suppress the sexual instincts that needed liberating not only in men but in women as well. In its own way, suffragism was as counterproductive, as lacking in sense, as antisuffragism. Each side tried to maintain a form of censorship that had afflicted Europe since the Renaissance: an application of the law of Christ in breach of the law of the Father; a suppression of the flesh (the female principle) by the spirit (the male). For Lawrence, the need for a reconciliation of flesh and spirit in "the law of Consummate Marriage" was made especially urgent by the outbreak of the Great War. Ironically, it was this event that prompted Emmeline Pankhurst and her allies to abandon the battle of the sexes: in the first week of the war, the Women's Social and Political Union (WSPU) suspended its activities, and in October 1915 its magazine, the *Suffragette,* was patriotically renamed *Britannia.* The ease with which many suffragists were co-opted by the war effort suggests that Lawrence's misgivings were not entirely unjust. Indeed, similar reservations have been expressed by Susan Kent, who has argued that in the postwar era suffragists lost the battle over sexual discourse precisely because they defined votes for women as their primary objective.[48]

Revising *The Rainbow* in ways that emphasized the rituals of sex war, Lawrence heightened the novel's engagement with this contentious public issue. Dissatisfied as he was with the arguments of both sides, he cannot have been surprised to find Helena Swanwick, one of the most progressive suffragists of the day, among those who censured the book for immorality.[49] Swanwick's pious objection to Anna Brangwen's dancing will merely have provided further evidence of suffragism's submission to the flesh-denying law of Christ that reigned over modern British culture. Suffragists like Swanwick and reactionaries like James Douglas were natural allies when it came to judging a book that tested the limits for literary treatment of sexual themes; radicals and conservatives were equally invested in censoring the body, in repealing "the great Law of the Womb," because they were following the same script, the same sacred text. Lawrence wanted to rewrite that script to reveal what he later called "the changing rainbow of our living relationships" (*P1*, p. 532). In *The Rainbow* he traces this process by dramatizing the sexual rituals inscribed in English law and in the English novel. The censor's efforts to uphold public morals and public decency at the 1915 trial were an attempt to keep those rituals sacred.

Savage Rites: *The Rainbow*

Adapting Lawrence's description of the Bible as "a great confused novel" (*P1*, p. 535), George H. Ford characterized *The Rainbow* as "a great confused bible."[50] It is entirely appropriate that a novel once derided as immoral should be described in this way: *The Rainbow* was attacked in 1915 because its author had trespassed on holy ground. Adapting Ford's phrase, we might say that the trial gave public expression to the confusion that occurs when an obscene book unnervingly resembles a sacred text.

The Rainbow is renowned for its ritual set pieces: the cornfield scene in which Will Brangwen proposes to Anna, Anna's dance before her bedroom fire, the bathing scene in "Shame," the stackyard scene in "First Love." In his account of the last scene, P. T. Whelan elegantly describes the effect of Lawrence's adaptation of sacred rituals, pagan as well as Christian: "Beneath the banal dialogue and commonplace occurrences is a world in which men and women reenact the ancient rites in their collective unconscious, swept by archetypal symbols into patterns of behavior in which their conscious mind has no part."[51] It is no accident that censorious eyes were drawn in 1915 to an episode like the lesbian bathing scene. Attired in modern battle dress, Lawrence's characters perform the ancient rites with a savagery (to recall James Douglas's objection) that threatened the sexual conventions of the time and subverted the war effort. It was the reenactment of these rites that prompted the reviewer J. C. Squire to ask whether Lawrence had fallen under the spell of German psychologists.

The Rainbow seemed especially controversial in 1915 because it restaged certain modern rituals as well. As we have seen, Lawrence vehemently opposed the ways in which modern existence ritualized a lifeless ideology of separate spheres. In a well-known letter of 1914, Lawrence announced that *The Rainbow* was a vehicle for imagining an alternative: the theme of the novel was, he said, "woman becoming individual, self-responsible, taking her own initiative" (*L2*, p. 165). The term "self-responsibility" also appears in "A Study of Thomas Hardy," where it denotes the burden of the quest for "the Law of the Holy Spirit," which demands that the individual submit to his or her own law and then seek out the law of another. As is often recognized, the declared theme of *The Rainbow* challenges the ideology of separate spheres by presenting active agency as a possibility open to women. The rituals enacted in the novel may be seen as leading away from the known world to a state of "becoming." Self-responsibility is a matter of process, at odds with the closure sought by censorious legal systems and modes of knowledge designed to achieve a certain calculable result. Lawrence submits old and seemingly new rites to the law of becoming, which frustrates ends previously sought and releases new possibilities. *The Rainbow* is a book of trials that renders inherited concepts of law obsolete.

Lawrence's statement of intent indicates a particular concern with women. What is perhaps most intriguing in the context of wartime censorship is the novel's restaging of the rites, or trials, of motherhood. Lawrence's philosophy of self-responsibility, as expressed in "Hardy," resists the equation of femininity with maternity that is found in sacred cultural texts: "That she bear children is not a woman's significance. But that she bear herself, that is her supreme and risky fate: that she drive on to the edge of the unknown, and beyond" (*STH*, p. 52). In the spirit of this pronouncement, *The Rainbow* gradually detaches womanhood from motherhood. The reviewer Clement Shorter's claim that the lesbian episode in "Shame" was unfit for family fiction indicates how the specter of nonreproductive female sexuality alarmed both the prosecutor, who read out Shorter's piece in court, and the judge, who banned the novel. The standards of public morality and public decency demanded that women fulfill their reproductive function, and that novels show them doing so. We have seen how the Great War exacerbated these sexual and religious anxieties: after the slaughter inflicted by its unholy enemy on the battlefields of northern France, the British population would have to regenerate itself. Yet *The Rainbow* resists the supposed inevitability of reproduction, and so frustrates the desire for closure, for a certain calculable result, that it embodies. Lawrence's novel implies that maternity, like other aspects of character, may be less a function than a performance, or, to appropriate Judith Butler's words, *"a corporeal style"*: "the repeated stylization of the body, a set of repeated acts within a highly rigid regulatory frame that congeal over time to produce the appearance of substance, of a natural sort of being."[52] Depicting the sex wars of three generations of Brangwens, *The Rainbow* emphasizes the patterns of continuity and repetition that shape human experience. Yet, as Butler argues, it is within the patterns of repetition ("a highly rigid regulatory frame") that change becomes possible. Dramatizing the process of change, *The Rainbow* insinuates that "the obligatory frame of reproductive heterosexuality" is no more, though no less, than a "regulatory fiction."[53] In this way, Lawrence wages a subtle war on common assumptions about the gendered self, assumptions taken for granted by detractors and censors on both sides in the battle of the sexes.

In some ways, the new opening chapters of *The Rainbow*, which deal with the first embattled generation of Brangwens, would not have upset Edwardian readers reared on the ideology of separate spheres. Reenacting the sexual rituals of the Victorian world, these chapters seem to leave those spheres intact by asserting irremediable differences between men and women. The young Tom Brangwen finds that in "the close intimacy of the farm kitchen, the woman occupied the supreme position," because men regarded her as their "anchor" and as "the symbol for that further life which comprised religion and love and morality" (*R*, p. 20). Yet the possibility of change is present from the start. While the Brangwen men are satisfied by "blood-intimacy," the women not only preserve domestic harmony but look to "the world beyond," where "men moved dominant and creative" (*R*, p. 11). The novel gradually moves outward from the domestic sphere into the active, creative world hitherto dominated by men. Breaking down the old stable ego of novelistic character, *The Rainbow* inches its way from the apparent stability of separate spheres to the verge of a new world as female characters, becoming individual and self-responsible, infiltrate "The Man's World" of public life and creativity.

At one level, the dualistic philosophy of "Hardy" and "The Crown" may be read as positing the deep gender divisions for which Lawrence is, in some quarters, notorious. In "Hardy," however, he observes that "the division into male and female is arbitrary, for the purpose of thought" (*STH*, p. 60). Male and female are categories that help us to see more clearly the fight of opposites, but they are not necessarily equated with man and woman respectively; like plants, human consciousness is bisexual. While sharply distinguishing between Tom and his Polish wife, Lydia, the opening chapters of *The Rainbow* dramatize this complication in Lawrence's thought. The marriage ultimately fulfills the law of the Holy Spirit, a union of the spirit and the flesh, of the male and the female. Yet, as many readers recognize, it is Tom who embodies the law of the female, the law of the flesh, while Lydia represents the male, the spirit. At the same time, Tom and Lydia enact a reversal of Edwardian sexual roles. It is Lydia who brings to the Marsh a knowledge of "the far-off world of cities and governments and the active scope of man" (*R*, p. 11); as a result of her previous marriage to Lensky, an activist in the Polish rebellion of 1863, she knows a larger world. Tom, meanwhile, is relatively passive, adopting the culturally "feminine" role, living in the blood rather than in the mind. Lydia has to struggle to get his "active participation, not his submission." It is on her initiative that they find "entry into another circle of existence, . . . through the doorway into the further space, where movement was so big, that it contained bonds and constraints and labours, and still was complete liberty" (*R*, p. 90).

If the opening chapters suggest that Lawrence is less interested in the literal aspects of gender than in their utility for thought, the same is true of the rituals of motherhood. In many ways Lydia is a conventional mother, living in the flesh. When we first meet her she already has a child, Anna, from her earlier marriage. And she provokes in Tom a sense of "new creation," of "metamorphosis" and "new birth," as if her presence inevitably suggested the maternal (*R*, pp. 32, 38, 39). In the proposal scene, however, Lawrence registers the transformation in their lives by combining the imagery of birth and maternity with the idea of "trespass": "He returned gradually, but newly created, as after a gestation, a new birth, in the womb of darkness. . . . And the dawn blazed in them, their new life came to pass, it was beyond all conceiving good, it was so good, that it was almost like a passing-away, a trespass" (*R*, p. 45). As Mark Kinkead-Weekes notes, Lawrence is playing on different meanings of "trespass": it signifies death and self-transcendence as well as offense (*R*, p. 501). The passage suggests that the fascination of childbirth lies not in the material facts but in the metaphorical possibilities for testing limits, for breaking old laws and creating new ones. Tom and Lydia are reborn in their marriage, and so establish themselves on a higher plane than was possible under the previous conditions of existence. It is this reborn state to which all Brangwens aspire.[54]

Similarly, when Lydia becomes pregnant with Tom's first child, Lawrence draws our attention to the sense of trespass, of transgressing established limits and creating anew. In an image anticipating the novel's final vision of the rainbow, Lawrence connects the estrangement that has come between Tom and Lydia with the idea of a broken covenant: "He [Tom] felt like a broken arch thrust sickeningly out from support" (*R*, p. 63). Eventually the arch is reconstructed, relieving Anna (also estranged from her pregnant mother) of her supporting role: "She was no more called upon to uphold with her childish might the broken end of the arch. Her father and her mother now met to the span of the heavens, and she, the child, was free to play in the space beneath, between" (*R*, p. 91). Rebuilt, the arch is transformed. The Brangwens have discovered ways of remaking the symbol of the old covenant as a sign of the law of consummate marriage, which Tom later celebrates in his tipsy speech at the wedding of Will and Anna. In the reenactment of the rites of marriage, the first generation starts to break from traditional Christian interpretations of the symbol for justice.[55]

The result is a family insulated not only against religious but against social laws as well: "neither Mrs Brangwen nor Brangwen could be sensible of any judgment passed on them from outside. Their lives were too separate" (*R*, p. 94). In the manuscript, Lawrence characterized the Brangwens as lawless (*R*, p. 568). But revising *The Rainbow* along the lines discovered in "Hardy," Lawrence altered "lawless" to "a law to themselves," implying that obedience to one's own law entails a rejection of external judgment (*R*, p. 97). The Brangwens constitute a domestic ideal, exemplary according to the social codes of Victorian and Edwardian England, yet their ideality is a function of their isolation from the outside world. Another revision underlined this point: in the manuscript, the Brangwens are "quite unaware" of the world, but in the published version they are "a small republic set in invisible bounds" (*R*, pp. 568, 97). The implication is that the English ideal can be realized only in a free state, sealed off from England itself. This freedom issues in attitudes to conventional religion that will not have pleased Lawrence's wartime readers. Lydia, who is half German, "had some fundamental religion," but she is careless of denomination: "She had been brought up a Roman Catholic. She had gone to the Church of England for protection. The outward form was a matter of indifference to her" (*R*, p. 97). And the young Anna uncannily anticipates the charges of indecency brought against Lawrence by leveling them at the sacred institution to which his censors deferred: "Whilst the religious feelings were inside her, they were passionately moving. In the mouth of the clergyman, they were false, indecent" (*R*, p. 99).

Lawrence was hardly unaware of the provocation contained in such passages; the revisions just noted indicate that the assault on conventional expectations was quite deliberate. Lawrence also knew that a price had to be paid in this world for trespasses made in the hope of transcending it: if one rewrites the law, one may be released from certain bonds, but one is no longer protected by the old safety clauses. The flood that kills Tom Brangwen is the revenge of the traditional religion rejected by his family, as if God has revoked His promise not to send another deluge. Tom is punished for presuming in his "facetious," drunken fashion to take the name of Noah, forgetting that in setting themselves apart from external judgment he and his family have rejected the divine justice promised to Noah (*R*, p. 227).[56] The revenge is also that of the contemporary world, which still abides by the old law. The flood is, as Paul Rosenzweig has noted, "a product of the devil of mechanization," of forces incarnated in Lawrence's time in the blasphemy of the war.[57] Tom's crime exemplifies the kind of offense against conventional morality that is committed throughout *The Rainbow*. Lawrence probably did not expect to get away with it any more than Tom does. In retrospect, Tom's death in the flood looks like a fictional analogue for the punishment subsequently inflicted on Lawrence: the censorship of his novel.

As it shifts focus to the second generation, Will and Anna, *The Rainbow* becomes more overtly provocative. Revisions to the chapters dealing with this phase of the Brangwen sex war heightened controversial aspects of the text, but even in places where Lawrence practiced self-censorship it often remained potentially scandalous. In this regard, the most striking example of Lawrence's muting of the text is the scene in chapter 6 ("Anna Victrix") when, naked before her bedroom fire, the pregnant Anna dances to God. That Lawrence later believed this episode had been found particularly offensive indicates a continuing awareness of the transgressive implications lingering in the published version, as if it had always been his intention to cause a scandal. Scandal there certainly was: Helena Swanwick drew attention to Anna's dancing, and it may well have been in James Douglas's mind when he censured *The Rainbow* for "the rigid pose of it all . . . the hard, stiff, pontifical worship of the gross" (*LCH*, p. 93). Within its explicitly theatrical frame, the dancing scene dramatizes the subversion of the sacred that upset Lawrence's contemporaries, subversion carried out, as is indicated in the language of Douglas's indictment, by a blending of the sacred with the erotic. The immediate problem is the presentation of the rites of maternity. On a broader plane, the episode also illuminates the vexed relationship between the private and public realms that characterizes the culture of censorship within which British modernism evolved.

It is not hard to see why Anna's dance was controversial in a culture determined to uphold public morals and public decency at home while fighting an enemy abroad. Lawrence implicitly compares the scene with the biblical story of David, "who danced before the Lord, and uncovered himself exultingly" (*R*, p. 170). In effect, Lawrence rewrites a sacred text in a form highlighting its latent eroticism. The blasphemy was more overt in the manuscript version: rather than "the unseen Creator," God is Anna's "unseen Lover"; David dances not "exultingly," but "shamelessly" (*R*, pp. 170, 585). In the Bible, the word "shamelessly" is used by David's wife, Michal, as a term of reproach, yet Lawrence's episode suggests unashamed sexuality. The manuscript also emphasizes Anna's romantic idealization of David: "As she sat by her bedroom window, watching the steady rain, her spirit was somewhere far off, with David. She had always loved David. It had haunted her, how he danced naked before the Ark, and the wife had taunted him" (*R*, pp. 169, 585). Anna's love of David expresses itself in imitation: "All the time she ran on by herself, being David" (*R*, pp. 170, 585). In the manuscript, then, she reenacts the story because it provides an objective correlative for her own situation and her feelings about it. The same applies to the published text, even though Lawrence toned it down. Anna's dance brings her exultation and a sense of superiority over Will; it allows her to "annul" him, to prevent him from joining her in communion with God. Implicitly likened to Michal, Will is the unwanted spectator, made to feel that his presence is a "violation" (*R*, p. 171). Some readers see Will, like Tom, as an incarnation of the flesh, but in this scene he seems to represent the censorious spirit which, according to Lawrence, has dominated European civilization since the Renaissance.[58]

Will's censorious intrusion highlights the paradoxical theatricality of this episode. Anna's objection to Will's presence—that she is dancing for herself, that she is doing what she likes in the privacy of her bedroom—belies the public aspect of her performance. She clearly has a specific spectator in mind: God. Will's intervention suggests that God is his substitute, a projection of the male, displacing the earthly husband in Anna's imagination. Will spoils the performance because he makes this spectatorship visible; the eroticism of the dance is heightened by the idea that God is the "unseen Lover." Anna projects God as a voyeur; Will ruins everything by bringing this covert theatricality out into the open.

As an analogue for Michal, Will emphasizes another blasphemous aspect of this episode: reversing the male and female roles of the biblical story, Lawrence implies that gender is an unstable theatrical artifice. Anna not only loves David, she *is* David; she plays his part. In a sense, the gender reversal makes the scene less scandalous than the biblical version, for it accords more nicely with conventional morality to make the sexual performer female rather than male, a point made in the Bible when Michal reproves David for dancing and leaping in the sight of the maids. Yet Lawrence's text is doubly transgressive because it highlights the erotic element of the sacred text. If Anna dancing to God represents a marriage of the religious with the sexual, how much more scandalous is the biblical scene in which David dances naked before the Ark, an affront to God and to the symbol for justice. Reviewing David's story in the light of Anna's, we are able to see more sharply its homoerotic subtext. As in Anna's display, the intended audience of David's performance is God, who is thus cast as a transcendental, bisexual voyeur, implicated in the polymorphous sexuality enacted on the human stage.

Lawrence's restaging of this episode (which does not appear in his 1926 play, *David*) is all the more blasphemous because it evokes the Virgin Mary as a figure of motherhood.[59] Anna combines the biblical roles of Mary and David, with the result that the Virgin's divine fertility is neutralized by David's sterility. In the second installment of "The Crown," published in *The Signature* on 18 October 1915, Lawrence wrote:

> And David never went in unto Michal any more, because she jeered at him. So that she was barren all her life.
>
> But it was David who really was barren. Michal, when she mocked, mocked the sterility of David. For the spirit in him was blasted with unfertility; he could not become born again, he could not be conceived in the spirit. Michal, the womb of profound darkness, could not conceive to the overweak seed of David's spirit. David's seed was too much of darkness, it bred and begot preponderant darkness. The flood of darkness set in after David, the lamps and candles began to gutter. (*RDP*, pp. 268–69, 470)

Again, there are striking points of likeness between Will and the jeering Michal, as between David and Anna, who wants to triumph over her husband. In dancing to God, however, the egoist merely worships a "reflection . . . of the worshipper's ego." As Lawrence put it in the 1925 version of "The Crown," to triumph is to wear "the crown of sterile egoism" (*RDP*, p. 269). In *The Rainbow*, Anna dons the Davidian mask, which, as we see in "Hardy" and the Italian essays, paradoxically censors the spirit. It is a mask of triumph that negates the law of consummate marriage.

"The Crown" also draws the war into its frame of reference. This theme is implicit in the 1915 text, which adduces Agamemnon, Caesar, and Napoleon, as well as David, as asserting the "absoluteness of the flesh" (*RDP*, p. 470). It is made explicit in the 1925 version:

> He who triumphs, perishes. As Caesar perished, and Napoleon. In the fight they were wonderful, and the power was with them. But when they would be supreme, sheer triumphers, exalted in their ego, then they fell. Triumph is a false absolution, the winner salutes his enemy, and the light of the victory is on both their brows, since *both* are consummated.
>
> In the same way, Jesus triumphant perished. Any individual who will triumph, in love or in war, perishes. There is no triumph. There is but consummation, in either case. (*RDP*, p. 269)

The implication is that insofar as each embodies the impulse to triumph, love and war amount to much the same thing. In *The Rainbow*, Anna's desire to annul her husband represents the mechanical sterility that Lawrence saw in all war, Caesarean, Napoleonic, or modern. A reading of the dancing scene in the context of the Great War highlights its scandalous effects. As the daughter of Noah (Tom), Anna is a figure of regeneration, presumably a welcome sight to

Lawrence's wartime readers. Yet Lawrence represents her as a dead end, an embodiment of sterile egoism. This point is underlined at the end of the chapter by her satisfaction in child-rearing, and by her relinquishing of "the adventure to the unknown"; she can see "a rainbow like an archway" in the distance, but she does not pass under it (*R*, pp. 182, 181). The novel continues to explore the theme of "woman becoming individual, self-responsible, taking her own initiative," but according to these criteria Anna can no longer be the center of interest. As an end in itself, reproduction is insufficient because it entails closure, a censorship of possibility. In Anna, maternity becomes a repeated act, which she accepts as her defining characteristic but which debases the law of the female. The "great Law of the Womb" becomes the vehicle for a mechanical performance of once sacred rites. This was not the family fiction that Lawrence's censors had in mind; indeed, it was just this sort of "impious denial of life" that caused the novel to be banned.

Throughout their marriage, Will and Anna dramatize the legal battles described in "Hardy," "The Crown," and *Twilight in Italy*. They reenact the war between the sexes; at the same time their marriage constitutes a restaging of the conflict between David and Christ, flesh and spirit, self and social love. The second generation's search for what Lawrence called consummate marriage is described insistently in terms of legal metaphors and images. Lawrence constantly reminds us of the need to resist rules and laws that stifle the self, and of the need to seek out the law of the Holy Spirit. The struggles of Will and Anna register the weight of this burden in a modern world filled with the spirit of negation.

From the beginning, Will represents the impulse to cling to conventional, duty-bound habits of mind, to the male law of the spirit, which we see in his censorious violation of Anna's dancing. Paradoxically, the effect is to make Will look more feminine: his restraint recalls the relative passivity of Tom Brangwen in the previous generation. Conversely, Anna, like Lydia, is the more active partner. The second generation dramatizes its polarity more fully, as if to compensate for the historical process by which the general axioms separating the sexes are starting to disappear. Anna, with her lax, slovenly ways, is noticeably more persistent than her mother in disrupting the man's sense of order. In the early days of their marriage, Anna has the upper hand. While "they were a law unto themselves," there is an imbalance in favor of the law of the female, the law of the flesh, which provokes doubts in Will's "orderly, conventional mind" (*R*, pp. 134, 139). Will cannot "get rid of a culpable sense of licence on his part"; "he could not help feeling guilty, as if he were committing a breach of the law"; he feels "unmanly" (*R*, pp. 134, 137). The "inner reality" discovered with Anna feels more alive than the outside world, "as though this house were the Ark in the flood, and all the rest was drowned" (*R*, p. 136). Yet Will feels secure only because the "world *was* there, after all." Like a prisoner in the dock, he cannot resist the sense that he is "accused" (*R*, pp. 136, 137).

Will intuits the possibility of healing the breach between the flesh and the spirit, between male and female. Watching "with wonder whilst his Tablets of

Stone went bounding and bumping and splintering down the hill," he envisages marriage as a miraculous transformation of a world enclosed by the rind of dead forms:

> He surveyed the rind of the world: houses, factories, trams, the discarded rind; people scurrying about, work going on, all on the discarded surface. An earthquake had burst it all from inside. It was as if the surface of the world had been broken away entire: Ilkeston, streets, church, people, work, rule-of-the-day, all intact; and yet peeled away into unreality, leaving here exposed the inside, the reality: one's own being, strange feelings and passions and yearnings and beliefs and aspirations, suddenly become present, revealed, the permanent bedrock, knitted one rock with the woman one loved. It was confounding. Things are not what they seem! When he was a child, he had thought a woman was a woman merely by virtue of her skirts and petticoats. And now, lo, the whole world could be divested of its garment, the garment could lie there shed away intact, and one could stand in a new world, a new earth, naked in a new, naked universe. It was too astounding and miraculous.
>
> This then was marriage! The old things didn't matter any more. One got up at four o'clock, and had broth at tea-time and made toffee in the middle of the night. One didn't put on one's clothes or one did put on one's clothes. He still was not quite sure it was not criminal. But it was a discovery to find one might be so supremely absolved. (*R*, pp. 139–40)

Will's perception of a new world, which looks forward to Ursula's vision of the rainbow at the end of the novel, is marked by the same desire for authenticity, the impulse to cast off transient appearances and scratch below the surface, that Lawrence himself expressed elsewhere. "Things are not what they seem!": marriage, though a convention, momentarily establishes itself as the route to a different plane, a higher reality, which transcends the false, ephemeral forms and conventions of everyday existence. Will communicates the sexual element of that new reality by imagining it as a woman whose garments are shed so that the man may see her naked. He imagines the encounter between flesh and spirit that brings the supreme absolution of consummate marriage. The image of the Tablets of Stone intimates that steps toward this state may be taken only when the old religious law is abolished. At the end of the passage Will's doubts, signs of lingering adherence to that law, emphasize the connection in Lawrence's mind between the transgression of existing laws and the attainment of true divinity. The phrase, "supremely absolved," was added in revision in place of "delightedly criminal" (*R*, pp. 140, 578); this change may be taken as significantly altering the meaning of the passage, but it may be seen also as equating supreme absolution with delight in criminality.

Reaching the impasse illustrated by the dancing scene, the second generation dramatizes the historical process by which the fight of opposites is reduced to a state of negation analogous, in Lawrence's terms, to the cultural stalemate signified by the Great War. From one vantage it seems just to read Will's interest in the church as a sign of adherence to the medieval law of the flesh. But to Anna his transports of religious emotion represent extreme abstraction and selflessness, which Lawrence associated with the modern flesh-censoring epoch.

In Anna's eyes, Will's love of the old sacred things bespeaks subservience to a "ready-made duty" that she finds abhorrent (*R*, p. 146); Will seems to retreat into an abstract, spiritual recess. Anna counters with excessive self-assertion, the sterile egoism of David. The result is nullity, corresponding to the state of the world in 1915: Anna may be Anna Victrix, but, as Lawrence wrote in the 1925 version of "The Crown," "[a]ny individual who will triumph, in love or in war, perishes" (*RDP,* p. 269).

The only way to break this deadlock is through excessive force, violent transgression of the sexual conventions that the blasphemy of the war was fought to maintain. As Cornelia Nixon has shown, when in April 1915 Lawrence revised the chapters dealing with the second generation, he heightened the violence of their sex war and made them more conscious of the corruption into which they fall. At the same time, Will now assumed a more active, independent role. In the March typescript he "seemed to hurt her [Anna's] womb callously," but now he does so "to take pleasure in torturing her"; what had been "ugly" and "vicious" now became "evil" and "malignant" (*R*, pp. 142, 579).[60] The result of this violence is acceptance of a new sensuality stemming from Will's malevolence. Initially, Anna strenuously resists this spirit, battling with her husband in "The Cathedral" (a chapter added in 1915) in "horrible, murderous" fights, followed by a passion between them that is "just as black and awful" (*R*, p. 194). In the expanded encounter at the end of chapter 8 ("The Child"), Will "with infinite sensual violence gave himself to the realisation of this supreme, immoral, Absolute Beauty, in the body of woman" (*R*, p. 220). G. Wilson Knight and Jeffrey Meyers have linked this passion, with its imagery of darkness and unplumbed depths, with anal sexuality, and surely the suggestions are strong:

> But still the thing terrified him. Awful and threatening it was, dangerous to a degree, even whilst he gave himself to it. It was pure darkness, also. All the shameful things of the body revealed themselves to him now with a sort of sinister, tropical beauty. All the shameful, natural and unnatural acts of sensual voluptuousness which he and the woman partook of together, created together, they had their heavy beauty and their delight. Shame, what was it? It was part of extreme delight. It was that part of delight of which man is usually afraid. Why afraid? The secret, shameful things are most terribly beautiful.
>
> They accepted shame, and were one with it in their most unlicensed pleasures. It was incorporated. It was a bud that blossomed into beauty and heavy, fundamental gratification. (*R*, p. 220)

Meyers points out how surprising it is that at the *Rainbow* trial the authorities did not remark on the "hints of sodomy" in this scene, "either because they failed to notice it or," he quips, "because the suggestion was too awful to contemplate."[61] Had the authorities seen the revised typescript of *The Rainbow,* they might have noted that in rewriting the second of these paragraphs for publication Lawrence laid a new stress on Will's and Anna's conscious acceptance of shame. In the typescript, the paragraph begins: "They blotted out shame, and were free of it, even in their most unlicensed pleasures. The shame simply did not exist" (R, p. 607). In the published version, what was once "blotted out" is now "accepted"; what "simply did not exist" is "incorporated." The change suggests a notion the authorities would have found even more difficult to contemplate: shame, if accepted, heightens sexual pleasure. Further, as the conflict between Will and Anna intensifies, so too does the organic vitality of their relationship: the new sensuality "was a bud that blossomed into beauty and heavy, fundamental gratification."

This passage represents a covert assault on inherited concepts of justice, an attempt to clear the ground to facilitate the new justice proclaimed in *Twilight in Italy*. Shame is not only "immoral and against mankind"; it is associated with "the rolling, absolute beauty of the round arch" (R, p. 220). Evoking the shape of the rainbow, this image implies that shame may bring the possibility of a new covenant to replace the old one. The flood that kills Tom Brangwen in the next chapter ("The Marsh and the Flood") suggests that the old covenant has been broken. But this breach is necessary to rejuvenate a dying world. The "inward life" of Will and Anna is "revolutionised": "The children became less important, the parents were absorbed in their own living" (R, p. 220). Will is free to express his creativity in the public arena by giving woodwork classes; conduct normally considered immoral and against mankind enables him to reenter that arena in a new, more animated way. It is at this moment that Will and Anna are reborn, though not as completely as Tom and Lydia, since the new sensuality falls short of the union of flesh and spirit achieved by their forebears (we see an image only of the arch, not of the rainbow itself).[62] At some level, Will's desire "to be unanimous with the whole of purposive mankind" (R, p. 221) merely represents subservience to the pursuit of goals, to the ideology of mechanical production, which, as is clear in "Hardy," Lawrence considers a futile preoccupation of the male (STH, pp. 25, 94). While limited, however, the renewal of Will's and Anna's marriage suggests that their experience of "shame" is a necessary step toward the absolute justice of the two infinites, the marriage of body and spirit.

"Shame," a term often associated in early-twentieth-century Britain with sexual deviance, preoccupied the authorities at the 1915 trial. The court may have missed the scandalous implications of the passage in "The Child," but the lesbian episode in chapter 12, titled "Shame," was a more obvious target, and it duly received full attention. As we have seen, lesbianism was not recognized by British law, and it was regarded as an unacceptable subject for fiction. In chapter 12, Lawrence ritualizes such deviance; the bathing scene involving Will's and Anna's oldest daughter, Ursula, and her teacher, Winifred Inger, is presented as a spectacle that seems to demand a response from the audience. In 1915 it was inevitable that the response would be one of condemnation. In fact, publishers steered clear of the most provocative parts of this chapter for many years afterward. In the American edition of December 1915, B. W. Huebsch suppressed several sentences describing contact between the two women. Martin Secker followed suit in the British edition of 1926, a move repeated by all other British publishers until 1949, and by their American counterparts until 1981.[63]

The bathing episode in "Shame" is a restaging of a relatively modern ritual, which, even in its more familiar guise, transgressed Edwardian sexual codes. The difference is that Lawrence's bathing scene involves women; such episodes usually featured men, as in E. M. Forster's *A Room With A View* (1908). Paul Fussell has shown that sexually charged bathing scenes, common in the writings of Great War soldier-poets as "a type of the pastoral oasis or a rare 'idyllic moment,'" hark back to Victorian celebrations of the vulnerable male body.[64] Lawrence himself included a male bathing scene in his first novel, *The White Peacock* (1911); as in *A Room With a View,* the episode is clearly homoerotic. After bathing, the narrator, Cyril Beardsall, is rubbed dry by his friend George Saxton, prompting these reflections: "we looked at each other with eyes of still laughter, and our love was perfect for a moment, more perfect than any love I have known since, either for man or woman." *The White Peacock* also relates this homoeroticism to prewar Aestheticism and Decadence by alluding throughout to such artists as Aubrey Beardsley, Edward Burne-Jones, and the Rossettis. Before rubbing Beardsall dry, for instance, Saxton tells him that he is "like one of Aubrey Beardsley's long, lean ugly fellows."[65] Lawrence may have had this tradition in mind when later describing Rawdon Lilly rubbing oil over the lower body of the ailing Aaron Sisson in *Aaron's Rod,* a novel that satirizes another form of decadence: postwar Bohemianism. Unlike *The White Peacock* and *Aaron's Rod,* however, chapter 12 of *The Rainbow* seems to have scandalized its readers because, in reviving memories of prewar decadence, it exacerbated them by recasting that decadence as lesbian.

Reading *The Rainbow* in the context of the Great War, it is not hard to imagine the kinds of anxiety aroused by the following passage from "Shame":

> And the elder held the younger close against her, close, as they went down, and by the side of the water, she put her arms round her, and kissed her. And she lifted her in her arms, close, saying softly:
>
> "I shall carry you into the water."
>
> Ursula lay still in her mistress's arms, her forehead against the beloved, maddening breast.
>
> "I shall put you in," said Winifred.
>
> But Ursula twined her body about her mistress.[66]
>
> After a while the rain came down on their flushed, hot limbs, startling, delicious. A sudden, ice-cold shower burst in a great weight upon them. They stood up to it with pleasure. Ursula received the stream of it upon her breasts and her belly and her limbs. (*R,* pp. 315–16)

This was one of the passages doctored by Huebsch, who excised the sentences ("Ursula lay still . . . twined her body about her mistress") most clearly indicating passionate bodily contact. It was bad enough in 1915 simply to portray active female sexual desire, a specter that took concrete form in Marie Stopes's enormously popular *Married Love* (1918). Occurring at a time when the British government was concerned about increases in divorce rates and illegitimate births,[67] Stopes's own trial in 1923 revealed postwar anxieties that grew out of the context in which *The Rainbow* was first received. The target of Stopes's unsuccessful libel suit, Dr. Halliday Gibson Sutherland, compounded his denunciation of her contraceptive methods by reminding the court that she had gained her doctorate in Munich, as if to suggest some connection between sexual immorality and the German threat: "In the midst of a London slum, a woman, who is a Doctor of *German* Philosophy (Munich) has opened a birth-control clinic, where working class women are instructed in a method of contraception described by Professor McIlroy as 'the most harmful method of which I have had experience.'"[68] The bathing scene in Lawrence's novel provoked anxieties anticipating those exposed at the Stopes trial, and it exaggerated them by raising the possibility of a female sexuality oriented toward other women: the scene fills the vacuum created by the absence of a generation of young British men by suggesting that female desires may be satisfied without them. In addition to displacing a generation of British males, Lawrence's depiction of lesbianism may have aggravated another anxiety, which was revealed quite graphically by subsequent opposition to Stopes's advocacy of contraception: Where might the next generation come from? Lesbianism, which meant women who did not fulfill their maternal function, promised not generation but termination.

Jeffrey Meyers has suggested that in citing the "Shame" chapter at the *Rainbow* trial the court was missing the point, that "Lawrence condemns this lesbianism."[69] While at some level this reading is hard to deny, ambiguities in Lawrence's treatment of lesbianism suggest that the court may not have been entirely wrong in reading the episode as subverting conventional notions of sexuality and gender. Winifred is not always portrayed in a negative light. When we first meet her she is described as "a rather beautiful woman, . . . clever, and expert in what she did, accurate, quick, commanding" (*R*, p. 311). Ursula adores Winifred's "fine, upright, athletic bearing and her indomitably proud nature: . . . She was proud and free as a man, yet exquisite as a woman" (*R*, p. 312). Winifred is also likened to the goddess Diana, which suggests that the bathing scene is a reenactment of an ancient drama as well as a more recent one. Like Diana, Winifred turns viciously on modern man, as we see in a passage that echoes Lawrence's own view of masculinity in modern industrial Britain. Noting earlier in the chapter Winifred's interest in "the Women's Movement," Lawrence writes:

"The men will do no more—they have lost the capacity for doing," said the elder girl. "They fuss, and talk, but they are really inane. They make everything fit into an old, inert idea. Love is a dead idea to them. They don't come to one and love one, they come to an idea, and they say 'You are my idea,' so they embrace themselves. As if I were any man's idea! As if I exist because a man has an idea of me! As if I will be betrayed by him, lend him my body as an instrument for his idea, to be a mere apparatus of his dead theory. But they are too fussy to be able to act: they are all impotent, they can't *take* a woman. They come to their own idea every time, and take that. They are like serpents trying to swallow themselves because they are hungry." (*R,* p. 318)

The images of impotence and devouring reanimate, in modern form, the mythical tale of Diana and Actaeon, who was punished for watching the goddess bathe. The passage implies that Actaeon's later counterparts may be even easier prey than he was: "They are like serpents trying to swallow themselves." In the modern world, the possibility of a vital sex war has been undermined by the absolute impotence of British males, a notion likely to aggravate British officials concerned about the source of the next generation.[70]

In a powerful irony, Winifred moves in a direction contrary to the terminal impulses feared by Lawrence's censors: she marries the younger Tom Brangwen, the manager of the Wiggiston colliery, who wants "to propagate himself" (*R,* p. 326). Cynthia Lewiecki-Wilson reads this marriage as "an ironic homage to the force of patriarchy," which "spawns the deadly forces of capitalism as well as the mechanical reproduction of the social unit, and decadent, 'perverted' sexuality too."[71] There are also other reasons why Lawrence's contemporaries would have found this variation on the marriage plot less than reassuring. For it is in marrying Tom that Winifred reveals what is wrong with her. Like Tom, and like all British males, she is the slave of the machine; in propagating the species she will simply be contributing to a system that produces the brutalized creatures Ursula encounters at St. Philip's School. Lawrence implies that, contrary to the view of his censors, Winifred very much belongs to the moribund tradition of the family and to the fictions it creates about itself. It is this subservience that is the source of Winifred's corruption. Like Tom, she illustrates what happens when the law of the womb is distorted by the abstract principles of the spirit: "She would make a good companion. She was his mate" (*R,* p. 327).

It is telling that "Shame" should end with the word "mate": Winifred is thus identified as a potential mother. Yet, as in "Anna Victrix," the implication is that in accepting this status Winifred is sealed off as a dead end. Rather than seeking out her own law, she accepts a set of received rules. Winifred's smooth transformation from lesbian to mate suggests that femininity is no more than an act, a series of interchangeable roles. While it may have comforted wartime readers to see a lesbian return to what Judith Butler calls "the obligatory frame of reproductive heterosexuality," it cannot have been so reassuring to think that the roles of wife and deviant might be played with such ease by one character, or that there might be no essential difference between a woman who loves men and a woman who loves other women. Winifred's marriage suggests that reproductive sexuality is merely a matter of performance, a powerful demonstration of the deep instability intrinsic to such a model of identity.

Winifred's partner in crime in the lesbian episode, Ursula Brangwen, is often hailed as Lawrence's feminist heroine, the woman who rejects marriage, has a miscarriage, and becomes "individual, self-responsible, taking her own initiative."[72] College-educated, sexually liberated, Ursula achieves a degree of independence that is beyond that of her mother and grandmother. The relationship with Winifred is generally regarded as an important stage in her development, but also as one she must outgrow. The lesbian episode is one of many trials to which Ursula is subjected. The test in this case is to see that Winifred, while attractive, perpetuates a false law that manifests itself in the perversions of the machine. The bathing scene dramatizes an ordeal that is reenacted in their visit to Wiggiston (a modern industrial hell), in Ursula's spell as a teacher at St. Philip's School, and in her student days at the University College of Nottingham: "Her very life was at test" (R, p. 358). The repetition forms the kind of pattern that Lawrence's contemporaries found so monotonous, but Ursula has to be tested again and again if she is to break through the existing system of laws and seize the initiative. It is through the process of trial and retrial that Ursula becomes a woman.

Ursula's trials actually begin before Winifred appears. The first sign that she is to be tested is the arrival of Anton Skrebensky; the episode with Winifred is an entr'acte between acts one and two of his struggles with Ursula, which constitute the third phase of the sex war. The sex scenes with Anton form a drama, enacted and reenacted with increasing ferocity. The treatment of Skrebensky in these scenes implies a withering critique of the military and imperial ideology he serves as a British soldier in the Boer War, a critique that must have aggravated Lawrence's wartime readers. The repeated sex duels with Ursula become the sort of savage rite that James Douglas attacked so bitterly in his review for the Star. The repetition of this rite is necessary for Ursula's attack on the laws of identity, sexuality, and reproduction. In search of her own law and the law of the Holy Spirit, Ursula must constantly reproduce herself; the process of becoming a woman requires the continual reenactment of an ordeal whose terms are gradually altered in the performance. As Skrebensky finds out to his cost, the terms must be changed if Ursula is to survive; the system of laws by which he abides must itself be put on trial.

It is Anton's arrival that rouses Ursula into sexual consciousness. That their love contests will become increasingly theatrical is intimated at the same instant: Ursula sees that in order to take her place in the world she needs to self-dramatize. Skrebensky thrills her "with a new life": "For the first time, she was in love with a vision of herself: she saw as it were a fine little reflection of herself in his eyes. And she must act up to this: she must be beautiful. Her thoughts turned swiftly to clothes, her passion was to make a beautiful appearance. Her family looked on in amazement at the sudden transformation of Ursula" (R, p. 272). Ursula is aware from the beginning that being a beautiful woman, an object of desire, is a matter of acting up. While the ensuing rites of desire become almost uncontrollably savage, there is a hint even now of her ability to exert self-control. Eventually, she takes control of Skrebensky, too.

To act up is to perform, but it is also to make trouble; it is an expression of dissatisfaction and rebellion. These are exactly Ursula's feelings when she begins her relationship with Skrebensky, and from the outset she assumes the role of troublemaker. At a low ebb as "the cloud of self-responsibility gathered upon her," Ursula plays this part in ways that seem designed to generate charges of blasphemy in wartime Britain. Christianity, once "a glorious sort of play-world," has become "a tale, a myth, an illusion," which no longer matches up with lived experience: "There could, within the limits of this life we know, be no Feeding of Five Thousand" (*R*, p. 263). Ursula responds to Christ with "sensuous yearning," yet "she knew underneath that she was playing false, accepting the passion of Jesus for her own physical satisfaction" (*R*, p. 267). With Anton, whom Ursula imagines as one of "those Sons of God," arrives the illusion of release from the realm of false acting into a "world of passions and lawlessness," a world in which it is perfectly acceptable to make love in church (*R*, pp. 271, 277). Ultimately, however, Skrebensky serves the same function in Ursula's imagination as Christ. As Lawrence makes clear in a phrase added to the typescript, Anton exists, like Christ, in "her own desire only" (*R*, p. 309). Christ and Skrebensky are both projections of a woman's desire; they fit the same imaginary portrait of inadequate masculinity. Some readers have seen Skrebensky as another incarnation of the law of the flesh,[73] but the parallel with Christ implies that he represents the spirit, like Winifred and the younger Tom Brangwen. In an image anticipating the terminal desires of "Shame" and Ursula's miscarriage, Anton's self is described as "dead, still-born, a dead weight in his womb" (*R*, p. 304). Unlike Tom and Lydia, and even Will and Anna, he cannot be reborn. He is an abortion, grotesque proof that the primeval law of the womb has been violated, that a false spirit has censored the body.[74]

Openly critical of war and hostile to the values for which Britain was fighting in 1915, Ursula repeatedly makes trouble for Skrebensky in a relationship that is highly ritualized. Some critics have traced a development in this novel from gesture (in the first generation) to speech (in the third).[75] But the greater articulacy of Ursula and Skrebensky is itself rendered in theatrical form, as we see in their frequent debates, a mode characteristic of the sophisticated world of *Women in Love*. These debates have the dramatic charge of trials. Ursula is being tested, but she seizes the initiative by taking the part of prosecutor, while Skrebensky tries to defend himself and the values of British civilization. Skrebensky is a mouthpiece for conventional, body-censoring views; he justifies military imperialism by invoking such concepts as community and duty, mechanical fabrications of the modern industrial age. As F. R. Leavis noted, Skrebensky is a "hollow man," whose "good-citizen acceptance of the social function as the ultimate meaning of life" is deeply connected to his "inadequacy as a lover."[76] But Ursula explicitly rejects Skrebensky's received values. Soldiers are dismissed as embodiments of the rigid abstraction visible elsewhere in the modern industrial world: "I hate houses that never go away, and people just living in the houses. It's all so stiff and stupid. I hate soldiers, they are stiff and wooden. What do you fight for, really?" Skrebensky's defense of the system merely convinces Ursula that he amounts to nothing: "'It seems to me . . . as if you weren't anybody—as if there weren't anybody there, where you are. Are you anybody, really? You seem like nothing to me'" (*R*, p. 289). Ursula then turns on democracy and imperialism, the institutions that Lawrence's contemporaries were trying to save in the Great War. Democracy she denounces as "meagre and paltry, . . . unspiritual"; only "degenerate races," she declares, "are democratic" (*R*, pp. 426, 427). The sole aim of colonial imperialism is to impose its own corrupt form of government on other countries, "to make things there as dead and mean as they are here" (*R*, p. 428). Imperialism is the means by which degenerate British democracy spreads its contagion; fighting for the nation, Skrebensky is just one more wooden soldier in that charade. In his devotion to these diseased abstractions, Skrebensky demonstrates subservience to the law of the spirit, which represses the body. He is guilty of failing to seek his own law, and therefore of negating the possibility of consummate marriage. Hence Ursula's verdict: "There seemed some shame at the very root of life, cold, dead shame for her" (*R*, p. 307). The charge of terminal desire is used to indict Skrebensky before Winifred appears.

The role of judge in this case was filled by Lawrence himself, and increasingly, as an examination of his wartime revisions makes clear, he took Ursula's side. In revision, Skrebensky became an easier target because he had to be shot down. In 1915 Lawrence accentuated Skrebensky's hollow corruption by introducing an element of perverse sexuality. Lawrence insinuated into Skrebensky's sexuality the "marshy, bitter-sweet corruption" associated elsewhere with the younger Tom Brangwen and Winifred Inger. Returning from the Boer War for the second act of his sex war with Ursula, Anton tells her that the darkness in England "is soft, and natural to me, it is my medium, especially when you are here" (*R*, p. 413). He exploits his medium in order to work on Ursula, to whose blood he transmits the "hot, fecund darkness" of Africa, so that "a turgid, teeming night, heavy with fecundity in which every molecule of matter grew big with increase, secretly urgent with fecund desire, seemed to come to pass" (*R*, p. 413). Lawrence connected such adjectives as "marshy," "corrupt," and "teeming" with the homosexuality he encountered at Cambridge in March 1915. Cambridge provoked dreams of beetles, which he associated with the "corruption" of men loving men: "It is this horror of little swarming selves that I can't stand: Birrells, D. Grants, and Keynses [*sic*]" (*L2*, p. 319). Lawrence claimed that he "never considered Plato very wrong, or Oscar Wilde," until confronted by John Maynard Keynes, "blinking from sleep, standing in his pyjamas": "And as he stood there gradually a knowledge passed into me, which has been like a little madness to me ever since" (*L2*, pp. 320–21). This knowledge informs "the hot, fecund darkness" that Skrebensky passes to Ursula in the "turgid, teeming night." In the terms of Lawrence's indictment, such associations suggest an enfeebled masculinity, a notion all the more scandalous in wartime Britain for being concentrated on the figure of a British soldier.

Ursula's verbal contests with Anton are acted out in the savage rites of their sexual encounters. Revising these violent scenes in the summer of 1915, Lawrence again weighted the scales to make Ursula even more dominant, Skrebensky more vulnerable. Lawrence put a new emphasis on the language of armed conflict, leaving Ursula triumphant and Skrebensky emasculated. Some of the most striking revisions occur in "First Love," particularly in the stackyard scene, in which Ursula "annihilates" her lover. She becomes "cold," "bright as a steel blade," "corrosive," "salt-burning," "poison," the antithesis of Anton's "inertia," "soft iron," and "dross." Ursula takes on the qualities of the moon, its "cold and hard and compact brilliance," as well as its impersonality; Skrebensky loses his edge. The one-sidedness of this episode became especially pronounced when Lawrence revised the manuscript: "A [hunter's madness and determination came over him too] <darkness, an obstinacy settled on him too, in a kind of inertia>. He sat [dark] <inert> beside her" (*R*, pp. 297, 626). In the revised version, Skrebensky no longer has the active, predatory instincts of the hunter: now he is a "blind, persistent, inert burden," weighing on Ursula "like a loadstone" (*R*, p. 296). When Ursula "received all the force of his power," and "even wished he might overcome her," Skrebensky is not up to the task; when his "will was set and straining with all its tension to encompass her and compel her," there is nothing to indicate that he has the power to do so (*R*, p. 297). The phrase, "If only he could compel her," indicates that Skrebensky's desire for dominance is mere wishful thinking: Ursula is entirely "beyond him as the moonlight was beyond him, never to be grasped or known" (*R*, p. 297). Such scenes cannot have pleased those who sat in judgment on *The Rainbow* in 1915.

In these terms, the most compelling scene occurs in chapter 15, "The Bitterness of Ecstasy," in which Ursula's victory over Skrebensky is consummated on the beach. As in the stackyard scene, the ritual element of this episode is quite marked: "He felt as if the ordeal of proof was upon him, for life or death" (*R*, p. 444). In effect, Anton, having lost the first trial, has been granted a retrial. Written between 1 February and 2 March 1915,[77] the beach scene seemed especially likely to arouse controversy, which Lawrence realized only too well, as did his American publisher, B. W. Huebsch, who made even more cuts in this chapter than in "Shame." Not only is the scene explicit in its representation of sex, but it portrays Ursula's triumph over her soldier-lover by drawing on images of war in a manner that might have been construed in 1915 as antiwar. As in "First Love," forces are deployed heavily in Ursula's favor. Anton experiences the sensation of reduction, as under the moonlight he "felt himself fusing down to nothingness" (*R*, p. 443). Meanwhile, Ursula, who "seemed to melt into the white glare, towards the moon," acquires the moon's impersonal destructive power, and becomes "like metal": Skrebensky hears "her ringing, metallic voice, like the voice of a harpy to him." Now Ursula, who prowls, "ranging on the edge of the water like a possessed creature," has Skrebensky in her grip (*R*, p. 444). Yet again, he fails the test. Under the impersonal glare of the moonlight, Ursula carries out his punishment:

> She lay motionless, with wide-open eyes looking at the moon. He came direct to her, without preliminaries. She held him pinned down at the chest, awful. The fight, the struggle for consummation was terrible. It lasted till it was agony to his soul, till he succumbed, till he gave way as if dead, and lay with his face buried partly in her hair partly in the sand, motionless, as if he would be motionless now for ever, hidden away in the dark, buried, only buried, he only wanted to be buried in the goodly darkness, only that, no more. (*R*, pp. 444–45)

In the long last sentence, Skrebensky appears reduced to the state of one of the war dead, or of a fatally wounded soldier seeking in burial refuge from further destruction. The analogy of the war is apposite, for a swooning Skrebensky "felt as if the knife were being pushed into his already dead body" (*R*, p. 445).[78] The war imagery expresses the arid impersonality into which Ursula's relationship with Skrebensky has fallen. Implying the barrenness of the sexual activity on which contemporary family fiction was founded, Lawrence subtly undermines the sense of domestic security necessary to a successful war effort. The depiction of Evelyn Daughtry's death in "England, My England" was risqué, but the war imagery in *The Rainbow* was more insidiously transgressive.

Ursula's annihilation of Skrebensky has consequences not calculated to soothe wartime British anxieties. Inevitably, Ursula calls off their impending marriage, terminating the marriage plot found in respectable family fiction. Rejected by Ursula, Skrebensky persists in his attempts to meet the requirements of that plot, and succeeds by marrying his colonel's daughter. But this is clearly an apology for marriage, a sign of Anton's lifeless insistence on pursuing a goal that he identifies with the ends of empire. The verdict on his marriage seems designed to upset Lawrence's wartime censors.

The indictment is so severe that Ursula, too, is forced to undergo further ordeals, to act out the last rites of Lawrencean justice. For, having appropriated the roles of prosecutor and executioner in the trials of Skrebensky, Ursula is not immune from punishment; after the beach scene she is tainted by Anton's arid inertia. The heroine is still very much on trial herself. In her zeal to secure Anton's fate, she has forced herself into a position as extreme and distorted as his. If he was the spirit, she was the body; she still has a long way to go in her development toward self-responsibility. Finally, however, Ursula acquits herself by showing that she understands the terms on which she must continue her quest for higher justice. She reveals her fitness not only by vanquishing Skrebensky but by displaying healthy skepticism of the idea that love itself is a goal, which, once achieved, becomes the cornerstone of safe domesticity. Anton makes clear his adherence to this view (another abstraction) by his actions after the beach scene. Strikingly, his feelings on this subject are shared by two characters not readily associated with him: Ursula's colleague at St. Philip's School, Maggie Schofield, and her college friend, Dorothy Russell. Both of these characters have suffragist sympathies; Dorothy is a member of the WSPU. Yet like Anton, Maggie and Dorothy see love as "an end in itself" (*R*, pp. 382, 440). Ursula disagrees, implying that suffragism serves the same goal-oriented ideology as the despised patriarchy. For Ursula, love is "a way, a means" (*R*, p. 382): hence her rejection not only of Skrebensky but also of Maggie's brother, Anthony. Ursula is a "traveller" who sees love as a continuous process, life as a series of trials. Even if consummate marriage is impossible at present, it is better to be a law unto oneself than to obey a moribund system of laws. It is not hard to see how the verdict on Skrebensky would have angered wartime readers; the extension of this judgment to include Maggie and Dorothy suggests that Lawrence sought to offend suffragists like Helena Swanwick as well as her more patriarchal colleagues.

In helping to deliver this inclusive verdict, Ursula exhibits her understanding of Lawrencean justice; she now faces one more trial of her own, a final, abortive restaging of the rites of maternity. It is hard to tell whether Ursula's pregnancy and miscarriage in chapter 16 ("The Rainbow") are real or imaginary, but she clearly experiences a violent physical upheaval, which Lawrence likens to a trial: "She was as if tied to the stake. The flames were licking her and devouring her" (*R*, p. 448). Having been chained to the body in the battles with Skrebensky, Ursula must undergo one last physical ordeal to escape its constraints; she must demonstrate her commitment to the laws of self-responsibility by reenacting the maternal role. Yet the termination of this pregnancy suggests that the role has played itself out; it imposes limitations that can no longer contain Ursula's potential for growth. Ursula's tribulations prepare us for the concluding vision of the rainbow, in which Lawrence suggests it is possible to pry open closed systems, to break out of old, encrusted forms into new life:

> And the rainbow stood on the earth. She knew that the sordid people who crept hard-scaled and separate on the face of the world's corruption were living still, that the rainbow was arched in their blood and would quiver to life in their spirit, that they would cast off their horny covering of disintegration, that new, clean, naked bodies would issue to a new germination, to a new growth, rising to the light and the wind and the clean rain of heaven. She saw in the rainbow the earth's new architecture, the old, brittle corruption of houses and factories swept away, the world built up in a living fabric of Truth, fitting to the over-arching heaven. (*R*, pp. 458–59)

The journalist James Douglas attacked Lawrence for perverting a "symbol of strange beauty," but what Douglas saw as the "lower nature" is incorporated into this vision. The new germination intimates a new kind of life associated with Ursula, who, in experiencing the rainbow vision, is reborn as a woman. In the process of rebirth, Ursula sends the exhausted, mechanical roles of wife and mother to their graves. In this way she takes to its conclusion the novel's subversion of Edwardian sexual ideology and, by implication, its refutation of the related ideologies of war and empire. To put the case legally, Ursula's imagination opens up the possibility of a state no longer ruled by mechanical systems of law, a state where male and female, spirit and flesh, are joined in absolute justice. It is a form of justice that is inconceivable under the rules of interpretation upheld by Lawrence's censors in November 1915.[79]

One commentator has recently warned against overestimating the feminist implications of the ending of *The Rainbow*; Ursula, he observes, resumes the search for a male counterpart in *Women in Love*, the second part of what was originally conceived of as one novel.[80] The point serves as a useful reminder of Lawrence's aesthetic orientation toward process rather than fixed goals: the rainbow, an image of hope, projects us onward into the future. But the sight of the rainbow also allows us to pause, to take stock of what has been achieved,

before moving on. At the end of the novel, the lone survivor of three generations of sex war is Ursula, who has grown into a self-responsible woman by
outlasting the ordeals of modern life; her survival means that the system of laws
governing the world has been permanently disfigured, that it is possible to think
of law in a new way. It is important to remember, moreover, that the compositional history of these novels was not known to Lawrence's censors; indeed,
their response to *The Rainbow* helps us to see the controversial aspects of this
work more clearly. Even if the compositional history had been available in
1915, *Women in Love* would hardly have revived wartime readers sickened,
like the reviewer Clement Shorter, by "the strong meat contained in . . . *The
Rainbow*."[81] After *The Rainbow* it was not so easy to adhere rigidly to the
script for family fiction that censors wanted to preserve. In his reworking of
that script, Lawrence had made the regulatory frame of sexual identity a little
more flexible; the "cages and censorships of woman's existence," defended by
Marian Cox in her attack on German culture, had been rendered a little less
safe. Lawrence's contemporaries were quite correct to read the savage rites of
The Rainbow as challenging the values of wartime Edwardian culture; that
was exactly what Lawrence wanted to do. But Lawrence was not the only
modern author rewriting the regulatory fictions of sex and gender. While *The
Rainbow* was on trial, James Joyce was at work on his own sex novel, another
major modernist text censored for obscenity.

2

Obscenity and Nonreproductive Sexuality: *Ulysses* and the *Little Review* Trial

When Margaret Anderson and Jane Heap agreed with Ezra Pound that the *Little Review* should undertake the serial publication of *Ulysses,* they fully expected their decision to result in the suppression of their magazine. They also believed *Ulysses* was worth it; as Pound said, *Ulysses* was "obscure, even obscene, as life itself is obscene in places, but an impassioned meditation on life."[1] For Anderson, *Ulysses* embodied "direct opposition to the prevalent art values in America," which she saw as the primary function of the *Little Review,* and at first she was committed to publishing Joyce's work uncut.[2] Despite subsequent editorial interference, first by Pound and later by Anderson herself, *Ulysses* succeeded in landing the two women editors in a New York courtroom. In September 1920 a lawyer complained to the district attorney that his daughter had received an unsolicited copy of the July–August issue of the *Little Review,* containing the concluding part of "Nausicaa," the thirteenth episode of *Ulysses,* in which Gerty MacDowell exhibits herself before the masturbating hero, Leopold Bloom. The district attorney called in John S. Sumner, secretary of the New York Society for the Prevention of Vice, and after a preliminary hearing in October 1920 the trial was set for February 1921. Despite hearing testimony that *Ulysses* would not corrupt the mind of a young girl, the three judges found Anderson and Heap guilty of publishing "indecent matter," and fined them $50 each.[3]

The publication history of *Ulysses* is inseparable from the history of the novel's censorship, for it appeared and evolved in the context of censorship. *Ulysses* was dogged by censors until 1934, when an American court upheld the verdict of Judge John M. Woolsey, who had legalized its publication one year earlier. In fact, the first installment of Joyce's novel appeared in the *Little Review* in the aftermath of an earlier censorship controversy. In October 1917 the U.S. Post Office had seized the *Little Review* issue containing Wyndham Lewis's story, "Cantleman's Spring Mate," in which a cynical British soldier seduces a young woman but abandons her when she becomes pregnant. When Judge Augustus Hand (who delivered the court's opinion in the 1934 case) upheld the legality of this action, Anderson and Pound condemned his decision, Anderson by declaring opposition to the prevalent art values in America, Pound in an essay called "The Classics Escape." In this piece, which appeared in the same issue of the *Little Review* as the first episode of *Ulysses*, Pound ridiculed Judge Hand's opinion that modern literature should answer to the courts while the classics "are ordinarily immune from interference, because they have the sanction of age and fame and USUALLY APPEAL TO A COMPARATIVELY LIMITED NUMBER OF READERS." In Pound's eyes, the classics had "in the beginning lifted mankind from savagery"; it was absurd to prevent living writers from contributing to that process. Pound concluded: "No more damning indictment of American civilization has been written than that contained in Judge Hand's 'opinion.'"[4]

Pound also attacked Hand for suppressing Lewis's story under a statute that accommodated literary obscenity under the same roof as contraceptives and abortion. Pound expressed amazement at learning that one's "works might be classed in law's eye with the inventions of the late Dr. Condom."[5] He believed that in suppressing "Cantleman's Spring Mate" under section 211 of the U.S. Criminal Code, Hand had endorsed a ludicrous confusion of literature with abortion and contraception—a confusion symptomatic of the deplorable condition of American society. Hand's decision seemed to imply that "a campaign for free literature" was necessarily "mixed up with a campaign for Mrs Sanger, birth control, etc." As Pound put it: "I object to a law which doesnt keep the two issues distinct. AND a country which cant distinguish between the two is in a bloody rotten state of barbarism."[6]

Despite such remonstrances about the obscenity law, it is strangely fitting that *Ulysses* was suppressed under a "statute which," as Pound said, "lumps literature and instruments for abortion into one clause" (*PQ*, p. 132). This event is what Pound called a "Luminous Detail,"[7] for debates about abortion and contraception are also, among other things, debates about the body—specifically, about censorship of the female body and of the discourses of that body. In a certain sense, Pound himself was more than willing to acknowledge literature's bodily ties, for he linked literary genius with seminal fluid: "the power of the spermatozoide," he wrote, "is precisely the power of exteriorizing a form." This interest in the creative properties of semen may partly explain Pound's reluctance to see a relation between literature and abortion; abortion obstructs procreation in a manner analogous to what he perceived as women's resistance to genius, the masculine force that shaped civilization. Of such resistance, Pound confessed: "Even oneself has felt it, driving any new idea into the great passive vulva of London."[8] But he was not alone in seeing the female body as a problem of modern civilization. In the aftermath of the Great War, the female body and the related issues of abortion and contraception seemed particularly vexatious because they were inextricable from the moral and demographic questions facing postwar society. J. B. Yeats attributed the suppression of "Cantleman's Spring Mate" to the hysterical atmosphere of war.[9]

Lewis's evocation of unwanted pregnancy must have seemed an unwelcome provocation at such a time, and in this light the censorship of his story does not seem so surprising. Although, unlike *The Rainbow,* Lewis's tale portrays the soldier as sexually dominant in ways that most readers expected, it offended them by representing Cantleman's liaison as part of an evolutionary mating process that renders irrelevant mere social conventions like marriage. But, as the case of Marie Stopes shows, one did not necessarily avoid censure just by advocating marriage. While popular with the public, Stopes's *Married Love* (1918) and *Contraception* (1923) were considered obscene because her treatment of marital sex involved open discussion of female desire and contraception. As a result Stopes faced court cases on both sides of the Atlantic, first her unsuccessful libel suit against the British doctor Halliday Gibson Sutherland in 1923, then two American obscenity trials in 1931.[10]

Beginning publication in the *Little Review* of March 1918, *Ulysses* entered the realm of public discourse in the context of such debates. Questions of censorship visibly intersected with issues of sex and gender in the March 1918 number, which contained not only Pound's essay and the first chapter of *Ulysses,* but also the second part of Ford Madox Ford's "Men and Women," an attack on Otto Weininger's misogynistic, extremely popular book, *Sex and Character* (1903). Weininger had defined femininity as negative, nonexistent, illogical, passive, as "nothing more than sexuality."[11] As Ford saw, Weininger gave men an excuse for throwing out the woman question with which the liberals among them were supposedly engaged. Ford perceived that Weininger affirmed the propriety of censuring, and censoring, a suffragist movement that, as Susan Kent has argued, sought to overthrow the dominant view of women as sexual objects.[12] Further, by equating women with sexuality Weininger reduced them to their reproductive function: "Sexuality uses the woman as the means to produce pleasure and the children of the body."[13]

From its initial appearance in this discursive context, *Ulysses* evolved in ways suggesting different approaches to women and sexuality. The novel implies the unexpected appropriateness of "lump[ing] literature and instruments for abortion into one clause" by reexamining the terms within which sexologists like Weininger made their extravagant yet often unquestioned claims. Particularly in the episodes beginning with "Nausicaa" and ending with "Penelope," Joyce portrays femininity as a series of texts constructed from other texts, an intertextual system comprising different forms and levels of cultural discourse about sex and sexuality, biology and psychology, society and religion. In condemning *Ulysses,* the judges at the 1921 trial were attempting to protect readers such as the daughter of the lawyer who complained about "Nausicaa"; Joyce's episode reveals the contradictions and ultimate futility of that attempt. Presenting the mind of Gerty MacDowell, "Nausicaa" portrays ideas of pure young womanhood as fantasies produced by texts—the sentimental, romantic discourse generating and framing Gerty's consciousness—that sanction prudery but also generate sexual desires. Those desires may be largely unconscious, but insofar as they express nonreproductive inclinations they are allied with contraception and abortion. Joyce's restaging of the pornographic process in "Nausicaa" shows illicit desires emerging from the same source as, even depending on, the public morality that supposedly prohibits them.

Insofar as Joyce's text offers an understanding of femininity, it does so by revealing the failings and contradictions of institutional discourses that claim such understanding. In this way "Nausicaa" exposes a gendered distribution of power relations that is to be found as readily in the procedure of the 1921 trial as in pornography. "Nausicaa" also suggests possibilities for disrupting, or aborting, those power relations by playing up the ways in which socially sanctioned concepts of gender identity depend on performance, on (in the words of Judith Butler) a "*stylized repetition of acts*," which "constitute the illusion of an abiding gendered self." As Butler argues, "gender identity is a performative accomplishment compelled by social sanction and taboo," and the abiding gendered self is a product of social sanction. Since gender is no more than a repetition of acts, "the possibilities of gender transformation are to be found in the arbitrary relation between such acts, in the possibility of a different sort of repeating, in the breaking or subversive repetition of that style."[14] Drama requires a script, which each performance interprets and, in effect, rewrites. By exploiting its performative fluidity, "Nausicaa" implies that the concept of gender derives from a cultural script that is always open to such rewriting. Joyce's interpretation of the script for femininity reveals its "postulation of a true gender identity" as what Butler calls a "regulatory fiction."[15] Joyce also suggests that by rewriting the regulatory fictions of gender and sexual identity, it is possible to resist the censorship of personal freedom and intellectual possibility that such fictions imply.

Promoting this reexamination of our ways of reading gender, sexuality, and the body, *Ulysses* complements and complicates the process by which Joyce's stylistic and formal innovations make us become more sophisticated, because more self-conscious, readers. In other words, one of the more obviously political aspects of the text is inseparable from its function as avant-garde art, an art that disrupts and deregulates previously accepted forms of expression by refocusing our attention on the act of reading itself. Claiming to find "Nausicaa" unintelligible, the judges at the 1921 trial were responding to *Ulysses* as an obscure literary experiment. Yet their condemnation of the work as obscene implied not only that they failed to comprehend the episode, but also that its content directed attention beyond the limits of sanctioned discourse. Assaulting sensibilities reared on the staples of traditional fiction, *Ulysses* renders intelligible what scandalized contemporary readers marked as off-limits or obscene: the unrepresentable and the unspeakable, the unknowable and the unthinkable. And in making them recognize obscene elements, *Ulysses* implicates readers in the pornographic process reenacted in "Nausicaa." While compelling readers into this transgressive act, Joyce's novel reveals the inseparability of conventional notions of aesthetic intelligibility from the social, political, and moral norms commonly attributed to literary tradition. As an experimental work, *Ulysses* frustrates those norms, and so aborts the expectations of readers who insist on enforcing them. Hugh Kenner has noted that in retrospect Joyce's hostile early reviewers seem to have been affronted by "a discontinuity between

Ulysses and English story-telling."[16] That is one way of saying that insofar as Joyce's experimental modernism was a literature of deregulation or discontinuity, it was inherently abortive or contraceptive. In this sense, *Ulysses* actually provokes the confusion of literature with antiabortion rhetoric that Pound deplored in U.S. obscenity law. Through such provocation, *Ulysses* encourages a close analysis of reproductive discourse, an analysis that illuminates the conventions, the underlying social and textual artifices, determining readerly and judicial expectations. Inviting readers to scrutinize the reproductive discourse underpinning the obscenity law, *Ulysses* provides a tacit commentary on its own 1921 trial. Joyce suggests that the grounds on which the trial was conducted were both contingent and inherently unstable.[17]

Ulysses in the *Little Review*: A History of Publication and Censorship

Like so much experimental modern literature, *Ulysses* was first steered into print by Ezra Pound. But Joyce's novel was unique in persuading Pound that it was worth the trouble it would inevitably cause. Pound saw in Joyce's work the "hard, clear-cut" realism that seemed to be missing in nearly all modern writing. "Clear thought and sanity," Pound wrote, "depend on clear prose"; if one wanted an explanation for the parlous state of modern German culture, one needed to look no further than modern German prose.[18] In Pound's terms, there would have been no confusion of literature and instruments for abortion in the U.S. Criminal Code if those responsible for drafting the law had been able to write clear prose. Joyce, who wrote with the "hard clarity of a Stendhal or a Flaubert," looked like the perfect antidote to this malaise;[19] the only writer who could touch him was the author of "Cantleman's Spring Mate" and *Tarr* (1918), "the most vigorous and volcanic English novel of our time."[20]

Pound's advocacy of *Ulysses* developed out of his own encounter with censorship in the wake of the *Rainbow* trial. Fearing that he too would be prosecuted, the printer employed by Elkin Mathews, publisher of Wilde's *Salome,* refused to print certain poems and phrases in the British edition of Pound's *Lustra* (1916). Pound was anxious as well: "we'll all of us be suppressed, à la counter-reformation, dead and done for," he declared (*PJ*, p. 75). That these concerns were provoked by Lawrence may have been especially galling, for Pound found in his stories not "clear hardness," but a "loaded ornate style, heavy with sex, fruity with a certain sort of emotion" (*PJ*, p. 32). It is important to note that the Pound who made these comments in 1915 was not the pre-1914 Pound, who had said of Lawrence: "As a prose writer I grant him first place among the younger men."[21] As A. Walton Litz has shown, however, Pound and Lawrence had begun to drift apart in 1914, and probably would have done so even without the extra push provided by the emergence of Joyce.[22] The suppression of *The Rainbow* gave Pound another incentive to distance himself from Lawrence. To appease Mathews he tried to distinguish his own "clean cut satire" from the "sexual overloading" to which he attributed the sales of Lawrence's novel (*PJ*, p. 282). *Lustra* shows that Pound was

not averse to indulging in sexual overloading of his own, but Lawrence implicitly lacked the clean, concrete, direct attributes he desired. A certain "concrete
expression" was necessary because "[b]eauty unrelieved goes soft and sticky"
(*PJ*, p. 283). What Pound wanted in *Lustra* was the hard definition, the firm
contours, announced by the opening of "Coitus":

> The gilded phaloi of the crocuses
> are thrusting at the spring air.[23]

But Pound bowed to the wishes of his publisher. Mathews agreed to print two-
hundred copies including all but four poems ("The Temperaments," "Ancient
Music," "The Lake Isle," and "Pagani's, November 8"), which he would sell to
those requesting an unabridged edition; a second impression omitted nine more
poems and changed the title of "Coitus" to "Pervigilium." To Pound, losing
such poems as "The Temperaments," which details the multiple cuckolding of
Bastidides and the "Nine adulteries, 12 liaisons, 64 fornications and something
approaching a rape" of Florialis, meant censoring out the book's virility. In the
shorn public edition, "the pretty poems and the Chinese softness" now pre-
dominated; the tone of this "*castrato*" volume was "debilitated."[24] Though
Pound did not explicitly make the connection, his problems with *Lustra* nicely
illustrate the analogy between censorship and contraception suggested by his
later remarks on the passive, resistant aspects of femininity: the publisher's
interference obstructed the flow of Pound's genius.

In the years following the difficulties with *Lustra,* Pound's creative energies
indeed ran dry, but his imaginative sterility did not prevent him from seeing in
Joyce's prose a possible cure for the larger cultural afflictions of American
society. *Dubliners* (1914) and *A Portrait of the Artist as a Young Man* (1916)
had already presented a "clear diagnosis" of the situation in Ireland[25]; perhaps
Ulysses would generate a sense of style to save America and Europe from
future Woodrow Wilsons. As Pound noted when describing Joyce's style: "The
mot juste is of public utility" (*PJ*, p. 200). Lewis may have been "an over-
abundant source," his mind "far more fecund and original" than Joyce's,[26] but
Joyce, "cold and meticulous," issued the bald statement that civilization (especially American civilization) desperately needed: "Getting back to Joyce. It still
seems to me that America will never look *anything,* animal, mineral, vegetable,
political, social, international, religious, philosophical or ANYTHING else, in the
face until she gets used to perfectly bald statement" (*PQ*, p. 148).

Pound wrote these last words to John Quinn, the New York patron of the
arts and lawyer who defended "Cantleman's Spring Mate" and *Ulysses* in
court. Pound found in Quinn someone who shared many of his values and
assumptions about art, an ally to help administer Joycean medicine to an ailing
American culture. Quinn was the "grown man" for whom Pound wanted to
write poetry, and to whom he proposed hoisting a banner that stated: "No
woman shall be allowed to write for this magazine" (*PQ*, pp. 92, 53). Pound
confessed that "there are about six women writers whose work I should regret
losing but," he continued, "the ultimate gain . . . in vigour.—in everything—

might be worth it" (*PQ*, p. 54). "Vigour," or "energy" (as Pound put it in another letter), was understood to be a distinctly masculine quality that naturally allied itself with Quinn's pragmatic "business" qualities. Quinn brought out those qualities in Pound. Pound came to believe that bald statements, which are also inherently masculine, might be uttered without obscenity, for, as he told Quinn, "the *energy* in Joyce, W[yndham]. L[ewis]. & myself is what upsets people. . . indecency has nothing to do with it" (*PQ*, p. 176). Consequently, when Quinn warned him that Joyce's language should be toned down, Pound took it upon himself to edit parts of *Ulysses* before sending them on to the *Little Review*: he deleted "some twenty lines" from the jakes episode at the end of "Calypso." As the pressure to censor *Ulysses* mounted with the seizure of the issues containing "Lestrygonians" and "Scylla and Charybdis," Margaret Anderson deleted the Croppy Boy's erection in "Cyclops" (the issue was seized anyway).[27] Meanwhile, as *Ulysses* took stylistic directions uncongenial to Pound's notions of sane realism, Joyce continued to go "rather far" toward obscenity (*PQ*, p. 176). Joyce was outraged at all editorial interference; Pound, pretending to be sympathetic, told Quinn that he could "see perfectly well that if *every* possible physical secretion is to be affichéd in course of the work, even this calamity must happen to Mr. Bloom." Pound went on: "Perhaps *everything* ought to be said ONCE in the English language At least J. seems bent on saying it. . . . Who am I to tamper with a work of genius" (*PQ*, p. 185). But Pound did tamper with "Nausicaa": "I did myself dry Bloom's shirt," he told Quinn (*PQ*, p. 202). Pound had learned from his experience with *Lustra*. To Quinn, ever alert to the realities of business, Pound seemed a model of good sense, even if (as it turned out) his tampering proved in vain.

Pound and Quinn also shared a contempt for what the latter called "the pseudo-Bohemianism of Washington Square": "a vulgar, disgusting conglomerate of second- and third-rate artists and would-be artists, of I.W.W. agitators, of sluts kept or casual, clean and unclean, of Socialists and near Socialists, of poetasters and pimps, of fornicators and dancers and those who dance to enable them to fornicate." Quinn perhaps goes further than Pound would have done in condemning perceived sexual license, but the author of the Hell Cantos will have appreciated his conclusion about an effete, decadent culture: "I'd rather scrape up manure on the street than endure their nauseating drivel at a table for an hour" (*MNY*, p. 285). Like the Pound of such poems as "The Garden" and "Portrait d'une Femme," Quinn identified that culture with a soft, indeterminate, feminine influence at odds with the hardness and clarity he valued both in legal practice and (again like Pound) in art. "The poetry of the practice of law for me," Quinn wrote in February 1920, "is the clear analysis and correct statement of facts and the clear application of rules of law to the facts. I hate vagueness in law as much as I hate sloppiness in art" (*MNY*, p. 458).

Like Pound, Quinn saw in *Ulysses* the hardness and clarity he desired. At the preliminary hearing in October 1920 he "contrasted the strong hard filth of a man like Joyce with the devotion to art of a soft flabby man like Wilde" (*MNY*, p. 449). The comparison of Joyce with Wilde tells us a great deal about Quinn's assumptions and the context in which he arrived at them. In the immediate context of the *Ulysses* trial, Wilde denoted the effeminacy and sexual deviance that Quinn associated with Washington Square.[28] Such connotations were also infused with broader implications linking the degenerate artistic circles of New York with those of Britain. During the Great War, Wilde's name was often invoked by the British authorities as a pretext for suppressing suspicious art, art that seemed all the more suspect for its manifest connections with 1890s Decadence. As we have seen, that Decadence was commonly regarded as French in origin, though during the war it was blamed on Germany. In Britain the war was seen as having a cleansing effect on this "wave of diseased degeneracy." Similar feelings insinuated themselves into the American cultural scene as well. A 1916 review of the year's poetry in the *New York Times Book Review* attributed the arrival of vers libre in America in 1915 to the war: swept from British shores by the war, the review explained, such literary fads as Imagism, Futurism, and Vorticism had taken up residence in America. Now, thankfully, "the main current of song" had reasserted itself in the United States; the aberration of free-verse-making was over, and Edwin Arlington Robinson was back in the limelight.[29] The appearance of *Ulysses* disturbed the literary status quo on both sides of the Atlantic. Evidently the war had failed in its cleansing motion, for the novel, true to its oft-noted encyclopedic nature, seemed to contain all the worst vices. When *Ulysses* was published in Paris by Sylvia Beach's Shakespeare and Company (1922), reviewers greeted it as the product of "a French sink," "Zolaesque," a piece of "literary Bolshevism," the work of "a perverted lunatic who has made a speciality of the literature of the latrine."[30] One critic saw in Joyce's novel another sign of immorality which, signifying nonreproductive sex, gave extra spice to the aroma of sexual deviance: "From certain angles *Ulysses* is an abortion."[31] These notices clearly indicate that Quinn's praise of *Ulysses* as strong hard filth did not reflect larger attitudes. Yet in contrasting Joyce with Wilde in these terms, Quinn was attempting to ward off such associations, to suggest that unlike Wilde (the most notorious literary faddist of them all), Joyce belonged in a robust, healthy cultural environment.[32]

Quinn's problem at the *Ulysses* trial was that the two women responsible for publishing the novel were associated with an American version of the effeminate, deviant art signified by Wilde's name. Margaret Anderson later recalled that the *New York Times* had described the *Little Review* as "a decadent art magazine that delights in publishing the filth of diseased contemporary writers."[33] Although he was subsidizing the magazine, Quinn shared something of this aversion. He particularly disliked Jane Heap, whom he considered "a typical Washington Squareite" (*MNY,* p. 287). When he praised Heap and Anderson, as in a 1917 letter to Pound, it was for their masculine qualities: "I like the spunk of the two women, their industry, their courage" (*MNY,* p. 289). But too often they displayed the effete, impractical qualities of "pseudo-Bohemianism." They exhibited a "wilful" lack of "business sense" by ignoring Quinn's warnings that the serial publication of *Ulysses* jeopardized its chances of being published as a book. What appalled Quinn most of all was the fact that Anderson and Heap were lovers, as he revealed to Pound in a letter of 16 October 1920: "I don't mind the aberrations of a woman who has some openness and elasticity of mind . . . in whose excretions there may occasionally be cream; but, by God! I don't like the thought of women who seem to exude as well as bathe in piss, if not drink it, or each other's."[34] When Quinn praised Joyce's strong hard filth, he meant something not only masculine but safely heterosexual as well.

The 1920 hearing and 1921 trial highlighted these issues in a manner suggesting that the battle was as much between two deviant women and a male heterosexual establishment as between the forces of censorship and the supporters of James Joyce. Quinn skirmished with Heap and Anderson as soon as legal proceedings began. Acutely aware of the strength of the case against the *Little Review,* Quinn wanted to take a pragmatic line and to argue (as he was to do in court) that while *Ulysses* was disgusting, it was not obscene, and that since the average reader would not understand the book, he or she would not be corrupted by it. But the two editors were determined to create as much of a stir as possible. Responding to their summons, they horrified Quinn by making defiant speeches, and declaring that the prosecution "would be the making" of the *Little Review* (*MNY,* p. 447). In response, Quinn waived examination for both women at the preliminary hearing. Judging by his account of that hearing, he was already ceasing to take the defense seriously. In a letter to Pound dated 21 October 1920, Quinn described the courtroom as "an amusing scene," with Heap and Anderson as stock characters in a disreputable stage farce:

> There was Heep [*sic*] plus Anderson, and plus heaps of other Heeps and Andersons. Some goodlooking and some indifferent. The two rows of them looking as though a fashionable whorehouse had been pinched and all its inmates haled into court, with Heep in the part of the brazen madame. The stage was also filled with police officers in blue uniforms with glaring stars and buttons, women and men by tows [*sic*] and threes awaiting arraignment or sentence, niggers in the offing, chauffeurs awaiting hearings; pimps, prostitutes, hangers-on and reporters—also whores, on the theory of "Once a journalist, always a whore."(*MNY,* p. 448)

Quinn's disgust for his deviant clients colored his perception of the entire proceedings. He tried to keep Anderson and Heap out of the picture as much as possible. When he stood up to speak and found them at his side, he sent them unceremoniously back to their seats.

Quinn's treatment of Anderson and Heap, which they considered outrageous, partly sprang from a disagreement about how to mount a credible legal defense of their actions. But the procedural quarrel was intimately related to sexual politics, a realm in which Quinn had more in common with the three male judges than with Anderson and Heap. When on 14 February 1921 the prosecuting assistant district attorney, Joseph Forrester, proposed to read aloud the allegedly obscene passages from "Nausicaa," one of the judges pointed at Anderson and objected that such material should not be uttered in the presence of an innocent young woman. Quinn explained that Anderson was one of the defendants, but the judge retorted that surely she could not have understood what she was printing. Despite their technical disagreement, the judge and Quinn shared some fundamental ideas about social propriety. For Anderson to understand what she was printing, her character would have to deviate from a socially sanctioned script; Quinn's disgust at her lesbianism was anchored in a similar assumption that pure femininity conformed to a certain set of conventions, a particular cultural text. Had the judge known what Quinn knew about the private lives of the defendants, he might not have been so ready to presume Anderson innocent in the manner he clearly intended. Knowing what he did, Quinn was keen to keep the participation of such a woman to a minimum; the fewer opportunities she had to incriminate herself, to display her nonconformity, the better her chances of acquittal.

In Anderson's eyes, Quinn's only success was his duping of the judges into thinking her "personal purity" quite unimpeachable.[35] Otherwise she was as unimpressed by the lawyer's performance as by the intellectual display put on by Judges Kernochan, McInerney, and Moss, which was, by all accounts, extremely mediocre. The judges, Anderson claimed, did not "know the difference between James Joyce and obscene postal cards." When they entered the court, she wondered: "Why must I stand up as a tribute to three men who wouldn't understand my simplest remark?" Noting that in this case the only function of the judges was "to decide whether certain passages of 'Ulysses' (incidentally the only passages they can understand) violate the statute," Anderson mused parenthetically: "Is this a commentary on 'Ulysses' or on the minds of the judges?" Answering her own question, Anderson perhaps summed up the role into which she had been compelled not only by the judges but by John Quinn: "But I must not dream of asking such a question. My function is silence." Like Radclyffe Hall, silenced during the 1928 trial of her lesbian novel *The Well of Loneliness,* Anderson found herself excluded from legal and literary debate lest her voice deviate from the conventions of contemporary social (and sexual) discourse. As at the Hall trial, that exclusion was consistent with the nature of the case: in many ways, the *Little Review* trial, like the Hall trial, concerned a work that failed to deliver a socially acceptable representation of female sexuality.

Yet Quinn's explicit statements about sexual politics belied the extent to which his allegiance to *Ulysses* allied him with his clients. Like Anderson and Heap, but unlike the judges at the 1921 trial, Quinn believed that *Ulysses* would revolutionize an enfeebled and (in his terms) feminized culture, that it would liberate intelligent readers from the shackles of exhausted novelistic conventions. Such considerations, apparently of a purely aesthetic nature, modified and complicated the manifest sexual politics of Quinn's disagreement with Anderson and Heap. When Quinn argued in court that *Ulysses* was "neither written for nor read by school girls," he was ostensibly accepting the prosecution's premise that Joyce's novel should not be read by young girls, and concurring with the judge's assumption that a supposedly innocent reader like Anderson would not understand it. Yet insofar as any reader could be said to understand *Ulysses,* at least two women clearly did so: Anderson and Heap. And it was equally clear to Quinn that at least four men did not understand it:

the three "ignorant" judges and the "apoplectic" prosecutor, Joseph Forrester.[36] If, in its assault on a feminized culture, *Ulysses* ended the idea of novels for ladies (as, Joyce said, *The Waste Land* did for the "idea of poetry"),[37] its new virile readership did not exclude actual women, even though it purportedly annihilated their polite, chaotic essence. Heap and Anderson, as Quinn said to Pound, had "spunk." Despite Pound's and Quinn's fantasies of a literature without women, the limited appeal of their cultural project compelled them to admit their alliance with, and dependence on, particular women, especially Heap and Anderson at the *Little Review* and Harriet Shaw Weaver and Dora Marsden at *The Egoist*.[38] Pound was attracted to the *Little Review* in the first place partly because he sympathized with its "direct opposition to the prevalent art values in America." Whatever their differences in conceiving the precise form of that opposition, he agreed with Anderson and Heap that the literary establishment should be overthrown. And sharing a version of Pound's cultural elitism, Anderson and Heap agreed with him that *Ulysses* tested the intelligence of its readers. "How could any one begin to discuss Joyce except with a person who has an intense grip on modern thought?" Heap asked. "The earth slimes with a slightly-informed protoplasm called humanity: informed with a few instincts. Some few have become aware of cerebral irradiations. Fewer attain active cerebration."[39] A similar elitism underpinned Quinn's argument in court: "the average person reading the July–August number would either understand what it meant, or would not. If he understood what it meant, then it couldn't corrupt him, for it would either amuse or bore him. If he didn't understand what it meant, then it could [not] corrupt him" (*MNY*, p. 449). The assumption was that most readers would fall into the latter category, along with those who found *Ulysses* unintelligible, and with the judge who groaned, "it sounds to me like the ravings of a disordered mind—I can't see why any one would want to publish it." The people who did want to publish it, male like Pound and Quinn, or female like Heap and Anderson, knew that they were few and far between.[40]

Heap expressed this sense of elite culture in "Art and the Law," an essay written in the period between the 1920 hearing and the 1921 trial. Art, she argued, represents a supreme principle of order that distinguishes it from the other activities of humankind. To try to combat it with the legal system was absurd and utterly futile: "What legal genius to bring Law against Order!" she exclaimed. The efforts of John Sumner of the Society for the Prevention of Vice to protect "our young girls" was merely one "chivalrous" example of such pointless activity, riddled with contradictions that led Heap to regard the *Ulysses* case as "rather ironical": "We are being prosecuted for printing the thoughts in a young girl's mind. Her thoughts and actions and the meditations which they produced in the mind of the sensitive Mr. Bloom. If the young girl corrupts, can she also be corrupted? . . . If there is anything I really fear it is the mind of the young girl."[41]

In Heap's hands, *Ulysses* sounds a little different from the book promoted by Pound and Quinn, for her elitism permits, even demands, an awareness of the potentially explosive elements in cultural scripts for femininity—elements unacknowledged by the court or by her lawyer, yet clearly displayed in Joyce's text. Like "Nausicaa," Heap suggests that the mind of the young girl is not an essential gendered category but a cultural text which, constructed according to particular conventions and excluding the socially unacceptable, has definite limits. In "Nausicaa" those limits, signifying the bounds of public taste in art and of accepted conceptions of gender and sexuality, are on open display. That Heap should point to these issues is entirely appropriate to the circumstances of the 1921 trial, in which two women were prosecuted for corrupting the mind of another woman by printing a representation of the mind of a fictional woman. The cultural fiction enabling the prosecution—that the daughter of a New York lawyer could be corrupted by Joyce's text—sustained the corollary fiction that the defendants could not have understood what they were printing (though they could still be fined for printing it). Yet "Nausicaa" implicitly questions this notion of uncomprehending female innocence by exploiting the subversive potential inherent in cultural scripts for femininity. According to the assumptions governing the trial, the words and behavior of the defendants could be intelligible only insofar as they fitted the template for the mind of a young girl. In "Nausicaa," Joyce uses that template as the basis for the figure of Gerty MacDowell, but he makes it look inescapably artificial, hopelessly contrived. Its apparent reality, essential to its capacity for signifying the psychological interior of female identity, is exposed as an illusion fabricated through a rigorous process of selection that silently censors all unwanted elements. The mind of the young girl represented a nexus of powerful social forces; "Nausicaa" opened those forces to question by laying bare the covert censorship on whose invisibility their power depended. Joyce's text turned the tables on its censors, exposing their attempt to uphold the authority of certain forms of social discourse. Simultaneously revealing the limits of such discourse, Joyce points to the vulnerability of the mind of the young girl to reinterpretation and rewriting. In the process, he indicates that censorious readers may be unwitting accomplices in that rewriting.

Peep Shows and Confessions in "Nausicaa"

In *Joyce's Anatomy of Culture,* Cheryl Herr writes that Joyce understood culture, particularly Irish culture, as "suppression of various kinds." Culture "makes the threat of censorship so pervasive," she argues, "that it becomes part of the motivation for art; to understand his own oppression, the artist describes the institutions responsible for it."[42] These dynamics of art and censorship bear with special force on Joyce's "Nausicaa" episode. Gerty MacDowell is the product of various intersecting, and often apparently conflicting, public discourses. Her birth is the result of immaculate conception; she is the child of textual intercourse. I borrow these metaphors from the languages of Christianity and sexuality to emphasize the institutional discourses most integral to the construction of this character: Roman Catholicism and pornography. It is the meeting of these two regulatory discourses that produces the regulated fiction of Gerty's mind.

Joyce's restaging of the pornographic process in "Nausicaa" implies that pornography's encounter with Christian morality is conflictual but also collaborative. That is to say, pornography, which represents nonreproductive sexual activity, finds its complement in the religious institution whose discourse on reproduction supposedly outlaws such activity. For the romantic fantasies associated with Gerty articulate desires generated by pornography in a manner not only inoffensive to Church doctrine, but actually reproduced by Catholic discourse about sex. In this way, Joyce suggests that, like all forms of textual discourse, pornography and Catholicism are interdependent, generating and sustaining each other, regardless of the overt claims one might make about the other. This interdependence illuminates the representational limits of each discourse, and so reveals the point where interpretation becomes both possible and necessary. Playing off pornography against Catholicism, Joyce sets in motion an illicit transaction that sponsors the production of Gerty MacDowell and at the same time creates a space in which, in order to perform her role, she must interpret it. An important part of what Thomas Richards describes as Joyce's fascination with "linguistic determinism" is the way in which discursive regulation generates potential resistance, even some sort of agency, as well as passive submission.[43] "Nausicaa" intimates that there may be limits to the extent to which cultural scripts for femininity can enforce passivity on their objects, even when the object looks as conventionally passive as Gerty. "Nausicaa" also catches Joyce's readers looking at this fabricated object of sexual curiosity, implicating them in the scandalous collusion between pornographic and religious discourses. It is the interpretative activity of the reader, negotiating a course between the moral imperative of Church doctrine and the gratificatory pleasures of pornography, that generates the obscenity of Gerty's performance. In this way, the implications of "Nausicaa" extend beyond the Irish context described by Cheryl Herr to the American trial of 1921, an event provoked by Joyce's text and structured by institutional discourses about sex.

On the face of it, the alleged obscenity of "Nausicaa" seems to be no more than the product of the apparently conscious, deliberate behavior of Joyce's protagonists. Between them, Gerty MacDowell and Leopold Bloom set up a peep show: she exhibits her underwear by leaning back ostensibly to watch a firework display, while he masturbates and fantasizes. The voyeuristic implications of Bloom's role are played out at length in the second half of the episode, when the narrative shifts focus from Gerty's consciousness to his; as Fritz Senn has observed, "Nausicaa" is a chapter of glances.[44] The beach scene is also implicitly blasphemous. Joyce uses the sounds of a temperance retreat to counterpoint the pornographic scene unfolding on the beach. Blasphemies associated with individual characters compound the profanity of this juxtaposition: Gerty thinks there should be women priests, Bloom ponders the sexual allure of male priests for the female members of their congregations. In view of this double frame for the episode's action, it is hardly surprising that the British journalist James Douglas, instrumental in bringing to court first *The Rainbow* and later *The Well of Loneliness,* should have written of *Ulysses:* "its unclean lunacies are larded with appalling and revolting blasphemies directed against the Christian religion and against the holy name of Christ."[45]

The joining of pornographic with religious discourse as a double frame for "Nausicaa" highlights some of the problems of censorship and freedom attending on Gerty MacDowell. Joyce clearly attributes to Gerty an element of self-consciousness, suggesting that to some extent she stage-manages her own performance. Her self-display is coupled with scandalous awareness of matters supposedly unintelligible to the minds of male New York judges, let alone to young girls. Gerty entertains Bloom by playing up her role as womanly spectacle:

> But Gerty was adamant. She had no intention of being at their beck and call. If they could run like rossies she could sit so she said she could see from where she was. The eyes that were fastened upon her set her pulses tingling. She looked at him a moment, meeting his glance, and a light broke in upon her. Whitehot passion was in that face, passion silent as the grave, and it had made her his. At last they were left alone without the others to pry and pass remarks and she knew he could be trusted to the death, steadfast, a sterling man, a man of inflexible honour to his fingertips. His hands and face were working and a tremour went over her. She leaned back far to look up where the fireworks were and she caught her knee in her hands so as not to fall back looking up and there was no one to see only him and her when she revealed all her graceful beautifully shaped legs like that, supply soft and delicately rounded, and she seemed to hear the panting of his heart, his hoarse breathing, because she knew too about the passion of men like that, hotblooded, because Bertha Supple told her once in dead secret and made her swear she'd never about the gentleman lodger that was staying with them out of the Congested Districts Board that had pictures cut out of papers of those skirtdancers and highkickers and she said he used to do something not very nice that you could imagine sometimes in the bed. But this was altogether different from a thing like that because there was all the difference because she could almost feel him draw her face to his and the first quick hot touch of his handsome lips. Besides there was absolution so long as you didn't do the other thing before being married and there ought to be women priests that would understand without your telling out. . . .[46]

From the outset Gerty is "adamant" about her intentions and strives to arrogate active agency to herself. She "revealed" herself to Bloom. And, as Kimberly Devlin observes, Gerty engages in a "counter female voyeurism . . . anticipated by Bertha Supple's furtive spying on 'the gentleman lodger.' "[47] Bloom is watching Gerty, but she is watching him, and he knows it: "She looked at him a moment, meeting his glance." In this sense, Bloom's voyeurism seems to depend on Gerty's permission, as if the scene expresses her desires and operates under her control.

At another level, Gerty merely appears to rehearse the role of pornographic object, which suggests that her self-consciousness is manufactured by a larger cultural discourse. Gerty often seems to be the passive vehicle of inherited scripts for femininity, willingly accepting the terms of the aroused male observer. It is not merely a question of her being watched by Bloom; the entire episode is shaped by voyeurism. From the very start she is exhibited before the reader as an object of curiosity participating in a carefully orchestrated drama. The process by which she is displayed begins with the withholding of her name until, two pages after her appearance with Cissy Caffrey and Edy Boardman, Joyce relieves our pent-up curiosity. By the time Joyce gives her name, the forces shaping her identity are already in motion. When the narrative asks, "But who was Gerty?" (*U*13.78), we are already familiar with the clichés of sentimental fiction molding her consciousness, because the narrative has been drawing on them all along. As we read on, we find a character immersed in the fashion magazines and sentimental novels of a popular culture that imprisons her. Of course, every character in a novel is confined to a world of fiction, but "Nausicaa" heightens the effect, for here Joyce makes a point of showing us that freedom and agency are illusions generated by texts. The implication is that Gerty is nothing if not censored.

The idea that Gerty's self-display is the product of severe constraint would have surprised the judges at the *Little Review* trial and, no doubt, Judge Martin T. Manton, who dissented from the 1934 decision in favor of *Ulysses*.[48] Yet, like any pornographic show, Gerty's performance is a regulated fiction. The repetition of the performance, as in a peep show or a striptease, is supposed to naturalize it, but "Nausicaa" exhibits the mechanisms designed to produce this effect. The linguistic determinism of the episode illustrates this point. For instance, Gerty's awareness that Bloom is masturbating seems to grant her active agency, but this agency is generated by the romantic clichés shaping her consciousness: "she knew he could be trusted to the death, steadfast, a sterling man, a man of inflexible honour to his fingertips." A sentence Joyce added in revision ("His hands and face were working and a tremour went over her") only makes more explicit what is suggested by the pun on "fingertips." The pun's overt verbal restraint is wonderfully consistent with the euphemistic aspect of Gerty's romanticism: she would not say outright that Bloom is masturbating, since that would be to diminish the heroic stature with which her narrative endows him. While making a dirty joke, Joyce also stresses Gerty's entrapment within the clichés of a worn-out novelistic style, manipulating language to show how much Gerty is manipulated by it.

This linguistic manipulation is connected with a larger ideological oppression, which compels Gerty to defer to the authority of social and religious institutions. The pun on "fingertips" is one among a number of euphemisms that Gerty uses to refer to menstruation and sex: "all that other," "the other thing," "that other thing" (*U*13.665–66, 709, 713–14). These euphemisms operate in Gerty's mind through the sanction of the Church, as becomes clear when she tries to reconcile her provocative behavior with Catholic doctrine: "Besides there was absolution so long as you didn't do the other thing before being married." As long as her virginity remains intact, she can lean back as far as she likes, but only because (she thinks) the Church allows her to. If her exhibitionism implies liberation into supposedly unintelligible territory, that territory is still circumscribed by the sexual ideology of the Church. Invoking

Church doctrine to justify her conduct, Gerty reaffirms her entrapment in a narrow cultural space, a space whose limitations are signified by the censored form of speech through which she communicates.

By placing these constraints on Gerty, the Church paradoxically combines forces with pornography, another discourse that requires the muting of women's speech. These two discourses may seem mutually exclusive, but in Gerty's narrative they work dialectically toward a common goal: the codification and control of female sexuality. Gerty illustrates this unlikely alliance by simultaneously embodying the seemingly opposed roles of angel and whore, roles inherited from Victorian sexual ideology. Gerty perpetuates this ideology in her thoroughly conventional attitude to the fallen woman: "From everything in the least indelicate her finebred nature instinctively recoiled. She loathed that sort of person, the fallen woman off the accommodation walk beside the Dodder that went with the soldiers and coarse men with no respect for a girl's honour, degrading the sex and being taken up to the police station" (U13.660–64). Gerty's avowed defiance of social convention goes no further than her claim that she and Bloom "would be just good friends like a big brother and sister without all that other in spite of the conventions of Society with a big ess" (U13.665–66). At home, her customary role is that of angel in the house: "A sterling good daughter was Gerty just like a second mother in the house, a ministering angel too" (U13.325–26). It seems that if only Gerty were not lame, her transition from daughter to wife and mother would be a smooth one. Yet it is in playing the role of ministering angel that she "tacked up on the wall . . . Mr Tunney the grocer's christmas almanac," before which she goes to the toilet (like Bloom in the jakes) or, perhaps, masturbates (like Bloom on the beach):

> the picture of halcyon days where a young gentleman in the costume they used to wear then with a threecornered hat was offering a bunch of flowers to his ladylove with oldtime chivalry through her lattice window. You could see there was a story behind it. The colours were done something lovely. She was in a soft clinging white in a studied attitude and the gentleman was in chocolate and he looked a thorough aristocrat. She often looked at them dreamily when she went there for a certain purpose and felt her own arms that were white and soft just like hers with the sleeves back and thought about those times because she had found out in Walker's pronouncing dictionary that belonged to grandpapa Giltrap about the halcyon days what they meant. (U13.334–44)

Insinuating nonreproductive sexual desires, Gerty's certain purpose suggests that even she is in danger of falling from her angelic pedestal. While arousing Gerty's desire, however, the picture of sentimental romance encourages her self-projection into a conventional role, that of the ladylove, who rightly accepts attentions given in the spirit of oldtime chivalry. The representation of heterosexual romance as a reproduction of a long-standing ritual lends an air of stability to these proceedings, which fulfill the requirements of a Victorian sexual ideology that underwrites both Church doctrine and pornography. Gerty's romantic self-projection helps to engender such meanings. Conceiving of her life according to the narrative implied in the picture ("You could see there was a story behind it"), she transforms Bloom, the masturbating voyeur, into "a man among men," "a manly man," "her dreamhusband" (*U*13.207, 210, 431): in her narrative, he becomes Ulysses. Thus, transgressive, non-reproductive sexuality seems to be rewritten in socially and doctrinally acceptable terms, as a mode of reproducing socially sanctioned meanings.

Gerty's performance also suggests that such roles are subject to cultural and commercial mediation. Acting out the script inferred from the picture in Mr. Tunney's almanac, Gerty reproduces a commercial, mass-produced romantic fiction. In "buying" this reproduction, Gerty unwittingly transports herself into a mass cultural fantasy and becomes, in effect, the dupe of the person who "sold" it to her. It is perfectly appropriate, as Suzette Henke observes, that Gerty should be attracted to Bloom, who makes his living by selling commercial advertisements and so depends on public gullibility.[49] The function of Mr. Tunney's almanac in relation to Joyce's readers further underscores this point. Necessarily mediating the visual image via language, the text emphasizes the reader's removal from the fictional scene, but the author and his fiction depend on our gullibility, on our willingness to "buy" the product, just as Bloom relies on that of the public to make a living. The picture in the almanac demonstrates the degree to which sexual fantasies are inseparable, in a consumerist society, from multiple layers of mediation.

The mediated nature of Gerty's performance is brought home by her account of Bertha Supple's gentleman lodger. Gerty has learned from Bertha that the lodger masturbated over newspaper pictures of skirtdancers. That the mediated objects of the lodger's desire should be professional performers highlights the manner in which sexual acts are necessarily staged. Gerty replicates this performance for Bloom, to whom she presents a picture just as the skirtdancers do to the lodger. While Gerty apparently fails to see this correspondence, it is suggested to the reader, for whom Gerty's narrative is already mediated by the conventions of fiction. By establishing such connections, Joyce creates for Gerty a role of larger cultural import than her sentimental musings might have indicated: her image indicates the horizons within which identity must always be constituted in a mediating, and mediated, commercial culture.[50]

Talking about her romantic experiences as if they were the most natural things in the world, Gerty misses the way in which such experiences are always mediated by the forces of social construction. Karen Lawrence has criticized Joyce for unnecessarily interrupting the grand progress of his novel's stylistic experiments merely to expose the limitations and blindnesses of this unsophisticated character. She contends that "by condescending to the mind and style of Gerty MacDowell," the episode "suggests that there is some Olympian ground upon which the writer and reader can stand to be exempt from the charges of stupidity."[51] Particularly when reviewed in the light of the Bloom narrative later in the episode, however, Gerty serves an important purpose in Joyce's critique of modern culture, a critique that casts doubt on the possibility of such exemption. She provides a graphic demonstration of the way in which, to use Judith Butler's terms, the performative accomplishment of sex and gender operates as "a compelling illusion, an object of *belief*," a regulatory fiction whose fictionality is "obscured by the credibility of its own production."[52] This credibility is sponsored by a stylized repetition of acts, which constitutes identity: if Gerty's sex show reminds us of the lodger's pictures of skirtdancers, the more likely we are to accept this state of affairs as natural and unalterable. And yet it is only by working within these confines that transformation or subversion is possible.

Credibility is further guaranteed by the assent of the spectator, especially when he accepts illusion as reality. As Gerty limps along the Strand, Bloom muses: "Pity they can't see themselves. A dream of wellfilled hose. Where was that? Ah, yes. Mutoscope pictures in Capel street: for men only. Peeping Tom. Willy's hat and what the girls did with it. Do they snapshot those girls or is it all a fake?" (*U*13.792–96).[53] It is uncertain in this passage whether Bloom would prefer a snapshot to a fake, but it is clear that to arouse his desire, representations of women as sexual objects must be mediated; the distinction between snapshot and fake is one of degree, not of kind. The distinction is similarly moot in another passage, which emphasizes that for Bloom narratives of desire must be staged if they are to create erotic appeal: "See her as she is spoil all. Must have the stage setting, the rouge, costume, position, music. The name too. *Amours* of actresses. Nell Gwynn, Mrs Bracegirdle, Maud Branscombe. Curtain up. Moonlight silver effulgence. Maiden discovered with pensive bosom. Little sweetheart come and kiss me" (*U*13.855–59). Gerty arouses Bloom's desire because she creates an aura of stage setting, while still transmitting desires of her own; her sex show transforms itself into an object of belief in Bloom's mind. Hence Gerty succeeds where, for Bloom, other women sometimes fail.

Although he recognizes the theatricality of the process by which women arouse male desire, Bloom is partially blind to an important aspect of that process: the performativity of his own voyeurism. His blindness is partial because it is motivated, but also because he is aware that Gerty knows what he is doing, half-concealed in the twilight: "Did she know what I? Course. Like a cat sitting beyond a dog's jump" (*U*13.908–9). Bloom's arousal, like Gerty's, is heightened by the self-consciousness produced by that knowledge. Yet his perception is, like hers, limited. Moreover, in revealing Bloom's circumscribed vision, Joyce urges his readers to attend more self-consciously to their own performance. For, in the first part of "Nausicaa," Bloom occupies a double function. He is the spectator at Gerty's sex show, but as masturbating voyeur he too performs, for the reader.[54] At the beginning of the episode, Bloom's only (and barely disclosed) function seems to be that of observer: unnamed, he has no apparent identity except that of "the gentleman" (*U*13.76-77), and his presence goes completely unmentioned for nearly two pages. But if Bloom's unseen presence initially seems synonymous with a transparent narrative eye, as the episode proceeds that transparency is gradually shown to be an illusion, the effect of theatrical artifice. To begin with, Bloom is clothed in garments taken from Gerty's wardrobe of romantic clichés, and the fact that he is wearing funeral dress merely fuels Gerty's sentimental impulses: "There was the allimportant question and she was dying to know was he a married man or a widower who had lost his wife or some tragedy like the nobleman with the foreign name from the land of song had to have her put into a madhouse, cruel only to be kind" (U13.656–59). It is only after her performance has ended that his name is disclosed:

> Then all melted away dewily in the grey air: all was silent. Ah! She glanced at him as she bent forward quickly, a pathetic little glance of piteous protest, of shy reproach under which he coloured like a girl. He was leaning back against the rock behind. Leopold Bloom (for it is he) stands silent, with bowed head before those young guileless eyes. What a brute he had been! At it again? A fair unsullied soul had called to him and, wretch that he was, how had he answered? An utter cad he had been! He of all men! But there was an infinite store of mercy in those eyes, for him too a word of pardon even though he had erred and sinned and wandered. Should a girl tell? No, a thousand times no. That was their secret, only theirs, alone in the hiding twilight and there was none to know or tell save the little bat that flew so softly through the evening to and fro and little bats don't tell. (U13.741–53)

This paragraph suggests that Bloom's conscience is easily appeased, partly because what has happened seems to be "their secret, only theirs." But is it only theirs? Joyce often leaves us uncertain about the speaker of a particular passage, and this one seems to be a case in point, for it occurs just as the narrative starts to shift from Gerty's consciousness to Bloom's. The narrative styles associated with these two protagonists melt into each other, so that no single speaker controls the flow of discourse. At moments like this, the episode operates as a larger consciousness, in which Bloom's role, like Gerty's, is simultaneously performative and spectatorial. "Nausicaa" hardly suggests "some Olympian ground upon which the writer and reader can stand to be exempt from the charges of stupidity": since Bloom's role as performer is inseparable from his function as spectator, the same could be said of the reader. Reading "Nausicaa," we participate in a kind of peep show. That is our secret.

Bloom's role as analogue for the reader has important implications for our reading of the text, for if he is an essential part of the pornographic performance of "Nausicaa," we too are implicated in the process of creating obscenity. Although such thoughts may not have pleased the court in 1921, "Nausicaa" apparently endorses Havelock Ellis's statement: "Nothing is in itself obscene apart from the human observer."[55] "Nausicaa" seems calculated to arouse readerly curiosity by teasing us with half-complete pieces of information. We are told that "three girl friends were seated on the rocks," but then for more than sixty lines we hear only of two, Cissy Caffrey and Edy Boardman. Gerty MacDowell is not introduced until her name enters the dialogue of the other characters. By the time the narrator asks, "But who was Gerty?," she has already become the object of curiosity, whom we wish to see displayed before us. The shift of focus from Gerty to Bloom at the end of her self-display abruptly signals what has already been indicated by her counter-voyeurism: he has been watching all along. It also draws attention to the reader's role. Following Gerty's movements through the narrative eye, we have been looking through Bloom's eye as well. To see him leaning against the rock in full view is suddenly to see oneself, to realize that one has been caught peeping. Gerty's counter-voyeurism doubles the effect, for her glances at Bloom are ours: Joyce's readers have it both ways. "Nausicaa" thus undermines the idea, so crucial to the supposed impartiality of obscenity trials, that reading may be a matter of objectively processing information.

Reading is often equated with voyeurism; "Nausicaa" draws special attention to the sexual politics of this process. The narrative eye through which we view the events of "Nausicaa" may sometimes look transparent, but its shifting interests and motives are always associated with a gendered viewing subject: often Bloom, sometimes Gerty, and sometimes both at the same time. In this sense we may read "Nausicaa" as a tacit commentary on its readers, and also on its author. For, if Bloom acts as the reader's surrogate, he also stands in for his male creator, James Joyce, whose gender constitutes the first filter through which Gerty's consciousness must pass. If the representation of Gerty is a snapshot taken through a male lens, it might be described, with equal justice, as a fake. "Nausicaa" encourages us to see the difference between snapshot and fake as one of degree rather than of kind. Joyce's text also asks us to consider what such a difference amounts to. Jules Law has argued that Judge Woolsey's 1933 decision acquitting *Ulysses* of obscenity betrayed the gender bias inherent in legal definitions of the "normal" reader: "the law is concerned only with the forensically 'normal'—that is, the masculine—response to pornography." *Ulysses* examines such biases, Law contends, by offering "an exemplary display of the evasions and deferrals our culture makes in reproducing its most fundamental distinctions."[56] "Nausicaa" also tests our ability, and willingness, to recognize how our view of events is constructed according to the masculine position in patriarchal culture. In this sense "Nausicaa" is calculated to provoke and exploit a masculine response to pornography. At the same time, Gerty interrupts this visual narrative by returning Bloom's gaze. In this way Joyce challenges us to reflect critically on the implications of our spectatorship, and to recognize its subversive possibilities.

Such reflection might have been especially problematic for a court attempting in 1921 to protect the forensically "abnormal" (or feminine) reader from corruption by *Ulysses*. The danger facing the court was that women readers might attain masculine consciousness, or that "masculine" might become indistinguishable from "feminine." Any such transformation would threaten the grounds for the distribution of power, which is crucial to the authority of the legal system. If women infiltrated the masculine position, sexual distinctions would be blurred and the structure of power destabilized. The young female reader who instigated legal proceedings in 1920 was responding to "Nausicaa" in the manner sanctioned by a patriarchal culture: seeing the unfamiliar, she correctly concluded that it was obscene. Readers like Margaret Anderson and Jane Heap could not be counted on to behave in the same way. That they were publishing *Ulysses* was an unpromising sign; by silencing them, the court prevented them from giving further proof of their errancy. In this sense the

1921 verdict may be seen as an attempt to uphold a cultural distinction be-tween the masculine and feminine spheres. Yet the fact that the trial happened at all suggests that the distinction was a precarious fiction.

"Nausicaa" must have been particularly troubling because its narrative pro-cedures encouraged transgressive acts of reading such as those of Anderson and Heap, women readers who saw in *Ulysses* a powerful weapon with which to wage war on "the prevalent art values in America." The editors of the *Little Review* trespassed into territory normally reserved for men, but Joyce's experi-mental novel sponsors this cultural transvestism. "Nausicaa" dramatizes such activity in Cissy Caffrey, about whom there is "a lot of the tomboy": she "whistle[s], imitating the boys in the football field"; she makes Gerty blush by "saying an unladylike thing" (*U*13.480, 754, 265). But Joyce does not limit oscillation between gender roles to female characters. His men can be equally susceptible to sexual indeterminacy. Indeed, Joyce indicates that men may not be powerful enough to withstand female raids on their authority.

Here Joyce implicates the Church in the questions raised by a secular obscenity trial, for the man whose authority he renders most vulnerable, and whose gender he leaves most unstable, is the Roman Catholic priest. The connection between the Church and the history of sexuality has been elucidated by Michel Foucault, who argues that confession is central to the structure of Western sexual discourse. The confessional, Foucault observes, is one of the "useful and public discourses" that turns desire into discourse and so regulates sex.[57] Scru-tinizing the sexual dynamics of confession, Joyce unsettles the larger structure of sexual power by implying that the priest's cassock is a sign of ambiguity because it resembles a woman's dress: for Joyce, the man who possesses an apparently unimpeachable authority over women is no less abnormal than the female penitent. Finding in the Church the same structures of power as in pornography, Joyce draws on the example of the priest to expose a larger instability in patriarchal power. Examining that power, he suggests that the gender distinction on which it rests may be open to question. Revisiting the Church, Joyce quietly poses new questions about male authority over female behavior, the very authority on which the court drew when judging Anderson and Heap in 1921.[58]

The Gerty MacDowell narrative points to the sexual dimension of the Church's authority when she muses: "Besides there was absolution so long as you didn't do the other thing before being married and there ought to be women priests that would understand without your telling out" (*U*13.708–11). These remarks not only indicate the power exercised by the Church over female sexual activity, but also point to the fact that this power was invested exclu-sively in men. Gerty would prefer to confess to a female priest; even if the confessional structure remained the same she would rather put herself in another woman's power than in a man's. As it is, however, only male priests have the authority to grant or deny absolution. In this sense, Catholic confes-sion reproduces the gendered structures of power and pleasure that we find in pornography.

In a suggestive essay, Mary Lowe-Evans explores Joyce's treatment of confession and the confessional box as "intriguing symbols of sexual power." Uncovering a "historic link between confession and contraception," Lowe-Evans argues that Bloom reveals contradictions in the Catholic position on sex. While priests can refuse absolution to the woman who allows her husband to practice birth control, they supplant the husband's role during confession by "substituting unproductive discourse for productive intercourse." Lowe-Evans notes that in "Oxen of the Sun," women are "satisfied with the titillation of confession" and therefore "lose interest in real, productive sexual intercourse." Bloom ponders the sexual allure of priests in "Nausicaa" when wondering whether women "get a man smell off us":

> What though? Cigary gloves long John had on his desk the other day. Breath? What you eat and drink gives that. No. Mansmell, I mean. Must be connected with that because priests that are supposed to be are different. Women buzz round it like flies round treacle. Railed off the altar get on to it at any cost. The tree of forbidden priest. O, father, will you? Let me be the first to. That diffuses itself all through the body, permeates. Source of life. And it's extremely curious the smell. Celery sauce. Let me. (U13.1034–41)

If mansmell is associated with human origins, it does not do any good to have it permeating the bodies of priests, who are supposed to be different, or celibate. Lowe-Evans persuasively argues that by distracting women from productive intercourse, Joyce's priests contribute to the Irish depopulation lamented in "Cyclops" by the Citizen. In this way, she contends, Joyce portrays the celibate priest as the "ultimate birth-controller," and "transforms the confessional into artificial contraceptive."[59]

Doctrinally, Gerty MacDowell's self-display and orgasm, like Bloom's masturbation, exemplify the sinful, nonreproductive sex that confession was supposed to regulate. Yet at one level their public display of contraceptive sexuality dramatizes the functions of confession in Roman Catholicism and so reverses the historical equation described by Foucault: "Nausicaa" demonstrates the link between power and pleasure by turning discourse into desire. The confessional box itself operates in a manner similar to that of the peep show. The priest's privileged access to women's sexual secrets replicates the structure of power exhibited in pornography, in which the male gaze supervises the production of female sexuality. Like the Peeping Tom, the priest is an invisible observer of the female object. Both confession and peep show are forms of surveillance as characterized by Foucault: each is concerned with "contacting bodies, caressing them with its eyes," and thus with producing "a sensualization of power and a gain of pleasure."[60] Moreover, like the voyeur's pornographic gaze, the priest's observation is mediated by the cultural filters of gender construction. That the act of reading cultural inscriptions of femininity may be contraceptive is underscored by the fact that Bloom, whose perspective is linked to our view of Gerty, masturbates during her performance. The same activity might be imputed to the priest in the confessional box. Bloom's thoughts wander in this direction in "Lotus-Eaters": "Confession. Everyone wants to. Then I will tell you all. Penance. Punish me, please. Great weapon in their hands. More than doctor or solicitor. Woman dying to" (*U*5.425–27). The pun on the priest's "[g]reat weapon" makes a connection between phallic and ideological power, the significance of which has been elaborated more recently by Jacques Lacan. In the context of confession, to wield this "weapon" is potentially to undermine the priestly function by opening it up to the very scrutiny that it supposedly exercises over the penitent. In this way, the structural kinship of confession with the peep show may bring the moral power of the priest under threat.

The confessions of "Nausicaa" dramatize these problems. The priest's great weapon is wielded by Bloom, whose body confesses its secrets to Gerty even as her body displays its own secrets to him. While she puts herself in his power, he concedes part of that power by imparting illicit knowledge of his own body; indeed, by returning his glance, Gerty actually takes that knowledge. Consequently, their relationship establishes itself on a reciprocal basis that subverts the structure of Catholic confession. This menace informs "their secret, only theirs, alone in the hiding twilight." The hiding twilight, moreover, lends their congress a privacy analogous to that of the confessional box, in which their bodies can speak to each other in perfect intimacy. Gerty is not only a penitent but a surrogate female confessor, who returns the gaze, and derives contraceptive sexual pleasure from the encounter. As Bloom muses afterward, "it was a kind of language between us" (*U*13.944). What "Nausicaa" emphasizes is the surprisingly equal terms on which Bloom and Gerty conduct their conversation.

In "Lotus-Eaters," Bloom notices that when women exit from the confessional box, they take repentance astonishingly lightly: "Then out she comes. Repentance skindeep. Lovely shame. Pray at an altar. Hail Mary and Holy Mary. Flowers, incense, candles melting. Hide her blushes" (*U*5.430–32). Dramatizing confession, "Nausicaa" suggests that the process may be relatively untroubling. One might expect, for instance, that blushing, the body's means of confessing shameful sexual knowledge, would preclude the presence of divinity, but in "Nausicaa" the body aspires to the condition described by Roland Barthes in "Striptease": "The end of striptease," Barthes wrote, "is . . . to signify . . . nakedness as a *natural* vesture of woman, which amounts in the end to regaining a perfectly chaste state of the flesh."[61] As Bloom and Gerty approach orgasm at the end of her self-display, "her face was suffused with a divine, an entrancing blush from straining back" (*U*13.723–24). Here divinity enhances, or is equivalent to, the entrancing effect of Gerty's blush. Guilt seems to be forgiven remarkably quickly. As Bloom observes in "Lotus-Eaters," repentance is only skindeep, and so perhaps is the sin itself; perhaps all one can say of shame is how lovely it is. In "Nausicaa," to be sure, the only sins afflicting the erotic scene are skindeep ones: "she was trembling in every limb from being bent so far back that he had a full view high up above her knee where no-one ever not even on the swing or wading and she wasn't ashamed and he wasn't either to look in that immodest way like that because he couldn't resist the sight of the wondrous revealment half offered like those skirtdancers behaving so immodest before gentlemen looking and he kept on looking, looking" (U13.727–33). It is illuminating that in the revised text Bloom is bewitched by a "wondrous revealment" rather than by a "revelation"; the verbal infelicity implies the fallen, unspiritual nature of the spectacle before him. Yet he is transfixed by Gerty as if she really does represent a vision of divinity, of flesh in its perfectly chaste state, and it is her unblushing frankness that enables his enchantment. The implication is that, in this Church, shamelessness passes for divinity.

Even more scandalous, "Nausicaa" hints that the divine aspect of Gerty's charms is borrowed from the Virgin Mary. The first few lines of the episode suggest Gerty's presence by conjuring up the image of the Virgin. As the sun sets, it casts its dying glow over a scene that includes "the quiet church whence there streamed forth at times upon the stillness the voice of prayer to her who is in her pure radiance a beacon ever to the stormtossed heart of man, Mary, star of the sea" (U13.6–8). Garry Leonard has remarked that the image of Mary signifies "the perfect 'feminine' commodity" and "someone eternal—'The Woman.'"[62] The Virgin also sponsors the Victorian ideal of the angel in the house, an ideal apparently embodied by Gerty. Mary is undefiled, but she is a mother, too; as a beacon to the stormtossed heart of man, she provides the moral guidance sought by those who pray in church. In this way Mary authorizes the social authority of man, whose freedom to exercise power in the public domain is enabled by the assurance of moral harmony at home. Associating Gerty with images of the Virgin, Joyce's narrative disturbs this equilibrium. Bloom in particular comes to see Gerty, wearing a "neat blouse of electric blue," as a Virgin figure, yet in his eyes she also marries divinity to the erotic: "His dark eyes fixed themselves on her again, drinking in her every contour, literally worshipping at her shrine" (U13.563–64). For Bloom, worshipping at Gerty's shrine means deriving erotic pleasure from her body, a body supposedly denied in traditional images of the Virgin. This blasphemy exposes a contradiction in the discourse of the Virgin, whose image is produced by the male gaze of Roman Catholicism.[63] "Nausicaa" implies that this gaze is always eroticized. That our view of Gerty is filtered through Bloom is doubly significant because his voyeurism replicates that of the consumer of pornography as well as that of the onanistic confessor. This alliance of Catholic and pornographic discourses underlines the way in which images of femininity, blushing, shameless, or apparently divine, are projected along the axis of male desire. The image of the Virgin Mary brings this desire home where (according to Victorian morality) it belongs, by providing a beacon to guide it in an acceptable direction. Gerty invokes this morality, but undermines it by displaying a sexual body that the discourse of the Virgin was designed to deny. The Virgin does not blush, because her body has no sins to confess; in this sense her body is not sexual at all. Gerty's self-exhibition recuperates sexuality, however, by denying its association with shame. Gerty suggests that the body's sins are merely skindeep, that its only blemishes are its blushes. In effect, she modifies traditional images of the Virgin by adding touches of color that enhance her spellbinding powers over the gazing male. Gerty is Joyce's new icon of immaculate femininity, to whom the Blooms of the world can confess their sins without incurring the wrath of their Creator. And Gerty is immaculate *because* she lacks Mary's maternal function: she transforms Mary into a cipher for nonreproductive sexuality.

In this way, "Nausicaa" threatens an image of femininity that was central to the regulated fiction invoked at the *Little Review* trial in 1921. Gerty's activities are not the same as those of Margaret Anderson and Jane Heap, of course, since her self-display ostensibly performs an unproblematically heterosexual function. And, on account of their lesbianism, the editors of the *Little Review* would hardly have been thought immaculate. But in the terms suggested by "Nausicaa," the transgression of Anderson and Heap may be allied with Gerty's self-display because lesbianism represents another face, even the endpoint, of the nonreproductive sexuality whose specter Gerty raises. In this light, Gerty's performance looks all the more transgressive because it links the image of the Virgin with the most scandalous implications of a female desire detached from woman's maternal function: the lesbianism of Anderson and Heap. Altering the margins of the woman's script, Joyce implies the possibility of desires that, as far as the court knew in 1921, were quite inconceivable.

Maternal Confessions in "Oxen of the Sun"

While the *Little Review* trial contested the representation of female sexuality, several of the episodes following "Nausicaa" continued Joyce's restaging of the more and less covert ways in which a patriarchal culture enacted and settled that contest. After completing "Nausicaa," Joyce resumed this project in "Oxen of the Sun," an episode of stylistic extravagance generated by one simple event, ironically juxtaposed with the masturbation in the previous episode: Bloom visits the maternity hospital where Mina Purefoy gives birth to her child. Cast as a parodic history of English prose, the narrative filters the birth through the boisterous, chauvinistic debates of a group of medical students. Written some months before proceedings were started against the *Little Review*, "Oxen" did not appear in its entirety before the court put a stop to its publication: though the first four-hundred lines of the new episode appeared in the *Little Review* of September–December 1920, a second installment was shelved when the court delivered its verdict. But while its own birth was strangled by the trial, "Oxen" subtly reexamines the sexual discourses that facilitated this act of censorship. As Richard Brown has suggested, the episode provides "a history of the science of birth as well as a history of English prose style."[64] The coincidence of these two histories allows Joyce to display the stylistic basis of scientific discourse, and to reveal its limitations. Through Bloom, moreover, Joyce suggests potential resistance to the coercive and censorious effects of these discourses. Style, Joyce implies, is limiting, but it can be enabling as well.

We may begin to locate resistance by noting two incongruities, both of which are apparent in the account I have just given. First, the stylistic extravagance of "Oxen of the Sun" seems disproportionate to its minimal action;

second, that action, the birth of a child, appears inappropriate in a chapter whose theme, drawn from an episode in *The Odyssey* and elaborated here in the prose parodies, is slaughter. The point, however, is deceptively simple (and it applies to the whole novel). Since no style can fully represent reality, all styles are masks representing aspects of it. Further, each mask should be discarded once it is no longer useful. "Oxen" offers glimpses of the birth of the Purefoy child by taking up one style, casting it off, and adopting another. Here, then, is the "polemic element" noted by Wolfgang Iser in his interpretation of the episode, which he reads as an attack on the "intrinsic tendency of style to edit observed realities." Exposing the editorial or censorious tendencies of style, Joyce implies that theories that try to capture the event narrated in "Oxen of the Sun" are similarly limited or, as Iser puts it, "manipulative" and "historically preconditioned."[65] The expansiveness of the episode's stylistic universe emphasizes this point.

The attack on stylistic censorship has moral and political implications, which are clarified by Joyce's exploration of reproductive rhetoric. Showing us the limitations of rhetorical styles, "Oxen" quietly announces that the moral positions implied by those styles are historically determined and inherently censorious. The episode's ever-expanding stylistic universe allows us to observe that the recurrence of anticontraceptive rhetoric signifies not natural law but a historically limited, pragmatic judgment. We can see, too, that while the repetition of this judgment seems to make it more secure, it increases the possibility of change. "Oxen of the Sun" reveals that what certain forms of rhetoric try to establish as fixed goals are part of a process, which spawns contraceptive as well as reproductive forms of sexuality. Reading "Oxen of the Sun" in the context of its production enables us to see all the more clearly that the *Little Review* trial, perpetuating and predicated on anticontraceptive rhetoric, was a similarly conditioned event. The trial sought ends that Joyce sets out to frustrate. "Oxen" implies the same lesson as *The Rainbow*: "All goals become graves."

Joyce encouraged readers to consider this episode in relation to concepts of law and criminality. According to Frank Budgen, Joyce interpreted the killing of the oxen in *The Odyssey* "as the crime against fecundity by sterilising the act of coition."[66] Some readers have inferred from this statement that Joyce meant to condemn contraceptive sexual activity.[67] Yet, as other critics have observed, things are not quite so straightforward.[68] The multiplication of styles in Joyce's "Oxen" episode militates against attempts to transmit clear moral messages. To read "Oxen" as anticontraceptive is to miss how relentlessly the episode exposes apparently definitive judgments as contingent on the historical conditions under which they are delivered. Joyce's stylistic experimentation renders such verdicts no more credible than the decision reached by his censors in 1921. Put in the context of the episode's unstable moral atmosphere, Joyce's statement about the slaying of Homer's sacred oxen implies that the crime against fecundity is an offense peculiar to those who seek to regulate sexuality by rhetorical and ideological means.

"Oxen of the Sun" dramatizes the conflicting impulses of naturalization and transformation, of censorship and resistance, in its development of plot and character, which proves inseparable from style. The multiplication of styles produces myriad identities: Bloom changes from an advertising agent into the medieval "traveller Leopold" in the parody of Mandeville, then into "Sir Leopold" in the parody of Malory, and so on (*U*14.126, 169–70). The multiplication of identity crosses sexual boundaries as well; even differences between the sexes are matters of style. The point is illustrated by Bloom, whose capacity for self-projection and self-dramatization marks him as a sympathetic figure quite unlike his vulgar, chauvinistic male companions at the hospital. In his performative fluidity, Bloom becomes a vehicle for a critique of reproductive and allied forms of rhetoric. In the process, he subverts the supposedly natural laws that regulate and censor sexual roles.

The medical students, whom Bloom joins at the hospital, treat the issue of a mother's safety and that of the unborn child merely as the occasion for abstract, and drunken, debate:

> For they were right witty scholars. And he heard their aresouns each gen other as touching birth and righteousness, young Madden maintaining that put such case it were hard the wife to die (for so it had fallen out a matter of some year agone with a woman of Eblana in Horne's house that now was trespassed out of this world and the self night next before her death all leeches and pothecaries had taken counsel of her case). And they said farther she should live because in the beginning, they said, the woman should bring forth in pain and wherefore they that were of this imagination affirmed how young Madden had said truth for he had conscience to let her die. And not few and of these was young Lynch were in doubt that the world was now right evil governed as it was never other howbeit the mean people believed it otherwise but the law nor his judges did provide no remedy. A redress God grant. This was scant said but all cried with one acclaim nay, by our Virgin Mother, the wife should live and the babe to die. In colour whereof they waxed hot upon that head what with argument and what for their drinking but the franklin Lenehan was prompt each when to pour them ale so that at the least way mirth might not lack. (*U*14.202–18)

The primary concern here seems to be that one should display one's reasoning powers and at the same time entertain one's auditors, so that "at the least way mirth might not lack." Apparently lofty, detached wit rapidly degenerates into graceless boasts and crude jokes, as we see when Dixon claims he "would ever dishonest a woman whoso she were or wife or maid or leman if it so fortuned him to be delivered of his spleen of lustihead": "Whereat Crotthers of Alba Longa sang young Malachi's praise of that beast the unicorn how once in the millenium he cometh by his horn, the other all this while, pricked forward with their jibes wherewith they did malice him, witnessing all and several by saint Foutinus his engines that he was able to do any manner of thing that lay in man to do" (*U*14.232–37). To boast about one's virility is to affirm one's fidelity both to Irish Nationalism and to the Roman Catholic Church, twin causes sharing one creed: "Copulation without population! No, say I!" (*U*14.1422). The apotheosis of this double fidelity is expressed in Mulligan's outrageous proposal to set up "a national fertilising farm to be named *Omphalos* with an obelisk hewn and erected after the fashion of Egypt and to offer his dutiful yeoman services for the fecundation of any female of what grade of life soever who should there direct to him with the desire of fulfilling the functions of her natural" (U14.684–88). Imagining himself reduced to a purely phallic function, Mulligan both entertains the crowd and affirms the myth of an essential masculinity that underwrites their political and religious loyalties. Naturally, there can be but one verdict on the birth of the Purefoy child: "In her lay a Godframed Godgiven preformed possibility which thou [Theodore Purefoy] hast fructified with thy modicum of man's work" (U14.1412–14). Since it fulfills the wishes of "One above, the Universal Husband" (U14.1318–19), childbirth is treated merely as evidence of male potency. The point is crudely driven home by Crotthers's tale of "old Glory Allelujurum," "an elderly man with dundrearies," who came to the hospital to enquire after his pregnant wife: "I cannot but extol the virile potency of the old bucko," Crotthers declares, "that could still knock another child out of her" (U14.891–93).

Like Stephen Dedalus, Bloom is set apart from the other men at the hospital by his refusal to laugh at their sexist humor. Bloom is the "[s]ingular" guest who muses over the fact that "the puerperal dormitory and the dissecting theatre should be the seminaries of such frivolity, that the mere acquisition of academic titles should suffice to transform in a pinch of time these votaries of levity into exemplary practitioners of an art which most men anywise eminent have esteemed the noblest" (U14.898–902). The students denigrate maternity in a fashion that seems especially ignoble to the man to whom the pain of losing his son, Rudy, is ever present: "To those who create themselves wits at the cost of feminine delicacy (a habit of mind which he never did hold with) to them he would concede neither to bear the name nor to herit the tradition of a proper breeding: while for such that, having lost all forbearance, can lose no more, there remained the sharp antidote of experience to cause their insolency to beat a precipitate and inglorious retreat" (U14.865–70). In this parody of Edmund Burke, Bloom's defense of femininity is conventionally chivalrous; it is a matter of delicacy and breeding. But his sympathy is quite different from that of the surgeon, who regards motherhood as nothing more than a vehicle for securing "the future of [the] race" (U14.832). The surgeon is able to utter this idea and still salute the students as he leaves the room; his rebuke is purely rhetorical and is therefore readily accepted by the students with gratuitous sentimentality. Bloom's defense of maternity is different because in suggesting his potential for imaginative sympathy with women, it leads him to project himself into the feminine position, to mimic woman's alterity, and so to overcome the limitations and censorships of the masculine role. The conventionality of Bloom's invocation of feminine delicacy indicates the transformative, and transgressive, potential of such sympathy. For if the maternal position is a cultural construct, the effect of intersecting historical discourses, Bloom can write himself into her narrative: "he rued for her that bare whoso she might be or wheresoever" (U14.240). His sympathy for the pregnant woman is literalized in "Circe," when he gives birth to "eight male yellow and white children" (U15.1821–22).

The sex of these hallucinatory offspring emphasizes the nature of Bloom's transformation.

Bloom's feminine sympathies imply a critique not only of the Church's position on birth control, but also of the allied, and often violent, cause of Irish Nationalism. Like the Church, Nationalism institutionalizes the oppression of Irish women by demanding that they produce the next generation of Irish males to fight the good fight against mainland Britain—a fight the Catholic Church, bitterly opposed to the Church of England, naturally condones. The surgeon's praise of motherhood as the means of securing the future of the race has a specifically Nationalist tinge, which may account for the alacrity with which the students accept his rebuke. The Nationalists' deplorable attitude to women is clearly connected to their violent political aims. Casting about for explanations for the demise of Ireland, they invoke stories in which women tempt men into betraying their country. In the "Nestor" episode, Mr. Deasy cites offenses from the Bible, Greek mythology, and Irish history to suggest that women are the root of all evil: "A woman brought sin into the world. For a woman who was no better than she should be, Helen, the runaway wife of Menelaus, ten years the Greeks made war on Troy. A faithless wife first brought the strangers to our shore here, MacMurrough's wife and her leman, O'Rourke, prince of Breffni. A woman too brought Parnell low" (*U*2.390–94). From the earliest Irish disaster, when MacMurrough persuaded Henry II to launch the first invasion in the twelfth century, to the fall of Charles Stewart Parnell at the end of the nineteenth, women have been to blame, as the Citizen affirms in "Cyclops."[69] It is apt that Bloom, with his maternal sympathies, should encounter violence at the hands of the Citizen, who laments the absence of Ireland's lost "twenty millions." The Citizen's belligerence underlines the point that while they blame women for their troubles, it is men who fight wars. In this sense we might read "Oxen of the Sun" as a criticism not only of the Irish Nationalist struggle but of all wars, including the event that gave special urgency to the debates about abortion and contraception informing the *Little Review* trial: the Great War.

Joyce makes the connection between Bloom's feminine sympathies and his opposition to violence at the end of the "Circe" episode as well. Taking Stephen Dedalus home after a violent encounter with a group of British soldiers, Bloom pays him maternal attentions:

Poetry. Well educated. Pity. (*he bends again and undoes the buttons of Stephen's waistcoat*) To breathe. (*he brushes the woodshavings from Stephen's clothes with light hand and fingers*) One pound seven. Not hurt anyhow. . . . (*U*15.4935–39)

This scene is rightly celebrated as Bloom's magical restoration to fatherhood, for as he watches Stephen's face he imagines it changing into that of his dead son, Rudy. Yet at his most paternal moment in the whole novel, Bloom is also playing mother, fulfilling a wish announced earlier in the episode: "O, I so want to be a mother" (U15.1817). In this bisexual role, a mélange of maternal and paternal styles, Bloom confounds the regulatory fictions that limit a character to one sex and one gender. At the same time, he counters the destruction wrought by British imperialists, whose violence, like that of the Irish Nationalists, is shown to be thoroughly reprehensible.[70]

Inevitably, Bloom's maternal sympathies are treated as cause for mockery by his fellows in the hospital. Amidst the ranks of male chauvinism, his dissent causes him to be cast as an "alien" (U14.906), and raises doubts about his sexual impulses—doubts justified, ironically, by his masturbation earlier in the evening. In the eyes of the students, Bloom pales in comparison with Theodore Purefoy, who in producing a child has proved his manhood and satisfied at one stroke the demands of Irish Nationalism and of Roman Catholicism. But Bloom does not buckle under these pressures. His opposition to this chauvinism implicitly criticizes a dual loyalty that treats women merely as the means of reproducing men to fight for God and country. Bloom thus occupies a position of resistance to patriarchy, the very position that Ezra Pound and John Quinn defined as feminine. It is here that Bloom's mimicry is most functional in relation to the historical context in which "Oxen" was written. Resisting the forces that reduce women to a subordinate position, Bloom breaks the patriarchal code underpinning not only the science of birth but also the 1921 trial of Margaret Anderson and Jane Heap.

"Circe": Bloom on Trial

The relevance of Bloom's sexual ambiguity to obscenity trials is suggested even more strongly in "Circe." In this phantasmagorical episode, set in Nighttown, Bloom finally meets Stephen Dedalus, but first he is put on trial for sexual perversion. Since Joyce was completing "Circe" at the very time that legal proceedings were instigated against his novel, it is tempting to think of Bloom's trial as a tacit commentary on actual events. Before leaping to the conclusion that Joyce wrote the episode with those events in mind, it is important to remember that, as Richard Ellmann reports, Joyce started writing it in June before the scandal began, and probably finished it in December (that is, after the October hearing, but before the February trial). Further, Joyce's friends in New York gave him only the sketchiest information about the legal proceedings. Yet Joyce did not send the manuscript to Pound until April 1921, two months after the trial had taken place. At the very least one can say that "Circe" explores questions of sexual normality similar to those raised by the 1921 trial. "Circe" invites further speculation because in many ways it recycles the drama of the episode ("Nausicaa") scrutinized in court. Bloom's trial functions as a secular forum for confession, which exploits the subversive potential of superimposing the conventions and structures of pornography on those of Catholic confession; it provides an arena for testing out possible reconfigurations of the human body and of human sexuality. In "Circe" Joyce implies that these performative structures may generate a limited freedom from the coercive power of the institutional discourses to which they belong. He suggests that

theatrical self-transformation may loosen the shackles of historical and biological determinism that bound the sexual discourses deployed at the *Little
Review* trial. In this way, "Circe" raises issues of freedom that are inevitably
brought into play by acts of censorship.

Bloom is put on trial after being arrested for "[u]nlawfully watching and
besetting" (*U*15.733–34). His alleged crime evokes his voyeuristic performance
in "Nausicaa," a connection underlined in "Circe" by Gerty MacDowell's
hallucinatory reappearance before the trial itself occurs:

> (*Leering, Gerty MacDowell limps forward. She draws from behind, ogling, and
> shows coyly her bloodied clout.*)

GERTY

> With all my worldly goods I thee and thou. (*she murmurs*) You did that. I hate you.

BLOOM

I? When? You're dreaming. I never saw you.

. . .

GERTY

> (*to Bloom*) When you saw all the secrets of my bottom draw. (*she paws his sleeve,
> slobbering*) Dirty married man! I love you for doing that to me. (*U*15.372–78, 383–
> 85)

Gerty's charges anticipate those leveled by a number of women who stand up at
Bloom's trial. Mary Driscoll, Mrs. Yelverton Barry, Mrs. Bellingham, and The
Honourable Mrs. Melvyn Talboys all accuse him of making indecent pro-
posals. Moreover, it appears not only that Gerty is one among many women
whom Bloom has ogled, but that his ogling characteristically involves imitating
the role of priestly voyeur. Bloom's sexuality always seems to inhabit the
mediated, mediating structures that characterize peep show and confessional.
Operating within those structures, however, Bloom threatens to destabilize the
sexual hierarchy they are supposed to support.

In a letter of 1924, Joyce's brother Stanislaus wrote of *Ulysses*: "It is undoubtedly Catholic in temperament. This brooding on the lower order of natural facts, this re-evocation and exaggeration of detail by detail and the spiritual
dejection which accompanies them are purely in the spirit of the confessional.
Your temperament, like Catholic morality, is predominantly sexual" (*JJ*,
p. 590). These remarks seem to apply most obviously to Stephen Dedalus,
whose refusal to pray for his dying mother is explained to him by Buck Mulligan in identical terms: "you have the cursed jesuit strain in you, only it's
injected the wrong way" (*U*1.209). Yet, as the "Circe" trial indicates, the same
comments may be as illuminating in relation to Bloom as they are in relation to
Joyce himself. The parallels between Bloom and Joyce suggest that the author
considered his own sexuality, his own normality, on trial, both in the episode
itself and perhaps in the New York courts, too. The charges leveled at Bloom
give him a profile closely resembling Joyce's, as revealed in a series of masturbatory letters to Nora Barnacle and in his furtive correspondence of 1918–1919
with Martha Fleischmann.[71] The sadomasochistic desires expressed in the let-

ters to Nora Barnacle and the voyeuristic impulses of the later correspondence evoke the spirit of the confessional in a manner quite similar to that of Bloom's own alleged communication with different women. According to Mrs. Bellingham, Bloom sent her an "obscene photograph" accompanied by a letter that sounds a lot like one of the author's: "It represents a partially nude señorita, frail and lovely (his wife, as he solemnly assured me, taken by him from nature), practising illicit intercourse with a muscular torero, evidently a blackguard. He urged me to do likewise, to misbehave, to sin with officers of the garrison. He implored me to soil his letter in an unspeakable manner, to chastise him as he richly deserves, to bestride and ride him, to give him a most vicious horsewhipping" (U15.1067–73). Bloom's wish for the vicarious pleasure of watching his wife engage in extramarital sex is similar to Joyce's attempts to persuade Nora Barnacle to have affairs with other men. For Bloom, as for Joyce, this pleasure also involves self-punishment: Dublin's modern Ulysses is as frantically jealous about Molly as Joyce was about his own wife. But as punishment, it is presumed to give pleasure to the person who metes it out as well as to the person receiving it. In this sense, Bloom's desire to exchange his wife for vicarious pleasure is akin to his plea for a most vicious horsewhipping. Both are forms of sadomasochistic pleasure which, like chastisement in the confessional, arouses the giver as much as the recipient.

Judging by the charges against him, Bloom carries the confessional apparatus with him wherever he goes. Mrs. Yelverton Barry indicates that he even takes it to the theater: "He said that he had seen from the gods my peerless globes as I sat in a box of the *Theatre Royal* at a command performance of *La Cigale*. I deeply inflamed him, he said" (U15.1018–21). The box at the theater suggests the confessional box; the image of the inflamed observer conjures up the sexually aroused priest, watching, unseen, like a voyeur at a peep show. Bloom's allegedly inflamed state seems related, like that of priest or voyeur, to a freedom to observe without being observed. It is significant, however, that Joyce evokes the confessional apparatus in the theater, for confession itself is theatrical. When Bloom spies on Mrs. Barry, he is playing a role, and in the process he necessarily casts her in one as well. But, as in the theater, these roles are inherently unstable. Begging Mrs. Bellingham to chastise him, to give him a most vicious horsewhipping, Bloom expresses a desire to reverse roles, imagining himself as miserable sinner, Mrs. Bellingham as priest. Sex and gender appear to be as unstable in the confessional as in any other theatrical structure. Implying that one can switch roles simply by changing costumes, by swapping a dress for a cassock, Joyce evokes the confessional in order to destabilize the sexual hierarchy it is supposed to enforce.

"Circe" heightens the theatrical instability of sex and gender by exaggerating and then undermining Bloom's masculinity. The sentence passed on him at the trial, death by hanging, casts him as the parodic embodiment of phallic masculinity: as we learn in "Cyclops," the hanged man is noteworthy for his erection (U12.455–78). The next sequence of events seems to affirm Bloom's cultural maleness. In a scene that externalizes his desire for social acceptance, he is transformed into the Lord Mayor and administers "open air justice" with the wisdom of a modern Solomon. Yet, in a process culminating in the birth of eight sons, Bloom's masculinity becomes deeply ambiguous. The trial effectively starts again as a group of doctors, acting as a panel of expert witnesses, diagnose a variety of sexual disorders. According to Mulligan, Bloom is bisexually abnormal, and shows signs of hereditary epilepsy and elephantiasis. Mulligan also finds "marked symptoms of chronic exhibitionism" and latent ambidexterity; he attributes Bloom's premature baldness to "selfabuse," and declares him "*virgo intacta.*" Madden diagnoses hypsospadia. According to Crotthers, Bloom's urine is albuminoid, his salivation insufficient, his patellar reflex intermittent. Dixon finally pronounces Bloom "a finished example of the new womanly man" (*U*15.1774–99). Thomas Richards has argued that nineteenth-century quack doctors "began to transform the female body into a specific site of advertised spectacle"; in "Circe" Bloom's body becomes a parodic spectacle advertising the gender-bending science of sexology.[72]

Bloom's body wears the medical symptoms of both sexes, but Joyce seems to evoke medical terminology to reveal how easily sex and gender elude definition and classification. Critics have traced some of this terminology to Havelock Ellis and Richard Krafft-Ebing. Ellis, for instance, associated ambidexterity with bisexuality, as Mulligan does in diagnosing Bloom, and Bloom's attraction to Gerty MacDowell may owe something to Ellis's account of a man who was attracted to lame women. Further, the name of Bloom's father, Virag, suggests viragitis, which Krafft-Ebing defined as the condition whereby a woman behaves like a man.[73] To this list we might add Dixon's pronouncement on Bloom as the new womanly man, a reversal (or semireversal) of viragitis perhaps deriving from Weininger's theory that Jews were womanly men. Bloom is a Jew, of course, and Joyce draws on other Weiningerian observations as well. Weininger thought that women and Jews shared a habit of placing books on the shelf upside down, as Bloom does and as Joyce's wife, daughter, and a Jewish friend, Ottocaro Weiss, all did; Ellmann reports that Joyce was delighted at finding a book placed upside down on Weiss's bookshelf.[74] But "Circe" also exposes the fictional basis of such ideas. As reported by the panel of doctors, Bloom's disorders seem to generate each other: one disorder suggests another, and so on. Yet the more disorders found by the doctors, the less credible their diagnosis becomes, for the more Bloom's body is scrutinized, the more it looks like a fiction, an illusion, fabricated by the impulse to diagnose. Bodies, it appears, are constructed by medicine as objects of belief, but "Circe" indicates that as medicine continues to insist on the credibility of its own fictions, their illusory nature is thrown into ever sharper relief. Joyce borrows from sexology so eclectically, and so randomly, that the fictionality and constructedness of his representation of the body become quite transparent. One might even say that his appeal to psychological jargon suggests that the diagnosing mind itself is fictitious.

Bloom's guise as the new womanly man has blasphemous implications as well. Under medical examination his body confesses secrets that "Nausicaa" associates with Gerty and, by implication, with the Virgin Mary. His self-abuse clearly relates to his own behavior in the earlier episode, but his chronic exhibitionism and status as *virgo intacta* are marks of Gerty's performance. The connection between Bloom and Mary is emphasized by Dixon's announcement that Bloom "is about to have a baby" (U15.1810): Joyce reallocates immaculate conception to his famously maculate hero. In addition to disturbing the sexual hierarchy of the confessional, Bloom's body reconfigures the structure of the male gaze, which the Church concentrates on the image of the Virgin Mother. He becomes his own Gerty, for his body is the object of erotic fantasy displaced onto an imaginary subject.

"Circe" carries the destabilizing and blasphemous effects of Bloom's bodily confessions even further in his whorehouse encounter with Bella Cohen. Bloom's role closely imitates the penitent's, and it is during this part of the narrative that he undergoes his famous sex change. Now narrative becomes confession. The confessor's role is filled by Bella, whose name accordingly changes to Bello, in whom Bloom, recounting his lurid past, invests the power of absolution and punishment. Bloom asks for Bello's "domination" (U15.2777); the latter complies by evoking the punitive, sadistic apparatus of the confessional, quenching a cigar on Bloom's ear, and declaring: "Ask for that every ten minutes. Beg. Pray for it as you never prayed before" (U15.2941). Insisting that Bloom accept such sadistic torture as penance, Bello demands the absolute candor that the Church requires of its penitents: "Say! What was the most revolting piece of obscenity in all your career of crime? Go the whole hog. Puke it out! Be candid for once" (U15.3042–43). Bello's insistence makes it clear that he (or she) expects gratification on hearing Bloom's confession: "Answer. Repugnant wretch! I insist on knowing. Tell me something to amuse me, smut or bloody good ghoststory or a line of poetry, quick, quick, quick! Where? How? What time? With how many? I give you just three seconds. One! Two! Thr . . . " (U15.3052–55). Bello's demand for erotic pleasure makes explicit what the priest, aided by the partition in the confessional box, conceals. His desire to penetrate the penitent's body graphically reveals itself in a mock auction, as he "*bares his arm and plunges it elbowdeep in Bloom's vulva,*" an act expected to arouse the spectator: "There's fine depth for you! What, boys? That give you a hardon?" (U15.3089–90). Bello is inflamed by the very idea of his victim's confessions, just as Bloom is by the sight of Mrs. Barry's "peerless globes" at the theater. But in devising a punishment for Bloom, Bello reiterates the instability of gender roles in this scene. Bloom, he decides, will be the brothel's chambermaid, a role that promises as much erotic gratification as anything experienced by the priest in confession. While this proposal preserves the confessional structure of power, it offers the victim opportunities for voyeuristic pleasure like that enjoyed by the priest. Especially for Bloom, always aroused by the sight of women's underclothes, the prospect of sousing and batting their "smelling underclothes," swabbing their latrines, and emptying their "pisspots" may not be uninviting.[75]

"Circe" also suggests possibilities for eluding or thwarting the coercive, censorious structures of pornographic and Catholic (as well as sexological) discourses, which for Bloom constitute what Stephen Dedalus calls the "nightmare" of history (U2.377). The full weight of this coercion is brought to bear when Bloom, having confessed his past transvestism and female impersonation, sees The Sins of the Past rise up against him with a litany of accusations: he left "[u]nspeakable messages" while he "presented himself indecently to the instrument in the callbox," he "encouraged a nocturnal strumpet to deposit fecal and other matter in an unsanitary outhouse," he offered "his nuptial partner to all strongmembered males," he spied on "loving courting couples" by the vitriol works, and he "gloat[ed] over a nauseous fragment of wellused toilet paper presented to him by a nasty harlot, stimulated by gingerbread and a postal order" (*U*15.3028–40). Like confession, however, this narrative is predicated on a faith in chronology that "Circe" seems to reject. For Bloom to be punished, he must have committed these sins in a past whose reality is thrown into doubt. For how does one distinguish past, present, and future from each other in this hallucinatory narrative? Critics have rightly pointed out that in some ways "Circe" proceeds at the level of naturalistic plot: Bloom and Stephen go to Bella Cohen's brothel in Nighttown, the latter breaks a lamp, Bloom pays for it, they flee outside; Stephen is knocked unconscious by a loud-mouthed British soldier, and is nursed home by Bloom. But at some level it is quite impossible to disentangle actual events from hallucinations, and it becomes unclear whether those hallucinations are Bloom's, as some of them seem to be, or projections of a larger narrative unconscious. At one point, for instance, "Circe" conjures up Blazes Boylan, who tells Bloom: "You can apply your eye to the keyhole and play with yourself while I just go through her a few times" (*U*15.3788–89). Implicitly, "her" means Molly: Bloom has been haunted all day by the knowledge that his wife has an afternoon appointment with Boylan, the notorious man-about-town. Boylan's offer, therefore, may be a projection of Bloom's doubts about his wife's fidelity. It may also refer to something that actually happened. Both of these conjectures may be correct, but there is no way of knowing. The blurring of the boundary between fact and fiction renders narrative chronology extremely uncertain. Vicki Mahaffey puts the case succinctly when noting that in "Circe," "costume changes replace narrative explication, as plot literally yields to disguise."[76] In an episode where fictions pose as facts, the appearance of Boylan and The Sins of the Past may be no more than one of those costume changes, a function of the theatrical apparatus supporting the entire narrative.

Founded on this unstable terrain, "Circe" hints that even within the conventions of its pornographic and confessional structures, a limited form of freedom may be possible. Paradoxically, this point is suggested quite powerfully by another scene evoking peep show and confessional, which occurs as the narrative dramatizes Bloom's fear of cuckoldry. Proposing that Bloom peep through the keyhole and masturbate, the hallucinatory Boylan intimates that Bloom fears cuckoldry yet desires it. Boylan insinuates that Bloom would enjoy watching the event because it will offer another opportunity for contraceptive sexual activity. Metaphorically, the scene places Bloom on both sides of the partition in the confessional box: he is the masturbating confessor, but he is also the penitent, punished for choosing contraceptive sex by being made to watch his wife engage in genuine reproductive sex with a true muscular torero. In other words, his punishment enables him to commit the crime against fecundity all over again. Bloom's desire for such pleasurable retribution is indicated by his cooperative answer to Boylan's offer: "Thank you, sir. I will, sir. May I bring two men chums to witness the deed and take a snapshot? (*he holds out an ointment jar*) Vaseline, sir? Orangeflower . . . ? Lukewarm water . . . ? (*U*15.3791–93). Bloom's response seems to confirm his complicitous desire to be cuckolded: why else has he stayed away from home all day? If Boylan is supposed to show him how a real man gets the job done, Bloom is willing to leave the task of reproduction to others and to keep different pleasures for himself. He wants not only to peep through the keyhole, but also to take a snapshot, which will enable him to reexperience the pleasures of voyeurism at some time in the future. What is more, he wants to share the present experience with two men chums; he might show the photograph to others as well (he gives Stephen a picture of Molly in "Eumaeus"). In this sense, Molly figures as the object of what Eve Sedgwick has called "homosocial exchange": like Bertha in Joyce's play, *Exiles* (1918), Molly is the medium for communicating desire between men. Reflecting on Richard Rowan's engineering of the affair between his wife, Bertha, and their friend, Robert Hand, Joyce makes this theme quite explicit in a note for *Exiles*: "The bodily possession of Bertha by Robert, repeated often, would certainly bring into almost carnal contact the two men. Do they desire this? To be united, that is carnally through the person and body of Bertha as they cannot, without dissatisfaction and degradation—be united carnally man to man as man to woman?"[77] Like Bloom, Rowan seems motivated in his machinations by voyeurism, which may be inseparable from homosocial desire. Affirming how deeply Bloom's sexuality is implicated in the voyeuristic structures informing peep show and confessional, Joyce's "Circe" episode releases nonreproductive desires, which the Church ostensibly condemns.

The freedom here sounds rather one-sided: Bloom seems to benefit at Molly's expense. Further, the illicit desires expressed in "Circe" are of a piece with what Richard Brown has aptly called the "contraceptive" sexual relationship that now exists between Molly and Bloom, a relationship that leaves Molly unsatisfied.[78] For more than ten years, as we learn in "Ithaca," the Blooms have not had "complete carnal intercourse, with ejaculation of semen within the natural female organ" (*U*17.2278–79). Though not sexless, a point underlined when Bloom, climbing into bed, kisses "the plump mellow yellow smellow melons of her rump" (*U*17.2241), the state of their marriage seems to please him more than her. Moreover, if their abstinence from complete carnal intercourse provides Molly with a motive to cuckold Bloom, the possibility of adultery simply fuels Bloom's inveterate jealousy. Bloom is jealous of every man who has dared even to look at Molly with desire, so that when "Ithaca," projecting Bloom's thoughts, enumerates her lovers, the list includes among its most unlikely members two priests, Father Corrigan and Father Sebastian of Mount Argus (*U*17.2133–42). In provoking such jealousy, however innocently, Molly actually increases Bloom's desire to wield power over her, and to control her.

Yet Bloom's cogitations at the end of "Ithaca" temper his jealousy with feelings of acceptance that imply an inclination to surrender the robes of power. This inclination tacitly criticizes the desire, displayed here as in the *Little Review* trial, to control female sexuality. Reflecting on Boylan, the only man whom he might reasonably suspect of supplanting his place in bed, Bloom experiences "[e]nvy, jealousy, abnegation, equanimity" (U17.2155). Bloom assumes that Molly has slept with Boylan, but he comes to see adultery as "not so calamitous as a cataclysmic annihilation of the planet in consequence of a collision with a dark sun," and as "not more abnormal than all other parallel processes of adaptation to altered conditions of existence" (U17.2180–82, 2190-91). Perceiving that he is but one in a series, Bloom takes the first step toward equanimity when he realizes that the idea of adultery depends on a narrative chronology that *Ulysses* persistently undermines:

If he had smiled why would he have smiled?

To reflect that each one who enters imagines himself to be the first to enter whereas he is always the last term of a preceding series even if the first term of a succeeding one, each imagining himself to be the first, last, only and alone whereas he is neither first nor last nor alone in a series originating in and repeated to infinity. (U17.2126–31)

To surrender the illusion of uniqueness is not to lose freedom but to gain it, to realize that one is not alone in the world and that one is not necessarily bound to a preordained role. It is also to give up the idea of purity, on which the concept of adultery depends. Finding equanimity, Bloom is liberated from the oppressive role of husband. No longer does he feel obliged to insist on his wife's purity and chastity. Although in "Circe" Bloom's loss of censor control appears quite grotesque, "Ithaca" suggests that in surrendering control he alleviates his own oppression and, perhaps, Molly's as well. Thus Bloom offers resistance to the censorious discursive structures deployed not only in his own trial but in the actual trial of Joyce's novel.

Freedom and Transformation in "Penelope"

Written in 1921 after the *Little Review* trial, the last episode in *Ulysses*, "Penelope," puts the transformative possibilities of Bloom's equanimity to the test by inviting a reexamination of the curiosity that leads many readers to return perpetually, like Bloom, to the subject of Molly's liaison with Blazes Boylan. "Penelope" appears openly to reject the taboos enforced at the trial, as if to indulge that curiosity: as Molly's mind courses over the day's events, the reader seems liberated into a sea of uncensored obscenity that D. H. Lawrence condemned as "the dirtiest, most indecent, obscene thing ever written."[79] Indicating, however, that curiosity and disgust are two sides of one coin, "Penelope" encourages readers to subject this kind of fascination to serious scrutiny. What are its motives? What needs does it serve? On what assumptions is it working? Providing a much-needed corrective to readings that describe this episode simply as a stream of consciousness, John Paul Riquelme has observed that "Penelope" returns to "mimesis of mind" without effacing the "mediating role" of style: "Style seems to have become the transparent medium for presenting plot and character. But that transparency is only a special kind of illusion, one that we experience as illusory by recognizing the seeming transparency to be also a mirror."[80] The mirror metaphor suggests that readers see themselves in Joyce's text, and also that what they see is framed; the mediating role of style is effaced only by particular readers reading under particular conditions. I would extend the point to the sexual politics of this episode. "Penelope" implies that the common critical obsession with the details of Molly's sex life comes from treating the episode's style as offering not a mirror for our own historically determined concerns, but a window onto female psychology. A careful reading of "Penelope" suggests that the fascination with Molly's sexual exploits is as much a product of male anxiety and fantasy, similar to what Bloom experiences, as of actual, verifiable events in the narrative. Like the anxieties exhibited at the *Little Review* trial, it is conditioned by the censorious discursive structures associated in *Ulysses* with confession and pornography. At the same time, "Penelope" warns us against assuming that Leopold and Molly Bloom are limited to the narrow gender roles defined by those structures. Rather than describing an inflexible, eternally constricting conventionality, "Penelope" constructs sexuality as a performance, which proves to be the ground on which transformation is possible.

It was Joyce himself who, in a series of comments to Frank Budgen, provoked the almost endless critical speculation about Molly's sexuality and marital infidelity. Joyce suggested that she represented the contradictory essence of femininity: inherently unfaithful, always shifting and changing shape, unfolding in waves, a stream of consciousness. Joyce wrote that Molly is "sane full amoral fertilisable untrustworthy engaging shrewd limited prudent indifferent *Weib. 'Ich bin der* [sic] *Fleisch der stets bejaht!'*" Richard Ellmann points out that the German phrase revises Mephistopheles's declaration in Goethe's *Faust,* "I am the spirit that always denies," into, "I am the flesh that always affirms."[81] While this revision, as Bonnie Kime Scott argues, implies a rejection of the Virgin Mary ideal,[82] it also provokes fantasies about a liberated female sexuality that have a lot in common with the Weiningerian theories attacked by Ford Madox Ford in the March 1918 issue of the *Little Review*. The "female principle," wrote Weininger, "is nothing more than sexuality." According to this theory, women experience "subjection to waves of feeling"; they have "no definite limits," and feel a "sense of continuity" with the rest of humankind.[83] Joyce's comments to Budgen suggest a continuity between Weininger's theory of female "instability and untruthfulness" and the contradictory surface of Molly's narrative. The nonlinear form of this narrative would thus reinscribe Molly within the same norms of femininity as the court invoked when judging "Nausicaa," and the two women who printed it, in 1921.

The critical fascination with Molly's sexual activity shares many of the voyeuristic impulses motivating both pornography and confession. The narrative suggests this connection when recalling a visit to Father Corrigan:

I hate that confession when I used to go to Father Corrigan he touched me father and what harm if he did where and I said on the canal bank like a fool but whereabouts on your person my child on the leg behind high up was it yes rather high up was it where you sit down yes O Lord couldnt he say bottom right out and have done with it what has that got to do with it and did you whatever way he put it I forget no father and I always think of the real father what did he want to know for when I already confessed it to God he had a nice fat hand the palm moist always I wouldnt mind feeling it neither would he Id say by the bullneck in his horsecollar . . . Id like to be embraced by one in his vestments and the smell of incense off him like the pope besides theres no danger with a priest if youre married hes too careful about himself then give something to H H the pope for a penance. . . . (*U*18.106–15, 118–21)

Through unnecessary prying, Father Corrigan betrays an unholy interest in the details of Molly's canal-bank encounter: his disinclination to "say bottom right out" implies as much titillation as reserve or embarrassment. "Penelope" confirms Bloom's observation in "Lestrygonians" that for female penitents, priests have a strange sexual allure, which is largely associated with their smell: "Id like to be embraced by one in his vestments and the smell of incense off him like the pope." Sexual contact with a priest has the added advantage of being purely contraceptive: "besides theres no danger with a priest if youre married hes too careful about himself." Even within this short passage, Molly's narrative bears out Mary Lowe-Evans's thesis that in Joyce's works priests often substitute unproductive discourse for reproductive intercourse; the recollection of Molly's confession dissolves imperceptibly into contemplation of the priest's contraceptive function in sexual discourse. In this sense the priest anticipates several Joyce scholars, whose fascination with the details of Molly's sexual experience imitates what the narrative recalls of Father Corrigan's curiosity. The memory of confession points to the Church as the source of this critical obsession. Endeavoring to account for female sexuality through an interrogation of Molly's experience, some critics have unwittingly mimicked the Church's attempt through confession to account for female sexuality, to censor female desire, and to install the female body not only as the object of, but as the necessary ground for, socially sanctioned male desires.[84]

Joyce's comments to Budgen suggest that he perpetuated this process, but an attentive reading of "Penelope" alerts us to the ways in which the construction of the female body is motivated by projections of male desire. While so much in this episode insinuates that Molly fulfills the fantasy of liberated female sexuality, the narrative includes musical allusions that ask us to reconsider the common assumption that she actually has sex with Boylan. Don Gifford notes allusions to Charles K. Harris's ballad "After the Ball" and to a duet in William V. Wallace's opera *Maritana*, both of which imply that female infidelity and betrayal are products of the jealous, self-deceiving male imagination.[85] The context in which "Penelope" alludes to "After the Ball" invites a ready comparison with Molly's own situation. The ballad tells the tale of an old man who has remained celibate under the erroneous assumption that many years ago he was deceived by his lover. The narrative anticipates the direct allusion to this tale when referring a few lines earlier to "some funny story about the jealous old husband," yet it also evokes Bloom, to whom Molly's mind turns as she recalls "those books he brings me the works of Master Francois Somebody" (*U*18. 484–85, 488). The image of Bloom also insinuates itself into the narrative as Molly remembers singing Wallace's duet, "O Maritana wildwood flower," which invokes the theme of the self-deceiving husband (*U*18.1297). The duet is sung by the heroine and her husband, who believes that she betrayed him before their marriage by becoming the king's mistress. Not only is the husband mistaken on this score, but he would not have married Maritana at all had they not been tricked by the villain of the piece.

These allusions have interesting implications. The allusion to *Maritana* compounds the theme of male self-deception expressed in "After the Ball" by showing another male character, in this case the villain, deceiving others simply for the sake of deceiving them. But most central here is the self-deception of jealous male lovers. The intertextual method of "Penelope" intimates that questions about Molly's sexuality, and about her fidelity to Bloom, are inextricable from the theme of male anxiety and fantasy. This method also alerts readers to the sexual politics of Joyce's strategies of representation. Insinuating the theme of male fantasy into its fabric, Joyce shows us how the text is constructed: the view of female psychology presented in "Penelope" is framed by male desires and male anxieties. Despite Joyce's comments to Budgen, and despite the appearance of its textual surface, "Penelope" implies that its own procedures for representing Molly's mind and body are mediated by structures of desire and power. In this sense "Penelope" confesses, and scrutinizes, not only our voyeurism but its own as well.

While "Penelope," like "Nausicaa," invites attention to the filters through which representations of femininity must pass, and suggests that all such representations are texts produced by other texts, this episode deconstructs the gendered identity it is often supposed to portray. Molly's narrative ascribes to masculinity the very instability that Weininger attributed to female psychology. Recalling Mulvey, the first man who kissed her, Molly insists that all men are deceitful, mutable, and inadequate when compared with women: "perhaps hes married some girl on the black water and is quite changed they all do they havent half the character a woman has" (*U*18.826–27). This reversal of Weininger's theory of female inconstancy may result from Molly's experience of Bloom, a "Deceiver" who "plots and plans everything out" (*U*18.318, 1008–9). According to "Penelope," Bloom is very much the new womanly man diagnosed by Dixon in "Circe." If his scheming qualities evoke the heroism of Odysseus, he sounds rather less than Odyssean as we hear of his feeble behavior during illness, and learn of his cowardice in the face of physical violence or the risks of adultery (*U*18.23, 31–32, 1000, 1253–54).

Molly's own behavior, as related in "Penelope," exploits an inconsistency in Weininger's theory of femininity. While positing sharp distinctions between male and female characteristics, Weininger conceded that they applied only to the "pure types of sex," for "male" and "female" are but "abstract conceptions which never appear in the real world."[86] In effect, Weininger understood the real world as a stage on which different sexual and gender identities are performed by actors, who do not necessarily conform to prescribed roles. Thus, the real world offers opportunities for resisting or destabilizing received sexual ideology. In "Penelope," Molly's performance suggests several points of potentially uncontainable instability. Her heterosexuality is thrown into doubt by her memory of Hester Stanhope, with whom she slept as a sixteen-year-old: "we were like cousins what age was I then the night of the storm I slept in her bed she had her arms round me" (*U*18.640–42). This memory recalls a note for *Exiles*, in which Joyce describes a "faint glimmer of lesbianism" in Bertha's friendship with "her dark-complexioned gipsy-looking girl friend Emily Lyons."[87] At another moment, Molly fantasizes about being a man, and expresses narcissistic excitement at the sight of her own breasts (*U*18. 1146–47, 1379). In many ways Molly is the manly female counterpart to her womanly husband. These two models of sexual instability cross paths, particularly through Joyce's extravagant use of flower imagery. Molly remembers Bloom calling her a "flower of the mountain" (*U*18.1576), but by name Bloom is a flower, too; he fulfills Molly's earlier (Bloomian) intuition that one day she would marry a man called Flower. In "Lotus-Eaters" Bloom's sex organ is described as "a languid floating flower" (*U*5.571–72).[88]

Collapsing Weiningerian distinctions between masculinity and femininity, "Penelope" suggests that such purportedly essential differences are produced by a system of seeing that censors sexuality under the compulsion (in the words of Judith Butler) of "social sanction and taboo." The narrative intimates that not only desire but the body itself is constructed by a gaze exerted by intersecting historical discourses. The dissolution of essential differences figured in the merging of Molly's and Bloom's sexual characteristics indicates that, while powerful, this system of seeing is entirely arbitrary. Their merging signals that within this system, sexual identity is an act whose major vehicle for self-expression, the body, is similarly located on the unstable ground of performance. Where Molly's performance of gender merges with Bloom's, it enacts a repetition that transforms the script on which their differences are supposedly founded. Reenacting the regulated fiction of femininity, Molly Bloom, like Gerty MacDowell, rewrites and deregulates it. The absence of individual limits, defined by Weininger as an essentially female characteristic, undermines the means by which institutional discourses attempt to censor sexuality. Driven by social sanction and taboo, the performative accomplishment of gender reinterprets the cultural script for femininity as the ground of transformation.

As the end of "Penelope" shows, *Ulysses* does not suggest that such transformation comes easily, or even consciously, to its characters. As far as we can tell, Molly utters her final "Yes" in the belief that Bloom has ordered her to get his breakfast the next morning, that he is reasserting himself as a conventional husband. This belief is the result of her mishearing his last sleepy mutterings in "Ithaca": "Going to dark bed there was a square round Sinbad the Sailor roc's auk's egg in the night of the bed of all the auks of the rocs of Darkinbad the Brightdayler" (*U*17.2328–30). As Cheryl Herr has noted, Bloom's mutterings "indicate that the presumed center of his consciousness is composed chiefly of elements from the peripheral and enclosing popular culture."[89] Molly seems as oblivious to this aspect of cultural conditioning as she is to the socially constructed nature of her interpretation of Bloom's words, an interpretation that highlights how readily she can adapt herself to the role of conventional wife.[90] Yet, despite its possible consequences for tomorrow's breakfast, the apparent miscommunication between the Blooms exemplifies an interpretative process that, in different circumstances, might prove liberating. It is a misinterpretation that signifies the uncertain nature of all textual interpretation: if, in this instance, it points Molly in a more conventional direction, on other occasions it may transform the script she is reading. And while Molly now believes herself compelled to act as if under male edict, her mistake suggests that scripts are not always as binding as we often take them to be, that they may not even be intended as binding. If some transformations are not realized at the level of conscious intention, they may still be powerful when enacted on the uncertain terrain of sex and gender.

It is in exploiting this terrain that "Penelope," like earlier episodes, unsettles the premises on which *Ulysses,* in mid-composition, was censored. "Nausicaa" quietly erodes the certainties on which the New York court depended when ruling the work obscene, but in the later episodes Joyce's inquiry into sexuality becomes increasingly explicit. "Circe" openly dramatizes the possibility of sex change; "Penelope" punctures commonly held theories of sexuality, deflating the censorious structures of power that supported them. And it is in puncturing those theories that "Penelope" admits the possibility of such crimes against fecundity as Margaret Anderson's and Jane Heap's; the assorted elements that form a character sometimes regarded as excessively heterosexual include a faint glimmer of lesbianism. While Gerty MacDowell's nonreproductiveness suggests the possibility of lesbianism by enacting a female sexuality unrelated to the woman's maternal function, "Penelope" implies that even a woman like Molly, whose maternity seems guaranteed by the existence of her children, may be susceptible to that most scandalous incarnation of female desire. "Penelope" might be read in this light as indirectly commenting on the sexual politics of the *Little Review* trial.

Restaging and transforming the cultural script for femininity, "Penelope" dramatizes a process analogous to that explored in another censored novel of the 1920s, *Lady Chatterley's Lover.* It is wonderfully ironic that *Lady Chatterley*'s author joined the courts in condemning the final episode of *Ulysses* as obscene. Despite his protest against Joyce's treatment of the subject, Lawrence's last novel raises questions about sex and gender similar to those posed by *Ulysses.* Contrary to Lawrence's polemic against the theatricality of the postwar world, *Lady Chatterley's Lover* locates sex and gender on the unstable ground of performance, reactivating the issues stifled by the suppression of the *Little Review. Ulysses* seemed to depart from the traditions of English storytelling, but it told new stories about sex and gender that, in his own way, Lawrence, too, would tell. What looks like an abortion from one angle may also be a different kind of birth, a new source of continuity.

3

Postwar Hysteria: The Case of *Lady Chatterley's Lover*

Lawrence pointed to a continuity between *Ulysses* and *Lady Chatterley's Lover* when stating his intention to do the same thing as Joyce but in a different way. Having read Joyce's novel, he told Compton Mackenzie: "This *Ulysses* muck is more disgusting than Casanova. . . . I *must* show that it can be done without muck." Mackenzie was prompted to ask: "Were Lady Chatterley and her lover conceived at that moment?"[1] Following Mackenzie, some critics have argued that in *Lady Chatterley's Lover* Lawrence tried to counteract Joycean obscenity with obscenity of his own making.[2] Lawrence found evidence in Joyce's work of "a would-be dirty mind" and "deliberate journalistic dirty-mindedness," which lacked "spontaneity or real life."[3] Joycean obscenity was sensationalistic; it pandered to what Lawrence, in "Pornography and Obscenity" (1929), called "mob-meaning."[4] Joyce, that is, located sexuality in the public domain; he falsified experience by turning it into a spectacle. "Real life," according to Lawrence, was to be found in the private world of "individual meaning." Joyce belonged in the theater of censorship; Lawrence himself did not.

Before he began to write *Lady Chatterley's Lover,* Lawrence was warned that his own work posed similar problems. Mackenzie told him "that if he was determined to convert the world to proper reverence for the sexual act by writing about it in a novel he would always have to remember one handicap for such an undertaking. . . . That except to the two people who are indulging in it the sexual act is a comic operation." Lawrence responded by conceding that Mackenzie might be right, and by making "a gesture of despair for the future of the human race."[5] In the event, Mackenzie's objection may have stiffened Lawrence's resolve to convert the world, to ask it to repudiate the inherently censorious mental habits that made sex look like a comic performance. What many readers found in *Lady Chatterley's Lover* was not a book that made them laugh but one that shocked them. To these readers, Lawrence's novel contained at least as much muck as *Ulysses*.

The controversy provoked by *Lady Chatterley's Lover* was exactly what Lawrence expected. Ideally, the book was to have appeared in an expurgated edition published in Britain by Martin Secker and in America by Alfred A. Knopf, accompanied by an unexpurgated version printed privately in Florence. But Lawrence himself said that the novel was "so improper, according to the poor conventional fools, that it'll never be printed."[6] Secker and Knopf accordingly turned it down. Lawrence hoped that the Florence edition, which was available by subscription only, would escape censorship, but its appearance in July 1928 immediately caused a scandal. Some London booksellers refused to handle the book, and it was clearly reaching only a few of its American subscribers. On 10 August officials at San Francisco confiscated five copies of the novel; Lawrence pronounced it "useless to mail copies to America" (*L6*, p. 525).

In Britain the press pounced. *The Sunday Chronicle* (14 October) wrote that the novel "reeks with obscenity and lewdness about sex"; *John Bull* (20 October) denounced it as "the most evil outpouring that has ever besmirched the literature of our country."[7] Rumors of suppression circulated in London for the rest of the year. On 18 January 1929 the British police seized six copies of the novel addressed to Lawrence's agent, Laurence Pollinger; the manuscript of a book of poems, *Pansies,* was intercepted in the mail a few days later. In a debate in the House of Commons on 28 February 1929, the Home Secretary, Sir William Joynson-Hicks, announced: "there is nothing which can properly be described as a literary censorship in this country."[8] But while there was no British trial for *Lady Chatterley* until 1960, nor an American trial until 1959, a literary censorship was clearly operating on both sides of the Atlantic. A bookseller in Cambridge, Massachusetts, was tricked into selling a copy of Lawrence's novel and then convicted for distributing obscene material; bookstores were raided in Philadelphia. The author lost out, too: because contraband literature was not protected by copyright, it was easy prey for pirates like the notorious American Samuel Roth, whose unauthorized edition of *Ulysses* had deprived Joyce of considerable royalties, just as Lawrence was deprived now.[9] Even more galling, perhaps, the piracy of *Lady Chatterley* led to renewed attacks on the novel. Under the headline, "Famous Author's Scandalous Book: Chapter Two of the Shame Epic" (19 January 1929), *John Bull* called for tighter controls over the pirated editions now reaching Britain from the United States (*L7*, p. 141).

The rest of Lawrence's career was clouded by scandal. His reputation as a "lurid sexuality specialist" was firmly entrenched in the popular imagination (*L5*, p. 611); the eye of the censor was fixed permanently on him. He was forced to omit several poems from Secker's July 1929 edition of *Pansies* (though these pieces were restored in a limited edition printed in August by P. R. Stephensen). Lawrence's paintings, which were exhibited at the Warren Gallery in London, were vehemently attacked in the press; thirteen pictures, deemed obscene because they showed pubic hair, were seized in a police raid on 5 July 1929. At Marlborough Street Magistrates Court on 8 August, Judge Frederick Mead ordered the destruction of four books of reproductions that had been published by Stephensen's Mandrake Press; the paintings themselves were saved only on condition that they were returned to their owners and no longer displayed in public. By the time of his death on 2 March 1930, Lawrence's name was virtually synonymous with scandal and censorship, as obituaries in the popular press made clear. Almost invariably such notices concluded their summaries of Lawrence's career by recounting his skirmishes with the law. The headline in the *Daily Express* highlighted the point: "D. H. Lawrence Dead. Stormy Life of Poet-Author-Painter. Banned Works."[10]

As Lawrence was well aware, he was not alone in being censored. In October 1928 he read press reports of moves by the Home Office against the sale and distribution of Radclyffe Hall's lesbian novel, *The Well of Loneliness*, which was tried and banned in November. There was, he noted, "great work going on for the *international suppression of indecent literature*"; the "censor-moron" was, as he put it, "loose" (*L6*, pp. 595, 613). But it was not only the popular press that saw his work as deliberately provocative. *Lady Chatterley* incited T. S. Eliot, Wyndham Lewis, Virginia Woolf, and James Joyce to unite in distaste for Lawrence's didacticism, which in their view rose to a fever pitch at odds with the strenuous discipline of great art. Eliot declared Lawrence "an almost perfect example of the heretic," while Joyce, whom Eliot considered "the most ethically orthodox" of modern writers, dismissed the novel he called "Lady Chatterbox's Lover" as propaganda: "I read the first 2 pages of the usual sloppy English which is a piece of propaganda in favour of something which, outside of D. H. L.'s country at any rate, makes all the propaganda for itself."[11] What Joyce called propaganda Woolf termed preaching: "And why does Aldous [Huxley] say he was an 'artist'? Art is being rid of all preaching: things in themselves: the sentence in itself beautiful: multitudinous seas; daffodils that come before the swallow dares: whereas L[awrence]. would only say what proved something."[12] Though believing strongly enough in freedom of expression to sign a 1929 petition pleading on behalf of Lawrence's paintings, Woolf could not reconcile Lawrence's polemical style with her own aesthetic criteria.[13]

The responses of both journalists and experimental modernists highlighted the public dimension of Lawrence's late work. His contemporaries seem to have regarded him as even more insistent than Joyce on creating a public sensation. At some level this was not the impression Lawrence wished to make. In a letter of 18 November 1927, for instance, he wrote of the need to "avoid all publicity" (*L6*, p. 223). The initial plan to have the unexpurgated *Lady Chatterley* printed privately, as opposed to the expurgated edition intended for the mass market, suggests that he wanted a relatively small, controlled audience for the uncensored version. Yet at another level Lawrence courted public controversy with this book, just as he had done with *The Rainbow*. As *Lady Chatterley* was twice rewritten, its author's vision became more concretely realized; at the same time the book looked increasingly as if it were designed to shock readers with frank evocations of sexual experience. The desire to shock pervaded Lawrence's later work. While composing *Lady Chatterley* he wanted to paint a picture that would kill those who refused to look at it. Imagining the carnage that would follow, he declared: "My word, what a slaughter!" (*L5*, p. 651). It cannot be accidental that several of Lawrence's paintings, notably *Leda and the Swan* and *The Rape of the Sabine Women*, depict rapes, as if he hoped his art would rape the spectator. Lawrence thought Joyce deliberately sensational, but he seemed to invite his contemporaries to view the sex and violence of his own work in the same way.

It is also significant that such violence appeared not in wartime but in the postwar era. In his famous essay "A Propos of *Lady Chatterley's Lover*" (1929), Lawrence provided a clue to his purpose: "in spite of all antagonism, I put forth this novel as an honest, healthy book, necessary for us today."[14] The sickness that made the book necessary was the modern urge to censor expressions of authentic sexual feeling, an urge that manifested itself in the "grey self-importance" of a "sincere Puritan" like Sir William Joynson-Hicks (*P1*, pp. 174–75). *Lady Chatterley's Lover* diagnoses Britain between the wars as a sick body suffering from the degeneracy that results when sex is turned into an object of what Lawrence considered genuine pornography, into an object, that is, of deliberation and self-consciousness. In Lawrence's terms, pornography is the product of a "vicious circle of secrecy" and "masturbation," which prizes the conscious mind and denies contact with the body (*P1*, p. 181). That contact can be restored, Lawrence suggests, only by discovering a new self through an exploration of sexual being. This exploration required the frankness that shocked early reviewers. To find a cure for the future, Lawrence had to wage war on his contemporaries; he had to shock Britain into healing its own inner disorders. It is with some satisfaction that he reports in August 1928 that *Lady Chatterley* "seems to have exploded like a bomb among most of my English friends, and they're still suffering from shell-shock." "But they're coming round already," he assured his correspondent, "and some few already feeling it was good for 'em" (*L6*, p. 505). One of Lawrence's most famous essays asks whether the novel is in need of surgery or a bomb; his frequent references to *Lady Chatterley* as a bomb imply that the most appropriate form of surgery is in fact a kind of war.[15]

Lawrence's notion of shock treatment as a cure for the ills of the world locates his late work quite specifically in the postwar world. It was at this time that thousands of ex-servicemen were suffering from shell shock as a result of their experiences in the Great War; Elaine Showalter reports that in the years 1919 to 1929 some 114, 600 British veterans supported their applications for pensions by citing disorders related to shell shock.[16] This connection between text and world has important implications for modern sexual politics, for, as Eric Leed observes, the symptoms of shell shock, or "male war neurosis," closely resembled those of the female malady, hysteria: "The symptoms of shell-shock were precisely the same as those of the most common hysterical disorders of peacetime, though they often acquired new and more dramatic names in war: 'the burial-alive neurosis,' 'gas neurosis,' 'soldier's heart,' 'hysterical sympathy with the enemy.' . . . [W]hat had been predominantly a disease of women before the war became a disease of men in combat."[17] The last phrase, "a disease of men in combat," is crucial, because it was in fulfilling the traditional stereotype of warlike masculinity that male soldiers acquired the symptoms of a condition that undermined the gender differences supporting that stereotype. As a result of playing the man's role, a soldier often ended up looking like a woman, displaying, as Showalter argues, the instability and emotionality traditionally associated with femininity, and appearing to resist both the war and the concept of manliness itself. Because shell shock could involve hysterical sympathy with the enemy, it threatened to subvert the battle lines defining the arena within which masculinity was to exhibit itself. Thus the link between shell shock and hysteria was not only medical but theatrical: displaying the symptoms of shell shock, one found oneself on the unstable ground of performance, in a region where roles that in the past had seemed fixed might become unsettled, reversed, entirely redefined, a region where enemies might trade places without regard for traditional loyalties.

Lawrence often attacked postwar society on these very grounds; "the modern hysteria, which," he told Maria Huxley, "affects men even worse than women," was a phenomenon he found *"nauseating"* (*L7*, p. 41). Yet for Lawrence, as Anne Fernihough has recently observed, art was a matter of "subterfuge" and "duplicity"; the artist's task was to evade the censorship of the conscious self, and to frustrate the intentions of "the wakeful man and moralist who sits at the desk."[18] *Lady Chatterley's Lover* is duplicitous because, in order to dramatize the problems of postwar society, to diagnose its sickness and find a cure, the novel appropriates the discourse of hysteria. It is a text of subterfuge because this discourse determines its narrative structure. This claim may seem surprising in the light of recent theoretical explorations of hysteria as an ambiguous position hospitable to feminism, especially when one considers attacks on Lawrence by critics like Kate Millett.[19] Read in the context of postwar hysteria, however, *Lady Chatterley* demands a revision of the flagrantly heterosexual, oppressively phallic image underlying both its early reception and much subsequent literary criticism. The novel resists the regulation of gender and sexuality; in the process it subverts the mechanisms of censorship that operate in the conscious artist as in the culture within which, and against which, he was writing. In these terms it is hard to say how different from *Ulysses* Lawrence's novel really is. But censors in the 1920s had trouble distinguishing between them as well.

Hysterical Lawrence

Readers today may be surprised to hear that *Lady Chatterley's Lover* is a hysterical text, but this idea would not have been news to readers and censors in 1928. For, in the eyes of many contemporaries, Lawrence himself was sick. This view persisted, in fact, for some time; at the 1960 trial at the Old Bailey, the prosecution cited Katherine Anne Porter's opinion that *Lady Chatterley's Lover* was "the fevered day-dream of a dying man . . . indulging his sexual fantasies."[20] Earlier attacks, such as the first *John Bull* review, had insisted on diagnosing Lawrence's sickness in culturally and historically specific terms, representing him as a composite of repugnant, un-English qualities: decadence, depravity, unmanliness.

Resorting to the familiar techniques of symptomatic reading, the initial assault on *Lady Chatterley's Lover* identified Lawrence's transgressions as offenses against British codes of morality. Echoing other contemporary publications, *John Bull* declared his whole oeuvre the production of a diseased mind . . . obsessed by sex," and pronounced *Lady Chatterley* "the fetid masterpiece of this sex-sodden genius." Exploiting a strategy used in wartime Britain in the war against modernism, the same review characterized *Lady Chatterley's Lover* as an un-British work whose nearest relation could be found only on the Continent: "The sewers of French pornography would be dragged in vain to find a parallel in beastliness. The creations of muddy-minded perverts, peddled in the back-street bookstalls of Paris[,] are prudish by comparison." As we have seen, it had been considered patriotic in wartime Britain to condemn modernism as Germanic and anti-British, but when the Great War was over there was no longer any need to specify Germany as the origin of Lawrence's disease: now the entire Continent could be blamed. *Lady Chatterley's Lover* had been printed by an Italian and "broadcast to the capitals of the Continent, where it ha[d] been snapped up eagerly by degenerate booksellers." *John Bull* claimed that the novel "sold like hot cakes, particularly in Paris." Implicitly, no true Englishman could have written *Lady Chatterley's Lover,* and if the novel found sympathetic readers at home it was only among "the most degenerate coteries in the literary world" and "British decadents," readers infected by Continental corruption.[21]

Certain members of artistic coteries were sympathetic to Lawrence. E. M. Forster famously described him as the "greatest imaginative novelist of his generation," a view that was reiterated in court in 1960 (*TLC*, p. 112). Forster praised Lawrence for the very reasons that Woolf and Joyce denounced him: what they called preaching or propaganda, Forster called prophecy. In Forster's view, Lawrence, "the only prophetic novelist writing today," conveyed a "rapt bardic quality" that approached the novelistic ideal of "melodic" form. There was no contradiction between the poetry and the preaching: "if he had not a message his poetry would not have developed. It was his philosophy that liberated his imagination, and that is why it is so idle to blame him for not keeping strictly to literature."[22] For W. B. Yeats it was the poetry of *Lady Chatterley* that stood out: "Those two lovers, the gamekeeper and his employer's wife, each separated from their class by their love, and by fate, are poignant in their loneliness, and the coarse language of the one, accepted by both, becomes a forlorn poetry uniting their solitudes, something ancient, humble and terrible."[23]

Despite Forster's injunction, many writers did blame Lawrence, and ironically this opposition commonly sprang up in the very same coteries.[24] But the most aggressive exponent of this view was another self-styled outsider, Wyndham Lewis. Lewis enjoyed the "exhilarating spectacle of his [Lawrence's] battle with antiquated and unreal prejudices of the puritan conscience," but spoke for many critics when he said: "It is not as a 'prophet' that I should praise Lawrence—it seems to me a finer thing to wish 'to be among the English poets' after you are dead, than 'to be among the prophets.'"[25] To Lewis, Lawrence's "frantic" prophesying and exaltation of the body appeared sensational and sentimental. Lewis vented such criticism in *Paleface* (1928) and *The Roaring Queen* (1936). *Paleface*, which was praised by T. S. Eliot as a "brilliant exposure" of Lawrence's "incapacity for what we ordinarily call thinking," parodies the idealized portraits of American Indians that Lewis found in Lawrence's *Mornings in Mexico* (1927).[26] In *The Roaring Queen*, Baby Bucktrout uses *Lady Chatterley's Lover* as a guidebook to seduction.[27]

It was in Lewis's criticism that the modernist critique intersected most visibly with the symptomatic readings of the popular press because he suggested, implicitly and explicitly, that Lawrence was suffering from postwar hysteria. Lewis hinted at this malady in *The Roaring Queen* by implying that Lawrence's prophetic art wanted resilience and masculine definition. Baby Bucktrout, who takes *Lady Chatterley's Lover* for protection against sexual inversion, discovers that the object of her desire, the gardener, has been seduced in the toolshed by another man. This homosexual parody of Lady Chatterley's visits to the gamekeeper's hut insinuates the instability of the sexual roles on which Lawrence's cure for modern sickness was founded. Such insinuations also found their way into Lewis's objections to Lawrencean prophecy, the "frantic" nature of which suggested hysteria: "the terrible disease that at last accounted for him, and which hunted him through life (much more than 'the world of men')—it was *that* also which was responsible (so it seems to me) for a good deal that was most hysterical and feeble in his work."[28] Though alluding here to a disease of the body, Lewis suggested that Lawrence's consumption was inextricable from the mind that produced the work, and that consequently much of the work, being hysterical and feeble, lacked artistic integrity. Donning the prophet's robes, Lawrence made himself into a hysterical spectacle, devoid of the firm contours of Lewis's muscular modernism.

Such responses to postwar Lawrence were common in the 1920s. In January 1926 the *Spectator* accused him of indulging in a "futile sort of girlish hysteria," and the same charge was filed by Thomas Earp in a commentary on Lawrence's "Introduction to These Paintings" (1929), which adduces fear of venereal disease as the cause of sexual repression in European painting. Earp wrote: "Mr. Lawrence occasionally lashes himself into an hysterical, exacerbated violence which not only detracts from the force of his argument, but gives an impression of merely fevered excitability rather than forceful reason" (*LCH*, p. 307). Lawrence did not take Earp's criticism kindly, and responded with a bitter parody: "I heard a little chicken chirp: / My name is Thomas, Thomas Earp! / And I can neither paint nor write / I only can set other people right."[29] As Carol Siegel has written, Lawrence believed "that all his censorship woes were caused by vicious male readers" (such as Earp), who saw him as "effeminate and so inferior."[30]

Lawrence's hysterical didacticism was not always perceived as a sign of effeminate weakness. Some readers associated these symptoms with male violence against women, a point made clear in two reviews of *The Woman Who Rode Away* (1928). Writing in the *Spectator,* Rachel Annand Taylor analyzed the "neurosis" that "half helps, half hinders him as an artist": "His personality is unquiet and feminine; hence he often degenerates into hysteric violence, hence he is so inimical to women, especially imaginative women, too like, and yet too unlike, to partake with him the composure of their dream."[31] Taylor viewed Lawrence as an explosive mixture of masculine battling with feminine qualities, and conceded that he was a "compelling visionary." Another reviewer, Ruth Suckow, was less sympathetic, arguing that in these stories Lawrence "gives rein again to his peculiar fear of women, his frequently hysterical emphasis upon the need for male domination to save this modern world in a Lawrencian savage sense."[32] *The Woman Who Rode Away* has often been invoked in this way. The tale ends poised on the point of the ritual slaughter of its heroine: the action is frozen as the protagonists wait for the evening sun to shine into the cave where the old Indian will strike her with a knife in an act symbolizing phallic penetration. The scene itself heightens the sexual symbolism. Before the ceremony, the heroine sees the cave "that like a dark socket bored a cavity, an orifice, half-way up the crag"; once inside the cave, she stands facing "the iridescent column of ice," which "hangs like a great fang."[33] To readers like Ruth Suckow, the violence anticipated by this scene vividly suggested that if Lawrence was waging a war against postwar Britain, it looked a lot like a sex war.

Although *The Woman Who Rode Away* does not necessarily recommend such violence, Suckow's and Taylor's readings of "hysterical" postwar Lawrence exemplified the common contemporary perception that literature after the war was antifeminist.[34] More recently, Sandra Gilbert and Susan Gubar have reiterated this point, citing Ezra Pound's association of femininity with the civilization for which the Great War had been fought: "There died a myriad," Pound wrote in "Hugh Selwyn Mauberley" (1920), "For an old bitch gone in the teeth, / For a botched civilization."[35] Susan Kent has shown that whereas the battle over sexual discourse had been central to the suffragist struggle of 1860 to 1914, feminists lost that battle in the years after the Great War by identifying the vote as their primary target. Kent argues that despite postwar legislation to open new avenues to women, their success in gaining the right to vote prompted both the decline of feminism as a mass movement and a new surge in antifeminist thought.[36] The forces of sex war were on the move again.

But it was not the same sex war. That the "hysteria" of Lawrence's prophetic demeanor seemed feeble and girlish to some readers but violent and antifeminine to others points to a sex war within literary criticism in the 1920s. Such conflict of opinion also indicates a deep ambiguity in the sexual discourse of postwar Britain. As we have seen, hysteria was the locus of exactly this sort of confusion, particularly in the aftermath of the Great War. It had been common practice before the war to recognize hysterical symptoms only in women; Otto Weininger, for instance, thought hysteria relatively rare in men.[37] Yet this shift in postwar discourse had been anticipated in a number of ways by Sigmund Freud. In "General Remarks on Hysterical Attacks" (1909), Freud had recognized that hysterical symptoms in women also suggested the possibility of theatrical exchange: "When one psychoanalyses a patient subject to hysterical attacks one soon gains the conviction that these attacks are nothing but phantasies projected and translated into motor activity and represented in pantomime." Citing the case "in which a patient tore off her dress with one hand (as the man) while she pressed it to her body with the other (as the woman)," Freud used the pantomimic trope to explicate the relation of hysterical fantasies to bisexuality: "The attack becomes obscured by the patient's undertaking the parts played by both the persons appearing in the phantasy, that is, through *multiple identification*."[38] Freud's apprehension of hysterical neurosis as obscured by multiple identification implies a connection between the subversion of gender and sexual roles and the undermining of battle lines: "hysterical sympathy with the enemy" (to recall one of the terms used for shell shock) may be related to the bisexuality revealed in identification with the masculine and feminine poles of gender. In this sense, hysteria reactivates sex war but blunts the instruments with which it is fought. Moreover, Freud thought that while women seemed more prone to hysterical attacks, men could be susceptible as well. As he observed in *Three Essays on the Theory of Sexuality* (1905), male hysteria was perhaps illuminated by "an unconscious tendency to inversion," which "is never absent."[39]

In *Sexual Inversion* (1897), Havelock Ellis stressed the theatricality of the connection between male sexual inversion and female hysteria. Observing the "tendency to dramatic aptitude—found among a large proportion of my subjects who have never been professional actors," Ellis added: "The dramatic and artistic aptitudes of inverts are, therefore, partly due to the circumstances of the invert's life, which render him necessarily an actor,—and in some few cases lead him into a love of deception comparable with that of a hysterical woman."[40] Implicitly, male hysteria is only a short step away from Ellis's stagey inversion. At the same time, the specter of inversion hovers in the background of this hysteria: *Sexual Inversion* is haunted by such figures as Oscar Wilde, whose downfall took place in the London courts only two years before Ellis's book appeared in print. According to the British authorities, *Sexual Inversion* was so haunted (and haunting) that it was suppressed in 1898, not to reappear in an English edition until the late 1930s.

In the eyes of many 1920s critics, such associations infected Lawrence's performance of hysteria. And while for Ellis the dramatic aptitude of the sexual invert signified a high degree of accomplishment, readers often construed Lawrence's display of hysterical symptoms as diminishing the potency of his art. Wyndham Lewis implied as much in *The Roaring Queen* when he parodied Connie Chatterley's sexual encounters with the gamekeeper. In a review of Lawrence's *Collected Poems* (1928), John Gould Fletcher tacitly linked what he considered the author's artistic decline with sexual weakness or deviance. Describing the poems as "oratorical *vers libres* of the Whitman type," and the "gospel of sex liberation" as something preached "to other men," Fletcher insinuated that such work promoted homoeroticism, the Whitmanian "manly love" that Lawrence had celebrated in an essay of 1921.[41] As James C. Cowan has noted, one of Lawrence's earliest medical readers, Joseph Collins, compared him not only with Whitman but also with Weininger and, in a barely veiled allusion, with Wilde. In *The Doctor Looks at Literature* (1923), Collins objected to "'the enigmatic aberration whose doctrines Mr. Lawrence is trying to foist upon an unsuspecting English-reading public,' that is, homosexuality."[42] In 1924 *The New Statesman* described Lawrence in terms reminiscent of Wilde by diagnosing his essays on American literature as exemplifying a "consciousness of one's audience that is too acute," which "is the normal characteristic of a highly civilised literature in which the social sense has developed the critical faculty to a degree that is incompatible with the production of highly creative art."[43] Here Lawrence emerges, Wilde-like, as the representative of a highly civilized literature, excessively conscious of the advanced society whose etiolation he embodies. For *The New Statesman,* as for Fletcher, Lawrence paid undue attention to the desires of his audience, a strategy making him vulnerable to the kind of readerly reinvention practiced by Lewis and by *John Bull.* Following Ellis, postwar models of sexual inversion suggested a strong link between, on the one hand, what Lewis considered Lawrence's failure to create muscular, masculine art and, on the other, the degenerate perversion that *John Bull* scented in *Lady Chatterley's Lover*: Lawrence's effeminacy implied homosexuality. When treading the boards of social prophecy, Lawrence may have presented an exhilarating spectacle, but he was often perceived as prone to hysterical sympathy with the most suspect kind of enemy. In the 1920s culture of censorship, he was bound to receive close attention from the authorities.

The Uses of Hysteria

For Lawrence the role of hysterical spectacle was, ostensibly, something to be resisted. Lawrence's deep anxiety about being cast in that role was evident in his histrionic reaction to his wartime medical examination, recorded in *Kangaroo.* He connected this "nightmare" with the war, which had created the conditions for such degraded rituals: "It was in 1915 the old world ended. . . . The integrity of London collapsed, and the genuine debasement began, the unspeakable baseness of the press and the public voice, the reign of that bloated ignominy, *John Bull.*" The result was a triumph for the "vast mob-spirit" of "the ghastly masses," a triumph for what postwar Lawrence equated with obscenity.[44] Lawrence came to associate obscenity not only with mob-meaning, but also with the mechanical, self-consciously theatrical sexuality of men and women in postwar society. For Lawrence this kind of sexuality was pornographic because it was produced by a "vast conspiracy of secrecy in the press," a conspiracy to be self-conscious about sex without being "fully and openly conscious." While readers and censors cast Lawrence as a hysterical spectacle, he used similar terms to diagnose their world as a no-man's-land where authentic sexuality disintegrated in a mire of carefully calculated poses and "attitudes," designed to guard the "dirty little secret" of sex (*P1,* p. 181).

It would be wrong to suggest that Lawrence's horror at the false artifices of the postwar world drove him to assault the theater per se. Lawrence himself was a playwright, and his biblical drama *David* (1926) evinces a strong theatrical will to reduce modern life to a series of stylized, formal essences. Even so, the postwar landscape showed how disturbing the effects of theater might be once released into the outside world. As a fixed place and institution the theater stabilized those effects, but translated into social terms it tended to do the opposite: if life itself was theatrical, a matter of playing roles and wearing masks, the theater represented a site of potentially uncontainable ambiguity. The reception of *David* was a prime example, provoking Lawrence to adopt the language of manifest antitheatricality. When the play was performed in London in 1927, Lawrence described the contemporary critic as "such a prig, one imagines he must either be a lady in disguise, or a hermaphrodite" (*L6*, p. 73). Yet such antitheatricality often betrayed Lawrence into adopting a theatrical posture. Lawrence created for himself an ambiguous position, a position of hysterical division, from which to deliver his diagnosis of the postwar world. In his struggles against the censorships of modern society, the artist of subterfuge and duplicity found that hysteria had its uses.

Lawrence frequently condemned the hysterical postwar no-man's-land as obscene. In a short poem called "Obscenity" (1929), he denounced the theatricality of no-man's-land as the "rind / of maquillage and pose" left by the "sewer" of "the caged mind," which polluted the body.

> The body of itself is clean, but the caged mind
> is a sewer inside, it pollutes, O it pollutes
> the guts and the stones and the womb, rots them down, leaves a rind
> of maquillage and pose and malice to shame the brutes. (*CP*, p. 463)

For Lawrence the male and female bodies constituted the two fundamental poles of existence, or what he called in a 1919 essay "the two principles." But those two poles had been eroded by the modern mind, so that life now was, as Macbeth says at the height of his tragedy, "a tale told by an idiot." In *Pansies*, Lawrence adapted Macbeth's words as he lamented that erosion:

> Modern life is a tale told by an idiot;
> flat-chested, crop-headed, chemicalised women, of indeterminate sex,
> and wimbly-wambly young men, of sex still more indeterminate,
> and hygienic babies in huge hulks of coffin-like perambulators—
> The great social idiot, it must be confessed,
> tells dull, meaningless, disgusting tales,
> and repeats himself like the flushing of a W.C. (*CP*, p. 522)

For Lawrence, to render the two principles of sex indeterminate was to deny the fundamental meaning of the human world. Consequently, the dramatic sex changes wrought in the men and women of postwar Britain signified what he called "modernity or modernism": "something that comes at the end of civilizations."[45] As described in "A Propos of *Lady Chatterley's Lover*," the postwar world resembled the no-man's-land between the Allied and German lines during the Great War, but it also looked very similar to the stage at the end of a Shakespearean tragedy: "it is like the end of a tragedy in the theatre. The stage is strewn with dead bodies, worse still, with meaningless bodies, and the curtain comes down" (*LCL*, p. 330).

In 1922 Lawrence confessed to reading "bits" of *Ulysses*; he pronounced the last part of Joyce's novel "the dirtiest, most indecent, obscene thing ever written."[46] If the Nighttown episode, "Circe," was among those bits, he will have encountered a prime example of what he considered modernist obscenity: the sensationalism produced by the self-conscious, mechanical workings of the caged mind, or (to steal the terms Lawrence used to describe Joyce) by the "schoolmaster with dirt and stuff in his head."[47] As we have seen, "Circe" recounts Leopold Bloom's rendezvous with Bella Cohen, a whorehouse madam, who alters her name to Bello, turns herself into a man, and proceeds to change Bloom into a woman, then a pig, and lastly a "charming soubrette with dauby cheeks, mustard hair and large male hands and nose, leering mouth." Pointing to the whores, Bello tells Bloom:

> As they are now so will you be, wigged, singed, perfumesprayed, ricepowdered, with smoothshaven armpits. Tape measurements will be taken next your skin. You will be laced with cruel force into vicelike corsets of soft dove coutille with whalebone busk to the diamondtrimmed pelvis, the absolute outside edge, while your figure, plumper than when at large, will be restrained in nettight frocks, pretty two ounce petticoats and fringes and things stamped, of course, with my houseflag, creations of lovely lingerie for Alice and nice scent for Alice.[48]

To emphasize its dramatic nature, Joyce presents the episode as the script of a play; correspondingly, gender and sexuality are represented as theatrical roles. Sandra Gilbert and Susan Gubar argue that by playing the woman's role Bloom enacts a "gender disorder," through which he learns "the necessity for male dominant-female submissive sexual order"; by wearing the soubrette's costume, they contend, Bloom realizes that, "through a paradoxical yielding to sexual disorder, the male, in particular, might gain the sexual energy he needed for ascendancy."[49] In Joyce's novel, however, the realization that identity may be no more than a role proves liberating: if life is theatrical, one may remake one's identity and so escape the forms of patriarchal domination that used to control it. *Ulysses* provides a route of escape from the nightmare of history, from which not only Stephen Dedalus but all of Joyce's characters are trying to awake. In *Ulysses* Joyce sets about unmaking and remaking history by exploiting the theatricality that for Lawrence made history, especially modern history, a nightmare.

The theatrical and often violent sex changes of Joyce's Nighttown dramatize aspects of postwar life that Lawrence found extremely troubling. In some ways the scene represents one manifestation of the hysterical babble to which, Lawrence believed, the modern world had been reduced: the "dull, meaningless, disgusting tales" told by the "great social idiot." If Lawrence read Joyce's Nighttown episode, he will have found a litany of the hysterical symptoms that he saw, as several of his essays make clear, in postwar public life. In "Cocksure Women and Hensure Men" (1928), Lawrence depicted modern woman as "out-manning the man" by rushing "to mad lengths about votes, or welfare, or sports, or business" (*P2*, p. 555): women exhibited hysteria in their frenetic activity in the public sphere, which was, as Lawrence put it in *The Rainbow*, "The Man's World." Meanwhile, the outmanned man displayed hysteria by taking on female characteristics: "Men are timid, tremulous, rather soft and submissive, easy in their very henlike tremulousness" (*P2*, p. 554). To a certain extent Lawrence's henlike man and Joyce's "new womanly man" were one and the same. Yet whereas Bloom's transformations prove potentially liberating, Lawrence casts modern man as the shell-shocked victim of war, trapped in the middle of no-man's-land: "Oh a no-man's-life in a no-man's-land / this is what they've given you / in place of your own life," he laments in *Nettles* (*CP*, p. 585). In Lawrence's view, the postwar world had become a battlefield for a grotesque new sex war in which roles were unsettled and reversed. Thus, in "Matriarchy" (1928) women are portrayed as bloodthirsty maenads assaulting enfeebled men, who "not only see themselves in the minority, overwhelmed by numbers, but . . . feel themselves swamped by the strange unloosed energy of the silk-legged hordes. Women, women everywhere, and all of them on the warpath!" (*P2*, p. 549). The situation described here is not unlike that in the first act of *Macbeth*, in which Lady Macbeth urges Shakespeare's reticent tragic villain to murder the defenseless King Duncan: men are dramatized as feeble victims, women as hysterical aggressors.

As Elaine Showalter has suggested, hysteria was the nervous disorder most readily associated with the feminist movement, the movement to which Lawrence refers when describing the "silk stockings" worn by emancipated women after the war.[50] As far as Lawrence could see, feminism amounted to little more than such dressing up: it was another sign of decay in a society on the verge of collapse. Feminism represented one of the temporary patterns into which women fell as a result of the postwar failure of prewar gender roles. In "Give Her a Pattern" (1928), Lawrence blamed modern men for this failure: "We shall see the changes in the woman-pattern follow one another fast and furious now, because the young men hysterically don't know what they want" (*P2*, p. 537). Implicitly, the hysterical, maenadlike violence of modern women was a consequence of the Great War. Not only had the display of warlike masculine qualities resulted in male hysteria, it had created the conditions for "the astonishing changes in women": "For years they go on being chaste Beatrices or child-wives. Then on a sudden—bash! The chaste Beatrice becomes something quite different, the child-wife becomes a roaring lioness!" (*P2*, p. 537). As a result of the "indifference" of feeble men, modern England was "nobody's country," beset by petty squabbling:

> Poor England! The men say it's no longer a man's country, it has fallen into the hands of the women. The women give a shout of scorn, and say *Not half!* and proceed to demonstrate that England would be a very different place if it *were* a woman's country—my word, a changed shop altogether. And between the two of them, men

and women, Old England rubs her eyes and says: Where am I? What am I? Am I at all? In short, do I exist?—And there's never a man or a woman takes the trouble to answer, they're all so busy blaming one another. (*P2*, p. 556)

Postwar England had become unstable, passive, emotional. It was a hysterical body that closely resembled Joyce's Nighttown, a theatrical realm where gender and sexual codes were alarmingly unstable.

Lawrence's polemic against this hysterical no-man's-land has often been treated as a declaration of sex war, for his assault on feminism seemed to draw on terms used in the growing postwar ranks of antifeminist men. Postwar Lawrence has been attacked not only by such contemporaries as the reviewer Ruth Suckow, but also by a number of more recent feminists. Hilary Simpson, for example, sees a connection "between the changing position of women in the war years and Lawrence's launching on his career as the prophet of male supremacy." She continues: "Like other male writers in the twenties, he declaims against the confusion of sexual roles, the masculinisation of women and the corresponding effeminacy of men; he questions women's attempts to enter the male world, especially politics; and he contrasts the new 'scientific' attitudes towards sexuality, maternity and child-rearing with the 'instinctive' behaviour of the past."[51]

A different approach has been suggested by Carol Siegel, who contends that Lawrence's assault was not on women themselves but on "the socially constructed" feminine, the "shell around the innate female." Siegel concedes that in depicting "the natural female state as furious rebellion," Lawrence practiced essentialism, but she observes that at "his most essentialist moments Lawrence seems most subversive of the ideologies that generally inform the representation of women in nonfeminist texts." Lawrence saw in women "an oppositely gendered force that would compel him to write"; it was this opposition that produced a vital conflict enabling and authorizing his art.[52] In the light of these insights it is possible to see how the relationship Lawrence imagined with his female readers resembled the creative "coming-together of the sexes," which he celebrated in "The Two Principles": "the birth of a softly rising and budding soul, wherein the two principles commune in a gentle union, so that the soul is harmonious and at one with itself," which "takes place in the youth of an era" (*P2*, p. 234). Lawrence's war on his readers was a war on false social contructions; it had to be fought in order to bring about a new era of peace between manhood and womanhood. Lawrence wrote in "The Real Thing" (1929) that sex is "the great uniter, the great unifier"; sex war was simply the result of the world's loss of faith after the Great War (*P1*, p. 197).

Lawrence's overt antifeminism was closely connected to his explicit rejection of the false constructions of the postwar world, a rejection made clear by his conclusion in "Cocksure Women and Hensure Men" that life could not continue to operate in its present mode: "It is all an attitude, and one day the attitude will become a weird cramp, a pain, and then it will collapse" (*P2*, p. 555). But Lawrence, too, had an attitude. He staged his sex war on the theatrical terrain of public discourse, a terrain that threatened to disrupt such oppositions as that between masculinity and femininity, to unsettle his relationship with readers, even to redefine his own identity. It is within this discourse that Lawrence makes himself heard, that his voice becomes intelligible. His diagnosis of modern society as hysterical was predicated on a theatrical relationship with his audience, on what many contemporaries considered his own hysteria. Siegel has suggested an analogy between Lawrence's fear of public exposure and the anxiety that women authors often experienced when publishing in the mass market.[53] In this case the hysterical woman on display was Lawrence, exposed before the public eye, prey to diagnosis as the diseased author of degenerate works.

Lawrence established complicity with the world of attitudes by performing the polemical role that, in the eyes of many contemporaries, diminished his artistic power. Publishing such outspoken pieces as "Matriarchy" and "Cocksure Women and Hensure Men" in the British press was a way of making money, of course, but it also entailed an implicit acknowledgment of social discourse, of the need to engage in dialogue in order to persuade others to see things as he saw them.[54] Tacitly recognizing that his prophetic role defined itself in social space, Lawrence granted the theatrical and frequently sexual terms in which public discourse was conducted. Entering the public arena, he situated himself on the unstable ground of performance, where gender and sexuality became matters of uncertainty. If, as Siegel suggests, furious rebellion was the natural female state in Lawrence's writings, it was also symptomatic of a postwar hysteria through which he stage-managed his own sex change. Rather than simply a revolt against the pattern given her by feeble postwar man, modern woman's fury was synonymous with Lawrence's own diatribe against the condition of England.

Lawrence's double-edged relationship with public discourse is illuminated by two of his so-called leadership novels, *The Lost Girl* (1920) and *The Plumed Serpent* (1926), works embodying (and propelling) his turn away from Britain. The "new conception of human life" explored in these novels is notorious for supposedly promoting female submission to patriarchal domination.[55] In *The Lost Girl*, the vaudeville actor Cicio tries to bend Alvina Houghton to his will; in *The Plumed Serpent*, Don Cipriano demands submission from Kate Leslie. Distilling male and female characters into their supposedly essential elements, Lawrence seems to polarize the sexes to such an extent that sex war is inevitable. Yet such an essentialist strategy may prove, in Carol Siegel's words, "subversive of the ideologies that generally inform the representation of women in nonfeminist texts." Lawrence allows the narratives of the divided poles to compete with each other, pitting the implicitly male narrator's impulse toward domination against the critical intelligence of a resistant female character. Lawrence does not force the reader to make a particular choice; he lets us decide. Like *Women in Love, The Plumed Serpent* concludes inconclusively, with Kate Leslie suspended between submission to the cult of Quetzalcoatl and resistance to its dream of male mastery. It is this suspension that guarantees the structural and artistic integrity of the novel.

In the leadership novels, moreover, the division of the sexes is ritualized in a theatrical manner that destabilizes the separate spheres of domestic femininity and public masculinity. Daniel Albright has noted that in *The Lost Girl* ritual cohabits easily with the everyday: living "half in theater and half in common life," Alvina creates with Cicio "a simple ongoing ritual *à deux.*"[56] In this sense, Lawrence is not far from Joyce, for whom theatricality implies the possibility of limited freedom. What Lawrence seeks in ritual is freedom from the conscious, caged mind that he saw in Joyce as in feminism. In *The Plumed Serpent,* ritual sexuality is dramatized in a quest for "blood consciousness," which will combat the conscious mind; victory over the latter will bring the disappearance of the rigid categories of public and private behavior to which it gave rise. But, as we see at the end of the novel, the conscious mind continues to lurk in the wings during these scenes; the theatrical rituals of *The Plumed Serpent* remain potentially overdetermined by the censorious operations of the mind.

In *The Plumed Serpent,* the caged mind appears to be the woman's, Kate Leslie's, yet Lawrence's use of the female body in this novel suggests that its new conception of human life includes the potential for sex change. Don Ramón, the leader of the Quetzalcoatl cult, is described by his new wife, Teresa, as a "column of blood," but he also possesses a womb: "When a man is *warm* and brave—then he wants the woman to give him her soul, and he keeps it in *his* womb, so he is more than a mere man, a single man. I know it. I know where my soul is. It is in Ramón's womb, the womb of a man, just as his seed is in my womb, the womb of a woman. He is a man, and a column of blood. I am a woman, and a valley of blood" (*PS,* p. 412). At one level this transplant operation seems to constitute a ritual appropriation of woman's source of creativity, and an attempt to forge an independent destiny for a cult of male marriage; to be sure, Teresa herself urges Kate to submit to Cipriano. But here, as elsewhere, the male will-to-power is countered by Kate's critical intelligence: "The slave morale! she said to herself. The miserable old trick of a woman living just for the sake of a man. Only living to send her soul with him, inside his precious body! And to carry his precious seed in her own womb! Herself, apart from this, nothing" (*PS,* p. 412). Lawrence's reconfiguration of the human body engenders a greater reciprocity between male and female forms, a larger interdependence. This reconfiguration is all the more startling for its being imagined through such polarized sexual metaphors as the womb and the phallic column of blood. Projecting a body liberated from biological constraints, Lawrence envisions liberty from the caged mind of contemporary sexual ideology. The appropriation of the womb suggests enslavement to that ideology, but it also enables an arresting image of freedom. Choosing the womb for the new male form, Lawrence makes his image of manhood prone to the female malady: hysteria, from the Greek word for womb (ὑστέρα), means "suffering in the womb" (ὑστερικός). In ritualizing hysteria, *The Plumed Serpent* creates a theater for enacting sex change.

Such reviewers as Ruth Suckow and Rachel Annand Taylor were seeing signs of this sex change in Lawrence's texts when they noted the coexistence of his "feminine" side with his "peculiar fear of women"; in effect, they read his texts as indicative of the sexual confusion that he denounced in postwar culture. Lawrence's postwar novels actually encourage such an interpretation. While those works explore possibilities for creating a world of male domination, they also dramatize an oppositional female voice, the voice of the womb, which, liberating the caged mind, also unhinges rigid gender constraints. In this sense Lawrence's texts made it possible for critics to read him symptomatically as "unquiet and feminine," as someone suffering from "girlish hysteria"—in other words, as part of the condition that ostensibly he deplored in the censorious culture of modern Britain.

This strange continuity between Lawrence's diagnosis of British society and the contemporary portrait of hysterical Lawrence may be understood as a form of "transference," the name Freud gave in *Studies on Hysteria* (1895) to the process by which his own presence revealed itself in the symptoms of his patients. Transference is a model for dissolving not only the supposed barrier between doctor and patient, but also the gender distinctions this barrier enforces; it describes the theatrical exchange by which Lawrence could be seen as suffering from the sexual disorders he observed in the postwar culture of censorship.

Lawrence the conscious artist would have scoffed at this suggestion. Transference would have been merely another example of Freud's reduction of human activity to the sexual motive, which Lawrence regarded as but one more form of censorship. In *Psychoanalysis and the Unconscious* (1921) and *Fantasia of the Unconscious* (1922), Lawrence offered an alternative to Freudian "rationalism" by celebrating the "religious or creative motive." He believed that divinity revealed itself through "the real phallic feeling and consciousness," which was "more than sex": only the "phallic reality" constituted true knowledge of the unconscious. Phallic reality was "warm and spontaneous," whereas sex, as Freud understood it, could be "any sort of cerebral reaction, mere cerebration transferred to the sexual centres" (*L6*, pp. 327, 320). With regard to *Lady Chatterley's Lover*, Lawrence insisted, "I don't call my novel a sex novel: It's a phallic novel," a novel with the "real phallic insouciance and spontaneity" lacking in sex today (*L6*, pp. 324–25). In Lawrence's terms, the revelation of the religious or creative motive through the phallic reality transcended the crude physical facts that fascinated Freud—the same facts, of course, that finally killed the consumptive novelist. Lawrence would deny what psychoanalysis would show: his own presence in the narrative of postwar social disease.

Despite Lawrence's ostensibly transcendent aspirations, he participated in a hysterical process that proved useful in his salubrious attack on British society. He explored the relation between disease and cure in his last story, *The Man Who Died* (1929). Drawing on the author's own brushes with death, the tale describes Christ rising from the tomb to pursue "the greater life of the body," which he had mistakenly abandoned in his former life for the claims of the spirit. His resurrection promises the greatest healthiness: the establishment of "contact" with the body of Isis, so that "the man and the woman were fulfilled of one another." The risen Christ is phallic, for he supplies what Isis has sought, the missing piece of the dismembered body of Osiris: "the last reality, the final clue to him, that alone could bring him really back to her." While Christ cures Isis of her want, however, she heals his wounds as well; as he says, she is the "woman who can lure my risen body, yet leave me my aloneness." They establish contact, but at the same time each concedes the autonomy of the other's soul.[57] Given the strong autobiographical element of *The Man Who Died,* the figure of the resurrected phallic Christ suggests that Lawrence imagined his own suffering as the source of a potential solution to a more universal malady. Through the mythic union of Christ and Isis, Lawrence creates a vision of a more perfect relation between man and woman than is possible in the current world of postwar decay.

The Man Who Died sheds light on Lawrence's attempt in *Lady Chatterley's Lover* to cure modern Britain. Diagnosed as hysterical by many of his readers, Lawrence in turn imagined the production of hysterical symptoms as a way of finding a remedy for postwar obscenity. He described *Lady Chatterley* as a "beneficent" and "very necessary" bomb launched at its corrupt British audience (*L6,* p. 316). It was in redeploying the same metaphor to describe *Lady Chatterley*'s effects on its first readers that he conceived of the novel as inducing shell shock: "[*Lady Chatterley*] seems to have exploded like a bomb among most of my English friends, and they're still suffering from shell-shock. But they're coming round already: and some few already feeling it was good for 'em" (*L6,* p. 505). As a bomb, *Lady Chatterley* gave its readers the jolt they needed to start them off on the road to recovery. Invoking the condition afflicting thousands of soldiers returning from the Great War, Lawrence reinvented the shell shock observed in his readers as a sign not simply of disease but of potential well-being. In a letter of 1913 he had written that "[o]ne sheds ones sicknesses in books" (*L2,* p. 90); in 1928 he hoped that one of his books would force a whole culture to shed its sicknesses.

Diagnosing shell shock, Lawrence read the symptoms of hysteria as a way of understanding the postwar world and as the source of a cure for its underlying malaise. He appropriated the discourse of hysteria in order to imagine the long-term benefits of this new war zone, from which would emerge the resurrected two principles, authentic manhood and womanhood. Those principles may originate in a splitting of the self similar to what Freud discerned in hysteria, but whereas Freud understood the cure as the reintegration of the unconscious self into the consciousness, Lawrence envisioned the unconscious as released from the shackles of the conscious self, blossoming anew.[58] For Lawrence, the production and analysis of hysteria would provide a key to unlock the new self, and as such it would represent the first step along the arduous road of recovery from the deep corruption of modern society. A novel that helped to mend those wounds would enable him to heal the rift that necessitated his declaration of war in the first place: the rift between himself and his readers.

It is clear in *The Man Who Died* that Lawrence regarded the phallus as essential to the healing process. Like Freud, whose methodology involved bringing to light certain repressed erotic truths and calling attention both to sexual organs and to the desire they arouse, Lawrence wished to resupply the sexual element that modern society had censored.⁵⁹ Seeing that element as the male organ, however, Lawrence understood its disappearance not as repression but as castration. Surveying the fragments and ruins of the postwar landscape, Lawrence saw this calamity everywhere. Britain was "a spunkless world" (*L7*, p. 165), a waste land populated by a "castrated" public that had lost its creative potential. His solution was to offer *Lady Chatterley's Lover* as phallic novel: "I do believe the phallic reality is good and healing, in a world going insane" (*L6*, pp. 319–20). The healing process would be enhanced by the shock induced by this reality. At the very time he was writing *Lady Chatterley's Lover*, Lawrence insisted on painting the phallus in each of his pictures: "I paint no picture," he said, "that wont shock people's castrated social spirituality" (*L5*, p. 648).⁶⁰

The castration imagery may be read as implying an exclusive concern with male readers, but Lawrence regarded castration and phallic reality as metaphors for understanding the malaise affecting all members of modern society: as he said, "the phallus itself is but a symbol" (*P2*, p. 456). As *The Man Who Died* shows, Lawrence believed that men *and* women had lost contact with phallic reality, to which he aimed to restore them. It is no accident that Lawrence used the bomb metaphor in a letter expressing impatience with two of *Lady Chatterley*'s earliest readers, both women, who objected to the novel's explicit representation of sex. Juliette Huxley and the typist Nelly Morrison each found *Lady Chatterley* pornographic, responding, Lawrence said, by going into a "green fury."⁶¹ Offering *Lady Chatterley's Lover* as a phallic novel, Lawrence was trying to bring to light the sexual truth of such castrated readers. In Freud's terms, Lawrence was seeking to restore what Huxley and Morrison had repressed, the penis. In Lawrence's own terms, the literal penis was transcended by the phallic reality, which promised a more universal remedy for "the catastrophe of our civilization" (*P1*, p. 175).

When Lawrence's contemporaries banned his "healthy," "necessary" novel, it was clear that the catastrophe had extended to the sphere of literature. Such acts of censorship made more visible a sickness that afflicted modern life at every level; for Lawrence, the assaults of *John Bull* and Sir William Joynson-Hicks only highlighted the need for a cure. For many readers, however, the novel itself was the problem and warranted the measures taken to ensure its suppression.

Lady Chatterley's Lover

Contemplating the eventually abandoned possibility of expurgating his phallic novel for general consumption, Lawrence vented his frustration with the castrated reading public: "I'm sick of cutting myself down to fit the world's shoddy cloth" (*L6*, p. 222). For Lawrence, "cutting myself down," or self-censorship, meant castration: in 1929, he referred to the proposed expurgated version as the "castrato public edition" (*L7*, p. 399), a phrase echoing Pound's description of the shorn edition of *Lustra*.[62] While communicating hostility, however, Lawrence's words reveal a desire to engage his audience, a desire that had previously issued in concessions to what readers and publishers would accept. To ensure that *Sons and Lovers* saw print in 1913 he had allowed Edward Garnett to make extensive cuts, which have only recently been restored (to mixed reviews) in the Cambridge edition of the novel. And until Secker and Knopf turned down *Lady Chatterley's Lover*, Lawrence had been eager to see this work reach a wider public in expurgated form. Yet the rejection by his publishers released Lawrence from the need to cut himself down; for the time being, his only option was to go ahead with the unexpurgated Florence edition. This version made few concessions to public taste, but in Lawrence's terms it was the novel's offensive, transgressive nature that made it more likely to engage its audience. We have seen that Lawrence measured the vitality of sexual relationships partly by the conflict they generated; because the uncensored version of *Lady Chatterley* departed more violently from canons of respectability, it was more liable than an expurgated text to explode in the public consciousness, to shatter old barriers, to create new possibilities. In the short term, Lawrence was caught in the after-shock of this explosion, and the novel was banned. But his duplicitous text had set in motion a countercurrent that would resist coercive notions of the acceptable and subvert the laws governing the theater of censorship.

Comparing the first and third versions of *Lady Chatterley*, Frieda Lawrence testified to the growth of the author's desire to engage his audience. In the foreword to *The First Lady Chatterley*, first published in America in 1944, she observed: "*The First Lady Chatterley* he wrote as she came out of him, out of his own immediate self. In the third version he was also aware of his contemporaries' minds."[63] In fact, Lawrence was so aware of his contemporaries' minds that when the Florence edition was reproduced in Paris in May 1929, he included his essay, "My Skirmish with Jolly Roger," which discussed the suppression and piracy of the novel and attacked censorious modern attitudes to sex. This essay was later expanded and retitled "A Propos of *Lady Chatterley's Lover*"; its appearance now, advertised as "Written Especially and Exclusively as an Introduction to this Popular Edition," shows how rapidly Lawrence assimilated the issue of censorship into his presentation of the novel. This turn in *Lady Chatterley*'s publishing history was simply an extension of the development noted by Frieda Lawrence. As Lawrence revised the novel, his personal vision gradually sharpened, demanding more "realistic" detail, but the same changes also led him to address the reader more directly. The rewritten *Lady Chatterley* represents a new polemical art that communicates with the reader in moral and political, as well as in aesthetic, terms. It was this recast novel that offended so many readers. At the same time, the recasting of the work propelled Lawrence himself into the prophetic role that provoked the explicitly aesthetic objections of other modernists and the political objections of many recent critics. On aesthetic as well as moral grounds, the rewritten *Lady Chatterley*, like the revised version of *The Rainbow*, was more likely to antagonize its audience than the earlier versions had been. Antagonism, however, created grounds for dialogue, and in dialogue readers might be forced to break their own rules.

The aggressive, polemical aspects of *Lady Chatterley* were heightened by two strategies that Lawrence employed in revision. One was to make the novel more concrete and explicit in its presentation of sex scenes, a measure that included using the "unprintable" language to which hostile readers drew attention in 1928 and at the 1960 trial. Lawrence insisted that such language was essential to his cure for the sexual wounds of postwar Britain: "The words that shock so much at first don't shock at all after a while. . . . [T]he words merely shocked the eye, they never shocked the mind at all. People with no minds may go on being shocked, but they don't matter. People with minds realise that they aren't shocked, and never really were; and they experience a sense of relief" (*LCL,* p. 307). The other strategy entailed dividing the novel's characters into what Michael Squires has called "elect" and "damned" categories.[64] As he rewrote the novel, Lawrence emphasized this moral hierarchy, making the novel more schematic, its message more direct. Whereas *The First Lady Chatterley* allows some sympathy for the impotent Clifford Chatterley, the final version of the novel clearly denounces him, as Lawrence put it in "A Propos," as "a pure product of our civilisation" (*LCL,* p. 333). During the rewriting process, Clifford increasingly came to represent the caged mind, which had produced a theatrical no-man's-land, a world in which fundamental sex roles had been perverted into hysterical attitudes of the modern mental consciousness.

In many ways, *Lady Chatterley's* solution to the problems of the modern world rests squarely on a traditional sexual ideology of male domination and female submission, which agreed with the conservative assumptions of many of Lawrence's detractors in the 1920s. Those readers were more unhappy about the manner in which the novel presented its solution than about the solution itself. Recast in a more polemical guise, however, *Lady Chatterley* was no simple vehicle for its author's prescriptions, for the revised novel dramatized ways of opposing a traditional sexual hierarchy. Rendering his characters abstract parts of an argumentative whole, Lawrence underlined their artificial, fictional nature; he emphasized the extent to which they are contrivances of their creator's mind, playing assigned roles in a morality play. As a result, the novel highlights the constructedness and theatricality of the characters through which the author urges a return to a purportedly natural sexual hierarchy. That hierarchy is also made to look less secure by Lawrence's enactment of a "furious rebellion," to use Carol Siegel's phrase, against modern civilization. In his fury, Lawrence resembles Connie Chatterley, who directs her anger at the false world of Wragby Hall and artificial sexual identities. Adopting what the novel itself defines as a female role, Lawrence's narrator undercuts his own attempt to sharpen distinctions between the sexes. As a result, the novel mirrors the theatrical no-man's-land which, at the level of didactic argument, Lawrence condemns. Indeed, the novel's didacticism is part of its theatricality, for Lawrence's narrator constructs the case against modern Britain by using the stage techniques of the social prophet. Through these conflicts and contradictions,

Lawrence furnishes a hysterical text: spliced between antitheatrical arguments and the theatrical strategies on which those arguments depend, *Lady Chatterley's Lover* destabilizes the sexual hierarchy that ostensibly Lawrence advocates as a solution to the problems of postwar Britain. Frustrating the censorship of authorial intention, and thus performing what Lawrence considered a central function of art, *Lady Chatterley* shows the attempt to regulate sexuality being opposed at every turn by an enemy within, an object of hysterical sympathy, conniving at deregulation. In the process, *Lady Chatterley* dramatizes the possibility of resistance to a culture of regulation and censorship that ensnared Lawrence in 1928.

One of the major effects of Lawrence's rewriting is that, unlike the first two versions, the final *Lady Chatterley* poses the question of hysteria quite directly in its presentation of Clifford Chatterley, a revision that dooms Clifford to damnation. At the end of the final version, Clifford responds as a "hysterical child" to his rejection by Connie. The narrative explicitly links this reaction with the effects of modern warfare: "The face in the bed seemed to deepen its expression of wild, but motionless distraction. Mrs Bolton looked at it and was worried. She knew what she was up against: male hysteria. She had not nursed soldiers without learning something about that very unpleasant disease." Mrs. Bolton, Clifford's nurse, realizes that her patient's hysteria is the effect of shock, a delayed reaction to what "[a]ny man in his senses must have *known*": "his wife was in love with somebody else, and was going to leave him." His hysteria, a "crisis of falsity and dislocation," is "a form of insanity" (*LCL*, p. 289).

Clifford's insanity, his hysterical blindness to the palpable facts of human life, results from a willful severing of "inner intuitive knowledge from [his] admitted consciousness" (*LCL*, p. 288): he is guilty of willed, mental consciousness. His body, one among the many strewn across the stage in the tragedy of postwar life, is polluted by his caged mind; it belongs to no-man's-land. Brought home from France "more or less in bits," Clifford is a victim of modern war, but his mind hardens into a shell that negates the possibility of "organic connection" or "touch" (*LCL*, pp. 5, 17). He becomes one of the "cerebrating make-shifts, mechanical and intellectual experiments," castigated by Tommy Dukes, that well-meaning but inadequate spokesman for the Lawrencean "democracy of touch" (*LCL*, p. 75).

Some readers have objected that Lawrence was cruel to make Clifford paralyzed; others have seen that paralysis as a piece of heavy-handed symbolism detracting from the artistic integrity of the novel. Lawrence noted in "A Propos of *Lady Chatterley's Lover*": "literary friends say, it would have been better to have left him whole and potent, and to have made the woman leave him nevertheless." Lawrence claimed that he did not know whether the symbolism was "intentional," but rereading the first version of the novel he "recognized that the lameness of Clifford was symbolic of the paralysis, the deeper emotional or passional paralysis, of most men of his sort and class, today" (*LCL*, p. 333). While Clifford is "a pure product of our civilization," his impotence seems consistent with the general landscape surveyed in the ride to Tevershall in chapter 11:

> Tevershall! That was Tevershall! Merrie England! Shakespeare's England! No, but the England of today, as Connie had realised since she had come to live in it. It was producing a new race of mankind, over-conscious in the money and social and political side, on the spontaneous intuitive side dead, but dead. Half-corpses, all of them: but with a terrible insistent consciousness in the other half. . . . How shall we understand the reactions in half-corpses? When Connie saw the great lorries full of steel-workers from Sheffield, weird distorted smallish beings like men, off for an excursion to Matlock, her bowels fainted, and she thought: Ah God, what has man done to man? What have the leaders of men been doing to their fellow men? They have reduced them to less than humanness, and now there can be no fellowship any more! It is just a nightmare. (*LCL*, p. 153)

Clifford is, of course, one of those leaders. As time goes on, he devotes more and more of his relentless mental energy to the mines, which he runs according to an outmoded, paternalistic theory of class relations; despite being a victim of the war, he practices the ways of thinking that caused it. In helping to make the colliers half-corpses, Clifford transforms them into mirror images of the shattered fragments of his own being, images that reflect the insanity of society at large, with its "two great manias," money and "so-called love" (*LCL*, p. 97). Clifford's lingering love for Connie is but another symptom of the "disease" of self-consciousness running amok in society; it exemplifies the "vicious circle of masturbation" that Lawrence condemned in "Pornography and Obscenity" (*P1*, p. 181).

Clifford's hysterical self-consciousness makes him, as Lawrence put it, "purely a personality" (*LCL*, p. 333). In an essay of 1919 Lawrence described personality as a social mask, an effect of theatrical artifice. Noting that "*Persona*, in Latin, is a player's mask, or a character in a play," he wrote:

> The old meaning lingers in *person*, and is almost obvious in *personality*. A person is a human being *as he appears to others*; and personality is that which is transmitted from the person to his audience: the transmissible effect of a man.
> . . . Never trust for one moment any individual who has an unmistakable *personality*. He is sure to be a life-traitor. His personality is only a sort of actor's mask. It is his self-conscious *ego*, his *ideal* self masquerading and prancing round, showing off. He may not be aware of it. But that makes no matter. He is a painted bug. (*P1*, pp. 710–11)

In *Lady Chatterley's Lover*, Clifford is the arch-life-traitor, who parades his insane, self-conscious ego, as Connie sees, in a "display of nothingness" (*LCL*, p. 50). When Lawrence rewrote the novel for the last time, he accentuated this theme by turning Clifford into a writer of stories whose theatrical apparatus guarantees success with contemporary readers; they seem "curiously true to modern life—to the modern psychology," because "the field of life is largely an artificially-lighted stage today" (*LCL*, p. 16). The dazzling surfaces of Clifford's stories provoke a violent distrust in Connie that the narrative tacitly endorses: "It was weird: and it was nothing. This was the feeling that echoed and re-echoed at the bottom of Connie's soul: it was all nothing, a wonderful display of nothingness. At the same time, a display. A display, a display, a display!" (*LCL*, p. 50). In some ways Clifford resembles Proust and Joyce, self-conscious modernists attacked by Lawrence in "Surgery for the Novel—or a Bomb" (1923). In his "peculiar talent for perspicuous personal gossip, clever and apparently detached" (*LCL*, p. 101), Clifford sounds like the impersonal narrator described by Flaubert as "God in the universe, present everywhere and visible nowhere," or the Creator, "indifferent, paring his fingernails," imagined by Stephen Dedalus in Joyce's *Portrait*.[65] For Lawrence, such aspirations toward impersonality merely conceal the mental consciousness at the center of an overbearing ego; though giving the appearance of detachment, Clifford's stories function as masks, which express his own mechanical personality.

The narrative of *Lady Chatterley's Lover* consistently condemns the theatrical apparatus of the social self or personality, which expresses, in its display of nothingness, the modern tyranny of mind over body, and the consequent distortion of the body's natural sexual configuration into an image of hysteria. At least as egregious as Clifford in this respect is his friend Michaelis, a playwright and Connie's first partner in adultery, who appears only in the third version of the novel. The narrative attacks Michaelis not as the representative of all playwrights, but for doing to drama what Clifford does to fiction, for making a display of nothingness. What is worse, Michaelis does it with even more success:

> Michaelis had seized upon the figure of Clifford as a central figure for a play: already he had sketched in the plot, and written the first act. For Michaelis was even better than Clifford at making a display of nothingness. It was the last bit of passion left in these men: the passion for making a display. Sexually, they were passionless, even dead. . . . They wanted, both of them, to make a real display—*their* display—a man's own very display, of himself, that should capture for a time the vast populace. (*LCL*, pp. 50–51)

Derek Britton suggests that Lawrence modeled Michaelis on Michael Arlen, whom he met just before rewriting the novel in late 1927. Lawrence, he notes, described Arlen as "a (sad) dog," a metaphor used to characterize Michaelis. For Britton, Michaelis signals a movement toward a "less class-bound distribution of passionlessness and warm-heartedness" in the final version of the novel.[66] Yet described as the "caddish and bounderish" author of "smart society plays," who finds favor with the "bitch-goddess Success," Michaelis also recalls Oscar Wilde (*LCL*, pp. 20, 21). Connie suspects that Michaelis wears his sadness as "a sort of mask" (*LCL*, p. 28); Wilde was a master of masks, and in *The Importance of Being Earnest* he made capital out of displaying nothingness. Michaelis sounds very much like one of Wilde's characters: he is "external man," who maintains "his hard, erect passivity" even during sex. It is telling that while Michaelis's inadequacy reveals itself most glaringly in sexual activity, he writes letters conveying "the same plaintive melancholy note as ever, sometimes witty, and touched with a queer sexless affection" (*LCL*, p. 29). The word "sexless" suggests a lack of masculine potency; "queer" intimates the deviant desires with which Wilde's name had been associated since his 1895 trials. Michaelis, "touched with a queer sexless affection," seems to have stepped straight from the fin de siècle into the pages of Lawrence's last novel. What is particularly disquieting about this character is how he indicates the extent to which the theatrical apparatus of the queer modern personality haunts sexual acts in the hysterical postwar world.[67]

As an antidote to these afflictions the novel proposes the phallus, which has "no independent personality behind it" (*LCL*, p. 136). Lawrence imagined the phallus as a bridge between man and woman or, as he put it in the second version, as a "third creature" (*JTLJ*, p. 238). In Connie it awakens another self, "burning molten and soft and sensitive in her womb and bowels" (*LCL*, p. 135). The phallus counters female as well as male corruption: it overcomes the beaked vagina of the keeper's first wife, Bertha Coutts, another hysterical personality who parades her depraved sexuality before the public eye. The phallus seems to cure hysteria, for when in the fourth encounter Connie finds that "the quick of all her plasm was touched," she is "born: a woman" (*LCL*, p. 174). The shock of repeated exposure to phallic reality releases womanhood from the accumulated layers of social artifice. Guaranteeing an authenticity to which neither Clifford nor Connie has access, the phallus represents the antithesis of the hysterical modern personality. It signifies an attempt to create a regulatory fiction that will counteract the misguided laws of the contemporary world. But the novel also asks us to examine this fiction critically.

In the novel's didactic scheme, the purveyor of phallic reality is Clifford Chatterley's gamekeeper, Oliver Mellors, whose stature increased in revision as that of hysterical Clifford dwindled. When, gun in hand, Mellors strides into action, he seems the opposite of his emasculated counterparts. Critics have noted a number of warlike qualities marking him as well equipped for the task assigned him. Keith Cushman, for example, sees in Mellors "an archetypal image of maleness" associated with "an earlier heroic tradition of combat that has been destroyed by modern industrialism"—destroyed, that is, by the forces of Clifford Chatterley.[68] Whereas Clifford has returned from the war more or less in bits, Mellors has survived intact, potent, dominant.

The keeper's potency and dominance readily translate themselves into the regulated language of sex war, for the novel revives this ritual conflict in a way that draws attention to the postwar context in which Lawrence was writing. Early in the novel, Connie discovers Mellors mistreating his young daughter, who bewails his killing of a poaching cat. In a moment of better humor, Mellors later admits that anger is integral to his character. His aggression takes sexual form in the first encounter, as he forces Connie into a suitably passive, submissive role:

> With a queer obedience, she lay down on the blanket. Then she felt the soft, groping, helplessly desirous hand touching her body, feeling for her face. The hand

stroked her face softly, softly, with infinite soothing and assurance, and at last there was the soft touch of a kiss on her cheek.

She lay quite still, in a sort of sleep, in a sort of dream. Then she quivered as she felt his hand groping softly, yet with queer thwarted clumsiness, among her clothing. Yet the hand knew, too, how to unclothe her where it wanted. He drew down the thin silk sheath, slowly, carefully, right down and over her feet. Then with a quiver of exquisite pleasure he touched her warm soft body, and touched her navel for a moment in a kiss. And he had to come into her at once, to enter the peace on earth of her soft, quiescent body. It was the moment of pure peace for him, the entry into the body of the woman.

She lay still, in a kind of sleep, always in a kind of sleep. The activity, the orgasm was his, all his: she could strive for herself no more. Even the tightness of his arms round her, even the intense movement of his body, and the springing of his seed in her, was a kind of sleep, from which she did not begin to rouse till he had finished and lay softly panting against her breast. (*LCL,* p. 116).

In *The First Lady Chatterley,* this moment is narrated with comparative reticence, but now Lawrence refers directly to entry and orgasm. Sharpening the concrete details of the scene, such changes register the growing specificity of Lawrence's vision. The revisions also have important implications for his readers. If the relatively muted first version was more palatable to conventional tastes, the revised passage is so revelatory that, in comparison, it seems designed to violate them. Significantly, however, the passage does not redistribute sexual power so as to threaten the conservative ideology that shaped postwar sexual discourse. Although Connie shows signs of shaking off her inertia (the phrase, "she could strive for herself no more," indicates that she has been striving), Mellors remains the active party; he alone gets satisfaction. While too frank for many of Lawrence's contemporaries, this restaging of heterosexual rites reinforces an ideology of male domination that found ready acceptance in postwar Britain.

Yet, as in *The Man Who Died,* Lawrence's male protagonist emerges as a tower of strength only after recovering from a previously frail condition. Like Joe Boswell in *The Virgin and the Gipsy* (1926), Mellors's role is that of the "resurrected man," who nearly died of pneumonia: Lady Chatterley's lover has "died once or twice already" (*LCL,* p. 216).[69] Mellors is still scarred by the effects of this experience. When Clifford's motorchair malfunctions in the wood, the keeper strains himself to breaking point in his efforts to get it going again, despite the exhortations of Connie, who has seen "what a pathetic sort of thing a man was, feeble and small-looking, when he was lying on his belly on the big earth" (*LCL,* p. 188): "The keeper put a stone under the wheel, and went to sit on the bank, his heart beating and his face white with the effort, semi-conscious. Connie looked at him and almost cried with anger. There was a pause and a dead silence. She saw his hands trembling on his thighs. . . . At last he sighed, and blew his nose on his red handkerchief. 'That pneumonia took a lot out of me,' he said" (*LCL,* p. 191).

Keith Cushman observes that "the resurrection motif, with its religious overtones, is central to Lawrence's powerful vision of human renewal and the life of the body."[70] But while, in his fragile body, Mellors represents the ulti-mate source of salvation, he does so only after being nursed back to health by the woman with whom he will form the perfect union. After their first encoun-ter the keeper regrets that Connie has forced him to abandon his not-so-splendid isolation: "She had connected him up again, when he had wanted to be alone. She had cost him that bitter privacy of a man who at last wants only to be alone" (*LCL*, p. 118). But she has connected him up and restored his sexual consciousness, his phallic potential. Connie becomes as indispensable to Mellors as Mrs. Bolton is to Clifford. Imitating a common postwar scenario, Mellors's situation partly mirrors that of the childish hysteric, Clifford. That Mellors imagines Connie's "tenderness" as vulnerable before the outside world reflects his own insecurity; he experiences "a dread of exposing himself and her to that outside Thing that sparkled viciously in the electric lights" (*LCL*, p. 120). While Mellors possesses the potential for phallic reality, it is Connie who enables him to realize it. In August 1928, the reviewer Ruth Suckow censured Lawrence for "his frequently hysterical emphasis upon the need for male domination. . . ."[71] What is hysterical here, however, is the novel's division between a call for such domination and voices of resistance, which expose male vulnerability and dependence. *Lady Chatterley's Lover* inscribes rules of conduct only for them to be broken.

It is through the contemplation of male fragility that the theatrical apparatus of the self-conscious, hysterical personality, linked in Lawrence's imagination with obscenity, returns to haunt his attempt to create an ideal manhood. Even before Connie and Mellors become lovers, the narrative presents the keeper's divine yet vulnerable body as if under the critical (though eroticized) female gaze. In a scene recalling erotic bathing scenes in *The White Peacock* and *The Rainbow,* Connie receives a shock when she sees the keeper who, "washing himself, utterly unaware," becomes a public spectacle at the very moment when he presumes privacy: "She saw the clumsy breeches slipping away over the pure, delicate white loins, the bones showing a little, and the sense of aloneness, of a creature purely alone, overwhelmed her. Perfect, white solitary nudity of a creature that lives alone, and inwardly alone. And beyond that, a certain beauty of a pure creature. Not the stuff of beauty, not even the body of beauty, but a certain lambency, the warm white flame of a single life revealing itself in contours that one might touch: a body!" (*LCL*, p. 66). In *The First Lady Chatterley,* Connie responds to this surprise encounter as to pure revelation: "Never mind his stupid personality! His body in itself was divine, cleaving through the gloom like a revelation" (*FLC*, p. 27). Consequently, in the first version the "pure body" comes to represent something that transcends the world of "mechanical personalities" (*FLC*, p. 28). In Lawrence's rewriting of this scene, Connie's response becomes more complex, especially in the final version. The sight of the keeper's body remains an occasion for wonder: "in some curious way, it was a visionary experience," and she "received the shock of vision in her womb." At one level Lawrence emphasizes Connie's femininity by locating her response in her womb. Yet it is in the womb that one suffers from hysteria, the vehicle of sex change. Correspondingly, in the final version Connie's attitude is divided against itself, as she takes on qualities more readily associated with Clifford: "But with her mind, she was inclined to ridicule. A man washing himself in a back yard! No doubt with evil-smelling yellow soap!—She was rather annoyed. Why should she be made to stumble on these vulgar privacies!" (*LCL*, p. 66). Here Connie acquires some of Clifford's cold intellectual aggression, as well as his social snobbery; in the terms of the sexual discourse that Lawrence wants to overhaul, she is masculinized. These revisions undoubtedly highlight the degree of visionary experience required to project Connie onto the higher plane of phallic reality: she labors too much under the sway of Wragby Hall's overcivilized perversion. Allowing her critical perspective to gather force, however, Lawrence sets in motion another narrative, which challenges the alternatives on offer. This challenge is all the more testing because it is articulated not through the despised Clifford but through Connie, in whom Lawrence invests his hopes for redemption. In the third *Lady Chatterley,* Connie comes to resemble the heroine of *The Plumed Serpent,* Kate Leslie, whose wavering resistance to the cult of Quetzalcoatl checks that novel's impulse to dream of male mastery.

Thus it is all the more disconcerting when, in the fourth encounter, Connie casts Mellors as a sexual performer, with herself as a critically detached, "queer" spectator. Connie's queerness may be a result of bad habits acquired during the abortive affair with Michaelis. By 1928, though, the word "queer" signified female as well as male sexual inversion, as was made clear by its repeated appearance in Radclyffe Hall's banned novel, *The Well of Loneliness.* Perhaps such insinuations color Connie's perception as she observes Mellors in the "ridiculous performance" of lovemaking:

> And this time the sharp ecstasy of her own passion did not overcome her, she lay with her hands inert on his striving body, and do what she might, her spirit seemed to look on from the top of her head, and the butting of his haunches seemed ridiculous to her, and the sort of anxiety of his penis to come to its little evacuating crisis seemed farcical. Yes, this was love, this ridiculous bouncing of the buttocks, and the wilting of the poor, insignificant, moist little penis. This was the divine love! After all, the moderns were right when they felt contempt for the performance: for it was a performance. It was quite true, as some poets said, that the God who created man must have had a sinister sense of humour, creating him a reasonable being, yet forcing him to take this ridiculous posture and driving him with blind craving for this humiliating performance. Even a Maupassant found it a humiliating anti-climax. Men despised the intercourse act, and yet did it.
>   Cold and derisive her queer female mind stood apart. And, though she lay perfectly still, her impulse was to heave her loins and throw the man out, escape his ugly grip and the butting over-riding of his absurd haunches. (*LCL*, pp. 171–72)

Here, it seems, Lawrence responds to Compton Mackenzie's warning that the sexual act looked comic to the outsider, by making it ridiculous in the eyes of one of those involved. But Mackenzie is answered at another level as well. On this occasion, as in the second encounter, the failure is partly due to Connie's continuing subordination to what Lawrence considered a masturbatory self-consciousness: "Cold and derisive her queer female mind stood apart." In this sense, she recalls two sexual perverts who embody a deplorable mental consciousness in Lawrence's earlier fiction: Winifred Inger in *The Rainbow* and Hermione Roddice in *Women in Love*. Yet Mellors admits that he is at fault also. Comforting Connie as she weeps, he says: "Ta'e th' thick wi' th' thin. This wor a bit o' thin, for once" (*LCL*, p. 172). All is not lost: they make love again, and this time Connie is "born: a woman." But their encounters are given point by anxiety lest the moment supposedly reserved for the supreme revelation of phallic reality become another occasion for the man's reduction to a farcical spectacle before a female audience. Alarmingly quickly, the keeper's hut can be rearranged as a theater of sexual performance. Mellors, Lawrence's alternative to the hollow impotence of Clifford and Michaelis, is prone to their failings. Like Michaelis, he, too, may look queer.

Later in the novel, Mellors counters with a hysterical diatribe against lesbianism, implying that if he does look queer it is only because he is subject to the lesbian's perverted gaze. Mellors makes it clear that he considers queer female spectatorship a disturbingly prevalent threat to his masculinity. Comparing different kinds of women ("the sly sort," "the ones that love everything," "the hard sort," and "the sort that's just dead inside"), he turns to "the sort that puts you out before you really 'come,' and go on writhing their loins till they bring themselves off against your thighs": "But they're mostly the Lesbian sort. It's astonishing how Lesbian women are, consciously or unconsciously. Seems to me they're nearly all Lesbian—." In a belligerent declaration of sex war he declares: "I could kill them. When I'm with a woman who's really Lesbian, I fairly howl in my soul, wanting to kill her." Clearly, Mellors is more disturbed by queer women than by men:

> "But do you think Lesbian women any worse than homosexual men?"
> "*I* do! Because I've suffered more from them. In the abstract, I've no idea. When I get with a Lesbian woman, whether she knows she's one or not, I see red. No, no! But I wanted to have nothing to do with any woman any more. I wanted to keep to myself: keep my privacy and my decency." (*LCL*, p. 203)

Mellors realizes that Connie has forced him into the open, that his privacy is no longer sacrosanct. Although, when his "blood comes up," he's glad, even triumphant, that Connie came along, he is "sorry, from the outside," because he anticipates "all the complications and the ugliness and recrimination that's bound to come, sooner or later." Perhaps fearing that Connie (like Winifred Inger) sees through the lesbian eye, Mellors begins to comprehend the strange power of the visual and theatrical metaphors through which the narrative views him for much of the novel. Thus Lawrence invites us to observe how the actions of his hero are regulated by the conditions of performance.

A number of recent film theorists have tried to define the possibility of a female gaze, as opposed to the male gaze that installs woman as the regulated object of narrative desire. In *Lady Chatterley's Lover* Mellors anticipates such concerns, but for him they represent a dreaded alternative that sharpens his own desire for "resurrection of the body," for "tenderness." Mellors seems to oppose "touch" to the female gaze that he finds so coercive; when attained, touch will signify what he considers the ideal relation between a man and a woman. Yet Mellors's own narrative undergoes some strange inversions, particularly when he claims that his only previous experience of touch was in the army, between men: "I knew it with the men. I had to be in touch with them, physically, and not go back on it. I had to be bodily aware of them—and a bit tender to them. . . ." Mellors speaks of the "natural physical tenderness, which is the best, even between men; in a proper manly way." It is this tenderness that will lead to full sexual consciousness: "Sex is really only touch, the closest of all touch. And it's touch we're afraid of. We're only half-conscious, and half alive. We've got to come alive and aware" (*LCL*, p. 277). The phrase, "in a proper manly way," may qualify the implicit homoeroticism here, yet that qualification tacitly confesses an intimacy that does not limit itself to a heterosexual continuum. Mellors's words even suggest that manly love (to recall Lawrence's phrase in the essay on Whitman) is a necessary precursor to heterosexual relations. When the keeper refers to the proper manly way, he may mean simply the candor and openness that Lawrence found in Whitman. Such openness is proclaimed by Connie's artist friend, Duncan Forbes: "It's the one thing they won't let you be, straight and open in your sex" (*LCL*, p. 264). Mellors and Forbes are different, of course, because whereas the first acts on such doctrine, the second offers only "a soft stream of a queer, inverted sort of love," which makes him sound less like the keeper than like Michaelis (*LCL*, p. 270). But even for Mellors, there is no direct route to openness. If he is to evade the implicitly deviant female gaze, he must first steer a crooked course into no-woman's-land. That may be the way to clear the path for heterosexual love, but it also means fraternizing with other fragile men like the dead colonel.

Lawrence apparently lifts the veil from these speculations in a late uncollected poem, which declares that sodomy, synonymous here with homosexuality, "can be sane and wholesome / granted there is an exchange of genuine feeling." But get it on the brain, he warns, and it becomes "pernicious," just as "bawdy" and "whoring" do:

> bawdy on the brain becomes obscenity, vicious.
> Whoring on the brain becomes really syphilitic
> and sodomy on the brain becomes a mission,
> all the lot of them, vice, missions, etc., insanely unhealthy. (*CP*, p. 845)

In another draft of the same poem, Lawrence concedes: "In fact, it may be that a little sodomy is necessary to human life" (*CP*, p. 952). In "I Know A Noble Englishman," he goes as far as to say that almost all Englishmen are instinctively homosexual, only they are not usually prepared to admit it. Sodomy is so prevalent that: "If you ask me, / Don Juan was never anything but a self-thwarted sodomist, / Taking it out, in spite, on women" (*CP*, p. 949). According to these lines, sex war results from the repression of natural instincts, particularly the homosexual instincts of most men. These poems suggest that perhaps the only way to avoid sex war is to grant those instincts free expression, to allow men to experience tenderness between themselves before they venture into the realm of heterosexual relations.

Such affirmations are complicated in *Lady Chatterley*'s hysterical narrative because they are uttered within dramatic contexts that encourage an ironic, sometimes a comic, perspective. Significantly, Lawrence commonly identifies that perspective with the woman's point of view. At various moments Connie indicates that the keeper's declarations are not only extravagant but absurd. At the end of his antilesbian ravings, for example, Mellors says that he wants "to get under the table and die," to which Connie responds by asking: "Why under the table?" (*LCL*, p. 204). In the process she makes Mellors laugh, and so compels him to give a flatly commonsensical answer ("Hide, I suppose") that blunts the force of his anger. Despite its apparently grave tone, their continuing dialogue is frequently informed by such irony; Connie's rejoinder, "We *are* a couple of battered warriors," forces another laugh from her earnest lover (*LCL*, p. 205). The pattern for many scenes involving the lovers is that while Mellors does most of the talking, Connie's critical eye (or ear) counterpoints his phallic exhortations, deflating his didactic rhetoric. In the famous sixth encounter, Mellors rants about modern women, yet Connie is only "half listening, and threading in the hair at the root of his belly a few forget-me-nots." Mellors, overserious, is unable to respond in kind to her playfulness: "Ay! That's where to put forget-me-nots—in the man-hair, or the maiden-hair.—But don't you care about the future?" (*LCL*, p. 220). It is hard to imagine Connie more than half listening to this question; her answer ("Oh, I do, terribly!") sounds more humorous than sincere. Mellors either misses or ignores her tone, embarking instead on a diatribe against the doomed world, its mechanization, its hostility to human life. As far as Connie can tell, Mellors is in love with the sound of his own voice: "He had talked so long now—and he was really talking to himself, not to her" (*LCL*, p. 221). The keeper's earnest despair makes Connie feel uneasy, but after the rain dance and lovemaking later in the same scene, her response becomes more overtly comic: "'An' if tha shits an' if tha pisses, I'm glad. I don't want a woman as couldna shit nor piss.' Connie could not help a sudden snirt of astonished laughter, but he went on unmoved" (*LCL*, p. 223). On occasions such as these, Mellors's earnestness is truly astonishing, and laughable. The same conclusion is urged on us by Connie's laughter, her disarming smiles and muted ironies.

It is undeniable that the narrative often tends to endorse Mellors's voice and censor others. Michael Squires has persuasively argued that as Lawrence rewrote the novel, he refashioned Mellors in his own image, transplanting the causes for failure from the keeper to the external world, and accepting sensitivity and female elements as integral parts of his newly discovered ideal manhood. The result, as Squires suggests, is Lawrence's self-portrait as a "scarred, sensitive man," whose views we often feel compelled to share.[72] In Lawrence's as in Mellors's terms, Connie's critical detachment indicates a perverted, self-conscious will that atrophies the true sexual instincts; it is typical of what Lawrence considered the obscene attitude of authors like Joyce and of censormorons like the Home Secretary, Sir William Joynson-Hicks. The aftermath of the third encounter, for instance, amply justifies Mellors's hysterical fears about female sexuality. Having been roused to orgasm, Connie experiences a vision of the male's ritual dismemberment at the hands of Bacchanalian—that is, hysterical—women:

> Ah yes, to be passionate like a bacchante, like a bacchanal fleeing wild through the woods. To call on Iacchos, the bright phallos that had no independent personality behind it, but was pure god-servant to the woman! The man, the individual, let him not dare intrude. He was but a temple-servant, the bearer and keeper of the bright phallos, her own.
>
> So, in the flux of new awakening, the old hard passion flamed in her for a time, and the man dwindled to a contemptible object, the mere phallos-bearer, to be torn to pieces when his service was performed. She felt the force of the Bacchae in her limbs and her body: the woman gleaming and rapid, beating down the male. (*LCL*, p. 136)

While supposedly free of personality, the phallus is imagined nonetheless as performing a subservient role, its supposedly regenerative powers entirely subject to the female will. The male body remains vulnerable to the destruction that caused Clifford's paralysis, only this time the battle lines would be drawn according to gender rather than nationality.

Yet *Lady Chatterley's Lover* hardly presents these problems in cut-and-dried form. The novel operates a system of checks and balances, which restrain the dogmatic tendencies embodied in Mellors; if the keeper represents an attempt to introduce the rule of male law, the narrative resists it. Whereas both the narrator and the keeper often criticize modern women, their words may be construed differently when it is noted, for example, that they use the same language as Clifford does in his own attack on Connie at the end of the novel. In one of his most hysterical moments, Clifford bellows: "you're not normal, you're not in your right senses. You're one of those half-insane, perverted women who must run after depravity, the *nostalgie de la boue*." It is quite clear that the novel does not endorse this bullying point of view, for Clifford's moral rectitude is swiftly deflated: "Suddenly he had become almost wistfully moral, seeing himself the incarnation of good, and people like Connie and Mellors the incarnation of mud, of evil" (*LCL*, p. 296). At other times, both Mellors and the narrator raise their voices in similarly overbearing fashion. Indeed, one might apply to them, as to Clifford, the words of censure reserved by the reviewer Thomas Earp for Lawrence's "Introduction to These Paintings." Each man "lashes himself into an hysterical, exacerbated violence which not only detracts from the force of his argument, but gives an impression of merely fevered excitability rather than forceful reason" (*LCH*, p. 307). Ironically, Earp's attack helps us to appreciate the power of this work, in which the hysterical, exacerbated violence of Lawrence's characters undermines their claims on the reader's sympathy. The countercurrents of *Lady Chatterley's Lover* resist coercion, defuse violence, and deflect argument.

Many of Mellors's ideas find expression in Lawrence's poetry and nonfictional prose, but the author's hysterical sympathies embrace Connie as well, even when her point of view seems to cut against the grain of the novel's argument. There is a striking parallel between Lawrence's own thoughts on modern love and Connie's observations on Mellors's "ridiculous performance" in the fourth encounter: "It was quite true, as some poets said, that the God who created man must have had a sinister sense of humour, creating him a reasonable being, yet forcing him to take this ridiculous posture and driving him with blind craving for this humiliating performance. Even a Maupassant found it a humiliating anti-climax" (*LCL*, p. 172). Lawrence said much the same thing in his 1927 essay, "Making Love to Music," which was composed after the second *Lady Chatterley* but before the third. The sex act, he reiterates, is "[n]ot a consummation, but a humiliating anti-climax" (*P1*, p. 160): "Even a man like Maupassant, an apparent devotee of sex, says the same thing. . . . Surely, he says, the act of copulation is the Creator's cynical joke against us. To have created in us all these beautiful and noble sentiments of love, to set the nightingale and all the heavenly spheres singing, merely to throw us into this grotesque posture, to perform this humiliating act, is a piece of cynicism worthy, not of a benevolent Creator, but of a mocking demon" (*P1*, p. 161). Lawrence apparently rewrote the sentences from the third *Lady Chatterley* in light of this essay, making Connie's voice sound more like his own: authoritative, metaphysical, literary. For instance, the phrase, "Even a man like Maupassant," was imported from "Making Love to Music": it did not appear in the second version. In line with this adjustment, Connie's speculative tone becomes more formal. In the phrase, "It is quite true, as some poets said," she reveals an assurance missing in the more casual, colloquial meanderings of the second version ("And she would say to herself, as so many men, poets and all, have said . . ." [*JTLJ*, p. 72]). This revision resonates with additional force in the seventh encounter, when Connie, tacitly endorsed by the narrator, declares: "What liars poets and everybody were!" (*LCL*, p. 247). The general tendency of such alterations implies that in her observations on the copulating Mellors, Connie acts as the agent of authorial will, dissecting its male object, which lies prone before the edge of Lawrencean irony. At times Lawrence's treatment of his hero and heroine makes it hard to know who the enemy is.

That the author's face appears behind the mask of his heroine as well as his hero's should not surprise us if we recognize that in the novels of the 1920s Lawrence stretched self-expression so far that he triumphed over his characters, making them functions of his own personality. Daniel Albright points out that by this stage Lawrence had succeeded in creating the "impersonal" novel, which should "demonstrate the basic biophysical principles that govern indifferently the human temperament and the metallurgy of iron." Thus it is not a long step from Lawrence back to Wilde, who suggests in "The Decay of Lying" that people are fundamentally alike, and differ only in their accidental, external features.[73] The comparison with Wilde is apposite because it alerts us to the theatricality of Lawrence's narrative strategies. *Lady Chatterley*'s characters dramatize aspects of the authorial self; the differences between those aspects signify a radical division, a hysterical splitting, in Lawrence's own personality. While the novel condemns Michaelis and Clifford Chatterley for displaying their personalities, Lawrence resorts to the same devices to project his own voice above the din of a censorious modern age.

This aspect of *Lady Chatterley* is illuminated by Michael Squires, who observes that although the novel sets about "the demolition of 'personality,'" which "inhibits phallic awareness," the narrator "flaunts" a personality that is "almost purely mental, intellectual, analytical." Squires draws a parallel between the narrator's voice and Clifford's, noting that "Clifford is to the fictional world what the narrator is to its readers: forceful, assertive, opinionated."[74] To be sure, in exhibiting what Lawrence called mental consciousness, the narrator closely resembles not only the despicable Clifford but also Connie, when she takes a detached, critical view of the ridiculous Mellors in the second and fourth encounters.

Squires diminishes the force of his own insight, however, because in dismissing these contradictions as signs of hypocrisy and artistic weakness he overlooks the competing alternatives and hysterical fragmentations embedded in Lawrence's text.[75] Such fragmentation is visible in the dramatic situations explored in the novel, but it is also present in the erotic climax, the "night of sensual passion," which takes place on the eve of Connie's departure for Italy. Unlike the sex scenes earlier in the novel, this episode is narrated without explicit detail. Though hardly muting its erotic power, this aspect of the scene has aroused the disapproval of several critics, who specify the unnamed acts as anal intercourse and accuse Lawrence of trying to avoid an honest confrontation with the issue. The debate began soon after the 1960 trial, when Andrew Shonfield and John Sparrow contrasted the veiled, ambiguous language used here with the frankness and openness applauded by those who defended the novel in court:[76]

> In this short summer night she learnt so much. She would have thought a woman would have died of shame. Instead of which, the shame died. Shame, which is fear: the deep organic shame, the old, old physical fear which crouches in the bodily roots of us, and can only be chased away by the sensual fire, at last it was roused up and routed by the phallic hunt of the man, and she came to the very heart of the jungle of herself. She felt, now, she had come to the real bed-rock of her nature, and was essentially shameless. She was her sensual self, naked and unashamed. She felt a triumph, almost a vainglory. So! That was how it was! That was life! That was how oneself really was! There was nothing left to disguise or be ashamed of. She shared her ultimate nakedness with a man, another being.
>
> And what a reckless devil the man was! really like a devil! One had to be strong to bear him. But it took some getting at, the core of the physical jungle, the last and deepest recess of organic shame. The phallos alone could explore it. And how he had pressed in on her! (*LCL*, p. 247)

Shonfield contends that in making this passage ambiguous, Lawrence practiced a cowardly form of self-censorship. Yet such criticism is unconvincing because it implies that sex should be represented in a particular way. Freed in this late encounter from his own insistence on explicitness, Lawrence explores the erotic potential of language, developing what Eugene Goodheart calls his "graphic and indirect" style. Noting the success of Lawrence's metaphoric displacements in conveying the experience of passion, Goodheart observes that the ambivalence of many of his erotic scenes reflect neither self-censorship nor a fear of censorship, "but a sense of undiscovered and unknown terrain, what lies beyond the prohibitions that Lawrence has chosen to transgress." Shonfield's objection to the night of sensual passion in *Lady Chatterley's Lover* reveals his own failure to perceive that, as Goodheart puts it, "Lawrence's dogmatic manner conceals the uncertainties."[77]

The night of sensual passion betrays uncertainties in such phrases as "the real bed-rock of her nature" and "the core of the physical jungle," which conjure up images of previously unplumbed depths, hitherto untested limits. This language recalls the imagery of depth and darkness employed in *The Rainbow* when, in another passage carrying anal overtones, Will and Anna Brangwen renew their passion "with infinite sensual violence":

> But still the thing terrified him. Awful and threatening it was, dangerous to a degree, even whilst he gave himself to it. It was pure darkness, also. All the shameful things of the body revealed themselves to him now with a sort of sinister, tropical beauty. All the shameful, natural and unnatural acts of sensual voluptuousness which he and the woman partook of together, created together, they had their heavy beauty and their delight. Shame, what was it? It was part of extreme delight. It was that part of delight of which man is usually afraid. Why afraid? The secret, shameful things are most terribly beautiful.[78]

The conscious acceptance of shame by Will and Anna intensifies their sexual pleasure: "It was a bud that blossomed into beauty and heavy, fundamental gratification" (*R*, p. 220). The power of the passage derives from its unspecificity; to insist on a particular meaning would be to diminish the suggestiveness of the prose and to negate Lawrence's attempt to convey feelings that break the limits of linguistic expression. The description of sensual passion in *Lady Chatterley's Lover* tests the capacity of language in a similar way. Here "shame" refers readers back to *The Rainbow*, where it appeared as a euphemism for sexual deviance, but Lawrence purges it of its repressive apparatus, especially in this later passage. Shame dies in *Lady Chatterley's Lover* because the sexual body has exceeded the expressive potential of language. Now even the most explicit vocabulary appears inadequate.

In this way the novel raises questions about sexual language that the 1960 trial was not prepared to consider. The trial focused more directly on passages in which Lawrence used "four-letter words." Graham Hough, for instance, testified that Lawrence was trying to relieve the burden of shame that "the normally obscene words" had been made to carry in a guilt-ridden, Puritanical society (*TLC*, p. 44). Significantly, the prosecutor, Mervyn Griffith-Jones, touched on the night of sensual passion only when summing up, and even then he veered rapidly away from the subject, as if to suggest that when an author failed to give the clear warning signs represented by obscene language, it was best to leave well alone. C. H. Rolph observed afterward that Griffith-Jones's "unexpected and totally unheralded innuendo visibly shocked some members of the Jury" (*TLC*, p. 221). A similar sense of peril warned off Lawrence's contemporaries when *Lady Chatterley* first appeared in 1928. The novel seemed to make the ground explode beneath their feet, causing damage they could see and also, more troublingly, damage they could not see. As in fin-de-siècle responses to *Jude the Obscure,* obscurity was felt to conceal the most unspeakable obscenities. Like Hardy's novel, *Lady Chatterley's Lover* induced a sense of hysterical blindness; after reading this book it was hard to see where modern love was going.

Lady Chatterley's Lover itself addresses this problem. The final movement of the novel betrays an uncertainty, as if it has exhausted its own possibilities or at least has made it impossible to articulate them any further. Connie is pregnant, but, as we learn in the last encounter in London, procreation does not summarize the potential embodied in "the creative act that is far more than procreative" (*LCL,* p. 279). What is more, the description of the London encounter is curiously routine, lacking the strange power of the night of sensual passion or of the more explicit earlier scenes.[79] The characters themselves fall back on a now insufficient, "unprintable" vocabulary, graphically illustrated in the conversation between Mellors and Connie's father, Sir Malcolm Reid, and also in Mellors's final letter.

This letter is often read as bringing *Lady Chatterley* to a pointed conclusion and as expressing an unequivocal vision of the future.[80] The coincidence of the end of the novel with Mellors's last words ("with a hopeful heart") suggests such an affirmation; as at the end of Joyce's *Portrait,* all distance between the character's and the narrator's points of view seems to be eliminated. Whereas the night of sensual passion allows Lawrence to explore possibilities beyond language, Mellors's letter depends heavily on a mode of discourse whose inadequacy has been disclosed: the language of "fucking." This language, like the keeper's parting expression of hope, refers back to what has occurred earlier in the novel; when the keeper speaks of "the peace that comes of fucking," his words have an oddly retrospective tone, suggesting that if the sex war is over, then a crucial source of vitality has been lost (*LCL,* p. 301). The novel ends with a stasis that is troubling because the peace between the lovers coincides with their separation. If the salvation offered through their example is one of individual meaning, that meaning has become excessively individual; Mellors and Connie seem doomed, at present, to enjoy salvation separately, alone.

While the final separation intimates the difficulty with which personal salvation might extend into the diseased social sphere, the keeper's final letter also articulates *Lady Chatterley*'s anxiety about the threat posed by that society, an anxiety about the mob. In Lawrence's experience, the mob was naturally allied with the censor-moron; as he noted in "Pornography and Obscenity," it was Sir William Joynson-Hicks who announced, in an article on censorship, that "the ultimate sanction of all law is public opinion" (*P1*, p. 186). In many ways, Mellors's letter summarizes the novel's polemical diagnosis of a society that sanctioned such utterances. Mellors notes the perversion of sexual roles: "The women talk a lot more than the men, nowadays, and they are a sight more cock-sure. The men are limp, they feel a doom somewhere, and they go about as if there was nothing to be done" (*LCL*, p. 299). And as nature is out of joint, general industrial collapse must follow: "There's a bad time coming, boys, a bad time coming!" (*LCL*, p. 300). In response to this sense of imminent social apocalypse, Mellors dwells on the personal form of salvation discovered with Connie: "So I believe in the little flame between us. For me now, it's the only thing in the world. . . . It's my Pentecost, the forked flame between me and you" (*LCL*, pp. 300–301). Looking forward to reigniting this flame, the keeper hopes for a renewal of the feast of Pentecost, the undoing of Babel, in which the perplexities of spoken language are miraculously overcome. But the situation that requires Mellors to write the letter in the first place, his separation from Connie, compromises the privacy enjoyed earlier in the novel and to which he wants to return. Now the lovers must step out of the woodland of the Wragby estate and face the world. They have tried to erect barricades between themselves and English society, but those barricades are about to come down.

The imminent dissolution of the frontier between the public world and the private refuge of sexual love mirrors the larger dilemma confronting readers at the end of the novel. Ending with Mellors's retrospective letter, Lawrence seems to grant final authority to the spokesman for the self-contained realm of love, and so resist assimilation into the corrupt outside world. Yet this individual case is supposed to set an example for the world to follow: at some point, individual meaning should translate itself into more general terms. The problem is that through such translation, individual meaning would have to meet the insidious threat of mob meaning, and if there's a bad time coming, such an encounter is hardly to be relished. Hysteria characterizes the relation of public to private discourse in Lawrence's text to the very end: *Lady Chatterley's Lover* remains divided between an impulse toward the private and the demands of a public realm given to censure and, as the reception of the novel showed, to censorship.

Dramatizing this tension, the end of *Lady Chatterley* suspends the trials of modern love indefinitely. Exploring a new sexual world, the novel discovers only irresolution, implying that the case may never be settled. As a literary experiment, a trial run for Lawrence's vision of phallic reality, *Lady Chatterley* exposes the fallibility of censorious discourses that seek to regulate sexuality and the forms of literary expression to which it gives rise. Thus Lawrence's hysterical modernism rewrites the postwar culture of censorship within which it evolved. Lawrence was not the last to take on that culture. But he opened a case that other modern writers would reopen in their often embattled relationship with contemporary readers. The trial of *The Well of Loneliness* in November 1928 provided one more forum for this ongoing process.

4

"SUPPRESSED RANDINESS":
Orlando and *The Well of Loneliness*

On 16 November 1928, almost exactly thirteen years after Judge Dickinson banned *The Rainbow,* Bow Street Magistrates Court again became the scene for the suppression of allegedly obscene literature when Sir Chartres Biron ordered the destruction of Radclyffe Hall's *The Well of Loneliness,* a polemical novel pleading for social tolerance for lesbianism.[1] In Hall's words, "the book is a cry for better understanding, for a wider and more merciful toleration, for acceptance of these people as God has made them."[2] On the face of it, Hall's novel presented a very different case from either *The Rainbow* or *Lady Chatterley's Lover,* both of which ostensibly condemn lesbianism. Moreover, *The Well of Loneliness* eschews the explicit descriptions of sexual encounters that, in Lawrence's case, attracted the eye of the censor; *The Well* is notable for its decorous restraint in such matters. One might be tempted to think that Hall got into trouble simply for raising the issue of lesbianism, since female sexual inversion (as we have seen) was not legally recognized in early-twentieth-century Britain. Queen Victoria reputedly refused to believe it existed, and a 1921 proposal to extend the homosexuality law to women ran aground in the House of Commons for similar reasons; Samuel Hynes speculates that male members of Parliament found lesbianism "too gross to deal with."[3] Yet at least two other novels published in the autumn of 1928, Compton Mackenzie's *Extraordinary Women* and, more importantly, Virginia Woolf's *Orlando,* clearly broached the same subject while escaping official censure. In Hall's case, the aggravating factor seems to have been not the subject but the treatment. Whereas Woolf's fictional biography, like Mackenzie's satire, sets out to make readers laugh, *The Well of Loneliness* pleads the cause of sexual inversion by taking up an aggressively polemical stance. Paradoxically, this stance has more in common with Lawrence's than with Woolf's.

A summary of Judge Biron's ruling in *The Times* (17 November) suggests that Hall provoked the British authorities into legal action by preaching an unacceptable sexual doctrine in an earnest tone that sought to deny the possibility either of laughter or of moral censure:

> He agreed that the book had some literary merit, though defaced with certain deplorable lapses of taste. The mere fact that the book was well written could be no answer to these proceedings; otherwise the preposterous position would arise that, because it was well written, every obscene book would be free from proceedings. The mere fact that the book dealt with unnatural offences between women would not in itself make it an obscene libel. It might even have a strong moral influence. But in the present case there was not one word which suggested that anyone with the horrible tendencies described was in the least degree blameworthy. All the characters were presented as attractive people and put forward with admiration. What was even more serious was that certain acts were described in the most alluring terms.[4]

To advocate sympathy and tolerance for lesbians, Hall had made sure that her lesbian heroine, Stephen Gordon, appeared above reproach. Ironically, as Hall's biographer Michael Baker has noted, it was by making Stephen virtuous that Hall provoked moral objections.[5] If those virtues had been nonexistent, or at least laughable as in *Extraordinary Women, The Well of Loneliness* would have passed muster as having, if not a strong moral influence, at least not a bad one. As it was, however, Hall's novel seemed to follow *The Rainbow* and *Ulysses* in tending to deprave and corrupt its readers.

The question of the relation between obscenity and literature prompted some musings in the diary of Virginia Woolf, who attended Bow Street on 9 November, the first day of the Hall trial: "What is obscenity? What is literature? What is the difference between the subject & the treatment? In what cases is evidence allowable?"[6] Like many other London literati, including E. M. Forster and Vita Sackville-West, Woolf went to the *Well of Loneliness* trial prepared to take the witness stand and speak against the obscenity charges. Yet she was not quite as committed to the cause of Radclyffe Hall as some critics have suggested.[7] Like many of her Bloomsbury friends, Woolf seriously doubted Hall's qualifications as an artist, finding her work, like Lawrence's, too polemical. Bloomsbury's reservations ran so deep that Woolf wrote to Quentin Bell eight days before the trial: "Most of our friends are trying to evade the witness box; for reasons you may guess. But they generally put it down to the weak heart of a father, or a cousin who is about to have twins."[8] To Woolf's relief, she was saved from defending Hall's novel in court by the magistrate's decision that only he, and not the defense's array of learned witnesses, could rule whether *The Well* was obscene: "In what cases is evidence allowable? This last, to my relief, was decided against us: we could not be called as experts in obscenity, only in art" (*D3*, p. 207). When, as she put it, "the bloody womans trial" went to appeal on 14 December, Woolf did not attend (*L3*, p. 563).

Woolf's objections to *The Well of Loneliness* were not limited to an aesthetic sphere; they also highlight crucial differences between women in questions of sexual politics, questions that are ultimately inextricable from aesthetic ones. In keeping with what Alex Zwerdling has described as the "divided" nature of her response to social issues,[9] Woolf was reluctant to endorse in public the image of the "mannish lesbian," which, due in no small part to Hall, gained wide currency in Britain in the late 1920s. Hall's lesbianism, eclipsing alternative images in the public eye, owed much to the theories of Havelock Ellis, whose model of sexual inversion functioned within the normative sexological and legal discourse through which Hall's trial was conducted. By publishing the novel with Ellis's prefatory assurances that it "possesses a notable psychological and sociological significance," that it "presents difficult and still unsolved problems,"[10] Hall effectively situated *The Well* within that discourse. In contrast, Woolf's *Orlando,* a fictional portrait of her aristocratic friend, Vita Sackville-West, mocks all normative sex and gender codes, destabilizing the very grounds on which sexological as well as legal conventions were founded.[11] Whereas *The Well of Loneliness* presents lesbianism as an issue for the debating chamber, *Orlando* propels its readers into the realm of the imagination, a region of seeming fantasy. Demonstrating the extent to which Woolf engaged the "real world," Zwerdling has argued that *Orlando* is not typical of her achievement, that it embodies "the shallower aspects of Bloomsbury 'sophistication.'"[12] Yet the novel is not so untypical in this regard. Rather than an aesthete's evasion of unpleasant reality, *Orlando* transforms reality, and history, into a theater of seemingly infinite, protean possibility, which prompts another series of questions: What is gender? What is sexuality? What is the difference between normality and deviance?

It would be a mistake to think that Hall did not consider these questions. Although she is generally quoted as defining lesbianism as abnormal, she once wrote to Ellis: "after reading your latest book I incline to say 'What is normal?'" (3 September 1928). But Hall's primary concern is always to establish the "truth," to persuade others to accept lesbianism "as a condition which, since it occurs in nature must, even if unusual, be recognised as a natural fact" (18 April 1928). Intriguingly, Hall's insistence on fidelity to "natural fact" is predicated on a discourse of "sincerity" intrinsic both to the debates of the 1928 trial and to the critical practices of some later readers trying to construct a history of the lesbian novel. Arguing that *The Well* has helped to screen lesbian consciousness, and rendered it secondary, Catharine Stimpson follows Hall in insisting on a "severely literal" definition of lesbianism as a "physical presence in the world."[13] In this light it seems inevitable that *The Well* should occupy a central place even in an account such as Stimpson's, which tries to correct errors perpetrated, she contends, by the common acceptance of Hall's novel as the voice of lesbianism. Such models of lesbianism, which understand sexual identity as essentially stable and psychologically interior, have been challenged by Judith Butler, whose notion of gender as performance implicitly undermines their rhetoric of sincerity. In this sense Butler's project, as articulated in *Gender Trouble* (1990), is somewhat analogous to Oscar Wilde's assault on nineteenth-century "earnestness." Particularly in *The Importance of Being Earnest,* Wilde undercuts the discourse of sincerity, and the sturdy moral categories it was meant to guarantee, by recasting it in a transparently theatrical vehicle that displays its susceptibility to subversive interpretation. In *Orlando*

Woolf perpetuates Wilde's legacy by revisiting and transforming the discursive practices that constructed images of lesbianism in Hall's novel and in the 1928 trial. Where Hall points to natural fact, Woolf exploits the theatrical properties of sexual identity to create a whole world of performance that renders the rhetoric of sincerity ever more doubtful. *Orlando* thus implies that to screen lesbianism is not necessarily to render it secondary; rather, theatricality may offer some means of resisting the censorious effects of public discourse. Readdressing the question of sexuality, Woolf shakes the foundations on which Hall's book and trial were built. At the same time, she activates issues that are now the subject of some controversy in gay and lesbian studies.

The Well of Loneliness: Reception and Trial

The opening of the campaign against *The Well of Loneliness* revealed some important features of the early-twentieth-century culture of censorship within which Hall and Woolf were working. The early reception of Hall's novel suggests that, like Lawrence, she had transgressed by using fiction as a vehicle for preaching unacceptable sexual doctrines. Despite the manifest differences between Hall's treatment of lesbianism and Lawrence's, both authors seemed equally guilty of speaking in the wrong tone of voice. Robert Lynd, who resurrected the role he had played in the *Rainbow* scandal to lead the attack on Hall, lamented the solemnity with which modern writers dealt with "indecent" subjects. In a 1927 essay on "The Bounds of Decency," he issued a complaint about the "modern revolt against the old-fashioned notions of decency" that makes quite clear the reasons for his imminent attack on Hall's novel. That revolt, he wrote, "instead of being a defence of laughter against the laughterless, . . . nowadays invites the imagination into a sanctuary of gloom. It is not only serious: it is solemn." Lynd's words, which he applied elsewhere both to Joyce and to Lawrence, summarize a complaint commonly made about *The Well of Loneliness*: "To-day . . . it is . . . not the comic writers, but the writers who never make a joke, who seem oftenest to transgress the bounds of decency."[14] It is not hard to see why Lynd praised *The Importance of Being Earnest*, which might be read as providing a defense of laughter, yet applauded the censorship of Wilde's laughterless and more obviously transgressive play, *Salome*. It is equally easy to see how such works as *Orlando* and *Extraordinary Women* escaped censure at a time when Hall's notoriously laughterless novel came under scrutiny.

The similarity of the charges leveled at Hall and Lawrence astonishes even less when it is noted that another of the voices first raised against *The Well* was that of James Douglas, whose reviews of *The Rainbow* and *Ulysses* had been instrumental in ensuring the censorship of those works in Britain. Douglas, now the editor of the *Sunday Express*, savaged Hall's novel in a famous review of 19 August, declaring that he "would rather give a healthy boy or a healthy girl a phial of prussic acid than this novel." "Poison kills the body," he continued, "but moral poison kills the soul" (*RHCO*, p. 57). Douglas rehearsed the customary litany of abuses allegedly committed by Hall's novel: degeneracy, decadence, perversion, all vices tending to undermine the moral integrity of the English novel. What he found most offensive was that "inverts" like Hall displayed themselves so openly: "They flaunt themselves in public places with increasing effrontery and more insolently provocative bravado . . . they take a delight in their flamboyant notoriety" (*RHCO*, p. 54). Douglas was appealing to the very mentality that Hynes attributes to the members of Parliament who, unable to bear thinking about female acts of gross indecency, thought it best to meet lesbianism with silence. *The Well* had to be suppressed because it seemed to defy a tacit agreement to say nothing; it did not even provide the defense of laughter demanded by Robert Lynd.

Just as he had used the war in 1915 as a pretext for attacking the decadence of *The Rainbow,* Douglas reinforced his criticism of Hall's "degenerate" novel by exploiting postwar anxieties about sexuality. If any subject demanded silence, it was lesbianism, which threatened to compromise postwar Britain's need to regenerate its population. After the war, divorce rates increased alarmingly, and the family unit could ill afford further attrition by the diversion of female sexual desire from its proper objects, men, toward other women; any such erosion would undermine the imperialist cause for which the Great War had been fought.[15] Douglas's attack on *The Well of Loneliness* played on these concerns and attempted to reignite the wartime fighting spirit: "I know that the battle has been lost in France and Germany, but it has not yet been lost in England, and I do not believe that it will be lost. The English people are slow to rise in their wrath and strike down the armies of evil, but when they are aroused they show no mercy, and they give no quarter to those who exploit their tolerance and their indulgence" (*RHCO*, p. 55). Two months later, as we have seen, *John Bull* would employ similar tactics in a review of *Lady Chatterley's Lover.* Like *John Bull,* Douglas was enraged by the idea that English literature might be undermined by such noxious, implicitly un-English, influences, which must originate, if not in France or in Germany, then (the next worst thing) in Ireland: "Finally, let me warn our novelists and our men of letters that literature as well as morality is in peril. Fiction of this type is an injury to good literature. It makes the profession of literature fall into disrepute. Literature has not yet recovered from the harm done to it by the Oscar Wilde scandal. It should keep its house in order" (*RHCO*, pp. 57–58). It is no accident that the name of Wilde, an Irishman commonly associated with French decadence, should reappear here. As a spectacle of British masculinity and male sexuality, the Wilde scandal seemed the nearest thing to the catastrophe threatened by *The Well of Loneliness.* At least in Wilde's case the immediate problem, the homosexual himself, could be attributed to a foreign source. *The Well,* a novel about an English aristocrat and by an English aristocrat, who advocated tolerance for *female* inversion, was not so easy to explain. Such a deviation from the perceived norms of female sexuality threatened the domestic morality that women were supposed to guard. All Douglas could do was propose official censorship, declaring "we must banish their propaganda from our bookshops and our libraries," and hope that the problem would quietly disappear.

Douglas's pen soon achieved the desired effect. On 22 August Hall's publisher, Jonathan Cape, withdrew the offending novel, though he did manage to get it printed by the Pegasus Press in Paris and redistributed in Britain (a fact that emerged at the trial only to embarrass him and seal the case for the prosecution). Yet far from closing the lid on lesbianism, Douglas's success sparked off what the *Daily Herald* called "The Battle of a Book." The *Evening Standard,* in whose pages Arnold Bennett had already applauded *The Well* as "honest, convincing, and extremely courageous," protested against Douglas's call for censorship.[16] In another counterattack on Hall's behalf, the editor of the *Herald,* Arnold Dawson, praised *The Well* as "a restrained and serious psychological study" and attacked Douglas as a "stunt journalist" guilty of "hysterical hypocrisy."[17] While the *Daily Express* carried on Douglas's dirty work, the *Herald* recruited the services of H. G. Wells and George Bernard Shaw, several of whose plays, as I mentioned earlier, had been censored. Both writers were interviewed for a front-page article that contrasted Hall's "high-minded sincerity" with the "flippant and cynical manner" of Mackenzie's *Extraordinary Women,* a novel that parodied Hall in the figure of Hermina de Randan.[18]

While *Extraordinary Women* includes lesbian scenes more risqué than anything in *The Well of Loneliness,* Mackenzie insists on a "sense of the ridiculous," which may have saved him from censure; its indecencies were decently clothed, in Robert Lynd's words, by "a defence of laughter." But the qualities that reviewers perceived in *The Well*—its restraint, its seriousness, its sincerity—provoked unfavorable reactions not only in the popular press, but also in the more refined air of Bloomsbury. Like Lynd, E. M. Forster, Leonard Woolf, and Virginia Woolf regarded Hall's sincerity as a function less of aesthetic achievement than of polemical intention. Though interested, as Lynd was not, in Hall's intention, these readers thought she failed to transform it into satisfying artistic form. As soon as *The Well* appeared, Leonard Woolf dismissed it as "formless and therefore chaotic," a "ragbag" of emotions manufactured with "journalese or the tell-tale novelist's clichés"; he wrote that although it was an "extremely interesting" study of psychology, the novel "fails completely as a work of art."[19] And when E. M. Forster, author of the then unpublished homosexual romance *Maurice* (1914), visited Hall to propose a letter of protest against the suppression of *The Well,* he was reluctant to praise the novel as a work of art in the way she expected: "I could not come out strong on its merits as a work of art," he wrote to Arnold Bennett.[20] In an unsigned essay entitled "The New Censorship," Forster attacked the suppression as "an insidious blow at the liberties of the public," but he carefully avoided the question of aesthetic worth.[21] The issue of personal freedom, which Hall herself stressed in statements to the press, marked the outer limit of Bloomsbury's interest in what Virginia Woolf considered Hall's "meritorious dull book" (*D3,* p. 193).[22] Woolf wrote to Vita Sackville-West suggesting that *The Well* hardly seemed worth defending even on that score: "And no one has read her book; or can read it. . . . So our ardour in the cause of freedom of speech gradually cools, and instead of offering to reprint the masterpiece, we are already beginning to wish it unwritten" (*L3,* p. 520). Bloomsbury's deep hostility is captured in Woolf's diary account of Forster's visit to Hall, which describes her as screaming "like a herring gull, mad with egotism & vanity." Woolf records Forster's response to Hall in remarkably neutral tones: "he thought Sapphism disgusting: partly from convention, partly because he disliked that women should be independent of men" (*D3*, p. 193). For Bloomsbury tastes, *The Well* was simply too polemical, or polemical in the wrong way, and Hall's personal behavior merely emphasized that unpalatable fact.[23]

At the trial on 9 November, the apparent sincerity of Hall's novel counted heavily against it. When asked by Herbert Metcalfe, counsel for the defense, whether he agreed with the *Times Literary Supplement* that *The Well* was "sincere, courageous, high-minded, and often beautiful," Scotland Yard's Chief Inspector Prothero replied: "I do not. Sincere and courageous, yes; but not high-minded and beautiful."[24] Sincerity did not guarantee moral or aesthetic worth, for one might grant it while still condemning the novel. As we have seen, Judge Biron's objections to the book indicated that Hall's sincerity only made matters worse.

The concept of sincerity served an important function in the court's reading of *The Well of Loneliness*. We have seen how the *Rainbow* trial of 1915 read Lawrence's novel as an autonomous text, as if authorial agency were no longer a factor once the published work had reached the outside world. A similar process was effected at the *Well of Loneliness* trial. As in 1915, the defendant was not the author but the publisher, in this case Jonathan Cape, along with a representative of the Pegasus Press, Leonard Hill. One memorable moment during the second day (16 November 1928) underlined this fact. Having criticized the novel for painting sexual inverts in rosy colors, Judge Biron attacked Hall's depiction of lesbian ambulance drivers in the war for "reflecting on a number of women at the front, women of position and character." At this juncture, Hall, seated at the solicitors' table, cried out, "I protest, I emphatically protest." Hall's outburst provoked the following exchange:

> Sir Chartres.—I must ask you to be quiet.
> Miss Radclyffe Hall.— I am the author of this book—
> Sir Chartres.—If you cannot behave yourself in Court I shall have to have you removed.
> Miss Radclyffe Hall.—Shame![25]

Like Lawrence in 1915, Hall had no legal right in the matter; her presence in the courtroom gave her no interpretative authority over her work. Since her novel was sincere, the trial did not need further help from the author to identify its voice; noise in the courtroom would only distract its judiciously chosen readers from their task. After the trial, Hall rightly observed to Havelock Ellis: "In the eyes of the law I am non-existent" (2 December 1928).

The same point was reiterated when Hall took the case to an unsuccessful appeal at the County of London Sessions on 14 December.[26] Castigating *The Well* as "more subtle, demoralising, corrosive, corruptive, than anything that was ever written," the Attorney General, Sir Thomas Inskip, insisted: "obscenity must be judged by the standard of the laws of the Realm. The fact that someone who wrote a book did not intend it to be obscene does not matter" (*RHCO*, pp. 123–24). When the court upheld Biron's original ruling, the chief magistrate, Sir Robert Wallace, made it quite clear in his concluding speech that the court had deliberately enforced certain laws of literary interpretation in reaching a verdict: "The character of the book cannot be gathered from the reading of isolated passages. They give an indication as to the general tendency, but the book must be taken as a whole. The view of the Court is that this book is a very subtle work. It is one which is insinuating and probably more dangerous because of that fact. . . . Put in a word, the view of this Court is that this is a disgusting book when properly read" (*RHCO*, pp. 137–38). There are striking parallels here not only with the *Rainbow* hearing but also with the *Madame Bovary* trial of 1857. *The Well* is all the more dangerous because its poison is subtle and insinuating; its powers of suggestion may catch the reader unawares, just as *Madame Bovary* had done when it cast a spell on Ernest Pinard, counsel for the prosecution, seventy years before.[27] The only way to ensure that these powers are detected is to read the book properly, as a whole, and (as the British Attorney General advised) by ignoring such distractions as authorial intention. Thus, the trial and appeal illustrate a particular kind of reader-response, and even New Critical, reading that, although claiming to disregard matters extraneous to a closed textual system, nonetheless vigorously pursues certain interests with manifest social and political consequences in the outside world.

There are further crucial points of comparison here with the trials of 1857 and 1915 and also with the *Ulysses* trial of 1921. In putting the book, not the author, on trial, the authorities made it speak *for* the author; anything pertinent that the author had to say was to be found within its pages. Just as Lawrence's presence in court was not required in 1915, nor Flaubert's in 1857, Hall's word was not needed at her trial. Hall actually wanted to take the witness stand, and to that end wrote a long preparatory statement, but defense lawyers advised against it. When she protested in court against Judge Biron's interpretation of the novel, she was immediately silenced. Indeed, Hall was placed in a position analogous to that of Margaret Anderson and Jane Heap at the 1921 *Ulysses* trial, for she was denied a voice not only by her official antagonists but by her own side. Her wishes were ignored at various stages by the publisher, Cape, and by his lawyers, Herbert Metcalfe and Norman Birkett. Cape had withdrawn *The Well* from publication after sending an unsolicited copy to the Home Secretary, Sir William Joynson-Hicks, who had promptly banned the book. The first morning in court, Birkett denied that *The Well* dealt with "unnatural offences," and Metcalfe contended that the novel made it "perfectly clear that throughout the relations between the two women were purely of an intellectual character."[28] Ironically, in transforming the novel's representation of lesbianism into an asexual relationship that agreed with conventional British notions of propriety, Birkett and Metcalfe were following the line Wilde had taken at his second trial, when he defended the "love that dare not speak its name."[29] They were also repeating a strategy employed at the

Madame Bovary trial by Marie-Antoine-Jules Sénard, counsel for the defense. Sénard stressed Flaubert's depiction of the "disillusions of adultery" so as to represent the novel as a morally conservative, educative enterprise that reinforced the value of marriage, an interpretation that, as Dominick LaCapra has shown, plays down the innovative aspects of Flaubert's achievement to which the scandalized prosecutor drew attention.[30] Hall had insisted that her novel be defended according to her intentions, as a plea, she told Cape, for "those who are utterly defenceless, who being from birth a people set apart in accordance with some hidden scheme of Nature, need all the help that society can give them" (*RHCO*, p. 85). Unexpectedly finding herself contradicted in court, Hall spent the lunch-time recess haranguing Birkett, informing him in no uncertain terms that she wanted her message proclaimed in public.[31] The morning's backpedaling, however, had done irreparable damage. When Birkett changed his tune in the afternoon session, the inconsistency was so obvious that the case for the defense collapsed in ruins, leaving Judge Biron little difficulty when the time came, after a week-long recess, to find the defendants guilty and fine Cape and Hill costs of 20 guineas each.

Disagreements between Cape's lawyers and Hall were partly the result of a conflict of interests: the author wanted to convey her message to the public, while the publisher hoped to avoid being found guilty. But this conflict also illuminates the sexual politics of the trial. Silencing Hall, the judge and lawyers ensured the sovereignty of their own critical judgments over and above the issue of professed authorial intention; they also excluded the extraneous voice of a lesbian, who might challenge the judicial verdict that followed from those critical judgments. Having muted Hall, the judge and the supporting cast of lawyers turned the trial into a battle between male readers, whose critical debate would determine the question of lesbianism. Hall's text functioned as a body of symptoms; the court's task was to diagnose its particular malady and, by extension, its author's disease. Virginia Woolf observed in Judge Biron an uncanny resemblance to "a Harley St. specialist investigating a case," a likeness she may have associated, as Ellen Bayuk Rosenman speculates, with "a Harley Street doctor of her own invention, Sir William Bradshaw of *Mrs. Dalloway*."[32] The medical analogy might be extended to include all involved in the official proceedings: it was everyone's task to doctor the text.

This doctoring corresponds closely with the symptomatic readings practiced on *The Rainbow* in 1915, readings that themselves borrowed the terms of Max Nordau's fin-de-siècle scientific criticism. Yet it is here that Hall's intentions and her sincerity become particularly vexatious questions, for in a sense she connived at a scientific approach to literature. In a letter of 18 April 1928 she addressed Havelock Ellis as "the greatest living authority on the tragical problem of sexual inversion," and invited him to compose a preface for her novel. Ellis's preface, which is very much a work of scientific criticism, subsequently received favorable attention from Hall's reviewers; his opinions, generally used to argue that *The Well* dealt with a medically recognized problem, proved crucial to the defense at the 1928 trial. On Hall's instructions, Birkett took pains in court to distinguish between "perversion" and what Ellis had termed "inversion": a natural hormonal imbalance whereby an individual experiences desire only for members of the same biological sex. In her eagerness for Ellis's endorsement, Hall perpetuated an image of the mannish lesbian that functioned intelligibly within early-twentieth-century sexological discourse. As Rosenman suggests, one might say that Hall constructed her novel as a case study in deviance, doctoring the text so that ultimately Ellis's word would count for more than her own.

Granting priority to Ellis's commentary, Hall effectively asked him to authorize her novel so that it would be seen to perform his theory of female inversion. The sincerity exuded by the novel would simply reflect the degree to which Hall succeeded in mimicking the voice of the man she addressed as the greatest living authority on sexual inversion. At one level, this strategy appears to deny Hall her own say, implying that the sole function of her sincerity was to establish certain facts through a mimicry that absented her from the scene of literary and legal representation. At another level, however, playing doctor was quite close to Hall's idea of authorship. For if sincerity was above all a matter of facts, what better role model for the lesbian artist than Havelock Ellis, "the greatest living authority on the tragical problem of sexual inversion"? In a letter to Evguenia Souline, Hall poses as a doctor interrogating a female patient: "I have never felt an impulse towards a man in all my life, because I am a congenital invert. For me, to sleep with a man would be wrong because it would be an outrage against nature. We do exist—where's your medical knowledge?—and believe me, you must not think us 'perverted.' Have you ever heard of bisexuality? You may be that."[33] Seduction itself becomes scientific. Intimating the distinction between inversion and perversion on which Birkett insisted in court, Hall implies that such medical knowledge is the script from which her lesbian imagination springs. Thus, when the lesbian artist works in the mode of sincerity, sincerity itself becomes a kind of performance.

Ironically, having spoken for Hall in his preface, Ellis declined to take the witness stand at the November trial. Writing to Hall on 20 October, he complained that his stutter impaired his ability to speak in public. He also pointed out that, "being the author of a book on this very subject that has been judicially condemned, I am 'tarred with the same brush.'" "The less said about me," he added, "the better for you."[34] The book to which Ellis referred was *Sexual Inversion* (1897), unavailable in Britain until the late 1930s since its suppression in 1898 as a "lewd and obscene" work.[35] Coauthored with John Addington Symonds, *Sexual Inversion* dealt mainly with male homosexuality, but Ellis extended his theory of natural hormonal imbalance to include women, which meant recognizing his wife's lesbianism.[36] Studying his wife's body for these purposes, Ellis used what he called the "key of sincerity." Wayne Koestenbaum has noted Ellis's reluctance to employ this key for reading the gay male body, perhaps for fear of implicating himself in the homosexual, literary discourse with which Symonds perhaps associated the term. Koestenbaum suggests that Ellis may have felt free to scrutinize the lesbian body in this manner because it represented transgressive desires with which he, as a man, could not be tainted. The homosexual male body would not afford such luxurious distance; its insinuating tones might threaten Ellis's scientific, implicitly hetero-sexual, impartiality.[37] For these reasons *The Well of Loneliness* must have hit the right note as far as Ellis was concerned. It passed the test of sincerity and apparently limited its focus to female deviance. Judging by the affirmations sounded in the preface, Ellis perhaps regarded Hall's novel as a work that validated the claims he had made in the name of science. Lovat Dickson has seen Ellis's refusal to speak for *The Well* in court as cowardice, and he may be right[38]; Ellis may not have relished the prospect of reiterating his published opinions before a judicial tribunal for fear of damaging his own growing repu-tation. Yet he may have said quite enough by writing a preface; perhaps it was time to let the novel speak for him. In a sense, Ellis's theory of inversion was itself on trial in November 1928.[39]

As well as depriving Hall of the spokesman she wanted, Ellis's silence in-directly enhanced the authority of the critical and medical judgment exercised at her trial. These two branches of knowledge converged in Judge Biron's pronouncement on 16 November: "The whole note of this book is a passionate and almost hysterical plea for the toleration and recognition of these people who, in the view presented in this book, are people who ought to be toler-ated and recognized, and their practices tolerated and recognized, in decent society. . . ."[40] Describing *The Well* as almost hysterical, Biron apparently characterizes the novel as a woman's handiwork, for hysteria was understood to be the woman's disease. Hall's text seemed to articulate the ravings of diseased femininity.[41]

Yet the intertextual relationship between Hall and Ellis complicates this reading. Since *The Well* was published with Ellis's preface and was partly written to exemplify his theory of inversion, it is hard to say where the disease originates. The novel and the preface enter the same plea. Is Hall ill, then, because her novel says things better left to a medical man (a complaint uttered at the trial)? Does lesbian authorship violate the scientist's preserve? By endors-ing that authorship, Ellis arguably allows himself to be implicated in Hall's lesbian discourse, to be tainted by a malady to which he was supposedly immune. When Ellis excused himself from Hall's trial, he unwittingly diag-nosed himself as a hysteric: the stutter to which he attributed his fear of public speaking suggests the fragmented speech that Freud and Breuer interpreted as a symptom of hysteria. Ellis's reluctance to speak in public also evokes the bash-fulness conventionally associated with femininity. The female invert's disease, Hall's disease, showed itself in a woman looking and behaving like a man: if Ellis looked and sounded like that diseased woman, wasn't he ill also? As the early reception of *Lady Chatterley's Lover* reveals, hysteria suggested a theat-rical realm where sex and gender roles became unstable and ill defined, espe-cially in the years after the Great War, when thousands of shell-shocked vet-erans wore symptoms of the female malady. Ellis himself expresses these theatrical doubts and ambiguities in *Sexual Inversion,* likening the most ex-treme exhibitions of the dramatic aptitude he found in male inverts to the love of deception of a hysterical woman, an analogy with compelling implica-tions for female inversion.[42] If sexual inversion displays itself in a manner approximating female hysteria, then a woman's inversion may be one manifestation of her illness. Alternatively, if hysteria is less discriminating, as it seemed to be after the war, might not female inversion look like male hysteria? The *Well of Loneliness* trial insinuated these unsettling questions into the relation between Hall and Ellis. Who spoke for whom? Who spoke like whom? Sir Chartres Biron's judgment inadvertently introduced a note of uncertainty into the trial's reading of this novel, begging fundamental questions about the nature of sexual definition at the very moment when the case on lesbianism was officially closed.

The Well of Loneliness: Lesbianism in Fiction and History

The centrality of *The Well of Loneliness* in several critical accounts of lesbian literature suggests that the novel creates the kind of uncertainty that the 1928 trial was supposed to put to rest. But *The Well* has in turn become the site of a different uncertainty. Notably, Catharine Stimpson argues that Hall's novel is paradigmatic of the "narrative of damnation," which has been dominant, she claims, in the modern lesbian novel. Stimpson contends that "the narratives of damnation reflect larger social attitudes about homosexuality." "Often ahistorical," she urges, these narratives "can also extend an error of discourse about it: false universalizing, tyrannical univocalizing."[43] In Stimpson's view, *The Well* commits just this error, which has been repeated by those who have read the novel as the true voice of lesbian consciousness. In this sense, readings that locate *The Well* at the heart of a lesbian tradition might be traced back to the 1928 trial, which treated Hall's novel as representative of female inversion, and which therefore produced Hall as an archetype to contain and efface alternative images of lesbianism.

There are strong indications that Hall helped to perpetuate what Stimpson calls larger social attitudes. According to her statements of purpose, she wrote *The Well of Loneliness* without trying to foster the uncertainty and ambiguity that Judge Biron feared. To a certain extent she stood on the same ideological ground as her censors. One interview, which appeared in *The Daily Mail* shortly before *The Well* was published, indicates that Hall shared many assumptions about gender roles with the men who judged and condemned her novel. Affirming her belief that, "generally speaking, woman's place is the home," she asserted: "One of the most deplorable of post-war conditions is, to my mind, the forcing of the wife and mother type of woman into a business or professional career." This condition, Hall claimed, was encouraged "by the vast amount of nonsense that is written and talked about women's right to work." "To be a good wife and mother is the finest work a woman can do," she declared; it is "the work for which Nature intended [her]."[44] Such antifeminist pronouncements seem inimical to the spirit of the plea issued in *The Well of Loneliness*, yet they are closely related. Hall founded her plea for tolerance on the premise that female inverts were hapless freaks of nature, trapped unwittingly in the wrong body, in the wrong place and time. As she told an American woman reporter after the ban: "In the heart of every woman is the desire for protection. In the heart of every man is the desire to give protection to the woman he loves. The invert knows she will never enjoy this and because of her affliction will face social ostracism."[45] The role of wife and mother was perfectly natural for most women, Hall believed; those for whom it was unnatural needed sympathy and understanding.

Inevitably, such thinking shaped Hall's conception of women's roles within lesbian relationships. Her hope for the future was, she told Ellis, to see "inverts able to marry, so that their sex lives might be judged by the time-honoured normal standards" (2 December 1928). Lesbian relationships, Hall thought, should conform to the normal pattern found among heterosexuals: aggressive male and passive female, protector and protected. Here Hall was again following Ellis, for whom courtship represented an essential biological process. Michael Baker observes that by adapting this pattern to account for lesbianism, Hall created a contradiction: the female half of the lesbian relation may be (and according to Ellis should be) attracted to a "real" man, rather than to a woman who behaved like one. According to this schema, in other words, "lesbian relationships are inherently unstable."[46] Superimposing the heterosexual model, Hall threatened to make lesbian relations disappear.

As some critics have noted, *The Well of Loneliness* generates similar issues by framing the tale of its lesbian heroine, Stephen Gordon, within the conventions of heterosexual romance. Bearing a male name because her parents, expecting and wanting a boy, did not bother to change it when she was born a girl, Stephen adopts the aggressive male role in her subsequent sexual relationships with other women. Behaving in accordance with "the intuition of those who stand midway between the sexes, . . . so ruthless, so poignant, so accurate, so deadly," Stephen finds herself competing with men for women's attention (*WL*, p. 83). For the first of those women, Angela Crossby, the encounters with Stephen represent mere dalliance; as if to bear out Ellis's theory of courtship, Angela rejects Stephen for a childhood rival, the virile, bullying Roger Antrim. The pattern is repeated when Stephen's long-term "feminine" companion, Mary Llewelyn, is enticed away at the end of the novel by the heroine's former suitor, Martin Hallam. Mary seems to be faced with a tragic choice between Stephen's long-time devotion and Martin's safe, conventional heterosexuality, but Stephen relieves her of the burden, sacrificing her own happiness to ensure Mary's protection from the social ostracism that goes with female inversion. Far from achieving the customary happy ending, this romance ends in despair for the lesbian, the sacrificial lamb, begging God for the right to existence. But even this dénouement follows a stock variation of the heterosexual romance plot. Jean Radford observes that by using quasi-religious language and various other mannerisms (archaisms, syntactical inversions, an exclamatory style), *The Well* recalls many nineteenth-century novels of love and sacrifice.[47] This "renunciation of human love in favour of the divine," the supposedly ahistorical turn that Stimpson observes in the narrative of damnation, enacts Ellis's suggestion that the invert might transcend her condition by cultivating a soulful spirituality. Ironically, it was in making a martyr of Stephen that Hall aggravated her critics at the trial.

Hall manipulated the same pattern in two previous works—her first novel, *The Unlit Lamp* (1924), and *Miss Ogilvy Finds Herself,* a story written in July 1926 but not published until 1934—that deal surreptitiously with the theme of female inversion. In *The Unlit Lamp,* the relationship between the heroine, Joan Ogden, and her tutor, Elizabeth Rodney, clearly has lesbian overtones. Like Stephen Gordon, Elizabeth is an aggressive, "masculine" woman competing for the other, less assertive woman's affections. Elizabeth's opponents are Joan's grasping mother, Mary Ogden, and a persistent but ineffectual male suitor, Richard Benson. In fact, of the three competitors Richard is by far the least aggressive; in contrast, there is relatively little to choose between Elizabeth and Mrs. Ogden. Like Stephen Gordon, Elizabeth loses the battle; she even misses out on the physical consummation that Stephen fleetingly enjoys. In the earlier work, however, the victor is not the man but the mother. *The Unlit Lamp* gives an ironic twist to the plot on which *The Well* would be founded because here it is the "masculine" woman who takes a husband, though she does so out of defeat rather than physical attraction. Relinquishing all hope of wresting Joan from her mother, Elizabeth marries Richard's equally persistent brother, Lawrence, and accompanies him to South Africa. Meanwhile, Joan remains unmarried, doomed to a fate like that of the unsubtly named Beatrice Lesway, whose "untidy, art-serged body" Joan imagines as a "perpetual battleground" for the "two violent rival forces" of her character: "the brain of a masterful man and the soul of a mother."[48] Instead of becoming a doctor, Joan opts for a conventional female role just as Miss Lesway, compelled by her sense of defeat to espouse social orthodoxy, would have recommended: she nurses invalids, first her mother and then Oswald Rupert, an old man with the mind of a child. Elizabeth had predicted that Joan would console herself by playing the martyr. In the event, unconsummated passion leads both women to perform this role.

Presenting the tale of another implicitly lesbian woman, *Miss Ogilvy Finds Herself* seems to operate outside the conventions of heterosexual romance evoked by *The Unlit Lamp* and *The Well of Loneliness.* Yet even in this story, which Hall later described as providing the nucleus for aspects of her censored novel,[49] the same conventions impose themselves, structuring not the narrative itself but a dream sequence that ends with Miss Ogilvy's death. The narrative begins at the end of the Great War, when the aged heroine returns to England after working in France with the ambulance service. Having reviewed her childhood (which ended in her "odd" withdrawal from the "matrimonial market") and her prewar adulthood (during which, like Joan Ogden, she nursed an ailing mother), Miss Ogilvy now looks forward to a bleak future: "Wars come and wars go but the world does not change: it will always forget an indebtedness which it thinks it expedient not to remember" (*MOFH*, p. 12). Whether as a "queer little girl who loathed sisters and dolls, . . . preferring to play with footballs and tops, and occasional catapults," or as an adult woman who sees all too clearly how her contribution to the war effort will be erased from cultural memory, Miss Ogilvy expects society always to exclude her (*MOFH*, p. 6). Her last effort to find a place for herself leads her to somewhere "marked on her map by scarcely more than a dot" (*MOFH*, p. 17): an island off the Devon coast with one building (a hotel) and a cave. It is on this island that Miss Ogilvy has her dream, which transports her into a primitive, tribal world where she experiences animal passion, not with a woman but with a man. In its naturalistic setting, the dream evokes the instinct for raw physical passion, which has been repressed in the heroine's everyday life. The end of the story, when Miss Ogilvy is found "sitting at the mouth of the cave . . . with her hands thrust deep into her pockets," suggests that she has literally been killed by this repression. The dénouement may suggest that Miss Ogilvy is the victim of her own failure to realize the heterosexual desire, the supposedly authentic human sexuality, incarnated in her dream. But the story emphasizes that the "difficulties of her nature" arise from the repression of her inverted sexuality by the world in which she lives (*MOFH*, pp. 34, 8). Since it would not be natural for her to conform to normative heterosexuality, the crisis represented by the end of the story is inevitable. In effect, Miss Ogilvy is martyred by sexual conventions, which assert themselves even in her dream. These conventions are so powerful that they structure not only the conscious world but the unconscious as well, so that her own dream offers no shelter. Having found herself, Miss Ogilvy has no alternative but to die.

Ostensibly, in Hall's view, inner nature was all that separated her lesbian characters from the heterosexuals featured in conventional romances. If Stephen Gordon, Joan Ogden, and Miss Ogilvy had been boys, or conventional girls, there would have been nothing untoward in their lives; their condition was simply "a fact in nature—a simple, though at present tragic, fact."[50] Experience guarantees authenticity, as is implied at the end of book 2 of *The Well of Loneliness*, when Stephen's teacher, Puddle, urges her to political action: "You may write with a curious double insight—write both men and women from a personal knowledge" (*WL*, p. 205). This concern with natural being keeps at arm's length theories of the social construction of selfhood. However much Stephen is identifiable according to her role, her male clothing, her fencing, her horsemanship (attributes very similar to those of the young Miss Ogilvy), those appearances simply denote the deeper reality of her sexual nature; that she looks and often behaves like a young male aristocrat only confirms her inversion. Hall would have bitterly opposed any suggestion to the contrary, as her response to the "Colonel" Barker case in England indicates: "A mad pervert of the most undesirable type, with her mock war medals, wounds, etc.; and then after having married the woman if she doesn't go and desert her! Her exposure at the moment is unfortunate indeed and will give a handle to endless people—the more so as what I ultimately long for is some sort of marriage for the invert."[51] Using an inflated rhetoric more readily associated with scandalmongers such as the journalist James Douglas, Hall distinguished sharply between congenital inverts like herself and masqueraders like Barker.

It is interesting, then, that *The Well of Loneliness* should record so closely those outward social appearances, especially as they indicate the theatricality of social roles. The narrative often hints that Stephen's inversion is just such a role. One of the first signs of her inversion is the housemaid's observation: "She is a queer kid, always dressing herself up and play-acting—it's funny" (*WL*, p. 20). Stephen's favorite role is that of Admiral Nelson; like any tomboy, and like her fictional predecessor Miss Ogilvy, she finds herself in conflict with the conventions that determine gender roles in children's play. She envies the masculine pursuits of the young Roger Antrim, and grows impatient with his sister Violet's submissiveness. Dramatizing this conflict, however, the narrative implies that such roles are entirely arbitrary:

> Violet was already full of feminine poses; she loved dolls, but not quite so much as she pretended. People said: "Look at Violet, she's like a little mother; it's so touching to see that instinct in a child!" Then Violet would become still more touching. She was always thrusting her dolls upon Stephen, making her undress them and put them to bed. . . . And then Violet knitted, or said that she knitted—Stephen had never seen anything but knots. "Can't you *knit*?" she would say, looking scornfully at Stephen, "I can—Mother called me a dear little housewife!" Then Stephen would lose her temper and speak rudely: "You're a dear little sop, that's what you are!" For hours she must play stupid doll-games with Violet, because Roger would not always play real games in the garden. He hated to be beaten, yet how could she help it? Could she help throwing straighter than Roger? (*WL*, p. 47)

Violet's childhood femininity is a series of poses: she exaggerates her affection for dolls, and her incompetence in rudimentary knitting exercises is matched only by Roger's in boyish pursuits. The introduction of Stephen to the Antrims' world of childhood leisure does not merely put things out of joint; it exposes the purely constructed character of their assigned roles. How ironic, therefore, that in later life the Antrims should fulfill their roles in the adult world quite perfectly, Roger finally beating Stephen at his own game, the seduction of women, and redeeming his boyhood inadequacies by dying a heroic death in the Great War. Yet it is not entirely clear that Roger's success is an expression of natural male sexuality, rather than the effect of social conditioning.

A similar sense of uncertainty surrounds Stephen, whose romantic failure and survival of the war (in which, emulating Miss Ogilvy, she participated as an ambulance driver) apparently undermine her maleness. Recalling the unhappy childhood sight of the footman kissing her beloved housemaid Collins, Stephen becomes hysterical at seeing Angela Crossby embracing Roger:

> Then, as sometimes happens in moments of great anguish, Stephen could only remember the grotesque. She could only remember a plump-bosomed housemaid in the arms of a coarsely amorous footman, and she laughed and she laughed like a creature demented—laughed and laughed until she must gasp for breath and spit blood from her tongue, which had somehow got bitten in her efforts to stop her hysterical laughing; and some of the blood remained on her chin, jerked there by that agonized laughter. (*WL*, p. 195)

At one level, Stephen's hysteria perhaps registers the shock of encountering heterosexual love where she had expected to pursue her own lesbian affair. But what is this hysteria? What does it mean for Stephen to be hysterical? If hysteria were the female malady, then Stephen would simply be an image of diseased femininity. But in postwar Britain, as we have seen, hysteria signified an unstable, theatrical terrain where men might look like women, and where women might resemble men. Stephen's survival of the war suggests a kinship with such hysterics, particularly with the damaged males spawned by postwar British fiction: Christopher Baldry in Rebecca West's *The Return of the Soldier* (1918), Christopher Tietjens in Ford Madox Ford's *Parade's End* (1924–1928), Oliver Mellors in *Lady Chatterley's Lover* (1928), and (as we shall see) Septimus Smith in Woolf's *Mrs. Dalloway* (1925).[52] For Stephen as for these characters, survival compromises masculinity: it would be more manly, conventionally speaking, to die like Roger Antrim. That Roger redeems his childhood shortcomings in the act of dying, however, implies that to be manly is merely to play a role. Stephen's hysteria embodies such role playing in a most unsettling way: for Stephen, a woman with a masculine psyche, who inhabits "the no-man's-land of sex," hysteria might be a natural condition that signifies not diseased femininity or masculinity so much as diseased sexuality (*WL,* p. 79). Stephen's example suggests that gender may be ascribed to such sexuality only in theatrical terms. It is a sexual crisis that produces Stephen's hysteria: a woman who has played the man's part, she finds that part filled by a "real" man, and, "flawed in the making," she reacts with the laughter of "a creature demented" (*WL,* p. 204).

Miss Ogilvy Finds Herself anticipates *The Well of Loneliness* in these very terms, and explicitly locates such problems in the hysterical postwar world by invoking shell shock. Filled with grief, and closing the bedroom door for the last time, Miss Ogilvy stands still to consider this question: " 'Is it shell-shock?' she muttered incredulously. 'I wonder, can it be shell-shock?' " (*MOFH,* p. 23). Like Stephen's, Miss Ogilvy's crisis is sexual. Her dream only heightens her affliction, articulating the heterosexual plot that shocks the sexually inverted consciousness. These dynamics are literalized in *The Well* when Stephen finds Angela and Roger in each other's arms. Miss Ogilvy's dream and death may be read as the culmination of hysteria produced by sexual repression, which is even more pronounced after the war than before. Shaped by the sexual conventions of her time, Miss Ogilvy's own unconscious provides the heterosexual love plot that eliminates lesbianism by conjuring up the images of aggressive male and submissive female. The final movement of her dream implies that these images represent the true state, the biological essence, of the natural world.

In *The Well of Loneliness,* Stephen Gordon's hysterical display sharpens the tension between the natural and the contingent, a tension that Catharine Stimpson overlooks in her reading of this narrative of damnation. In one sense, Stephen's reaction seems to indicate that conflict between different sexualities naturally exists. Yet the novel also suggests that the pattern of Stephen's sexual failures depends on historical conditions unfavorable to lesbianism: inversion is "a fact in nature—a simple, though at present tragic, fact." Some critics have remarked that Hall's image of the mannish lesbian is a product of her historical context, but *The Well* itself dramatizes that sense of contingency and limitation.[53] Stephen's betrayal by Angela Crossby, who shows Stephen's love letter to her husband to divert his attention from her own affair with Roger, simply anticipates the heroine's self-sacrifice at the end of the novel. Each incident is the necessary outcome of a historical situation in which the force of social convention crushes the possibility of freedom for the "freak" of nature. When hysteria breaks out in Stephen, it registers the collision between nature and history, a collision that must end in tragedy. Hence Hall's anger at Leonard Woolf's "dastardly" review, which declared that since her ragbag of journalese and tell-tale novelist's clichés produced characters devoid of true emotional content, *The Well* failed to create "the emotions appropriate to their tragedy or comedy." Denying that *The Well* achieved tragic grandeur, Woolf implied that the novel failed to establish the historical premises essential for a persuasive exposition of Hall's polemical intentions.

Yet in registering Hall's sense of historical entrapment, *The Well of Loneliness* expresses a desire not simply to break the mold of history but to transcend it. This impulse also motivates E. M. Forster's homosexual romance, *Maurice,* of which Forster wrote: "A happy ending was imperative. . . . I was determined that in fiction anyway two men should fall in love and remain in it for the ever and ever that fiction allows. . . ."[54] Leaving the hero to roam the greenwood with the gamekeeper Alec Scudder, Forster releases the transcendent impulse in the manner desired so urgently, but ultimately unavailingly, by Hall's characters.[55] This impulse seems related to a general turn toward pastoralism that was "typical," as Suzanne Raitt has noted, "of the homosexual subculture of the 1920s and 1930s."[56] Throughout *The Well*, scenes depicting the harrowing consequences of present social conditions provoke fantasies of escape; each time, the offending encounter is sexual in some way. Stephen's reaction to seeing Collins with the footman is to hurl a flowerpot and flee wildly to the house. A horror-struck Stephen again flees to the house when Martin Hallam proposes marriage, prompting a fit of self-questioning ("What was she, what manner of curious creature, to have been so repelled by a lover like Martin?") that can only end in the answer, "'I don't know—oh, God, I don't know!'" (*WL*, pp. 99, 100). Flight becomes a necessity for Stephen with almost monotonous regularity. The sight of Angela and Roger kissing, the home that once afforded protection, England itself, all become unbearable to Hall's heroine, who goes to Paris with the faithful Puddle and later retreats with Mary to a Mediterranean villa. Seeing the possibilities for happiness in this world contract to nothing, Stephen eventually has no choice but to martyr herself for Mary's sake and to appeal to God for salvation: "Acknowledge us, oh God, before the whole world. Give us also the right to our existence!" (*WL*, p. 437). In Hall's terms, nothing could be more depressing, for, as Jean Radford argues, the closing appeal of *The Well*, while ostensibly made to God, "is in effect also addressed to the reader, that is, to *social* not metaphysical beings."[57] In Hall's novel, as in Forster's *Maurice,* the impulse to turn away from the present crisis is intelligible only in relation to historical forces. Just as the ever and ever of Forster's romance owes its force to the never and never of history, so Hall's fantasy of divine, transcendental salvation is produced by the experience of actual constraint and limitation. The 1928 trial of Hall's novel seems to have reinforced this experience, sealing off the route by which lesbianism might make its way into history, just as the conventions of tragic romance foreclosed such possibilities in fiction.

Orlando: Lesbianism in Fictional History

The Well of Loneliness and Virginia Woolf's fictional biography *Orlando* are often linked as lesbian novels. As some readers have remarked, the lesbian content of *Orlando* is not explicit.[58] But when the book appeared on 11 October 1928, the title character was quickly identified as the dedicatee, Vita Sackville-West, and in a now famous phrase Nigel Nicolson later described the work as "the longest and most charming love letter in history."[59] Seeing that *Orlando* was readily received as a lesbian work, many have been led to wonder how it escaped censure and became a best-seller at the very time when Hall's novel was condemned in the British courts.[60] Citing the much-quoted passages in Woolf's diary that describe *Orlando* as a "writers holiday" (*D3*, p. 177), one critic contends that the novel's style and tone ("a joke not to be taken too seriously") allowed Woolf to escape the disapproval that greeted the apparently more earnest *Well of Loneliness*.[61] Working on similar assumptions, another reader has characterized *Orlando* as "a work of fancy" that indicates "Woolf's continuing inability to give full acknowledgment to her own lesbianism," a judgment never passed on Hall, whose honesty is assumed.[62] Yet rather than simply asking us whether Woolf affirmed a lesbian identity, *Orlando* activates issues of expression and social visibility lurking in the question unwittingly provoked, as the satirist Beresford Egan pointed out, by the prosecution of *The Well of Loneliness*: What is lesbianism? (*RHCO*, p. 97).[63]

The difficulty of answering and even framing this question is indicated by Woolf's vacillation between the comic and the serious while writing *Orlando*. By the time she finished the book in March 1928, Woolf found that "it may fall between stools, be too long for a joke, & too frivolous for a serious book" (*D3*, p. 177). Leonard Woolf, *Orlando*'s first reader, took it more seriously than expected; he considered it a "satire," and "very original" (*D3*, pp. 184–85). Far from a sign of weakness, this vacillation is a cornerstone, a guiding principle, in the novel. And as Woolf wrote in the long essay composed at the same time as *Orlando*, "Phases of Fiction," comedy may restore some much-needed sanity after an excursion into romance, the genre to which *The Well of Loneliness* belongs: "how it [romance] needs the relief of comedy; how the very distance from common human experience and strangeness of its elements become ridiculous."[64] As these comments imply, romance extrapolates from common human experience as much as any other form does; made up of the most exaggerated kinds of strangeness, its image of life may be quite ridiculous. The same gloss might be put on Woolf's reading of *The Well of Loneliness*.

It is clear, too, that Woolf vacillated on the subject of "sapphism" (the term she often used for lesbianism). When in March 1927 she first conceived the idea of *Orlando*, or *The Jessamy Brides*, it was to be "an escapade after these serious poetic experimental books whose form is always so closely considered": "Sapphism is to be suggested. Satire is to be the main note—satire & wildness. . . . My own lyric vein is to be satirised. Everything mocked" (*D3*, p. 131). Woolf's early expressions of interest in Vita Sackville-West had a similar "frivolous" air. Relating Sackville-West's celebrated relationship with Violet Trefusis, the model for Princess Sasha in *Orlando*, Woolf wrote to Jacques Raverat in 1925: "I can't take either of these aberrations seriously. To tell you a secret, I want to incite my lady to elope with me next" (*L3*, pp. 155–56). She was forced to take Sackville-West seriously in September 1928, when they planned a holiday together in France. It was a prospect that caused Woolf some anxiety, and she was relieved when the vacation came to an end. Yet Woolf wrote to Sackville-West in February 1929 to proclaim the impact of *Orlando* in the United States: "The percentage of Lesbians is rising in the States, all because of you."[65] The society of women itself provided relief from the oppressively masculine atmosphere of "Bloomsbuggery" (Woolf's term for the cult of male homosexuality centering around Lytton Strachey). In another letter to Raverat, Woolf wrote: "Much preferring my own sex, as I do, or at any rate, finding the monotony of young mens' conversation considerable, . . . [I] intend to cultivate women's society entirely in the future" (*L3*, p. 164). Presumably, women's society would be the counterpart of Woolf's "anti-bugger revolution" (*D3*, p. 10). This society would not necessarily be exclusively sexual, but its sapphic overtones are suggested by a letter that, as Sherron Knopp has noted, suggests a close connection between Woolf's relationship with Sackville-West and the composition of *Orlando*:

> If I saw you would you kiss me? If I were in bed would you—
> I'm rather excited about Orlando tonight: have been lying by the fire and making up the last chapter. (*L3*, p. 443)

Woolf's excited reticence here might be encapsulated in a phrase Sackville-West once used to explain Woolf's illness after a 1929 trip to Berlin: "SUPPRESSED RANDINESS."[66] The hesitant, uncompleted phrase ("would you—") enforces a kind of self-censorship, which illustrates Woolf's typical reticence in dealing with sexual topics. This gap also indicates a space where sapphism is to be suggested, though not stated. The reluctance to state gives Woolf's letter its delicacy, its emotional and suggestive power; to state would be to risk blunting those fine edges. The same principles were at work when Woolf revised *Orlando* for publication. Woolf excised several details that made her challenge to conventional thinking about sexuality more overt. Such details included references to "the great season of Orlando's lusts" and his "red sensual lips," as well as a description of chastity as "a bore"; an allusion to Sappho was cut.[67] Hermione Lee has taken these excisions as evidence that "the finished version is slightly less *risqué*."[68] It would be more accurate, however, to say that in revision the novel became transgressive in more subtle, less outspoken ways.

This quality, defining a crucial difference between Virginia Woolf and Radclyffe Hall, also emerges in Woolf's early piece, "Friendships Gallery" (1907), and in a discarded draft for the "Chloe liked Olivia" section of *A Room of One's Own* (1929). In "Friendships Gallery," a romantic biographical spoof about Violet Dickinson that anticipates the more extended experiment in *Orlando,* Woolf suggests "that a blank means rather more than a full name for it is capable of feeling if you guess it aright."[69] A blank, in other words, may evoke the world of flesh and blood, the living person who is rather more than a name and is capable of feeling. This idea is charged with erotic possibilities in a passage that Woolf cut from the published version of *A Room.* As Ellen Bayuk Rosenman observes, the excised passage seems to refer to lesbianism and to the Hall trial. When the narrator reads at the bottom of the page, "Chloe liked Olivia; they shared a ———," she is prevented from going on because the pages "had stuck"; "while fumbling to open them," her imagination calls up images of policemen, magistrates, and a trial that declares the book obscene. At this point the pages "came apart," revealing to a grateful narrator the harmless information that Chloe and Olivia shared "only a laboratory."[70] Rosenman argues perceptively that along with the "teasing hesitation in naming what the women share," the "imagery of attachment and space creates a double image of lesbianism and its suppression"; the "secret space that the reader and the characters share before the turn of the page" indicates "the gaps left by censorship."[71] In the published version, the reference to male authority is pinned even more directly to the Hall trial, for now Woolf names the judge, Sir Chartres Biron, but the teasing hesitation of the draft has disappeared, too: as we all know, Chloe and Olivia shared a laboratory.[72] The relatively uncontroversial published version does not exert the pressure of Woolf's suppressed randiness with quite the same force.[73]

The space between the pages, the blank denoting something that one might like to say but cannot, represents a limited zone within which, for Woolf, the literary imagination might give tenuous, momentary expression to lesbian desires. When Sir Chartres Biron silenced Radclyffe Hall at the *Well of Loneliness* trial, he indicated that, unlike male homosexuality, lesbianism remained unspeakable in the public discourse of Britain between the wars; attempting to overcome the danger that modern books might "become so insipid, so blameless, so full of blank spaces and evasions that we cannot read them," the imaginative writer had to exploit the gaps left by official and self-imposed forms of censorship.[74] For Woolf, vacillation suggested a means to such exploitation: it offered to expand possibility, redraw the parameters within which sexuality is defined and suppressed, and so rewrite the vexed relationship between lesbianism and literary history. In this sense, vacillation in *Orlando* is analogous to hysteria in *The Well of Loneliness,* with the crucial difference that Woolf's vacillations undermine the possibility of issuing the medical and legal pronouncements to which, as Hall's novel and trial showed, hysteria made one susceptible. Consequently, Woolf's fictional biography may be read as dramatizing the problems of censorship in relation to lesbianism, yet as maintaining the delicate balance between the jokey and the serious on which the whole book turned. While contemplating the momentous issues that surfaced at the time of the Hall trial, and having delivered the *Room* lectures at

Cambridge, Woolf was able to write on 7 November 1928: "Orlando was the outcome of a perfectly definite, indeed overmastering impulse. I want fun. I want fantasy. I want (& this was serious) to give things their caricature value. And still this mood hangs about me. I want to write a history, say of Newnham or the womans movement, in the same vein. The vein is deep in me—at least sparkling, urgent" (*D3*, p. 203). Woolf wanted fun and fantasy, but felt urgent about her desire to give the caricature value of the things in which she sought refuge from the society of men: Newnham College and the women's movement. According to the spirit of *Orlando,* one can vacillate quite endlessly.

Writing of *Orlando,* Woolf told Sackville-West: "it sprung upon me how I could revolutionise biography in a night."[75] Woolf achieves that revolution by dramatizing and parodying the conventions of traditional biography, mocking the notion of quantifiable human experience, in order to create a space for imaginative speculation. Once opened, this space plays havoc with the separation of art and life that lay at the heart of critical assumptions enforced at the Hall trial. Woolf sets about this project by creating a bizarre, protean character who, living from the Elizabethan times to the date of publication (11 October 1928), freely crosses the boundaries usually found between different ages, nations, and sexes. Using the principle of vacillation, Woolf liberates Orlando from the historical ties that bind Radclyffe Hall's inverted heroine, Stephen Gordon, and dispels the notion that biography has for its object a single, unified identity. In the last chapter Woolf imagines a multiplicity of selves contained in one person, rendering futile any effort to compile an exhaustive, comprehensive biography: "For she had a great variety of selves to call upon, far more than we have been able to find room for, since a biography is considered complete if it merely accounts for six or seven selves, whereas a person may well have as many thousand."[76]

Woolf does not attempt to rationalize such leaps and bounds; on the contrary, *Orlando* makes an ostentatious display of transgressing historical and logical norms. On two occasions Orlando inexplicably falls asleep for seven days. After the first of these incidents, his reawakening (a mock resurrection) provokes wide-ranging metaphysical speculations on the nature of sleep, on life and death, which are then brushed aside as trivial hindrances to the story: "Having waited well over half an hour for an answer to these questions, and none coming, let us get on with the story" (*O,* p. 68). The second big sleep is the occasion of the famous sex change, the novel's strangely veiled dramatic climax, which, paradoxically, has no effect on the identity of Orlando, whose essential elements are joined in a seamless continuity. The theory, Woolf wrote in a manuscript note, was "that character goes on underground before we are born; & [leave] leaves something afterwords [*sic*] also" (*OHD,* p. 2): "Many people, . . . holding that such a change of sex is against nature, have been at great pains to prove (1) that Orlando had always been a woman, (2) that Orlando is at this moment a man. Let biologists and psychologists determine. It is enough for us to state the simple fact; Orlando was a man till the age of thirty; when he became a woman and has remained so ever since" (*O,* p. 139).

The sex change brings into the foreground the principle of uncertainty that underpins the structure of *Orlando*. "[H]orrified to perceive how low an opinion she was forming of the other sex, the manly, to which it had once been her pride to belong," Orlando seems "from some ambiguity in her terms" to be "censuring both sexes equally, as if she belonged to neither": "and indeed, for the time being she seemed to vacillate; she was man; she was woman; she knew the secrets, shared the weaknesses of each" (*O*, p. 158). This uncertainty merely expresses a vacillation that is present even in the contorted qualifications of the novel's jokey first sentence: "He—for there could be no doubt of his sex, though the fashion of the time did something to disguise it—was in the act of slicing at the head of a Moor which swung from the rafters" (*O*, p. 13).

While seeming to leave the essential principles of sexual difference unaltered, these vacillations create the possibility of nonheterosexual desire. Since the sex change leaves Orlando's identity untouched, the object of her desire is still a woman, the Princess Sasha. Becoming a woman is advantageous, for it allows Orlando to decipher signs whose intended meanings had seemed unintelligible to her previously male mind:

> And as all Orlando's loves had been women, now, through the culpable laggardry of the human frame to adapt itself to convention, though she herself was a woman, it was still a woman she loved; and if the consciousness of being of the same sex had any effect at all, it was to quicken and deepen those feelings which she had had as a man. For now a thousand hints and mysteries became plain to her that were then dark. Now, the obscurity, which divides the sexes and lets linger innumerable impurities in its gloom, was removed. . . . At last, she cried, she knew Sasha as she was. . . . (*O*, p. 161)

In this romance, however, love is simply a farcical game, the parts of lover and beloved merely suits of clothing one wears in order to strut upon the stage of life. It is sufficient to know what Sasha had thought and felt as a woman; hereafter, new adventures will lie in store, such as the renewal of Archduke Harry's pursuit of Orlando. Earlier in the novel the Archduke had appeared as Archduchess Harriet Griselda, but finding that Orlando is now a woman, he sheds his female disguise. In response to this revelation, "they acted the parts of man and woman for ten minutes," prompting Orlando to muse: "If this is love . . . there is something highly ridiculous about it" (*O*, p. 179).

In one sense, the ludicrous outcome of the Archduke's advances paves the way for Orlando's apparently more serious affair with Marmaduke Bonthrop Shelmerdine. Yet in submitting Orlando to the marriage and childbirth to which this relationship leads, Woolf mocks heterosexual romance, suggesting that the conventions mimicked by *The Well of Loneliness* may be empty. Marriage and childbirth, traditionally climaxes of feminine experience in the English novel, as they are in Quentin Bell's biography of Woolf, become relatively unremarkable features on the landscape of Orlando's journey through history, minor events, offered cursorily for the reader's delectation as mere curiosities of nineteenth-century society.[77] Writing on 12 October 1928 to Harold Nicolson, a loose model for Shelmerdine, Sackville-West described

Orlando as "an absolutely enchanting book," but faulted Woolf for "making Orlando 1) marry, 2) have a child": "Shelmerdine does not really contribute anything either to Orlando's character or to the problems of the story, (except as a good joke at the expense of the Victorian passion for marriage) and as for the child it contributes less than nothing, but even strikes rather a false note. Marriage & motherhood would either modify or destroy Orlando, as a character: they do neither."[78] The emphasis on the importance of motherhood is not surprising, given Sackville-West's maternal role in relation to Woolf, a role both women acknowledged in writing of each other.[79] But in *Orlando*, the maternal relation, and the marriage from which it conventionally springs, merely signify conformity to the Victorian age. The features of that age are recorded in a historical commentary that tacitly notes the emergence of the ideology of separate spheres in British society: "The sexes drew further and further apart. No open conversation was tolerated. Evasions and concealments were sedulously practised on both sides. And just as the ivy and the evergreen rioted in the damp earth outside, so did the same fertility show itself within. The life of the average woman was a succession of childbirths. She married at nineteen and had fifteen or eighteen children by the time she was thirty; for twins abounded. Thus the British empire came into existence. . ."(*O*, p. 229).The narrator parodically links these social modifications to changes in the natural conditions of the outside world, but to Orlando "the great discovery of marriage," by which people "were somehow stuck together, couple after couple, . . . did not seem to be Nature": "There was no indissoluble alliance among the brutes that she could see" (*O*, p. 242). Even so, she finds that a wedding ring is the only cure for the "tingling and twangling" that afflicts her left finger in the nineteenth century. As it turns out, the union with Shelmerdine could not have been more appropriate, for his sexual identity is as unstable as Orlando's. When Orlando declares her passionate love, the same "awful suspicion rushed into both their minds simultaneously":

> "You're a woman, Shel!" she cried.
> "You're a man, Orlando!" he cried. (*O*, p. 252)

This suspicion is quickly absorbed by the groundswell of the narrative's inexorable progress, and is entirely forgotten at the end when Shelmerdine makes a heroic final entrance in answer to Orlando's call (which, made with breast bared to the moon, reads like a parodic allusion to the beach scene in *The Rainbow*). But in accommodating these unconventional elements within its hyperconventional resolution, *Orlando* is simply following the ground rules of Shakespearean comedy, a key source for Woolf's title character. To defuse the social and sexual transgressions of the novel with an ostentatious final assertion of marital love is to tell the reader that, as in Shakespeare's play, things are as you like it. In *Orlando*, readerly anxieties about such matters are to be mocked.[80]

Appropriating the transvestite apparatus of Shakespeare's comic plots, Woolf suggests that in order to change from the female to the male role,

Orlando merely has to wear different clothes. After the sex change she adopts "those Turkish coats and trousers which can be worn indifferently by either sex" (O, p. 139).[81] But she finds that by alternating between distinctively male and female clothes she can multiply "the pleasures of life": "From the probity of breeches she turned to the seductiveness of petticoats and enjoyed the love of both sexes equally" (O, p. 221). Such conduct inevitably provokes laughter, as when Orlando throws off the male garb to reveal herself as a woman to the prostitute Nell, but here mirth is a pleasurable by-product of this theatrical mode, where the truest poetry is the most feigning. Orlando's outward appearance can undergo any number of transformations, which enhance the pleasure of her existence, or the text.

Composed of these multiple selves, Orlando's personality is every bit as theatrical as when defined by D. H. Lawrence as "the transmissible effect of a man," an "actor's mask," an "*ideal* self masquerading and prancing round, showing off."[82] While Lawrence regarded such surfaces as shallow and deceptive, Orlando finds them enabling and liberating. In an essay, "The New Biography," published in 1927, Woolf declared that the modern biographer needed to weld together the "granite" of truth and the "rainbow" of personality, but warned: "Truth of fact and truth of fiction are incompatible." And in "The Art of Biography" she faulted Lytton Strachey's "tragic history," *Elizabeth and Essex* (1928), for mixing invented facts with verified ones.[83] Yet in *Orlando* granite is entirely continuous with rainbow: truth seems identical to the glittering artifice, the sparkling fictions, of the central character's personality. In its defiance of Lawrencean stricture, *Orlando* is akin to *Ulysses*, which makes for an interesting alliance, as Woolf dismissed Joyce's novel as "the conscious and calculated indecency of a desperate man who feels that in order to breathe he must break the windows."[84] However desperate *Ulysses* seemed, it was pondering this work that prompted Woolf to remark: "it may be true that the subversive mind dwells on indecency."[85] *Orlando,* itself the product of a subversive mind, offers some striking parallels with one of Joyce's most conscious and calculated indecencies: the whorehouse scene in "Circe." The instability of sexual roles dramatized in "Circe" is analogous to that in *Orlando*. In *Orlando,* as in *Ulysses,* theatrical self-transformation allows one to throw off an assigned social role, to remake an identity, and ultimately to reject what Stephen Dedalus calls the nightmare of history: those received, official versions of the past that censor one's possibilities in the present and the future. In Woolf's novel, Orlando's personality ranges so freely that the whole of English history from the time of Elizabeth I seems to be remade in his or her rapidly changing image. The censoring force of history appears to be harnessed entirely to Orlando's whim, to whatever suit of clothing Woolf asks her character to put on.

In this way, *Orlando* would seem to override the coercive historical forces that dictate the unhappy dénouement of *The Well of Loneliness*. Yet while turning history into an effect of Orlando's variety performance, Woolf suggests that her character's apparently limitless freedom may be qualified. After all, if identity, rather than referring to some deep, essential self, consists entirely in what Lawrence termed the transmissible effect of personality, how is that effect achieved? Seeing Orlando's facility in alternating between male and female roles leads Woolf's narrator to wonder whether "it is clothes that wear us and not we them" (*O*, p. 188). Such conjecture implies even greater freedom: by wearing the same clothes we might eliminate sexual difference altogether, and so liberate human character from what Woolf, in "Women Novelists" (1918), called "the tyranny of sex."[86] When it is clothes that wear us, however, perhaps our roles are simply determined by whatever clothes are available: that is, they may be arbitrarily imposed from without. If we are worn by our clothes, we are constructed, and potentially censored, by some external agency, such as the sexual hierarchy that assigns particular clothes to the male and female roles. In this sense, the pleasures of Orlando's performance would appear to reside outside the protagonist herself. If the identity of Orlando merely consists in a series of external signs, then the pleasures of her multiple lives may belong to the reader who, interpreting those signs, is free to exert an authority over the text similar to that claimed over Hall's novel at the 1928 trial.

In the next paragraph the vacillating narrator rejects the idea that clothes wear us and, inclining to another view, reconsiders the possibility of an essential sexual identity submerged beneath the excesses of theatrical artifice:

> The difference between the sexes is, happily, one of great profundity. Clothes are but a symbol of something hid deep beneath. It was a change in Orlando herself that dictated her choice of a woman's dress and of a woman's sex. And perhaps in this she was only expressing rather more openly than usual—openness indeed was the soul of her nature—something that happens to most people without being thus plainly expressed. For here again, we come to a dilemma. Different though the sexes are, they intermix. In every human being a vacillation from one sex to the other takes place, and often it is only the clothes that keep the male or female likeness, while underneath the sex is the very opposite of what it is above. (*O*, pp. 188–89)

If there is an essential sexual identity, this passage suggests that its relation to outer appearances is completely arbitrary. If identity comprises an unchanged element, a stream that flows continuously beneath the ever-changing surface of life, its relation to sex and gender must always remain a dilemma, suspending us between the poles of sex and gender that usually make biography intelligible: "Whether, then, Orlando was most man or woman, it is difficult to say and cannot now be decided" (*O*, p. 190). A glance at the manuscript indicates that Woolf attached some importance to leaving the question open in this way. The manuscript reads: "Whether then Orlando was most man or woman it is difficult to say; but since she wore a woman's clothes the balance seemed to incline that way . . . (*OHD*, p. 150). The narrator steers toward an answer in the manuscript, but away from it in the revised text. During revision Woolf clearly decided to emphasize Orlando's sexual ambiguity. In this way she made the published text slightly more risqué than the draft.

Orlando's dilemma anticipates and complicates the androgynous mind of *A Room of One's Own*. In the latter work, androgyny signifies a condition in which "there are two sexes in the mind corresponding to the two sexes in the body"; these sexes "require to be united in order to get complete satisfaction and happiness" (*AROO*, p. 98). Ostensibly, Woolf's image of harmony, symbolized by a man and a woman together in a taxi, is "a natural fusion," a "union of man and woman," without hierarchy, without subservience to the single oppressive "I" of conventional narrative. In this essay, however, the vision of androgyny is conveyed through images of marriage, intercourse, and fertilization, a language borrowed from the supposedly repudiated sexual hierarchy. We are told that "a woman also must have intercourse with the man in her," and that "when this fusion takes place . . . the mind is fully fertilised" (*AROO*, p. 98). A few pages later this fusion is again depicted in sexual terms, this time as a marriage, whose pleasures seem to be viewed through male eyes: "Some marriage of opposites has to be consummated. The whole mind must lie wide open if we are to get the sense that the writer is communicating his experience with perfect fullness" (*AROO*, p. 104). Here, the mind is seen as a passive, implicitly female object, which lies wide open before the observing eye of the active male, trying to achieve a consummation. It is no accident, therefore, that *A Room of One's Own* acknowledges Coleridge as the original theorist of the androgynous imagination and follows him in nominating Shakespeare as its most perfect exemplar.[87]

In *Orlando*, the principle of perpetual vacillation releases the narrative from this patriarchal language: one cannot, and need not, decide to what sex Orlando most belongs. While there appear to be two sexes, two poles of gender, there is no preordained set of rules that fixes them in one place, or that assigns one identity to either pole. The novel underscores the point by putting it in a legal context. When Orlando returns from Turkey to England after the sex change, the problem of her identity becomes a matter for the courts, which have to consider the following charges: "(1) that she was dead, and therefore could not hold any property whatsoever; (2) that she was a woman, which amounts to much the same thing; (3) that she was an English Duke who had married one Rosina Pepita, a dancer; and had had by her three sons, which sons now declaring that their father was deceased, claimed that all his property descended to them" (*O*, p. 168). A hundred years later, the case is settled: Lord Palmerston annuls the marriage to Rosina, whose sons are disinherited; he declares Orlando female and entails her estates on future male heirs. In this comically protracted lawsuit, as Maria DiBattista argues, sex "becomes a legal fiction, like paternity and property rights."[88] Uncannily anticipating questions raised by the Hall trial, *Orlando* highlights the law's role in defining sexual identity. Woolf's vacillating novel implies that such legal judgments are artificial, arbitrary attempts to limit what cannot be limited.

In an insightful chapter on Orlando's vacillation, Rachel Bowlby notes that there is also "the question as to whether the sexes 'intermix' at one time (as would be implied by the androgynous model of *A Room*), or alternate over a period of the life of 'a human being.'"[89] This is an important observation, but Bowlby implicitly designates the period of vacillation as the second half of the novel, that is, after Orlando's sex change. This reading significantly affects her interpretation of Orlando's subsequent gender trouble. Bowlby suggests that the "capacity for vacillation is itself what marks her [Orlando's] femininity in the eyes of the biographer," prompting the further speculation that "as a woman," Orlando "is forever vacillating between the sexes, as if femininity is an inherently unstable position, or as if its very condition is that of putting on and off the identities of one or the other sex."⁹⁰ Just as one might question whether hysteria was solely the woman's disease in postwar Britain, one might ask, too, if Woolf's text limits vacillation to the feminine position. Bowlby herself notices that the first sentence of the novel (which I cited earlier) raises an unanswerable question about Orlando's sex. The sex change invites us to draw a query mark around the protagonist's entire career. It simply dramatizes an uncertainty that has been present all along, and its effect on the action is to make us more conscious of a possibility that the novel has raised throughout: as Orlando can disguise her womanhood by putting on men's clothes, it is equally plausible that her former male appearance concealed something female in her character. When, in addition to these qualifications, one takes into account the difficulty of determining the extent to which Orlando's cross-dressing is an active or a passive strategy, it is hard to rejoice unreservedly over Orlando's "endless dissimulation" as a means of subverting the patriarchal hierarchy of male dominance and female submission.

A similar point might be made about the potential space opened up for lesbian desire by the uncertainty of Orlando's sex. Clearly, lesbian relations become especially viable after the sex change. But as Orlando's manhood is equivocal at the beginning of the novel, his youthful amorous adventures might be interpreted as expressing deviant sexuality under the more respectable cloak of heterosexual romance. This possibility is strongly suggested by Woolf's source for Orlando's affair with Sasha, the relationship between Vita Sackville-West and Violet Trefusis, during which the former was known for masquerading in Paris as a man. In adopting a male guise, Sackville-West seemed to become what was conventionally regarded as the dominant party, but the man's was not necessarily the only active role: while the active partner in her relationship with Virginia Woolf, Sackville-West was also playing mother. Likewise, in *Orlando* the terms "active" and "passive" do not necessarily denote specific gendered identities, or even particular sexualities; they seem to float quite freely between various unfixed positions. But that freedom entails an element of undecidability, which makes it difficult to determine exactly how the novel articulates lesbian desire. A whole series of questions is begged. What is deviant desire? What is normal desire? Further, what is the feminine position, or the corresponding masculine position? Of course, the more ambiguous gender becomes, the harder it is to evaluate the deviance or straightness of a desire. If there is deviant desire in *Orlando,* it lies in the interstices of the plot's ostensibly heterosexual apparatus, in the gaps between what is and what cannot be said. To state it would be to undo its condition of possibility.

The dilemma of Orlando's sex highlights ambiguities in his or her identity, but it also raises questions about Woolf's vacillating narrator, who expounds one theory only to drop it and pick up another. At one juncture, the narrator claims to "enjoy the immunity of all biographers and historians from any sex whatever" (O, p. 220). As Bowlby observes, the context of this declaration suggests that "the neutrality of biographers and historians is parodied as only an impossible pose." It is not clear, though, that this pose covers "a certain sex underneath."[91] The biographer too operates as a figure of perpetual oscillation, as we see when Orlando joins Nell and other prostitutes to exchange "fine tales" and "amusing observations":

> for it cannot be denied that when women get together—but hist—they are always careful to see that the doors are shut and that not a word of it gets into print. All they desire is—but hist again—is that not a man's step on the stair? All they desire, we were about to say when the gentleman took the very words out of our mouths. Women have no desires, says this gentleman, coming into Nell's parlour; only affectations. Without desires (she has served him and he is gone) their conversation cannot be of the slightest interest to anyone. "It is well known," says Mr. S. W., "that when they lack the stimulus of the other sex, women can find nothing to say to each other. When they are alone, they do not talk; they scratch." And since . . . it is well known (Mr. T. R. has proved it) "that women are incapable of any feeling of affection for their own sex and hold each other in the greatest aversion," what can we suppose that women do when they seek out each other's society?
>
> As that is not a question that can engage the attention of a sensible man, let us, who enjoy the immunity of all biographers and historians from any sex whatever, pass it over, and merely state that Orlando professed great enjoyment in the society of her own sex, and leave it to the gentlemen to prove, as they are very fond of doing, that this is impossible. (O, pp. 219–20)

In this passage it is extremely difficult to pin the narrator down to a particular sex for more than a fleeting moment. The claim to sexual neutrality may be a male pose designed to give the air of impartial authority, perhaps akin to that of the judge and lawyers who settled the case of Radclyffe Hall. At the beginning of the episode, however, the narrator seems to shift uncertainly from the position of a female observer, who has access to women's quarters, to another realm where the voice is implicitly detached from the women ("they" as opposed to "we"), but not necessarily associated with the man whose unwelcome step is heard on the stair. Further, the voice of Mr. S. W., appealing to the supposedly objective authority of common knowledge and the quasi-scientific proof of Mr. T. R., parodies the claim to immunity that the narrator makes a few lines later. It is ironic, of course, that the narrator assumes a certain distance from gentlemen, who are very fond of proving things: throughout the novel, the anxious narrator betrays a comic concern for facts and truth.

The passage also hints at the suppressed randiness that Vita Sackville-West attributed to Woolf. The question as to what women do when they seek out each other's society is left hanging as the narrator diverts attention toward himself or herself, but having claimed immunity, the narrator lets it be known that "Orlando professed great enjoyment in the society of her own sex." We are not invited directly to inquire what "enjoyment" means, but it seems to reactivate the unanswered question of the previous paragraph. And while that question cannot engage the attention of a sensible man, it might interest the invisible biographer, who, as if to suppress any randiness before it reaches the wrong audience, exercises a tactful censorship over the content of the women's conversations ("but hist . . . but hist again"), but who is not necessarily excluded from the pleasures they offer.

Through the offices of the vacillating biographer, the mock censor of *Orlando*, the censorship of taboo sexual subjects emerges as an important subtext of the novel. Comically fussing over the scarcity of vital facts and information, the biographer pretends to get as close to the truth as possible, but this means fabricating and inventing. When the time comes to relate the events surrounding Orlando's sex change, we learn that "often it has been necessary to speculate, to surmise, and even to make use of the imagination" (*O*, p. 119). The narrator drops a veil over the sex change itself, lifting it only when the change is complete, and then affecting unconcern with the topic by declaring, "let other pens treat of sex and sexuality; we quit such odious subjects as soon as we can" (*O*, p. 139). On the surface, this ostentatious disavowal of interest in odious sexual topics mimics the conventional prudery of biographers and readers. At the same time, though, the narrator implies that we have been showing an unhealthy concern for matters that should be left, as was stressed at the *Well of Loneliness* trial, to scientists and psychologists. The narrator's disavowal parodies such gestures on the part of biographers, who often arouse the reader's interest only to deflect it with pretended moral piety. Springing from no other source than the desire to display his or her own impeccable moral standards, the disapproving frown of Orlando's biographer simply imitates a well-worn and seemingly hollow convention.

By invoking the imagination, the narrator not only effects a silent (and parodic) censorship of odious topics, but also implies that any historical record is riddled with gaps and evasions, which in turn may enforce a kind of censorship. The narrator comes into conflict with the fact-recording function that supposedly lies at the heart of a biographical enterprise. As Daniel Albright has observed, Woolf's biography of Roger Fry demonstrates her own respect for the importance of empirical facts, yet seeing that human perception may be nothing more than the distorted vision of the eye, she remained only half committed to the belief in an objective world that such respect would seem to require.[92] A similar skepticism motivates Orlando's parody of the naïve theory that biography constitutes an impartial process of marshalling and ordering factual evidence. A vacillation between empiricism and skepticism destabilizes the narrator's voice, denying it the tone of uncompromising authority. Woolf also entertained the possibility that this vacillation was gendered. In her first novel, *The Voyage Out* (1915), Terence Hewet tells the heroine, Rachel Vinrace, "You've no respect for facts, Rachel; you're essentially feminine."[93] According to this exclamation, the essentially feminine represents that vague, elusive region lacking the hard, definite outline of facts; meanwhile, its masculine counterpart would be akin to the confident, direct, logical "I," who provokes respect, boredom, and not a little hostility in the narrator of *A Room of One's Own*. In *Orlando*, the narrator's voice evolves as a curious mixture of these two conflicting impulses: we hear the yearning for empirical truth, but that yearning is constantly held in check, and perhaps undermined, by the realization that the record is necessarily incomplete, that the imagination must be called upon to supply what is missing. But since *Orlando* destabilizes the grounds on which gender is assigned, it is hard to distinguish these impulses from each other, as if one were feminine, the other masculine.

The theatrical instability of the narrator's role suggests some striking similarities with the vacillations of Orlando. Mimicking the tones now of conventional morality, now of the biographer or historian, the narrator puts on voices as easily as Orlando puts on clothes, adopting whatever role suits the occasion. Bowlby rightly argues that as figures of vacillation Orlando and the narrator are interchangeable. But rather than linked solely to femininity, as Bowlby contends, the vacillations of *Orlando* denote a more fundamental uncertainty about sex and gender roles, intimating a deeper ambiguity in the composition of the human personality. The apparent interchangeability of Orlando and the narrator further contributes to the indefinite nature of character, prompting one to ask where Orlando begins and the narrator ends.

In these ways, vacillation in *Orlando* bears close structural resemblances to hysteria, as a glance at Woolf's earlier novel, *Mrs. Dalloway* (1925), reveals. The chief locus of hysteria in that work is a male character, Septimus Warren Smith, who has returned from the Great War suffering from shell shock. Smith's torment culminates in suicide as he hurls himself from his window onto the railings below. This tragic dénouement is the flip side of the comic extravagance found in *Orlando*. Whereas in *Orlando* vacillation opens and magnifies possibilities for the human personality, *Mrs. Dalloway* demonstrates the grisly consequences of complete openness. Tortured by his loss of awareness of the boundaries of the self, Septimus exemplifies the character who, liberated from the disgusting body, lives only in the mind.[94] Such is the indefiniteness of character, however, suffering does not die with Septimus. Hearing the news of this unknown man's demise, Clarissa Dalloway feels an affinity with him: "She felt somehow very like him—the young man who had killed himself."[95] Citing Woolf's stated intention to build the novel upon the division between sanity and insanity, Phyllis Rose has argued that Septimus's visions of beauty are mad distortions of Clarissa's ecstatic vision of life, but in that case the gulf separating sanity from insanity is not wide.[96] *Mrs. Dalloway* effectively dramatizes Freud's model of transference by showing that one personality may be receptive to currents transmitted by another: Clarissa's sympathy with the plight of the unknown Septimus exemplifies the theatrical exchange suggested to Freud by his study of hysteria. Clarissa's identification with Septimus is a kind of hysterical sympathy that overrides biological and social constructions of sex and gender. There are, to be sure, some unlikely correspondences between Clarissa and Septimus. Her memories of her childhood friendship with Sally Seton mirror his suppressed homoerotic feelings for his friend Evans, who died in the war. Both are disenfranchised members of postwar society, she too old to take full advantage of recent changes made for the benefit of women, he wrecked by shell shock.⁹⁷ In these ways, the roles of Clarissa and Septimus, like those of Orlando and the narrator, are interchangeable.⁹⁸

Having noted these structural resemblances, how might one account for the contrast between the tragic consequences of hysteria in *Mrs. Dalloway* and the irrepressibly comic vein of vacillation in *Orlando*? One answer is suggested by the sight that provokes Clarissa's imaginative identification with Septimus: the renowned doctor, Sir William Bradshaw. To Clarissa, the doctor symbolizes an oppressive male authority that makes life intolerable. In this sense Clarissa's voice corresponds with that of Woolf, whose presentation of Bradshaw's meeting with Septimus anticipates her later comparison of the Harley Street specialist with the judge at the Hall trial. In Woolf's eyes, both doctor and judge embodied a repugnant form of social power: "So they [Bradshaw and Mrs. Smith] returned to the most exalted of mankind; the criminal who faced his judges; the victim exposed on the heights; the fugitive; the drowned sailor; the poet of the immortal ode; the Lord who had gone from life to death; to Septimus Warren Smith, who sat in the arm-chair under the skylight staring at a photograph of Lady Bradshaw in Court dress, muttering messages about beauty" (*MD*, p. 97). In the light of this passage, Sir William's proposal to send Septimus to a lunatic asylum sounds like a parody of the scientific critic's diagnosis of the madness of artists. Clarissa's intuition that Sir William must drive people to suicide is quite accurate: Septimus leaps to his death shortly after hearing the plan for his confinement. The plight of hysterical Smith, the criminal who faced his judges, resembles that of Radclyffe Hall, the "depraved" novelist whose case was considered, like his, better left to scientific experts. Yet while *Mrs. Dalloway* records the gory effects of the oppression inflicted on individuals by medical and, by implication, other forms of patriarchal discourse in the postwar years, *Orlando* systematically undermines the viability of such discourse, deconstructing its assumption of a single, authoritative voice. Narrator and narrated become so interchangeable that neither can be said to authorize the other. As historian, the narrator is able neither to judge nor to define Orlando, except insofar as that character reflects the shadowy structure of the purportedly biographical narrative. Rather than framer and framed, the narrator and narrated of *Orlando* are more like doubles, mirror images of one form.

While *Orlando* provides comic relief from the horrors of hysteria explored in *Mrs. Dalloway*, it is still necessary to ask to what extent the later work offers the world of art as consolation for the suffering experienced in the real world. If we see the narrator and Orlando as mutually generating doubles, then we seem to have an image of a cocoonlike realm sealed off from the world outside the text. Woolf herself announced that in writing Orlando she felt "the need of an escapade" (*D3*, p. 131). At one point after her sex change, Orlando gives thanks for her freedom from the man's world: "'Better is it,' she thought, 'to be clothed with poverty and ignorance, which are the dark garments of the female sex; better to leave the rule and discipline of the world to others; better to be quit of martial ambition, the love of power, and all the other manly desires if so one can more fully enjoy the most exalted raptures known to the human spirit, which are,' she said aloud, as her habit was when deeply moved, 'contemplation, solitude, love'" (O, p. 160). Explicitly commenting on the disempowerment of women in a patriarchal society, Orlando projects herself (perhaps not without irony) onto a transcendental plane of contemplation, solitude, love. Here a social and historical prohibition on women propels Orlando into a spiritual mode of existence that soars above the sordid world of men. Counting the costs as well as the benefits, however, a manuscript draft of the same passage reveals a more acerbic sense of this strategy:

> Heaven be praised she said; [feeling in] thanking Heaven she did not prance down Pall Mall on a war horse, sentence to death or wear 72 different medals on her breast: surely our choice is better than theirs: poverty, insignificance, nakedness: [those are] the [invisible] garments which cover us with invisibility & allow us to escape from all the [ties of pomp] & circumstance; to pass lonely & free on clouds where we are unnoted; to hover there (they passed a valley) unregarded, [peeking] watching, observing, lost in contemplation; to [escape from the d] odious ceremonies & disciplines (here they came to slip from mankind (who are as busy with their ceremonies & disciplines; & thus enjoy the most exalted of all states of mind—where they, with their wealth [& their comfort], & their importance must still be playing at soldiers in Pall Mall. (OHD, p. 126)

Like another passage in the manuscript, which refers caustically to such writers as Arnold Bennett and Desmond MacCarthy as "masculinists," the draft is unequivocally critical when alluding to patriarchy (OHD, p. 169). The word "nakedness" exposes the impoverished, disenfranchised state of women, in stark contrast to the splendid attire men wear when displaying their social power. As Woolf later put it in Three Guineas (1938), dress "not only covers nakedness, gratifies vanity, and creates pleasure for the eye, but it serves to advertise the social, professional, or intellectual standing of the wearer."[99] Compared with the pomp and circumstance of men's public lives, women's lives are shrouded in invisibility. Orlando ponders the fringe benefits of this condition: it is possible "to pass lonely & free on clouds where we are unnoted," and to observe from an unimpeded critical distance the "odious ceremonies & disciplines" on which men seem to thrive. Paradoxically, then, the social prohibition under which all women labor may grant the female artist some latitude. Yet it is significant that Woolf hints at these advantages by using the image of the cloud. An ethereal, bodiless form, the cloud evokes memories of Septimus Smith, who drifts so far into the recesses of the mind that he disintegrates. More crucially, as an image of freedom the cloud is inherently unstable: like the words painted in the sky in Mrs. Dalloway, clouds can dissolve and become illegible. In this sense the invisible refuge offered by the clouds nicely describes the position of women in society: an illegible sign, a censored presence, or absence, in the script of the world.

Phyllis Rose justly observes that when Orlando becomes a woman and finds herself excluded from the male freedoms of the world, a "note of didacticism enters."[100] Yet the published version of the novel is not as didactic as it would have been had Woolf included manuscript passages such as those discussed above. What I want to ask is: Why did Woolf revise those more explicit polemical overtones out of the novel? Leonard Woolf has testified to her "almost pathological hypersensitiveness to criticism, so that she suffered an ever increasingly agonizing nervous apprehension as she got nearer and nearer to the end of her book and the throwing of it and of herself to the critics."[101] Virginia Woolf herself expressed this apprehension by admitting her fear of "being downed in public" by reviewers (*D2*, p. 208). Her more overtly polemical works were sometimes censured even by sympathetic readers like E. M. Forster. Woolf rightly suspected that Forster declined to review *A Room of One's Own* on account of its "shrill feminine tone," and she expected to be "attacked for a feminist & hinted at for a sapphist" by other critics (*D3*, p. 262). Implying that feminism was some sort of disease, Forster declared in his 1941 Rede Lecture: "There are spots of it all over her work." Though describing *A Room* as "charming and persuasive," Forster opined that "feminism is also responsible for the worst of her books—the cantankerous *Three Guineas*—and for the less successful streaks in *Orlando*."[102] Even the tailored version of *Orlando* was too polemical for some.

Yet contributing in the wake of the Hall trial to a *Nineteenth Century and After* series called "The Censorship of Books" (April 1929), which also included essays by Forster and Havelock Ellis, Woolf realized that excessive pandering to a projected audience may incur the same effects as official censorship. Arguing, like Forster, that censorship should apply only to "books which are sold as pornography to people who seek out and enjoy pornography," Woolf, tongue in cheek, exclaimed: "Moreover, if modern books become so insipid, so blameless, so full of blank spaces and evasions that we cannot read them, we shall be driven to read the classics, where obscenity abounds."[103] Implicitly, blank spaces and evasions may appear in literature when an author buckles under the pressure of social forces, which converge in the censorship of works deemed obscene. That is, a work may internalize an anticipated prohibition, substituting self-censorship for the censorship exercised by social institutions, and so render itself illegible. One might read the illegibility of the self-censored work as analogous to the invisibility of women in society and in history. Woolf hints at this comparison in *Three Guineas,* when she remarks that the only public forum open to women, the press, is subject to male editorial control: "although it is true that we can write articles or send letters to the Press, the control of the Press—the decision what to print, what not to print—is entirely in the hands of your sex" (*TG*, p. 12).

Orlando dramatizes the problem of blank spaces in several ways. As the note of suppressed randiness runs through its pages, Woolf is engaged in a struggle to suggest without stating, and yet avoid the danger of making the book so elusive, so obscure, that it becomes insipid, blameless, even illegible. Where *Orlando* succeeds in carrying out Woolf's intention to suggest sapphism, it does so by vacillating, by casting doubt, by intimating that it may be nothing but a joke, so that any obscenity may pass unnoted like the unobserved female observer. In this fashion, *Orlando* poses the question, What is lesbianism?, and undermines the assumptions governing the legal and sexological discourses of the *Well of Loneliness* trial, yet appears innocent as to the verdict.

Coda: *Between the Acts*

In August 1939 Woolf wrote in her diary: "I have been thinking about Censors. . . . All books now seem to me surrounded by a circle of invisible censors."[104] To the very end of her career, Woolf contemplated the relation of writing to censorship. In her last, unfinished novel, *Between the Acts* (1941), she reactivated questions that had been generated by *Orlando*. While *Orlando,* exploiting the gaps left by censorship, potentially undermines its social prohibition, *Between the Acts* demonstrates how those gaps may render a work totally illegible. Framed by the tale of Giles and Isa Oliver's failing marriage, the central action of Woolf's final work concerns the annual pageant put on by the local villagers in the garden of an English country house, Pointz Hall, in June 1939. This year's pageant presents typical literary scenes from the various stages of English history so as to expose the brutality found in them by the author, the implicitly lesbian Miss La Trobe, whom Sandra Gilbert has described as "an ironic version of the lost Shakespearean sister Woolf imagined in *A Room.*"[105] In effect, Miss La Trobe illuminates what she considers the suppressed subtext of literary history. As far as the audience is concerned, the restoration of these supposedly censored elements in turn censors what they regard as authentic history. As one departing spectator asks after the performance, "why leave out the Army, as my husband was saying, if it's history?"[106] Another wonders: "Did she mean, so to speak, something hidden, the unconscious as they call it? But why always drag in sex. . ." (*BA*, p. 199). At the end of the performance, the actors turn mirrors on the audience to reveal them as nothing but "orts, scraps, and fragments," yet the spectators find the play itself a series of virtually unintelligible bits and pieces (*BA*, p. 188). To the audience, Miss La Trobe's polemical intentions remain quite obscure. The Reverend G. W. Streatfield tries to rationalize the play in terms similar to those expressed in *Orlando* by declaring that the orts, scraps, and fragments of our many selves add up to one harmonious whole, but now this idea rings false, for, as Daniel Albright observes, Streatfield is merely a stock clerical fool.[107] In its formal and interpretative daring, Miss La Trobe's play signally fails to substitute its own illusion for received history. As its author comes to realize, the play reaches the audience as a series of blanks and evasions, an illegible text:

> She could say to the world, You have taken my gift! Glory possessed her—for one moment. But what had she given? A cloud that melted into the other clouds on the horizon. It was in the giving that the triumph was. And the triumph faded. Her gift meant nothing. If they had understood her meaning; if they had known their parts; if the pearls had been real and the funds illimitable—it would have been a better gift. Now it had gone to join the others.
> "A failure," she groaned, and stooped to put away the records. (*BA*, p. 209)

The airplanes zooming through the skies overhead as Woolf wrote *Between the Acts* will have emphasized the irony of this image of the cloud: while the gift of art fades into increasing illegibility, war has resumed its rightful place in the historical process. Miss La Trobe's failure restores her to the familiar role of the outcast: "Nature had somehow set her apart from her kind" (*BA*, p. 211). The fate of her play expresses the plight of its author; its illegibility mimics the social invisibility of the polemical lesbian artist.

The issues dramatized in Miss La Trobe's play highlight a larger crisis addressed in *Between the Acts*: a crisis in the representation of history, or in the relation of art to the real world. The problem exposed by the failure of the play is that any attempt to represent history involves some form of censorship. Even when one tries to include the notion of history-as-process, as Miss La Trobe does by turning mirrors on the audience, the product is still fragmented and partial. Yet while Miss La Trobe's play is afflicted by partiality, the more all-encompassing visions of other characters in this novel are so impartial as to be ultimately indistinguishable from complete blankness. In *Between the Acts*, history is always on the point of deteriorating into the amorphousness of prehistory: when the action closes, Mrs. Swithin is perusing the same chapter on prehistoric man that she was reading at the beginning of the novel. Indeed, in a world on the brink of another apocalyptic war, prehistory seems barely distinguishable from posthistory: "'That's what makes a view so sad,' said Mrs. Swithin. . . .'And so beautiful. It'll be there,' she nodded at the strip of gauze laid upon the distant fields, 'when we're not'" (*BA*, p. 53). And Isa Oliver imagines a world of such formal abstraction that it is static, expressionless, formless: "'Where do I wander?' she mused. 'Down what draughty tunnels? Where the eyeless wind blows? And there grows nothing for the eye. No rose. To issue where? In some harvestless dim field where no evening lets fall her mantle; nor sun rises. All's equal there. Unblowing, ungrowing are the roses there. Change is not; nor the mutable and lovable; nor greetings nor partings; nor furtive findings and feelings, where hand seeks hand and eye seeks shelter from the eye'" (*BA*, pp. 154–55). Inhospitable even to the human eye, the world in Isa's vision is utterly indecipherable; it dissolves into "the heart of silence," or into "the heart of darkness, in the fields of night" (*BA*, pp. 49, 219). In Septimus Smith's deluded terms, it is a world of hysterical blindness that exhibits the devastating consequences of complete openness and indefiniteness; to leap into the void like Septimus would seem to be the only remaining possibility for an already fragmented life form. The fate of Septimus Smith suggests that in the end fragments and blankness add up to much the same thing. For the literary artist, the illegibility of fragments and the blankness of silence signal to an equal degree the failure of the verbal medium, a censorship of expressive possibility, and so the unattainability of the fullness and wholeness to which an attempt to represent history aspires. In the theater of censorship, Woolf implies, the modern writer experiments with ways of articulating something always in the face of being able to say nothing.

Notes

Preface

1. Evelyn Waugh, *Vile Bodies* (Boston: Little, Brown, 1958), pp. 22–23, 25.
2. Sir William Joynson-Hicks, quoted in "Indecent Books," *The Times* (6 March 1929): 11.
3. Sir William Joynson-Hicks, *Do We Need a Censor?* (London: Faber and Faber, 1929), p. 7.
4. D. H. Lawrence, "Pornography and Obscenity," in *Phoenix: The Posthumous Papers of D. H. Lawrence,* ed. Edward D. McDonald (New York: Viking Press, 1936), p. 174.

Introduction

1. Lawrence managed to publish only one more work of fiction in Britain during the war, the story "Samson and Delilah" (1917), which appeared, as did a few poems and "The Reality of Peace," in the *English Review*. His poetry fared better than his fiction in this period: *Amores* was published in 1916, followed by *Look! We Have Come Through!* in 1917 and *New Poems* in 1918.
2. *Maurice* was published in 1971, and was followed in 1972 by the stories included in *The Life to Come* (New York: W. W. Norton, 1987).
3. See C. H. Rolph, ed., *The Trial of Lady Chatterley* (Harmondsworth, England: Penguin Books, 1961). For other discussions of censorship as repression see Morris L. Ernst and Alan U. Schwartz, *Censorship: The Search for the Obscene* (New York: Macmillan, 1964); Edward de Grazia, *Girls Lean Back Everywhere: The Law of Obscenity and the Assault on Genius* (New York: Random House, 1992); Natalie Robins, *Alien Ink: The FBI's War on Freedom of Expression* (New York: Morrow, 1992). Even David Saunders, who rejects the argument that the nineteenth-century obscenity law was intended to repress sexual expression, falls back on this model to describe censorship in the modern era; "Victorian Obscenity Law: Negative Censorship

or Positive Administration?," in *Writing and Censorship in Britain,* ed. Paul Hyland and Neil Sammells (New York: Routledge, 1992), p. 163.

4. Biron, quoted by Vera Brittain in *Radclyffe Hall: A Case of Obscenity?* (London: Femina Books, 1968), p. 91.

5. Mead, quoted in "The D. H. Lawrence Paintings," *The Daily Telegraph* (9 August 1929): 5.

6. David Saunders, "The Trial of *Lady Chatterley's Lover*: Limiting Cases and Literary Canons," *Southern Review* 15, 2 (July 1982): 162–63.

7. See, for example, Jeffrey Weeks, *Sex, Politics and Society: The Regulation of Sexuality since 1800* (London: Longman, 1989), p. 117.

8. Dominick LaCapra, *Madame Bovary on Trial* (Ithaca, N.Y.: Cornell University Press, 1982), pp. 7–8.

9. Hans Robert Jauss, *Toward an Aesthetic of Reception,* trans. Timothy Bahti (Minneapolis: University of Minnesota Press, 1982), pp. 27, 42.

10. Richard Dellamora makes this connection when examining Swinburne's response to "sapphism" in Baudelaire's poetry; *Masculine Desire: The Sexual Politics of Victorian Aestheticism* (Chapel Hill: University of North Carolina Press, 1990), p. 70. Ernst and Schwartz suggest that when he proposed the bill, Lord Campbell was thinking of Dumas the Younger's *La Dame aux Camélias,* the source for the opera *La Traviata,* which was running in London at the time; *Censorship,* p. 25. In any case, the tainted source was French, and that was what bothered the British authorities.

11. De Grazia, *Girls Lean Back Everywhere,* pp. 52, 45.

12. Jeffrey Meyers discusses this preoccupation with Salome, especially that of Moreau and Huysmans, in *Painting and the Novel* (Manchester: Manchester University Press, 1975), pp. 84–95. Meyers also notes that the doomed hero of Wilde's novel *The Picture of Dorian Gray* (1890) "religiously" turns the pages of *A Rebours* as if he were experiencing revelation. Attention was drawn to this passage in court in 1895, as I explain below.

13. Kerry Powell, *Oscar Wilde and the Theatre of the 1890s* (Cambridge: Cambridge University Press, 1990), pp. 36–40. Powell notes that Pigott admitted allowing the performance of plays that were "veiled in the decent obscurity of a foreign language," and that he testified to the usefulness of censorship before a House of Commons Select Committee, which decided on 2 June 1892 that censorship "has worked satisfactorily" and should be extended "as far as practicable to the performances in music halls."

14. Pigott, quoted by John Russell Stephens in *The Censorship of English Drama, 1824–1901* (Cambridge: Cambridge University Press, 1980), p. 112. Also see Richard Ellmann's account of the censorship of *Salome* in *Oscar Wilde* (New York: Alfred A. Knopf, 1988), pp. 372–73.

15. The tribulations of Saint-Saëns's opera indicate that British culture was not alone in its distaste for biblical drama. Similar prejudices in France prevented *Samson et Dalila* from appearing on the Parisian stage until 1890, though it was performed in German at Weimar as early as 1877. For the same reason, early performances in New York and Brussels, as well as in London, were given in concert form only. The prevalence of such feelings in late-seventeenth-century France had meant that Racine never saw *Athalie* represented as he intended. After clerical intervention, the first performance took place in a schoolroom in 1691 without décor or costumes.

16. Quoted from Pemberton Billing's verbatim report of the trial in *Vigilante* (13 April 1918): 3; cited by Samuel Hynes, *A War Imagined: The First World War and English Culture* (New York: Atheneum, 1991), p. 227. Also see Regenia Gagnier,

Idylls of the Marketplace: Oscar Wilde and the Victorian Public (Stanford, Calif.: Stanford University Press, 1986), pp. 153–54.

17. Hynes, *A War Imagined*, pp. 16–17.

18. A comparison with Walt Whitman may be appropriate here, for Whitman's name often appeared in Victorian writing as a sign for gay desire; see Dellamora, *Masculine Desire*, pp. 86–93, and Gagnier, *Idylls of the Marketplace*, pp. 157–58.

19. In fact, Queensberry's handwriting was so unclear that the court had to ask him to read the message aloud. Another possible reading is: "For Oscar Wilde Ponce and Somdomite." But it was easier for Queensberry's attorneys to prove that Wilde had "pos[ed] as a sodomite" than that he had committed particular acts.

20. H. Montgomery Hyde, *The Trials of Oscar Wilde* (New York: Dover Publications, 1973), p. 326; cited hereafter as *TOW*.

21. On 5 July 1890 an anonymous review in the *Scots Observer* described *Dorian Gray* as written "for none but outlawed noblemen and perverted telegraph-boys." The review clearly implied a connection with the Cleveland Street affair, which had begun in September 1889 when two men were imprisoned for procuring boys to "commit divers acts of gross indecency" with the male clients of a London brothel. The brothel's clients included aristocrats like Lord Arthur Somerset. But when the *North London Press* named the Earl of Euston as one of those clients, he sued the editor, Ernest Parke, for libel. Parke was found guilty and sentenced to a year in prison. The severity of the sentence was attributed by some commentators to Euston's noble birth; Parke had made a similar complaint about the treatment of Somerset, who had been allowed to escape to the Continent. For further discussion of this scandal see Ed Cohen, *Talk on the Wilde Side: Toward a Genealogy of a Discourse on Male Sexualities* (New York: Routledge, 1992), pp. 123–27, and H. Montgomery Hyde, *The Love That Dared Not Speak Its Name: A Candid History of Homosexuality in Britain* (Boston: Little, Brown, 1970), pp. 127–33. For the *Scots Observer* review of *Dorian Gray*, to which Wilde replied in the letter cited below, see *The Letters of Oscar Wilde*, ed. Rupert Hart-Davis (New York: Harcourt, Brace, and World, 1962), p. 265; cited hereafter as *LOW*.

22. Dellamora, *Masculine Desire*, p. 212.

23. In reply to Carson's questions about *A Rebours*, Wilde said: "Not well written, but it gave me an idea" (*TOW*, p. 114). Clarke protested against such questions at the time, and his objection was sustained by Judge Charles.

24. Clarke was again reinforced on this point by the judge, who in summing up told the jury that Wilde's authorship of *Dorian Gray* was irrelevant to the present case, even though the novel was not as "wholesome" as the works of Sir Walter Scott and Charles Dickens (*TOW*, p. 215).

25. See Cohen, *Talk on the Wilde Side*, especially pp. 143–46.

26. André Gide, *Oscar Wilde: In Memoriam (Reminiscences)*, trans. Bernard Frechtman (New York: Philosophical Library, 1949), p. x.

27. Wilde, of course, did not miss the irony. When, as the third trial was about to begin, his friend Robert Sherard remarked, "you have got your name before the public at last," he replied laughingly, "Yes. Nobody can pretend now not to have heard of it" (*TOW*, p. 233).

28. Describing performances of *Earnest* in the context of late Victorian consumerism, Gagnier writes: "the theater as collective and spectacular artifact, including both the stage and the opulently accoutred audience, reflects the conspicuous consumption that is the world of the play." Thus, she suggests, Wilde "sent an audience in pursuit of its own manufactured image"; *Idylls of the Marketplace*, pp. 8, 134.

29. W. H. Auden, *Forewords and Afterwords*, selected by Edward Mendelson

(New York: Random House, 1973), p. 323. The homoerotic significance of Bunburying has also been pursued by Christopher Craft in "Alias Bunbury: Desire and Termination in *The Importance of Being Earnest*," *Representations* 31 (Summer 1990): 19–46.

30. William Green has argued that "Wilde had ample opportunity to avoid using it [Bunburying] in the play if he suspected it had any homosexual connotations which might have drawn attention to him. . . . Wilde could have substituted another name for Bunbury"; "Oscar Wilde and the Bunburys," *Modern Drama* 21, 1 (1978): 70. While Green seems too ready to shy away from the homosexual connotations of Bunburying, Joel Fineman has perhaps overstated the opposite view by claiming that it "was not only British slang for a male brothel, but is also a collection of signifiers that straightforwardly express their desire to bury in the bun"; "The Significance of Literature: *The Importance of Being Earnest*," in *Critical Essays on Oscar Wilde*, ed. Regenia Gagnier (New York: G. K. Hall, 1991), p. 113. Surely nothing is quite straightforward in *Earnest*. Kerry Powell has traced Bunbury, the imaginary invalid, and the imaginary brother Ernest to an unpublished farce called *Godpapa*, which played at the Court Theatre in London in 1891–1892. "Bunburying," Powell concludes, "if not the name itself, is highly characteristic of late-century farce. Characters form imaginary identities or engage in fictitious activities which enable them to invigorate their respectable but humdrum lives." In farces emphasizing the "sheer illicit fun of the secret life," Bunburying often "amounts to little more than a husband's philandering"; Powell, *Oscar Wilde and the Theatre of the 1890s*, pp. 124–28.

31. Oscar Wilde, *The Complete Works of Oscar Wilde* (New York: Harper and Row, 1989), p. 896; cited hereafter as *CW*.

32. Michel Foucault, *The History of Sexuality*, vol. 1: *An Introduction*, trans. Robert Hurley (1978; New York: Vintage Books, 1990), p. 43.

33. Cohen analyzes this and other conceptual shifts marked by the Labouchere Amendment in *Talk on the Wilde Side*, chapter 4.

34. Foucault makes this point in his discussion of the ancient Greek "aesthetics of existence"; *The History of Sexuality*, vol. 2: *The Use of Pleasure*, trans. Robert Hurley (New York: Pantheon Books, 1985), pp. 89–93. I use Foucault's term below to suggest a connection between Wilde and Greek homoeroticism. Foucault's argument that the Greeks were concerned not with the object of sexual choice but with the proper regulation of one's pleasures is suggestive for a reading of *De Profundis*, in which Wilde indicts himself not for taking his pleasures among his own sex, but for failing to exert due self-control; see *The Use of Pleasure*, pp. 85, 187–88. Wilde's use of the Platonic dialogue in "The Decay of Lying" and "The Critic as Artist" provides further intimations of his Greek heritage.

35. Oscar Wilde, *The Letters of Oscar Wilde*, ed. Rupert Hart-Davis (New York: Harcourt, Brace, and World, 1962), p. 402.

36. Cesare Lombroso, *The Man of Genius* (New York: Garland, 1984), p. 170.

37. Unlike Nordau, Lombroso urged a compassionate attitude toward "insane" artists. Nature, he wrote, seems to have "intended to teach us respect for the supreme misfortunes of insanity"; ibid., p. 361.

38. Max Nordau, *Degeneration* (New York: D. Appleton, 1895), p. 317. The theatricality of hysteria was deliberately exploited by Jean-Marie Charcot, who literally put his patients on show. For a general discussion of "hysterical" theatricality see Elaine Showalter, *The Female Malady: Women, Madness, and English Culture, 1830–1980* (New York: Pantheon Books, 1985), pp. 150–55.

39. Nordau, *Degeneration*, p. 25.

40. Havelock Ellis, *Sexual Inversion* (1897); reprinted in *Studies in the Psychology of Sex,* vol. 1 (New York: Random House, 1942), p. 296. Ellis's book was suppressed after the trial of a London bookseller, George Bedborough, in 1898. Ellis recorded his views on the case in *A Note on the Bedborough Trial* (London: The University Press, 1898).

41. Wilde's talking, in other words, was not a cure but a symptom.

42. Craft, "Alias Bunbury," p. 35.

43. Craft shows that Wilde was familiar with the terminology of "Urning"; ibid., pp. 38–39, 45–46. Nicholson's poem "Of Boys' Names" is quoted by Timothy d'Arch Smith in *Love in Earnest: Some Notes on the Lives and Writings of English "Uranian" Poets from 1889 to 1930* (London: Routledge and Kegan Paul, 1970), p. xviii. Smith takes his title, of course, from Nicholson's.

44. See W. B. Yeats, *The Autobiography of William Butler Yeats* (New York: Collier Books, 1965), p. 87.

45. See Lionel Trilling, *Sincerity and Authenticity* (New York: Harcourt Brace Jovanovich, 1972), especially pp. 103–4, and Joseph Conrad, *Heart of Darkness* (New York: Penguin Books, 1973), pp. 40–52. What Marlow finds "incomprehensible" is the sight of a man-of-war shelling the bush to no apparent effect. And noticing how little effect blasting has on the cliffs, he observes: "this objectless blasting was all the work going on." Marlow himself wastes no time before fighting the good fight: "I went to work the next day, turning, so to speak, my back on that station. In that way only it seemed to me I could keep my hold on the redeeming facts of life. Still, one must look about sometimes; and then I saw this station, these men strolling aimlessly about in the sunshine of the yard. I asked myself sometimes what it all meant." Committed to work, and interpreting the world as a cipher, Marlow is the archetypal nineteenth-century British Protestant. Correspondingly, his concern with the waste of colonial resources perhaps reflects 1890s British anxieties about a decline of trade, industry, and national power that seemed to indicate the waning influence of the work ethic itself.

46. Wilde's epigram is quoted by Hesketh Pearson in *Oscar Wilde: His Life and Wit* (New York: Harper and Brothers, 1946), p. 170.

47. Arguing along similar lines, Richard Dellamora writes that because Wilde's dandyism upset the "balance between the dual imperatives of leisure and work incumbent upon Victorian gentlemen," it was regarded as a "smear on aristocratic manliness"; *Masculine Desire,* pp. 199, 202.

48. Theodor Adorno, *Aesthetic Theory,* trans. C. Lenhardt, ed. Gretel Adorno and Rolf Tiedemann (London: Routledge and Kegan Paul, 1984), p. 17.

49. Hans-Georg Gadamer, *Truth and Method,* trans. revised by Joel Weinsheimer and Donald G. Marshall (New York: Crossroad, 1989), pp. 103, 144.

50. David Marshall, *The Figure of Theater: Shaftesbury, Defoe, Adam Smith and George Eliot* (New York: Columbia University Press, 1986), and *The Surprising Effects of Sympathy: Marivaux, Diderot, Rousseau and Mary Shelley* (Chicago: University of Chicago Press, 1988).

51. Joseph Litvak, *Caught in the Act: Theatricality in the Nineteenth-Century English Novel* (Berkeley: University of California Press, 1992), p. xii.

52. Judith Butler, "Performative Acts and Gender Constitution: An Essay in Phenomenology and Feminist Theory," in *Performing Feminisms: Feminist Critical Theory and Theatre,* ed. Sue-Ellen Case (Baltimore: Johns Hopkins University Press, 1990), pp. 270–71. Butler elaborates on these issues in *Gender Trouble: Feminism and the Subversion of Identity* (New York: Routledge, 1990), especially pp. 134–41.

53. Butler, "Performative Acts and Gender Constitution," p. 277.

54. Alex Zwerdling, *Virginia Woolf and the Real World* (Berkeley: University of California Press, 1986), p. 33.

Chapter 1

1. Unless otherwise indicated, all references to the trial are cited from the report in *The Daily Telegraph* (15 November 1915): 12; reprinted in Emile Delavenay, *D. H. Lawrence: L'Homme et la genèse de son œuvre. Les années de formation: 1885–1919. Documents* (Paris: Librairie C. Klincksieck, 1969), pp. 662–63.

2. Mark Kinkead-Weekes, Introduction, *The Rainbow* (Cambridge: Cambridge University Press, 1989), p. xxx; cited hereafter as *R*. Observing Lawrence's remarkably calm acceptance of this news, Kinkead-Weekes presents evidence that Methuen may have returned *The Rainbow* on the assumption that the recent outbreak of the Great War would hamper sales of all books, and that by giving the court the impression that obscenity had been the issue, he may have been trying merely to avoid harsh punishment. As my analysis will show, however, obscenity was clearly a pressing issue throughout the process of the novel's publication.

3. D. H. Lawrence, *The Letters of D. H. Lawrence*, vol. 2, ed. George J. Zytaruk and James T. Boulton (Cambridge: Cambridge University Press, 1981), pp. 369–70; cited hereafter as *L2*.

4. D. H. Lawrence, *The Letters of D. H. Lawrence*, vol. 1, ed. James T. Boulton (Cambridge: Cambridge University Press, 1979), p. 544; cited hereafter as *L1*.

5. D. H. Lawrence, *Study of Thomas Hardy and Other Essays,* ed. Bruce Steele (Cambridge: Cambridge University Press, 1985), p. 14; cited hereafter as *STH.*

6. H. D. [*sic*] Lawrence, "With the Guns," *Manchester Guardian* (18 August 1914); reprinted in Carl Baron, "Two Hitherto Unknown Pieces by D. H. Lawrence," *Encounter* 33, 2 (August 1969): 5–6.

7. D. H. Lawrence, "Him with His Tail in His Mouth," in *Reflections on the Death of a Porcupine and Other Essays,* ed. Michael Herbert (Cambridge: Cambridge University Press, 1988), p. 311; cited hereafter as *RDP.*

8. D. H. Lawrence, *The Letters of D. H. Lawrence*, vol. 3, ed. James T. Boulton and Andrew Robertson (Cambridge: Cambridge University Press, 1984), pp. 142–43; cited hereafter as *L3.*

9. D. H. Lawrence, *Twilight in Italy* (New York: Viking Press, 1958), p. 74; cited hereafter as *TI.*

10. Kingsley Widmer, *Defiant Desire: Some Dialectical Legacies of D. H. Lawrence* (Carbondale: Southern Illinois University Press, 1992), p. 136.

11. Unless otherwise indicated, I refer to the 1915 version of this work rather than to the 1925 text.

12. See Charles L. Ross, *The Composition of* The Rainbow *and* Women in Love: *A History* (Charlottesville: University Press of Virginia, 1979), pp. 45–46.

13. George P. Landow, *Images of Crisis: Literary Iconology, 1750 to the Present* (Boston: Routledge and Kegan Paul, 1982), p. 158. Also see Landow, "The Rainbow: A Problematic Image," in *Nature and the Victorian Imagination,* ed. U. C. Knoepflmacher and G. B. Tennyson (Berkeley: University of California Press, 1977), pp. 341–69; and Virginia Hyde's stimulating chapter on *The Rainbow* in *The Risen Adam: D. H. Lawrence's Revisionist Typology* (University Park: Pennsylvania State University Press, 1992), pp. 73–99.

14. Robert Lynd, in *D. H. Lawrence: The Critical Heritage,* ed. R. P. Draper (New York: Barnes and Noble, 1970), p. 92; cited hereafter as *LCH.*

15. See Frank Fowell and Frank Palmer, *Censorship in England* (1913; repr. New York: Benjamin Blom, 1969), p. 374. As is made clear by other information presented by these authors, the petition did not necessarily indicate a massive shift of public opinion on the issue. A similarly lengthy array of signatures was attached to a counter-petition expressing "confidence in the censorship as exercised under the Lord Chamberlain's supervision"; ibid., p. 378. This letter, designed as a preemptive strike, was published in daily newspapers earlier in the same year, though it did not reach the Home Secretary.

16. Following the suppression of *The Cenci,* Shaw became an ardent opponent of censorship; the preface to *The Shewing-up of Blanco Posnet* is perhaps the most notable of the many pieces he wrote about this issue. *Mrs. Warren's Profession,* written in 1893, was not publicly produced in Britain until 1925 (though it had been given two private performances in 1902); its American premier in 1905 led to prosecution in the courts.

17. See Jeffrey Meyers, *D. H. Lawrence: A Biography* (New York: Alfred A. Knopf, 1990), p. 189. Dickinson's bitterness on this score reemerged in 1918 when he sentenced Bertrand Russell to six months in Brixton jail for advocating British acceptance of Germany's peace offer.

18. See Harry T. Moore, *The Intelligent Heart: The Life of D. H. Lawrence* (New York: Grove Press, 1962), p. 258.

19. The phrase, "wave of diseased degeneracy," is from W. R. Colton, "The Effects of War on Art," *The Architect* 45 (17 March 1916): 200; cited by Samuel Hynes, *A War Imagined: The First World War and English Culture* (New York: Atheneum, 1991), p. 58. Pursuing the idea of the Great War as a war of cultures, Modris Eksteins has argued that Germany fought in search of spiritual liberation from the old order embodied by British culture. Eksteins contends that as the "foremost representative of innovation and renewal," Germany sought deliverance from the "vulgarity, constraint, and convention" of a fin-de-siècle world that persisted most powerfully in Britain; *Rites of Spring: The Great War and the Birth of the Modern Age* (Boston: Houghton Mifflin, 1989), pp. xv, 92.

20. Jean Finot, "La Solidarité Franco-Anglo-Italienne: Essai de réalisation d'un programme intellectuel de demain," *The Athenæum* (27 November 1915): 388.

21. Marian Cox, "Music and War-Kultur," *English Review* 21 (October 1915): 309–10.

22. D. H. Lawrence, "England, My England," *English Review* 21 (October 1915): 245.

23. There are a number of crucial differences between the 1915 and 1921 versions, the most obvious being the hero's change of name to Egbert. The attention given to the war was significantly reduced in the later text as well. The revised version was the title story in a collection published in 1922 by Martin Secker.

24. G. W. de Tunzelmann, in *Critics on D. H. Lawrence: Readings in Literary Criticism,* ed. W. T. Andrews (Coral Gables, Fla.: University of Miami Press, 1971), p. 18.

25. Moore points out that de Tunzelmann, whose real name was Georg Wilhelm von Tunzelmann, "was perhaps reacting against his own Germanic background"; *The Intelligent Heart,* p. 259. De Tunzelmann was not alone in this maneuver, as the example of Ford Madox Hueffer reveals. Hueffer not only changed his name to Ford but abandoned his prewar "social agnosticism" to attack German culture in *When Blood Is Their Argument* (London: Hodder and Stoughton, 1915). Ford's book in turn spurred on Ezra Pound in "Provincialism the Enemy" (1917, in Ezra Pound, *Selected Prose*

1909–1965, ed. William Cookson [London: Faber and Faber, 1973], pp. 159–73), an indictment of the German philological methods that, Pound argued, helped to cause the war; see James Longenbach, *Modernist Poetics of History: Pound, Eliot, and the Sense of the Past* (Princeton, N.J.: Princeton University Press, 1987), pp. 99–103.

26. Max Nordau, *Degeneration* (New York: D. Appleton, 1895), p. vii. Intriguingly, Nordau's arguments were anticipated by another victim of insanity, Friedrich Nietzsche, in *The Case of Wagner* (1888, in *The Birth of Tragedy and The Case of Wagner,* trans. Walter Kaufmann [New York: Vintage Books, 1967]).

27. In his excellent discussion of Nordau's "symptomatic" reading, Allon White observes that whereas Freud only gradually gained currency in prewar Britain, Lombroso won immediate popularity in the 1890s, and that this trend persisted during the first decade of the twentieth century. It should also be noted that, as White acknowledges, the term "symptomatic" reading is taken from Louis Althusser. See White, *The Uses of Obscurity* (London: Routledge and Kegan Paul, 1981), pp. 49, 4.

28. *The Signature* was a short-lived antiwar pamphlet organized in the autumn of 1915 by John Middleton Murry. "The helpless little brown magazine," as Lawrence called it in his 1925 "Note to 'The Crown,'" survived only for three issues (*RDP,* p. 249).

29. See John Carter, "The *Rainbow* Prosecution," *Times Literary Supplement* (27 February 1969): 216.

30. See Emile Delavenay, *D. H. Lawrence: The Man and His Work. The Formative Years: 1885–1919,* trans. Katharine M. Delavenay (London: Heinemann, 1972), p. 234. Kinkead-Weekes notes that in fact Methuen removed the novel from his advertisement as early as 28 October (*R,* p. l).

31. Sir John Simon, quoted in Edward Nehls, *D. H. Lawrence: A Composite Biography,* vol. 1 (Madison: University of Wisconsin Press, 1957), pp. 334–35.

32. See Delavenay, *D. H. Lawrence,* p. 241; Paul Delany, *D. H. Lawrence's Nightmare: The Writer and His Circle in the Years of the Great War* (New York: Basic Books, 1978), p. 158. Another critic sharing Delavenay's view is Alistair Davies; see "Contexts of Reading: The Reception of D. H. Lawrence's *The Rainbow* and *Women in Love,*" in *The Theory of Reading,* ed. Frank Gloversmith (Totowa, N.J.: Barnes and Noble, 1984), pp. 215–16.

33. D. H. Lawrence, *The Letters of D. H. Lawrence,* vol. 5, ed. James T. Boulton and Lindeth Vasey (Cambridge: Cambridge University Press, 1989), p. 611.

34. Diane Bonds, *Language and the Self in D. H. Lawrence* (Ann Arbor: University of Michigan Research Press, 1987), pp. 23–24.

35. As a reader for Duckworth's press, Garnett rejected Joyce's *A Portrait of the Artist as a Young Man* (1916) on similar grounds, dismissing it as too unconventional. Garnett's report provoked a violent response from Ezra Pound; see *Pound/Joyce: The Letters of Ezra Pound to James Joyce, with Pound's Essays on Joyce,* ed. Forrest Read (New York: New Directions, 1967), pp. 65–66.

36. Ross, *The Composition of* The Rainbow *and* Women in Love, p. 8.

37. Bruce Steele has shown, moreover, that the chapters are a set of drafts, not necessarily arranged in the order Lawrence would have wanted for publication (*STH,* pp. xxxiii-xxxiv).

38. In another passage dealing with this theme, Lawrence wrote: "the two must be forever reconciled, even if they must exist on occasions apart one from the other" (*STH,* p. 87). As Michael Black observes, the last phrase is a "lawyer-like provision for a realistic alternative"; *D. H. Lawrence: The Early Philosophical Works* (Cambridge: Cambridge University Press, 1992), p. 205.

39. My account of these works emphasizes points of likeness in their arguments, but it is important to note developments in Lawrence's dualism. As Michael Black observes, it is unclear in "Hardy" whether the desired reconciliation would be a synthetic state, combining Father and Son, or a successive one. Black argues that the movement traced in "Hardy," Father to Son to Holy Ghost, is a "temporal or evolutionary" sequence, whereas "The Crown" describes the third term as "perpetually hovering above," and thus defining, the eternal opposition between Father and Son. One might put it another way by noting that Lawrence came to see the third state as obliterating distinctions between synthetic and sequential states. See Black, *D. H. Lawrence*, pp. 223, 464.

40. D. H. Lawrence, *Kangaroo* (New York: Penguin Books, 1950), p. 240; cited hereafter as *K*. For further discussion of the "Nightmare" chapter, see Neil Myers, "Lawrence and the War," *Criticism* 4, 1 (1962): 44–58.

41. Delany, *D. H. Lawrence's Nightmare*, p. 376.

42. Edward Garnett, *The Trial of Jeanne D'Arc and Other Plays* (London: Jonathan Cape, 1931), p. 16.

43. Eve Kosofsky Sedgwick, *Between Men: English Literature and Male Homosocial Desire* (New York: Columbia University Press, 1985), especially pp. 3–17.

44. D. H. Lawrence, "Italian Studies: By the Lago di Garda," *English Review* 15 (September 1913): 226.

45. Simone de Beauvoir, *The Second Sex*, trans. H. M. Parshley (New York: Vintage Books, 1974), pp. 242–52; Kate Millett, *Sexual Politics* (New York: Ballantine Books, 1978), pp. 333–411. Some critics have seen Lawrence as sympathetic to feminism before the war but antagonistic afterward; see Hilary Simpson, *D. H. Lawrence and Feminism* (London: Croom Helm, 1982), especially pp. 64–78; and Cornelia Nixon, *Lawrence's Leadership Politics and the Turn Against Women* (Berkeley: University of California Press, 1986). In her study of Lawrence's so-called leadership phase, Judith Ruderman regards his "power doctrine" as incipient in *The Rainbow*; see *D. H. Lawrence and the Devouring Mother: The Search for a Patriarchal Ideal of Leadership* (Durham, N.C.: Duke University Press, 1984), p. 78. For other attacks on this front see John Middleton Murry, *Son of Woman: The Story of D. H. Lawrence* (London: Jonathan Cape, 1931), especially p. 118; Carolyn Heilbrun, *Toward a Recognition of Androgyny* (New York: Alfred A. Knopf, 1973), pp. 101–2; Faith Pullin, "Lawrence's Treatment of Women in *Sons and Lovers*," in *Lawrence and Women*, ed. Anne Smith (London: Vision Press, 1977), pp. 49–74. For defenses of Lawrence see Anaïs Nin, *D. H. Lawrence: An Unprofessional Study* (London: Black Spring Press, 1985); Norman Mailer, *The Prisoner of Sex* (Boston: Little, Brown, 1971), especially pp. 126–60; Peter Balbert, *D. H. Lawrence and the Phallic Imagination: Essays on Sexual Identity* (New York: St. Martin's Press, 1989), especially pp. 1–14; essays in *Lawrence and Women* by Lydia Blanchard, Harry T. Moore, and Mark Spilka.

46. Sandra M. Gilbert and Susan Gubar, *No Man's Land*, vol. 1: *The War of the Words* (New Haven, Conn.: Yale University Press, 1988), p. 30. Instructive in this regard is Gilbert and Gubar's reading of Lawrence's antiwar poem, "Eloi, Eloi, Lama Sabachthani?" (1915), which they oversimplify by identifying the sexist voice of the speaker with the author; see *No Man's Land*, vol. 2: *Sexchanges* (New Haven, Conn.: Yale University Press, 1989), p. 261. A number of readers have raised similar objections to Millett's reading of Lawence's fiction, notably Lydia Blanchard in "Love and Power: A Reconsideration of Sexual Politics in D. H. Lawrence," *Modern Fiction Studies* 21, 3 (Autumn 1975): 431–43. Also see Janet Barron, "Equality Puzzle: Lawrence and Feminism," in *Rethinking Lawrence*, ed. Keith Brown (Milton Keynes, England: Open University Press, 1990), pp. 12–22.

47. Susan Kingsley Kent, *Sex and Suffrage in Britain, 1860–1914* (Princeton, N.J.: Princeton University Press, 1987), especially chapter 6.

48. Ibid., p. 227.

49. Swanwick was a member of the National Union of Women's Suffrage Societies and editor of its official newspaper, *Common Cause,* from 1909 to 1912, but she left the organization because her arguments for women's sexual autonomy were "too advanced" for the rest of the Executive Board; ibid., p. 20.

50. D. H. Lawrence, "Why the Novel Matters," in *Phoenix: The Posthumous Papers of D. H. Lawrence,* ed. Edward D. McDonald (New York: Viking Press, 1936), p. 535; George H. Ford, *Double Measure: A Study of the Novels and Stories of D. H. Lawrence* (New York: Holt, Rinehart, and Winston, 1965), p. 134. Following Ford's reading of *The Rainbow* as a journey out of Eden toward the Promised Land, the "biblical" aspects of this novel have become familiar critical terrain. In particular, see Frank Kermode, "Lawrence and the Apocalyptic Types," *Critical Quarterly* 10 (1968): 14–38; and Virginia Hyde, *The Risen Adam,* pp. 73–99. Both Kermode and Hyde study Lawrence's use of biblical typology and its relation to the structure of history. Also see Michael Bell, *D. H. Lawrence: Language and Being* (Cambridge: Cambridge University Press, 1992), pp. 76–78.

51. P. T. Whelan, *D. H. Lawrence: Myth and Metaphysic in* The Rainbow *and* Women in Love (Ann Arbor: University of Michigan Research Press, 1988), p. 37.

52. Judith Butler, *Gender Trouble: Feminism and the Subversion of Identity* (New York: Routledge, 1990), pp. 139, 33.

53. Ibid., p. 136.

54. Heilbrun sees this kind of spiritual "ceremony of birth" as "characteristic of the modern novel in the years before the Second World War"; *Toward a Recognition of Androgyny,* p. 103.

55. As my commentary implies, Tom and Lydia stop short of complete self-fulfillment; they create possibilities explored by the next generation. For further discussion of this point see Mark Spilka, *The Love Ethic of D. H. Lawrence* (Bloomington: Indiana University Press, 1955), p. 97; and Mark Kinkead-Weekes, "The Marriage of Opposites in *The Rainbow,*" in *D. H. Lawrence: Centenary Essays,* ed. Mara Kalnins (Bristol: Bristol Classical Press, 1986), p. 27.

56. Kermode calls Tom Brangwen a "distorted antitype of Noah"; "Lawrence and the Apocalyptic Types," p. 21.

57. Paul Rosenzweig, "A Defense of the Second Half of *The Rainbow*: Its Structure and Characterization," *D. H. Lawrence Review* 13, 2 (1980): 155. Rosenzweig observes that the "implicit comparison with the Biblical flood is thus partially ironic." Also see Kinkead-Weekes, "The Marriage of Opposites," p. 27.

58. For a reading of Will as inhabiting the pre-Renaissance epoch of Law, see Whelan, *D. H. Lawrence,* pp. 123–25.

59. George Ford describes Anna's bedroom dance as "a modern Magnificat"; *Double Measure,* p. 131. Also see Whelan, who argues that the dance is "a denial of paternity," and that Anna's "pregnancy is a matter between her and the 'Unknown,' a miraculous event like the conception of Jesus." Whelan, moreover, likens Anna to the Bacchantes, who tore Pentheus (Will) to shreds for illicitly witnessing their rites; *D. H. Lawrence,* pp. 31–32.

60. Nixon, *Lawrence's Leadership Politics,* p. 56.

61. Meyers, *D. H. Lawrence,* p. 186. Also see G. Wilson Knight, "Lawrence, Joyce and Powys," *Essays in Criticism* 11, 4 (1961): 403–41.

62. See Spilka, *The Love Ethic of D. H. Lawrence,* pp. 105–6.

63. When Lawrence died in 1930, a British official drew attention to Secker's 1926 edition of *The Rainbow,* which was officially still banned. The authorities dropped the matter, rather than risk creating sympathy for the deceased author. See Home Office Papers, HO45/13944 (10, 25 March 1930), Public Record Office, Kew.

64. Paul Fussell, *The Great War and Modern Memory* (New York: Oxford University Press), p. 299. Fussell also notes that in "the tradition of Victorian homosexuality and homoeroticism . . . soldiers are especially attractive"; ibid., p. 278. For further discussion of bathing scenes see Timothy d'Arch Smith, *Love in Earnest: Some Notes on the Lives and Writings of English "Uranian" Poets from 1889 to 1930* (London: Routledge and Kegan Paul, 1970), pp. 169–72.

65. D. H. Lawrence, *The White Peacock,* ed. Andrew Robertson (Cambridge: Cambridge University Press, 1983), pp. 223, 222.

66. This line, restored in the Cambridge edition, was omitted from previous editions of *The Rainbow,* including the text published in 1915.

67. Samuel Hynes notes that in postwar Britain, national councils tried to gather evidence about divorce rates, as well as about illegitimate births and sexually transmitted diseases, in the hope of tackling these growing problems; *A War Imagined,* p. 371.

68. Sutherland, quoted in *Birth Control and Libel: The Trial of Marie Stopes,* ed. Muriel Box (South Brunswick, N.Y.: A. S. Barnes, 1968), p. 27.

69. Meyers, *D. H. Lawrence,* p. 185.

70. Earl Ingersoll further complicates our view of Winifred by linking her with the self-assertive heroine of Henrik Ibsen's play *Lady Inger of Östrat*; "*The Rainbow*'s Winifred Inger," *D. H. Lawrence Review* 17, 1 (Spring 1984): 67–69.

71. Cynthia Lewiecki-Wilson, *Writing Against the Family: Gender in Lawrence and Joyce* (Carbondale: Southern Illinois University Press, 1994), p. 101.

72. See Carolyn Heilbrun, *Toward a Recognition of Androgyny,* pp. 109–10; Lydia Blanchard, "Mothers and Daughters in D. H. Lawrence: *The Rainbow* and Selected Shorter Works," in *Lawrence and Women,* pp. 76–90; Janice Harris, "Lawrence and the Edwardian Feminists," in *The Challenge of D. H. Lawrence,* ed. Michael Squires and Keith Cushman (Madison: University of Wisconsin Press, 1990), pp. 66–75; Lewiecki-Wilson, *Writing Against the Family,* p. 102.

73. See, for example, Whelan, *D. H. Lawrence,* pp. 128–29, and Spilka, *The Love Ethic of D. H. Lawrence,* pp. 113–14.

74. Lawrence uses similar terms to describe the unsatisfied soul in "Hardy": "Give us a religion, give us something to believe in, cries the unsatisfied soul embedded in the womb of our times. Speak the quickening word, it cries, that it will deliver us into our own being" (*STH,* p. 44). Skrebensky's problem is that, embedded in the womb of his times, he cannot acknowledge the primeval "Law of the Womb." Also see "The Crown" (*RDP,* p. 255).

75. See, for example, Kinkead-Weekes, "The Marriage of Opposites," pp. 29–30, and Nigel Kelsey, *D. H. Lawrence: Sexual Crisis* (New York: St. Martin's Press, 1991), pp. 127–28.

76. F. R. Leavis, *D. H. Lawrence: Novelist* (New York: Simon and Schuster, 1969), p. 140. Also see H. M. Daleski, *The Forked Flame: A Study of D. H. Lawrence* (Madison: University of Wisconsin Press, 1987), pp. 107–9.

77. These dates have been established by Mark Kinkead-Weekes in "The Marble and the Statue: The Exploratory Imagination of D. H. Lawrence," in *Imagined Worlds: Essays in Honor of John Butt,* ed. Ian Gregor and Maynard Mack (London: Methuen, 1968), p. 415. Charles Ross agrees, and notes a new tone of apprehension in a letter of

2 March, the day on which Lawrence completed the original manuscript of the novel; *Composition,* pp. 32–35.

78. Julian Moynahan makes a similar point about another passage in the novel, which, as he notes, anticipates the treatment of Clifford Chatterley in *Lady Chatterley's Lover; The Deed of Life: The Novels and Tales of D. H. Lawrence* (Princeton, N.J.: Princeton University Press, 1963), pp. 61–62.

79. Some readers have claimed that the ending of the novel is an assertion of optimism unjustified by the earlier treatment of Ursula. Kinkead-Weekes, however, neatly sums up the case for the defense by observing that the rainbow in the Bible "was gratuitous too, and the promise is no more unconditional here than there"; "The Marriage of Opposites," p. 38. Also see Rosenzweig, "A Defense of the Second Half of *The Rainbow,*" pp. 150–60; Ronald Schleifer, "Lawrence's Rhetoric of Vision: The Ending of *The Rainbow,*" *D. H. Lawrence Review* 13, 2 (1980): 161–78; Ann McLaughlin, "The Clenched and Knotted Horses in *The Rainbow,*" *D. H. Lawrence Review* 13, 2 (1980): 179–86.

80. Balbert, *D. H. Lawrence and the Phallic Imagination,* pp. 77–80. Whelan, too, argues that the two novels belong to the same metaphysical universe, and he cites Lawrence's 1920 letter to Martin Secker: "*The Rainbow* and *Women in Love* are really an organic artistic whole, I cannot but think it would be well to issue them as *Women in Love,* Vol I and Vol II" (*L3,* p. 459). But, as Whelan concedes, we should not necessarily take Lawrence at his word here; *D. H. Lawrence,* pp. 175–76. Even if we were to do so, it is quite possible that Lawrence thought differently in 1915.

81. Several readers have criticized Lawrence for making Ursula more "traditional" in *Women in Love,* which is a sign, according to Cornelia Nixon, of his "turn against women"; see *Lawrence's Leadership Politics,* p. 22. In his defense of Lawrence, Balbert essentially sees the same development in Ursula's character. Michael Levenson argues perceptively that such readings are produced by a "*trompe l'œil* effect created by her energetic recoiling from the false revolutionaries around her"; *Modernism and the Fate of Individuality: Character and Novelistic Form from Conrad to Woolf* (Cambridge: Cambridge University Press, 1991), p. 154.

Chapter 2

1. Ezra Pound, *Literary Essays of Ezra Pound,* ed. T. S. Eliot (New York: New Directions, 1968), p. 416.

2. Margaret Anderson, "Judicial Opinion (Our Suppressed October Issue)," *Little Review* 4, 8 (December 1917): 48.

3. Accounts of the trial are to be found in "*Ulysses* Adjudged Indecent; Review Editors Are Fined," *New York Tribune* (22 February 1922): 13; "Improper Novel Costs Women $100," *New York Times* (22 February 1922): 13; Margaret Anderson, "*Ulysses* in Court," *Little Review* 7, 4 (January–March 1921): 22–25. As Brook Thomas has noted, the American court was employing the Hicklin standard; "*Ulysses* on Trial: Some Supplementary Reading," *Criticism* 33, 3 (Summer 1991): 381. This rule underwrote the indictment of *The Rainbow,* and reappeared, explicitly or implicitly, in the later trials of *The Well of Loneliness* (1928), *Lady Chatterley's Lover* (1959, 1960), and *Ulysses* (1933, 1934).

4. Ezra Pound, "The Classics Escape," *Little Review* 4, 11 (March 1918): 34.

5. Ibid., p. 32.

6. Ezra Pound, *Selected Letters of Ezra Pound to John Quinn, 1915–1924,* ed.

Timothy Materer (Durham, N.C.: Duke University Press, 1991), p. 142; cited hereafter as *PQ*.

7. Ezra Pound, "I Gather the Limbs of Osiris," *Selected Prose 1909–1965,* ed. William Cookson (London: Faber and Faber, 1973), p. 21.

8. Pound made these comments in the postscript to his translation of Rémy de Gourmont's *Natural Philosophy of Love* (1921); see *Pavannes and Divagations* (New York: New Directions, 1958), p. 204. For further discussion see James Longenbach, "Pound among the Women," *Review* 12 (1990): 135–36.

9. See B. L. Reid, *The Man from New York: John Quinn and His Friends* (New York: Oxford University Press, 1968), p. 314; cited hereafter as *MNY*.

10. In a nice coincidence, the American judge who twice dismissed obscenity charges against Stopes's books, John M. Woolsey, also permitted the publication of *Ulysses* in 1933.

11. Ford Madox Hueffer [Ford], "Men and Women," *Little Review* 4, 11 (March 1918): 36–51; Otto Weininger, *Sex and Character* (New York: G. P. Putnam's Sons, 1906), p. 90.

12. Susan Kingsley Kent, *Sex and Suffrage in Britain, 1860–1914* (Princeton, N.J.: Princeton University Press, 1987), pp. 3–5.

13. Weininger, *Sex and Character,* p. 237.

14. Judith Butler, "Performative Acts and Gender Constitution: An Essay in Phenomenology and Feminist Theory," in *Performing Feminisms: Feminist Critical Theory and Theatre,* ed. Sue-Ellen Case (Baltimore: Johns Hopkins University Press, 1990), pp. 270–71.

15. Ibid., p. 279.

16. Hugh Kenner, *Ulysses* (Baltimore: Johns Hopkins University Press, 1987), p. 172.

17. Jeffrey Segall takes a similar line in his recent study of Joyce's reception by various schools of twentieth-century American criticism. "The trajectory of his career and reputation in America," writes Segall, "offers a running, albeit implicit, commentary on the state of our criticism and our culture. In short, Joyce's books continue to read us"; *Joyce in America: Cultural Politics and the Trials of* Ulysses (Berkeley: University of California Press, 1993), p. 10.

18. Ezra Pound, "James Joyce. At Last the Novel Appears," *The Egoist* 4, 2 (February 1917): 22.

19. Ezra Pound, *Pound/Joyce: The Letters of Ezra Pound to James Joyce, with Pound's Essays on Joyce,* ed. Forrest Read (New York: New Directions, 1967), p. 39; cited hereafter as *PJ*.

20. Ezra Pound, "'Tarr,' by Wyndham Lewis," *Little Review* 4, 11 (March 1918): 35. Appropriately, Pound ended this review by comparing Lewis's protagonists, Tarr and Kreisler, with Joyce's Stephen Dedalus: "Only in James Joyce's Stephen Dedalus does one find an equal intensity, and Joyce is, by comparison, cold and meticulous, where Lewis is, if uncouth, at any rate brimming with energy, the man with a leaping mind."

21. Ezra Pound, *Letters of Ezra Pound, 1907–1941,* ed. D. D. Paige (New York: Harcourt, Brace, 1950), p. 22.

22. See A. Walton Litz, "Lawrence, Pound, and Early Modernism," in *D. H. Lawrence: A Centenary Consideration,* ed. Peter Balbert and Phillip L. Marcus (Ithaca, N.Y.: Cornell University Press, 1985), pp. 15–28.

23. Ezra Pound, *Personae: The Shorter Poems of Ezra Pound,* ed. Lea Baechler and

A. Walton Litz (New York: New Directions, 1990), p. 113. Pound's penchant for sexual overloading is also apparent in "Fratres Minores" (1914), which ridicules poets who "With minds still hovering above their testicles / . . . complain in delicate and exhausted metres / That the twitching of three abdominal nerves / Is incapable of producing a lasting Nirvana"; ibid., p. 78.

24. Ezra Pound, *Personae*, p. 102; *Letters of Ezra Pound*, pp. 81, 83. The unabridged American edition, published in New York in 1917, restored the poems omitted from the 1916 text, but "The Temperaments" was left out of the abridged version.

25. Pound, "James Joyce," p. 22.

26. Pound, quoted by Humphrey Carpenter, *A Serious Character: The Life of Ezra Pound* (Boston: Houghton Mifflin, 1988), pp. 278–79.

27. Anderson advertised her editorial censorship in a protesting footnote; see "Ulysses," *Little Review* 6, 1 (May 1919): 21.

28. Pound also used this term. On 31 October 1920 he wrote to Quinn agreeing that the fight against the suppression of *Ulysses* "should be DISSOCIATED from the aroma of Washington Square" (*PQ*, p. 199).

29. "The Year's Harvest of Noteworthy Poetry," *New York Times Book Review* (26 November 1916): 508–9. Interestingly, this article cited Lawrence's *Amores* (1916) as another example of "the cleansing effect of the war" in British poetry, for it "revealed on the whole a gayer personality than this author's novels had led us to expect."

30. The reviews concerned are reprinted in *James Joyce: The Critical Heritage*, ed. Robert H. Deming (London: Routledge and Kegan Paul, 1970), pp. 201, 195, 275, 192.

31. Harold P. Preston, "Ulysses," *Modern Review* 1, 1 (Autumn 1922): 41.

32. American literary trials continued to invoke Wilde as an exemplar of ephemeral, deviant art. Judge Crane's dissenting opinion in the 1922 case of Théophile Gautier's novel *Mademoiselle de Maupin* cited him as an author whose "polished style with exquisite settings and perfumed words makes it all the more dangerous and insidious and none the less obscene and lascivious." Crane added: "Oscar Wilde had a reputation for style, but went to jail just the same. Literary ability is no excuse for degeneracy"; quoted by Morris L. Ernst and Alan U. Schwartz, *Censorship: The Search for the Obscene* (New York: Macmillan, 1964), p. 64. As late as 1941 Van Wyck Brooks revived Wilde's ghost when he attacked Joyce, Eliot, and Pound for being "coterie writers": "Was not James Joyce, for one, the ash of a burnt-out cigar, were they not all of them ashes of the eighteen-nineties, aside from the matter of technique?"; quoted by Segall, *Joyce in America*, p. 70.

33. See Edward de Grazia, *Girls Lean Back Everywhere: The Law of Obscenity and the Assault on Genius* (New York: Random House, 1992), p. 16.

34. Quinn, quoted by Wayne Koestenbaum, *Double Talk: The Erotics of Male Literary Collaboration* (New York: Routledge, 1989), p. 119.

35. Anderson, "'Ulysses' in Court," p. 25. Unless otherwise indicated, the proceedings of the trial, and Anderson's reflections on them, are quoted from this source.

36. Quinn characterized Forrester as apoplectic when using him as the "chief exhibit" for the defense. Forrester's rage at *Ulysses,* Quinn argued, was an accurate reflection of the response that the novel was likely to provoke: "It may make people angry and make them feel as though they wanted to go out and tomahawk someone or put someone in jail, but it does not fill them with sexual desires." Quinn described the judges as ignorant when expressing his belief that he had persuaded them of his case: "I got two of the Judges, who were *consciously ignorant.* I failed with the third Judge, who was *unconsciously ignorant* . . ." (*MNY*, p. 455).

37. Joyce, quoted in Richard Ellmann, *James Joyce* (1959; New York: Oxford University Press, 1965), p. 510; cited hereafter as *JJ*.

38. *The Egoist* published Joyce's *Portrait* and excerpts from episodes 2, 3, 6, and 10 of *Ulysses*. Publication of *Ulysses* was limited by printers' fears of prosecution for obscenity and by complaints from subscribers that serial publication would devalue the novel's appearance as a book.

39. Jane Heap, "The Reader Critic," *Little Review* 5, 2 (June 1918): 57.

40. In a response to the seizure of the January issue containing part of "Cyclops," one *Little Review* correspondent affirmed that readers of *Ulysses* belonged to a small band of marginalized yet superior intellects, fortified by hardier, more robust "moral natures": "And what caused the suppression of the January issue? The Joyce, I suppose. I have been through the whole number very carefully and the 'Ulysses' is the only offender I can find. But why cavil about Joyce at this late day?—it would seem to me that after all these months he could be accepted, obscenity and all, for surely the post-office authorities should recognize that only a few read him, and those few not just the kind to have their whole moral natures overthrown by frankness about natural functions"; "Reader Critic," *Little Review* 6, 11 (April 1920): 61. Appropriately, this issue also contained the first part of "Nausicaa."

41. Jane Heap, "Art and the Law," *Little Review* 7, 3 (September–December 1920): 5–7.

42. Cheryl Herr, *Joyce's Anatomy of Culture* (Urbana: University of Illinois Press, 1986), p. 35.

43. Thomas Richards, *The Commodity Culture of Victorian England: Advertising and Spectacle, 1851–1914* (Stanford, Calif.: Stanford University Press, 1990), p. 224. I should add that Richards tends to deny the possibility of such agency, though at times he seems to concede it (see note 50).

44. Fritz Senn, "Nausicaa," in *James Joyce's* Ulysses: *Critical Essays,* ed. Clive Hart and David Hayman (Berkeley: University of California Press, 1974), p. 301.

45. James Douglas, *Sunday Express*; quoted by de Grazia, *Girls Lean Back Everywhere*, p. 26. De Grazia suggests that Douglas's review of the relatively unscandalous portions of *Ulysses* printed in *The Egoist* ensured that the novel would not be published in book form in Britain (see note 38).

46. James Joyce, *Ulysses: The Corrected Text*, ed. Hans Walter Gabler with Wolfhard Steppe and Claus Melchior (New York: Vintage Books, 1986), 13.687–711; cited hereafter as *U*. This text is slightly different from the version printed in the *Little Review* and read at the 1921 trial, but since few of the changes are significant for present purposes, I note them only where appropriate. For the 1921 text see *Little Review* 7, 2 (July–August 1920): 42–60.

47. Kimberly J. Devlin, "The Female Eye: Joyce's Voyeuristic Narcissists," in *New Alliances in Joyce Studies,* ed. Bonnie Kime Scott (Newark: University of Delaware Press, 1988), p. 136.

48. Judge Manton himself was later imprisoned for obstructing federal justice.

49. Suzette Henke, "Gerty MacDowell: Joyce's Sentimental Heroine," in *Women in Joyce,* ed. Henke and Elaine Unkeless (Urbana: University of Illinois Press, 1982), p. 135.

50. The relation between Gerty's sexuality and commercial culture is explored in detail by Thomas Richards and Garry Leonard. Richards sees Gerty as "wholly circumscribed" by commodity culture; *The Commodity Culture of Victorian England,* p. 234. Leonard, however, contends that Gerty "is painfully balanced between a wholehearted effort to believe in the 'old time chivalry' . . . and a shrewder attempt to

maintain her competitive edge in the sexual marketplace. . . ." Leonard rightly points out that Gerty criticizes other women's attempts to display themselves in order to exalt "the prospective worth of her own performance"; "Women on the Market: Commodity Culture, 'Femininity,' and 'Those Lovely Seaside Girls' in Joyce's *Ulysses*," *Joyce Studies Annual* 2 (1991): 55, 35. Mediating between Leonard and Richards, I would emphasize that for Joyce resistance to a particular culture is most effective when it comes from within.

51. Karen Lawrence, *The Odyssey of Style in* Ulysses (Princeton, N.J.: Princeton University Press, 1981), pp. 122–23.

52. Butler, "Performative Acts and Gender Constitution," pp. 271, 273.

53. "A mutoscope was a device for exhibiting a series of photographs of objects in motion," which produced "a rather jerky motion picture"; Don Gifford, with Robert J. Seidman, Ulysses *Annotated: Notes for James Joyce's* Ulysses (Berkeley: University of California Press, 1988), p. 394.

54. For other discussions of the reader's role in the voyeurism of this episode see Kimberly J. Devlin, "The Romance Heroine Exposed: 'Nausicaa' and *The Lamplighter*," *James Joyce Quarterly* 22, 4 (1985): 395–96; and Patrick McGee, *Paperspace: Style as Ideology in Joyce's* Ulysses (Lincoln: University of Nebraska Press, 1988), p. 94.

55. Havelock Ellis, "The Revaluation of Obscenity," in *More Essays of Love and Virtue* (Garden City, N.Y.: Doubleday, Doran, 1931), p. 119.

56. Jules David Law, "'Pity They Can't See Themselves': Assessing the 'Subject' of Pornography in 'Nausicaa,'" *James Joyce Quarterly* 27, 2 (Winter 1990): 219, 238.

57. Michel Foucault, *The History of Sexuality*, vol. 1: *An Introduction*, trans. Robert Hurley (New York: Vintage Books, 1990), pp. 20–25.

58. The law's gender distinction also applied to James J. Walker's famous anticensorship speech, which was delivered in the New York Senate in 1924 in circumstances similar to those of the *Little Review* trial. At the beginning of the year, New York Judge Robert F. Wagner had convicted Thomas Seltzer for publishing Arthur Schnitzler's *Casanova's Homecoming* (1918) and an anonymous Austrian work, *A Young Girl's Diary*, which included a preface by Freud. Legal proceedings began when the sixteen-year-old daughter of Judge John Ford took home a library copy of D. H. Lawrence's *Women in Love* (1920), which had been unsuccessfully prosecuted (along with Schnitzler's novella and the Austrian diary) in 1923. Lawrence's novel escaped censure in 1924, but fear for the mind of another young girl provoked renewed action against the other two works. In the wake of Judge Wagner's decision, the Clean Books League tried to introduce an obscenity law in the New York Senate, but Walker helped to ensure their failure by declaring: "No woman was ever ruined by a book." The cornerstone of Walker's argument, however, was his objection to governmental interference in the lives of individuals when "proper influences dominate their home." The implication was that women could be trusted so long as they were subject to the proper moral authority of father or husband. See de Grazia, *Girls Lean Back Everywhere*, pp. 72–77.

59. Mary Lowe-Evans, "Sex and Confession in the Joyce Canon: Some Historical Parallels," *Journal of Modern Literature* 16, 4 (Spring 1990): 571–72. Also see her *Crimes Against Fecundity: Joyce and Population Control* (Syracuse, N.Y.: Syracuse University Press, 1989), pp. 65–66.

60. Foucault, *The History of Sexuality*, p. 44.

61. Roland Barthes, "Striptease," in *Mythologies*, trans. Annette Lavers (New York: Noonday Press, 1972), pp. 84–85. Kimberly Devlin also describes the narrative of

"Nausicaa" as a striptease, but she equates such exhibitionism with "exposure" and "revelation": "The first half of 'Nausicaa' enacts a sort of narrative striptease, slowly unveiling more and more of Gerty's inner life"; "The Romance Heroine Exposed," p. 395. As Barthes emphasizes, however, striptease is all in the act; it does not "drag into the light a hidden depth."

62. Garry Leonard, "The Virgin Mary and the Urge in Gerty: The Packaging of Desire in the 'Nausicaa' Chapter of *Ulysses*," *University of Hartford Studies in Literature* 23, 1 (1991): 19.

63. Tony E. Jackson also makes this point in "'Cyclops,' 'Nausicaa,' and Joyce's Imaginary Irish Couple," *James Joyce Quarterly* 29, 1 (Fall 1991): 72.

64. Richard Brown, *James Joyce and Sexuality* (Cambridge: Cambridge University Press, 1985), p. 77.

65. Wolfgang Iser, *The Implied Reader: Patterns of Communication in Prose Fiction from Bunyan to Beckett* (Baltimore: Johns Hopkins University Press, 1974), pp. 193, 192.

66. Frank Budgen, *James Joyce and the Making of* Ulysses (Bloomington: Indiana University Press, 1960), p. 215.

67. Richard Ellmann, for instance, argues that "Oxen of the Sun" should be interpreted as follows: "the processes of nature and art are synonymous with each other; they imitate each other's fecundity and will not be sterilized"; Ulysses *on the Liffey* (New York: Oxford University Press, 1972), p. 140. Charles Peake describes Bloom as "the defender and advocate of fertility"; *James Joyce: The Citizen and the Artist* (Stanford, Calif.: Stanford University Press, 1977), p. 255.

68. See Brown, *James Joyce and Sexuality*, pp. 70–78, and Lowe-Evans, *Crimes Against Fecundity*, pp. 53–64.

69. The Citizen alludes to the tale of Dermod MacMurrough, the twelfth-century king of Leinster (*U*12.1157). After eloping with the wife of O'Rourke, another Irish chieftain, MacMurrough was deposed, but having fled to England he persuaded Henry II to launch the first invasion of Ireland; see Gifford, Ulysses *Annotated*, p. 39. The fall of Parnell after the Katherine O'Shea scandal is also evoked in a passage in "Eumaeus," which conjures up Bloom's fears about Molly's relationship with Blazes Boylan (*U*16.1359–1410). Joyce's critique of Nationalist sexism qualifies Bonnie Kime Scott's argument that the liberation of Irish women came through their work for the Nationalist movement; *Joyce and Feminism* (Bloomington: Indiana University Press, 1984), p. 29. In the light of *Ulysses*, one might argue that through such cooperation Irish women connived at their own oppression.

70. R. Barrie Walkley has treated Bloom's maternal tendencies as an instance of the couvade; "The Bloom of Motherhood: Couvade as a Structural Device in *Ulysses*," *James Joyce Quarterly* 18, 1 (Fall 1980): 55–67. Contending that *Ulysses* privileges paternity over maternity, however, Walkley overlooks the implications of the representation of antifeminism in "Oxen of the Sun." Walkley's interpretation of Bloom's last words in "Ithaca" as a reassertion of patriarchy also seems dubious to me, for reasons that will emerge.

71. See *Letters of James Joyce*, vol. 2, ed. Richard Ellmann (New York: Viking Press, 1966), pp. 431–36, and *Selected Letters of James Joyce*, ed. Richard Ellmann (New York: Viking Press, 1975), pp. 180–92. Ellmann provides a fine discussion of the letters to Fleischmann, but his account of the earlier correspondence with Nora Barnacle is rather cursory (*JJ*, pp. 462–67, 296). Brenda Maddox gives a full account of both sets of letters in *Nora: The Real Life of Molly Bloom* (Boston: Houghton Mifflin, 1988), pp. 97–108, 159–61.

72. Richards, *The Commodity Culture of Victorian England*, p. 206.

73. See Brown, *James Joyce and Sexuality*, p. 84, and Cheryl Herr, "'One Good Turn Deserves Another': Theatrical Cross-Dressing in Joyce's 'Circe' Episode," *Journal of Modern Literature* 11, 2 (July 1984): 265. Herr locates her discussion in the context of late-nineteenth- and early-twentieth-century dramatic transvestism. The theater of this period, she argues, "functioned as a refuge for those phenomena like cross-dressing that Victorian and Edwardian society wanted to see as having no more substance than theatrical illusions"; ibid., p. 263. Also see chapter 4 of her *Joyce's Anatomy of Culture*.

74. See the notorious chapter 13 of Weininger's *Sex and Character*. Also see Ellmann (*JJ*, p. 477). Marilyn Reizbaum has argued persuasively that Joyce invokes Weininger's theories only to expose their flaws; "The Jewish Connection, Continued," in *The Seventh of Joyce,* ed. Bernard Benstock (Bloomington: Indiana University Press, 1982), pp. 229–37. Robert Byrnes takes a similar line, arguing that in Bloom Joyce puts the models of Weininger and Krafft-Ebing to comic use. Byrnes reads the "Circe" trial, in which "a panel of sexologists diagnose Bloom with Krafft-Ebing's taxonomy," as a parody of such constructions; "Bloom's Sexual Tropes: Stigmata of the 'Degenerate' Jew," *James Joyce Quarterly* 27, 2 (Winter 1990): 303–23. Suzette Henke also interprets Joyce's use of Krafft-Ebing as parodic; "Joyce and Krafft-Ebing," *James Joyce Quarterly* 17, 1 (Fall 1979): 84–86. Henke and Byrnes both reject Stanley Sultan's view that Joyce rehearses Krafft-Ebing's theory of male perversion as a movement "from passivity to masochism to feminization"; see Sultan, *The Argument of Ulysses* (Columbus: Ohio State University Press, 1964), pp. 317–18. As will become clear in my own discussion, I side with Reizbaum, Byrnes, and Henke on these questions.

75. Bonnie Kime Scott discusses Bloom's punishment and perversions in relation to Roland Barthes' *Michelet*. She explains that for Barthes, Michelet attains the status of voyeur when he "becomes woman, lesbian," a process he fulfills by playing the part of chambermaid. Applying this analysis to "Penelope," Scott suggests that the reader may be "the ultimate, voyeuristic, Micheletian chambermaid"; "Joyce and Michelet: Why Watch Molly Menstruate?," in *Joyce in Context,* ed. Vincent S. Cheng and Timothy Martin (Cambridge: Cambridge University Press, 1992), pp. 122–37.

76. Vicki Mahaffey, *Reauthorizing Joyce* (Cambridge: Cambridge University Press, 1988), p. 148. Hugh Kenner discusses "Circe" in similar terms. He is especially illuminating when discussing the reader's difficulty in following the narrative line in "Circe," arguing that whereas naturalism and hallucination are usually regarded as two extremes of one continuum, Joyce treats them as parts of an undifferentiated dramatic surface. As to how much freedom is enabled by the theatrical procedures of "Circe," Kenner implies that it may be quite limited: "To change one must only (only!) change one's role." But, as Kenner seems to allow, small freedoms are better than none. See "Circe," in *James Joyce's* Ulysses: *Critical Essays,* ed. Clive Hart and David Hayman (Berkeley: University of California Press, 1974), p. 360.

77. James Joyce, *Exiles* (New York: Penguin Books, 1977), pp. 156–57. Ultimately it is unclear whether Bertha and Robert actually consummate their affair; it seems enough for Richard to entertain absolute uncertainty. In this sense, *Exiles* closely anticipates the dénouement of the triangular relationship between Bloom, Molly, and Boylan in *Ulysses*.

78. Brown, *James Joyce and Sexuality*, p. 67.

79. Lawrence, quoted by Dorothy Brett, *Lawrence and Brett: A Friendship* (Philadelphia: J. B. Lippincott, 1933), p. 81. Lawrence was not alone, of course, in singling out Molly's monologue. Intriguingly, those who found "Penelope" especially

offensive included several Soviet critics of the 1930s; see Segall, *Joyce in America,* pp. 31–32.

80. John Paul Riquelme, *Teller and Tale in Joyce's Fiction: Oscillating Perspectives* (Baltimore: Johns Hopkins University Press, 1983), p. 225.

81. Ellmann, *Selected Letters of James Joyce,* p. 285.

82. Scott, *Joyce and Feminism,* p. 158.

83. Weininger, *Sex and Character,* pp. 90, 191, 198.

84. The most obvious manifestation of the critical obsession with Molly's sex life might seem to be the "empirical" approach of David Hayman, in "The Empirical Molly," in *Approaches to* Ulysses: *Ten Essays,* ed. Thomas F. Staley and Bernard Benstock (Pittsburgh: University of Pittsburgh Press, 1970), pp. 103–35; and of Hugh Kenner, in "Molly's Masterstroke," in Ulysses: *Fifty Years,* ed. Thomas F. Staley (Bloomington: Indiana University Press, 1974), pp. 19–28. But I am thinking primarily of critics who see Molly as representing the archetypal "mystery" of femininity. See Stuart Gilbert, *James Joyce's* Ulysses: *A Study* (New York: Vintage Press, 1955), pp. 385–405; Budgen, *James Joyce and the Making of* Ulysses, pp. 262–66; Robert Adams, *Surface and Symbol: The Consistency of James Joyce's* Ulysses (New York: Oxford University Press, 1962), pp. 35–43; Robert Boyle, "Penelope," in Hart and Hayman, *James Joyce's* Ulysses, pp. 407–33; Marilyn French, *The Book as World: James Joyce's* Ulysses (Cambridge, Mass.: Harvard University Press, 1976), pp. 243–61.

85. Gifford, Ulysses *Annotated,* pp. 616, 629. Cuckoldry as the product of the jealous male mind is also the implicit theme of allusions in "Sirens" to an aria from Bellini's 1831 opera *La Sonnambula* (*The Sleepwalker*). The aria "Tutto è sciolto" ("All Is Lost") is sung by the heroine's fiancé, who wrongly believes that she has been unfaithful to him. Joyce's allusions are timed to coincide with the part of the day when Bloom (also a tenor, as was Joyce) thinks Molly is about to betray him (*U*11.610, 629, 635, 638–39); see Gifford, Ulysses *Annotated,* p. 292.

86. Weininger, *Sex and Character,* p. 26.

87. Joyce, *Exiles,* pp. 155–56. French points out this connection in *The Book as World,* p. 288.

88. This point is also suggested by Cheryl Herr's thesis that even Molly's menstruation, an apparently "incontestable" sign of femininity, is part of her performance of the woman's role, which Bloom mimics in his nosebleeding; "'Penelope' as Period Piece," *Novel* 22, 2 (Winter 1989): 130–42.

89. Herr, *Joyce's Anatomy of Culture,* p. 164.

90. For the argument that Molly is an utterly conventional woman see Elaine Unkeless, "The Conventional Molly Bloom," in *Women in Joyce,* pp. 150–68.

Chapter 3

1. Compton Mackenzie, *My Life and Times: Octave Five, 1915–1923* (London: Chatto and Windus, 1966), p. 167.

2. See Dennis Jackson, "*Lady Chatterley's Lover*: Lawrence's Response to *Ulysses*?" *Philological Quarterly* 66, 3 (Summer 1987): 410–16; Derek Britton, *Lady Chatterley: The Making of the Novel* (London: Unwin Hyman, 1988), p. 262. Robert Kiely noted some years ago how few critics discuss Lawrence and Joyce together without denigrating one at the other's expense. For a useful bibliography see Kiely, *Beyond Egotism: The Fiction of James Joyce, Virginia Woolf, and D. H. Lawrence* (Cambridge, Mass.: Harvard University Press, 1980), p. 237. Other interesting comparisons of Lawrence and Joyce are made by James C. Cowan, "Lawrence, Joyce, and the

Epiphanies of *Lady Chatterley's Lover*," in *D. H. Lawrence's "Lady": A New Look at* Lady Chatterley's Lover, ed. Michael Squires and Dennis Jackson (Athens: University of Georgia Press, 1985), pp. 91–115; and Zack Bowen, "*Lady Chatterley's Lover* and *Ulysses*," in ibid., pp. 116–35.

3. D. H. Lawrence, *The Letters of D. H. Lawrence*, vol. 6, ed. James T. Boulton and Margaret H. Boulton with Gerald M. Lacy (Cambridge: Cambridge University Press, 1991), pp. 507, 508, 548; cited hereafter as *L6*.

4. D. H. Lawrence, "Pornography and Obscenity," in *Phoenix: The Posthumous Papers of D. H. Lawrence*, ed. Edward D. McDonald (New York: Viking Press, 1936), p. 171; cited hereafter as *P1*.

5. Mackenzie, *My Life and Times*, p. 168.

6. D. H. Lawrence, *The Letters of D. H. Lawrence*, vol. 5, ed. James T. Boulton and Lindeth Vasey (Cambridge: Cambridge University Press, 1989), p. 651; cited hereafter as *L5*.

7. "Famous Novelist's Shameful Book," *John Bull* (20 October 1928): 11; "Lewd Book Banned," *The Sunday Chronicle* (14 October 1928): 1. Reprinted in Edward Nehls, *D. H. Lawrence: A Composite Biography*, vol. 3 (Madison: University of Wisconsin Press, 1959), pp. 262–65.

8. See D. H. Lawrence, *The Letters of D. H. Lawrence*, vol. 7, ed. Keith Sagar and James T. Boulton (Cambridge: Cambridge University Press, 1993), p. 6; cited hereafter as *L7*.

9. During July to October 1927, Roth published *Ulysses* in slightly expurgated installments in *Two Worlds Monthly*. Joyce's circle responded in an international protest. Among those who signed this document were T. S. Eliot, Havelock Ellis, E. M. Forster, Wyndham Lewis, H. G. Wells, Virginia Woolf, W. B. Yeats, and Lawrence. George Bernard Shaw refused to sign, as did Pound, who, Ellmann notes, "thought Joyce was putting personal advertisement ahead of the general evils of the copyright and pornography laws and using 'a mountain battery to shoot a gnat'"; see Richard Ellmann, *James Joyce* (1959; New York: Oxford University Press, 1965), p. 599. Roth ceased publication in the face of legal action, and on 27 December 1928 the Supreme Court of the State of New York banned him from using Joyce's name. In the meantime, Roth had offered to pay Joyce's way to New York "to answer my charges against him for his conduct in the matter . . ."; "An Offer to James Joyce," *Two Worlds Monthly* 3, 3 (September 1927): 181. For detailed treatment of the piracy of Lawrence's novel see Jay. A. Gertzman, "The Piracies of *Lady Chatterley's Lover*: 1928–1950," *D. H. Lawrence Review* 19, 3 (Fall 1987): 267–99.

10. *Daily Express* (4 March 1930): 3. For other examples see obituaries published on the same date in *The Times, The Daily Mail,* and *The Daily Telegraph.*

11. T. S. Eliot, *After Strange Gods: A Primer of Modern Heresy* (London: Faber and Faber, 1934), p. 38; James Joyce, *Letters of James Joyce*, vol. 1, ed. Stuart Gilbert (New York: Viking Press, 1957; rev. 1966), p. 309. The same charges could be leveled, of course, at *After Strange Gods*. As Christopher Ricks points out, Eliot himself came to see his book as heretical and declined to keep it in print. Ricks puts the case perfectly: "The book is desperately controversial, and one of the things of which it despairs is the possibility of worthwhile controversy"; *T. S. Eliot and Prejudice* (Berkeley: University of California Press, 1988), p. 77.

12. Virginia Woolf, *The Diary of Virginia Woolf*, vol. 4, ed. Anne Olivier Bell with Andrew McNeillie (New York: Harcourt Brace Jovanovich, 1982), p. 126.

13. The petition was signed by, among others, Lytton Strachey, John Maynard

Keynes, and Vita Sackville-West, none of whom felt any particular affinity with Lawrencean aesthetics; see Nehls, *D. H. Lawrence*, vol. 3, pp. 368–69.

14. D. H. Lawrence, *Lady Chatterley's Lover; A Propos of* Lady Chatterley's Lover, ed. Michael Squires (Cambridge: Cambridge University Press, 1993), p. 307; cited hereafter as *LCL*.

15. See D. H. Lawrence, "Surgery for the Novel—or a Bomb" (*P1*, pp. 517–20).

16. Elaine Showalter, *The Female Malady: Women, Madness, and English Culture, 1830–1980* (New York: Pantheon Books, 1985), p. 190.

17. Eric Leed, *No Man's Land: Combat and Identity in World War I* (Cambridge: Cambridge University Press, 1979), p. 163.

18. Anne Fernihough, *D. H. Lawrence: Aesthetics and Ideology* (Oxford: Clarendon Press, 1993), pp. 56–57. Fernihough is quoting from Lawrence, *The Symbolic Meaning: The Uncollected Versions of* Studies in Classic American Literature, ed. Armin Arnold (Arundel, England: Centaur Press, 1962), p. 18.

19. See Jane Gallop, "Keys to Dora," in *In Dora's Case: Freud—Hysteria—Feminism*, ed. Charles Bernheimer and Claire Kahane (New York: Columbia University Press, 1985), pp. 200–20; Kate Millett, *Sexual Politics* (New York: Ballantine Books, 1978), pp. 333–411.

20. C. H. Rolph, ed., *The Trial of Lady Chatterley: Regina v. Penguin Books Limited* (Harmondsworth, England: Penguin Books, 1961), p. 47; cited hereafter as *TLC*.

21. "Famous Novelist's Shameful Book," p. 11.

22. E. M. Forster, *Aspects of the Novel* (San Diego: Harcourt Brace Jovanovich, 1955), p. 143; and R. P. Draper, ed., *D. H. Lawrence: The Critical Heritage* (New York: Barnes and Noble, 1970), p. 344; cited hereafter as *LCH*.

23. W. B. Yeats, *The Letters of W. B. Yeats*, ed. Allan Wade (New York: Macmillan, 1955), p. 810.

24. In a 1921 review of *Women in Love*, John Middleton Murry expressed his oft-repeated claim that having become "a fanatic or a prophet," Lawrence was no longer interested in being an artist (*LCH*, pp. 168–72). Also see Murry's accounts of Lawrence's *Collected Poems* in *The New Adelphi* (December 1928): 165–67, and his *Son of Woman: The Story of D. H. Lawrence* (New York: Jonathan Cape 1931). In 1928 Raymond Mortimer compared Lawrence with Van Gogh as someone in whom "the missionary often obliterates the artist"; *The Nation and Athenæum* (9 June 1928): 332. See also "Mr. Lawrence's Pansies," *The New Statesman* (27 July 1929): 501–2; John R. Chamberlain, "D. H. Lawrence Shows Himself More Prophet than Artist," *New York Times Book Review* (3 June 1928): 2.

25. Wyndham Lewis, quoted by Jeffrey Meyers in *The Enemy: A Biography of Wyndham Lewis* (London: Routledge and Kegan Paul, 1989), p. 144; Lewis, "The Son of Woman," *Time and Tide* (18 April 1931): 472. The second piece is a review of Murry's book on Lawrence.

26. See Eliot, *After Strange Gods*, p. 58. Though eschewing the charge of hysteria, which was crucial to Lewis's critique, Eliot's own assault on Lawrence often followed Lewis in employing the symptomatic terminology of the popular press. In Lawrence, Eliot discerned "a distinct sexual morbidity," a baffling "insensibility to ordinary social morality," and frequent manifestations of the "effects of decadence." Lawrence's vision was "spiritual, but spiritually sick." The author of *Lady Chatterley's Lover*, Eliot concluded, "seems to me to have been a very sick man indeed"; ibid., pp. 58, 59, 39, 60.

27. Wyndham Lewis, *The Roaring Queen* (London: Secker and Warburg, 1973).

An interesting footnote to the history of twentieth-century censorship is the fact that Lewis's novel, due to be published by Jonathan Cape in 1936, was withdrawn for fear of libel suits. Some of the figures satirized were Arnold Bennett (Samuel Shodbutt), Brian Howard (Donald Butterboy, the Roaring Queen), Richard Sickert (Richard Dritter), and Virginia Woolf (Rhoda Hyman). Baby Bucktrout is thought to be based on Nancy Cunard.

28. Lewis, "The Son of Woman," p. 470.

29. D. H. Lawrence, *The Complete Poems of D. H. Lawrence,* ed. Vivian de Sola Pinto and Warren Roberts (New York: Viking Press, 1964), p. 680; cited hereafter as *CP*.

30. Carol Siegel, *Lawrence among the Women: Wavering Boundaries in Women's Literary Traditions* (Charlottesville: University Press of Virginia, 1991), p. 197.

31. Rachel Annand Taylor, "In Three Continents," *Spectator* (2 June 1928): 844. Taylor's diagnosis of Lawrence's "neurosis" was reiterated in the New York *Bookman* by William McFee, who commented that in his studies of neurotics, Lawrence "writes in a very neurotic way himself." "[N]o doubt," McFee opined, *The Woman Who Rode Away* was "great art, but it seems a little insane at times"; "Novels to the Fore," *Bookman* (July 1928): 569.

32. Ruth Suckow, "Two Temperaments," *The Outlook* (29 August 1928): 713. Some male readers made similar observations. Roger Chance thought Lawrence's views on sex "anti-feminine"; "Love and Mr. Lawrence," *Fortnightly Review* (October 1929): 500–11. W. H. Roberts considered Lawrence "a virile writer, making his appeal more directly to men than to women," who lavished on his male characters a sympathy that he denied his heroines; "D. H. Lawrence: Study of a Free Spirit in Literature," reprinted in *Renaissance and Modern Studies* 18 (1974): 5–16. Other critics saw things differently, though. Peter Quennell, for example, believed Lawrence's later works to have a feminist bias; "The Later Period of D. H. Lawrence," *Scrutinies,* vol. 2, ed. Edgell Rickwood (London: Wishart, 1931), pp. 124–37.

33. D. H. Lawrence, *The Complete Stories,* vol. 2 (New York: Penguin Books, 1976), pp. 579–80.

34. Susan French has suggested that the story leaves us "to draw our own conclusions"; "Lawrence's Women," *Times Literary Supplement* (5 February 1993): 15. French is replying to Brenda Maddox's argument that Lawrence's writing is unequivocally tainted by sexism; see Brenda Maddox, "Reluctant to Kiss," *Times Literary Supplement* (15 January 1993): 5.

35. Sandra M. Gilbert and Susan Gubar, *No Man's Land,* vol. 2: *Sexchanges* (New Haven, Conn.: Yale University Press, 1989), p. 319; Ezra Pound, *Personae: The Shorter Poems of Ezra Pound,* ed. Lea Baechler and A. Walton Litz (New York: New Directions, 1990), p. 188.

36. The Representation of the People Bill (1918) gave the vote to women householders and the wives of householders aged thirty or older. The vote was granted to women on the same basis as men in 1928. For Kent's discussion of these and other pieces of postwar legislation see *Sex and Suffrage in Britain, 1860–1914* (Princeton, N.J.: Princeton University Press, 1987), pp. 220–27. Also see Gilbert and Gubar, *Sexchanges,* pp. 47–82, and Samuel Hynes, *A War Imagined: The First World War and English Culture* (New York: Atheneum, 1991), especially pp. 367–76.

37. Otto Weininger, *Sex and Character* (New York: G. P. Putnam's Sons, 1906), pp. 265–66.

38. Sigmund Freud, "General Remarks on Hysterical Attacks," trans. Douglas Bryan, in *Dora: An Analysis of a Case of Hysteria* (New York: Collier Books, 1963),

pp. 153, 154. Also see Freud, *The Interpretation of Dreams,* trans. and ed. James Strachey (New York: Avon Books, 1965), pp. 182–84.

39. Sigmund Freud, *Three Essays on the Theory of Sexuality,* trans. and ed. James Strachey (New York: Basic Books, 1975), p. 32.

40. Havelock Ellis, *Sexual Inversion* (1897); reprinted in *Studies in the Psychology of Sex,* vol. 1 (New York: Random House, 1942), pp. 295–96.

41. John Gould Fletcher, "Night-Haunted Lover," *New York Herald Tribune Books* (14 July 1929): 6. Also see D. H. Lawrence, "Whitman," *The Nation and Athenæum* (23 July 1921): 616–18; reprinted in Lawrence, *The Symbolic Meaning,* pp. 254–64.

42. Joseph Collins, *The Doctor Looks at Literature: Psychological Studies of Life and Letters* (New York: George H. Doran, 1923), pp. 273, 284. See James C. Cowan, *D. H. Lawrence and the Trembling Balance* (University Park: Pennsylvania State University Press, 1986), p. 125.

43. J. F. H., "Mr. Lawrence's Criticism," *The New Statesman* (2 August 1924): 498.

44. D. H. Lawrence, *Kangaroo* (London: Penguin Books, 1950), pp. 240, 236.

45. D. H. Lawrence, *Phoenix II: Uncollected, Unpublished, and Other Prose Works,* ed. Warren Roberts and Harry T. Moore (New York: Penguin Books, 1978), p. 540; cited hereafter as *P2.*

46. Lawrence, quoted by Dorothy Brett in *Lawrence and Brett: A Friendship* (Philadelphia: J. B. Lippincott, 1933), p. 81.

47. D. H. Lawrence, *The Letters of D. H. Lawrence,* vol. 4, ed. Warren Roberts, James T. Boulton, and Elizabeth Mansfield (Cambridge: Cambridge University Press, 1987), pp. 340, 345. Derek Britton notes that in 1920 Lawrence also read the serialized version of *Ulysses* in the *Little Review; Lady Chatterley,* p. 8.

48. James Joyce, *Ulysses: The Corrected Text,* ed. Hans Walter Gabler with Wolfhard Steppe and Claus Melchior (New York: Vintage Books, 1986), 15.2972–80.

49. Gilbert and Gubar, *Sexchanges,* p. 334.

50. Showalter, *The Female Malady,* p. 145. Also see Gilbert and Gubar, *Sexchanges,* pp. 427–28.

51. Hilary Simpson, *D. H. Lawrence and Feminism* (London: Croom Helm, 1982), pp. 65, 105. Also see notes 45 and 46 in chapter 1 of this book.

52. Siegel, *Lawrence among the Women,* pp. 58, 16, 39. Also see Anne Fernihough's discussion of Lawrence and "the semiotic" in *D. H. Lawrence,* especially pp. 57–58.

53. Siegel, *Lawrence among the Women,* pp. 48–49. Also see Anne Smith, "A New Adam and a New Eve—Lawrence and Women: A Biographical Overview," in *Lawrence and Women,* ed. Smith (London: Vision Press, 1977), p. 20.

54. "Cocksure Women and Hensure Men" was published in *Forum* (New York) in January 1929. "Matriarchy" appeared in the London *Evening News* (5 October 1928), and several other essays were published in this and other British newspapers, even in those that attacked Lawrence. Most startlingly, "Give Her a Pattern" appeared in the *Daily Express* on 19 June 1929, just two days after this paper had described his paintings as such to "compel most spectators to recoil with horror"; "D. H. Lawrence as Painter / Censored Novelist's Pictures / Intimate Nudes," *Daily Express* (17 June 1929): 11. This tactic was calculated, of course, to make money for the *Daily Express.*

55. D. H. Lawrence, *The Plumed Serpent (Quetzalcoatl),* ed. L. D. Clark (Cambridge: Cambridge University Press, 1987), p. 415; cited hereafter as *PS.* Laurence Lerner, for instance, finds that "the action of the book comes down very firmly behind

the cult of Quetzalcoatl"; "Lawrence and the Feminists," in *D. H. Lawrence: Centenary Essays,* ed. Mara Kalnins (Bristol: Bristol Classical Press, 1986), p. 82.

56. Daniel Albright, *Personality and Impersonality: Lawrence, Woolf, and Mann* (Chicago: University of Chicago Press, 1978), p. 65. In some ways my argument here also complements Robert Kiely's discussion in *Beyond Egotism,* pp. 208–21. Kiely suggests that for Lawrence the only authentic form of theater was one that made the spectator come "up against the performer."

57. D. H. Lawrence, *St. Mawr and The Man Who Died* (New York: Vintage Books, 1953), pp. 209, 188, 182.

58. Freud and Breuer wrote: "The longer we have been occupied with these phenomena the more we have become convinced that *the splitting of consciousness which is so striking in the well-known classical cases under the form of* 'double conscience' *is present to a rudimentary degree in every hysteria, and that a tendency to such a dissociation, and with it the emergence of abnormal states of consciousness . . . is the basic phenomenon of this neurosis*"; *Studies on Hysteria,* trans. and ed. James Strachey (New York: Basic Books, 1957), p. 12.

59. In the fourth case history of *Studies on Hysteria* (Katharina), Freud "cleared up" the case by supplying the male sex organ as the answer to his final question, to which the patient did not reply: "What part of his body was it that you felt that night?" Freud "could not penetrate further" than Katharina's facial expression, but it was enough to satisfy him: "I owed her a debt of gratitude for having made it so much easier for me to talk to her than to the prudish ladies of my city practice, who regard whatever is natural as shameful"; *Studies on Hysteria,* pp. 131–32. Here, of course, is another example of transference: Katharina's "personal relation" with Freud comes to the fore, so that their dialogue becomes a displaced form of sexual intercourse. In this sense, Freud donates his own organ to supply what the patient lacks.

60. There has been widespread speculation about Lawrence's impotence, most famously in Dorothy Brett's account in an epilogue to *Lawrence and Brett,* cited by Meyers, *D. H. Lawrence,* p. 315. Brett's report complements 1920s portraits of Lawrence as girlish, hysterical, and requiring the treatment he proposed for British culture as a whole.

61. In disgust, Huxley volunteered "John Thomas and Lady Jane" as a title for the novel, advice that Lawrence perversely insisted on following until friends convinced him that it would further damage his already sullied reputation. Huxley's title is now used for the second version of the novel, first published in 1972. Morrison typed the first five chapters of *Lady Chatterley's Lover* but refused to continue because she found it indecent. To Morrison, Lawrence replied: "And remember, although you are on the side of the angels and the vast majority, I consider mine is the truly moral and religious position. You suggest I have pandered to the pornographic taste: I think not. To the Puritan all things are impure, to quote an Americanism" (*L6,* p. 260).

62. Frieda Lawrence later authorized an expurgated edition of *Lady Chatterley's Lover,* published in 1932 by Secker (London) and Knopf (New York), to combat the numerous pirated editions. For Pound's use of the term "*castrato*" see *Letters of Ezra Pound, 1907–1941,* ed. D. D. Paige (New York: Harcourt, Brace, 1950), p. 83.

63. Frieda Lawrence, Foreword, in D. H. Lawrence, *The First Lady Chatterley* (London: Penguin Books, 1973), p. 10; cited hereafter as *FLC.*

64. Michael Squires, *The Creation of* Lady Chatterley's Lover (Baltimore: Johns Hopkins University Press, 1983), p. 169.

65. Gustave Flaubert, *The Letters of Gustave Flaubert, 1830–1857,* ed. and trans. Francis Steegmuller (Cambridge, Mass.: Belknap Press of Harvard University Press,

1980), p. 173; James Joyce, *A Portrait of the Artist as a Young Man* (London: Penguin Books, 1976), p. 215. Connie attacks Proust directly in the final version of *Lady Chatterley* (*LCL*, p. 194). In the second version, as Dennis Jackson observes, she criticizes Joyce's *Ulysses* as well. See Jackson, "*Lady Chatterley's Lover*: Lawrence's Response to *Ulysses*?," p. 411, and D. H. Lawrence, *John Thomas and Lady Jane* (London: Penguin Books, 1973), p. 222; cited hereafter as *JTLJ*. In another interesting variation on this theme, Jennifer Swift reads Lawrence's novel as a response to T. S. Eliot; "The Body and Transcendence of Two Wastelands: *Lady Chatterley's Lover* and *The Waste Land*," *Paunch* 63–64 (December 1990): 141–71.

66. Britton, *Lady Chatterley,* p. 246. Also see Squires, *The Creation of* Lady Chatterley's Lover, p. 61, and Cowan, *D. H. Lawrence and the Trembling Balance,* p. 78.

67. The first uses of "queer" recorded in the *OED* suggest connections between sexual deviance and Wildean aestheticism: "A young man, easily ascertainable to be unusually fine in other characteristics, is probably 'queer' in sex tendency"; "*queer,* crooked; criminal. Also applied to effeminate or degenerate men or boys." Although the *OED* attributes these examples to American publications of 1922 and 1931, Wayne Koestenbaum has observed that "queer" carried such resonances in turn-of-the-century collaborative romances by Conrad and Ford, and by Robert Louis Stevenson and Lloyd Osborne; *Double Talk: The Erotics of Male Literary Collaboration* (New York: Routledge, 1989), pp. 145, 167.

68. Keith Cushman, "The Virgin and the Gipsy and the Lady and the Gamekeeper," in *D. H. Lawrence's "Lady,"* p. 158. Evelyn J. Hinz and John J. Teunissen see parallels between Mellors and Ares; "War, Love, and Industrialism: The Ares/Aphrodite/ Hephaestus Complex in *Lady Chatterley's Lover*," in ibid., p. 204.

69. See D. H. Lawrence, *The Virgin and the Gipsy* (New York: Vintage Books, 1984), p. 128.

70. Cushman, "The Virgin and the Gipsy," p. 158.

71. Suckow, "Two Temperaments," p. 713.

72. Squires, *The Creation of* Lady Chatterley's Lover, p. 65.

73. Albright, *Personality and Impersonality,* pp. 9, 19. *Lady Chatterley's Lover* represents the defeat of the "old stable ego of the character" that Lawrence imagined while writing *The Rainbow* in 1914.

74. Squires, *The Creation of* Lady Chatterley's Lover, pp. 178, 58.

75. Taylor Stoehr faults Lawrence along lines similar to those followed by Squires. Stoehr argues that Lawrence indulges in the very things for which he indicts others: dream, fantasy, self-consciousness, "mentalized sex"; "'Mentalized Sex' in D. H. Lawrence," *Novel* 8, 2 (Winter 1975): 101–22.

76. Andrew Shonfield, "Lawrence's Other Censor," *Encounter* 17, 3 (September 1961): 63–64; John Sparrow, "Regina v. Penguin Books Ltd.: An Undisclosed Element in the Case," *Encounter* 18, 101 (February 1962): 35–43. Sparrow argued (perhaps rightly) that had the prosecutor made his interpretation of this passage clear to the court, *Lady Chatterley* may well have been banned in 1960. Squires, too, regrets the indirection of the passage, attributing it to Lawrence's "fear of an enraged public"; *The Creation of* Lady Chatterley's Lover, p. 38. This is not a persuasive argument, since there is enough elsewhere in the novel to upset wary readers. Another well-known, though unsatisfactory, critical exchange on this topic began with Mark Spilka's review of Colin Clarke's *River of Dissolution* in "Lawrence Up-Tight, or the Anal Phase Once Over," *Novel* 4, 3 (Spring 1971): 252–67. See replies by Clarke, George Ford, and Frank Kermode in "Critical Exchange," *Novel* 5, 1 (Fall 1971): 54–70. Also see

G. Wilson Knight, "Lawrence, Joyce and Powys," *Essays in Criticism* 11, 4 (October 1956): 403–17. More recently, James Cowan has described this passage as representing "what . . . has been critically established as consensual anal intercourse"; *D. H. Lawrence and the Trembling Balance,* p. 154.

77. Eugene Goodheart, "Censorship and Self-Censorship in the Fiction of D. H. Lawrence," in *Representing Modernist Texts: Editing as Interpretation,* ed. George Bornstein (Ann Arbor: University of Michigan Press, 1991), p. 237.

78. D. H. Lawrence, *The Rainbow,* ed. Mark Kinkead-Weekes (Cambridge: Cambridge University Press, 1989), p. 220; cited hereafter as *R.*

79. For a different reading of the London encounter see Rosemary Reeves Davies, "The Eighth Love Scene: The Real Climax of *Lady Chatterley's Lover,*" *D. H. Lawrence Review* 15, 1–2 (Spring–Summer 1982): 167–76. Davies argues that the night of sensual passion represents but "a brief emergence of his [Mellors's] death-oriented side," which he has to accept before "the primacy of creation can occur." In the seventh encounter, Davies contends, Connie submits to Mellors so that he may come to terms with his "death-orientation." I am not sure, though, that this reading does full justice to the postcoital passage I cited earlier. This passage sheds very different light on the "neglected eighth sexual episode," which Davies sees as expressing Mellors's new feelings of confidence and acceptance.

80. Gerald Doherty's recent essay in *PMLA* exemplifies this reading of Mellors's letter: "It formulates a terminal wisdom to be held in reserve as the foundation for the future. Despite the tentativeness of this conclusion—after all, the lovers are still separated—*Lady Chatterley's Lover* is the sole Lawrentian novel to formulate an unequivocal message, to commit both the protagonists to it, and, in writing it into the future, to raise obsessively the question of its transmission"; "One Vast Hermeneutic Sentence: The Total Lawrentian Text," *PMLA* 106, 5 (October 1991): 1143.

Chapter 4

1. In January 1929, Hall's American publisher, D. S. Friede, was arraigned under Section 1141 of the New York State penal law, "relating to the circulation of indecent literature," but on 8 April, in the Court of Special Sessions of the City of New York, the defense won the case. See Vera Brittain, *Radclyffe Hall: A Case of Obscenity?* (London: Femina Press, 1968), p. 140ff; cited hereafter as *RHCO.*

2. Radclyffe Hall to Havelock Ellis, 2 December 1928; Harry Ransom Humanities Research Center, University of Texas at Austin. Unless otherwise indicated, I quote from this collection when citing Hall's correspondence.

3. Samuel Hynes, *A War Imagined: The First World War and English Culture* (New York: Atheneum, 1991), p. 375.

4. "Novel Condemned as Obscene," *The Times* (17 November 1928): 5.

5. Michael Baker, *Our Three Selves: The Life of Radclyffe Hall* (New York: William Morrow, 1985), p. 220.

6. Virginia Woolf, *The Diary of Virginia Woolf,* vol. 3, ed. Anne Olivier Bell with Andrew McNeillie (New York: Harcourt Brace Jovanovich, 1980), p. 207; cited hereafter as *D3.*

7. See Jane Marcus, *Virginia Woolf and the Languages of Patriarchy* (Bloomington: Indiana University Press, 1987), pp. 163–87; and Shari Benstock, "Expatriate Sapphic Modernism: Entering Literary History," *Lesbian Texts and Contexts,* ed. Karla Jay and Joanne Glasgow (New York: New York University Press, 1990), pp. 183–203. For these critics, Woolf's attention to Hall's case is an essentially affirmative

enterprise. Marcus even suggests that Hall is the "heroine" of *A Room of One's Own*. As will become clear, I regard such claims with some skepticism.

8. Virginia Woolf, *The Letters of Virginia Woolf*, vol. 3, ed. Nigel Nicolson and Joanne Trautmann (New York: Harcourt Brace Jovanovich, 1977), p. 555; cited hereafter as *L3*.

9. Alex Zwerdling, *Virginia Woolf and the Real World* (Berkeley: University of California Press, 1986), p. 33.

10. Havelock Ellis, "Commentary," in Radclyffe Hall, *The Well of Loneliness* (New York: Anchor Books, 1990), p. 6; cited hereafter as *WL*.

11. For discussion of the biographical sources of *Orlando* see Frank Baldanza, "Orlando and the Sackvilles," *PMLA* (1955): 274–79; and Howard Harper, *Between Language and Silence: The Novels of Virginia Woolf* (Baton Rouge: Louisiana State University Press, 1982), pp. 163–203. For discussion of the friendship between Woolf and Sackville-West see Joanne Trautmann, *The Jessamy Brides: The Friendship of Virginia Woolf and Vita Sackville-West*, Pennsylvania State Studies #36 (University Park: Pennsylvania State University Press, 1973); Hermione Lee, *The Novels of Virginia Woolf* (New York: Holmes and Meier, 1977), especially pp. 138–45; and Suzanne Raitt, *Vita and Virginia: The Work and Friendship of V. Sackville-West and Virginia Woolf* (Oxford: Clarendon Press, 1993).

12. Zwerdling, *Virginia Woolf and the Real World*, p. 28.

13. Catharine R. Stimpson, "Zero Degree Deviancy: The Lesbian Novel in English," *Critical Inquiry* 8, 2 (Winter 1981): 363–79.

14. Robert Lynd, "The Bounds of Decency," *Books and Writers* (Freeport, N.Y.: Books for Libraries Press, 1970), pp. 215, 222. Lynd comments on Joyce's humorlessness in the same essay, and in a later piece, "James Joyce and a New Kind of Fiction" (1935), he remarks: "When he quotes an obscenity he seldom quotes it with hilarity. He quotes it without prejudice on one side or the other, as an anthropologist might quote the saying of an African tribesman"; ibid., p. 147. Lynd's criticism on Wilde and Lawrence may be found in his *The Art of Letters* (Freeport, N.Y.: Books for Libraries Press, 1971), chapters 17 and 24, respectively.

15. See Hynes, *A War Imagined*, p. 371. Norah James's novel, *Sleeveless Errand*, blamed the loss of sexual control experienced by the heroine, Paula Cranford, on the war. This helps to explain why the book was banned even though, as the defense pointed out, it contrasted "the despair and hopelessness and waste" of Paula's life with the "normal life" of the married male protagonist, Bill Cheland. See James, *Sleeveless Errand* (Paris: Henry Babou and Jack Kahane, 1929), pp. 202–5; "Seized Novel Condemned," *The Times* (5 March 1929), p. 13.

16. Editorial, *Evening Standard* (20 August 1928): 6; Arnold Bennett, *Evening Standard* (9 August 1928): 7.

17. Arnold Dawson, "The Stunters and the Hunted," *Daily Herald* (20 August 1928): 4; "Novel Sent to 'Jix' for Judgment" (21 August): 1; "The Battle of a Book" (22 August): 5; "Should the Bible Be Banned?" (22 August): 7.

18. "Shaw and Wells in Banned Book Battle," *Daily Herald* (6 October 1928): 1. In *Extraordinary Women*, Mackenzie gives his character Hall's well-known hobbies ("spiritualism and gardening and collecting old furniture") and recalls an incident earlier in Hall's life by referring to an "attempted man-handling by the Society of Psychical Research"; *Extraordinary Women* (London: Hogarth Press, 1986), pp. 14–15. On Hall's problems with the Society of Psychical Research, see Lovat Dickson, *Radclyffe Hall at the Well of Loneliness: A Sapphic Chronicle* (London: Collins, 1975), pp. 80–96. Wyndham Lewis also parodied Hall in the deep-voiced female artist, with "a stiff

Radcliffe-Hall collar, of antique masculine cut," who lives in "this lonely well," "this palatial well of stern bachelor loneliness"; *The Apes of God* (1930; London: Penguin Books, 1965), pp. 234, 236, 239.

19. Leonard Woolf, "The World of Books. *The Well of Loneliness,*" *The Nation and Athenæum* (4 August 1928): 593. Hall called the review "a really dastardly attack, hitting below the belt with a vengeance"; quoted by Baker, *Our Three Selves,* p. 229.

20. Forster to Bennett, 31 August 1928. Still on the subject of Hall, Forster added that he wished "most heartily that I had never gone to see her." See letters in the Henry W. and Albert A. Berg Collection, The New York Public Library, Astor, Lenox and Tilden Foundations; cited hereafter as Berg.

21. [E. M. Forster], "The New Censorship," *The Nation and Athenæum* (1 September 1928): 696. In the next issue of this magazine, Forster and Woolf jointly published a letter on the same topic. It is worth noting, moreover, that Forster refrained from publishing *Maurice* not simply because it depicted homosexuality but because its homosexual lovers were allowed a happy ending. For all its heterodox stridency, *The Well of Loneliness* was, as Hall told Ellis, "a warning to any young and thoughtless girl," for "sexual desire often leads to a pack of trouble" (2 December 1928). Forster realized perfectly well that if a pessimistic work like Hall's novel could offend public opinion so easily, nothing would save his optimistic tale from suppression.

22. See the *Daily Herald* for interviews given by Hall on 21 and 24 August, and on 6 October.

23. Other notable reviewers who criticized *The Well* on these grounds were L. P. Hartley, in "New Fiction," *Saturday Review* (28 July 1928): 126–27; and Cyril Connolly, in "New Novels," *The New Statesman* (25 August 1928): 614–15.

24. "Alleged Obscene Novel. Proceedings at Bow-Street," *The Times* (10 November 1928): 9.

25. "Novel Condemned as Obscene," p. 5.

26. The appeal was attended by Rudyard Kipling and Marie Stopes. Vita Sackville-West looked in briefly, but soon became bored and went shopping instead.

27. Dominick LaCapra notes that Pinard was fascinated by Flaubert's portrait of Emma Bovary as a temptress who "lures the reader into the same temptations and immoral forms of behavior to which she succumbed"; *Madame Bovary on Trial* (Ithaca, N.Y.: Cornell University Press, 1982), p. 35. Ironically, as LaCapra observes, Pinard later published a book of his own obscene verse.

28. "Alleged Obscene Novel," p. 9; "*The Well of Loneliness* in Court," *Daily Express* (10 November 1928): 2.

29. See H. Montgomery Hyde, *The Trials of Oscar Wilde* (New York: Dover Publications, 1973), p. 201.

30. LaCapra, *Madame Bovary on Trial,* pp. 34–51. As I noted earlier, a book well suited to this line of defense was Norah James's *Sleeveless Errand,* which shows how adultery and promiscuity lead to disillusionment in the postwar era (see note 15).

31. In a letter to Gerard Hopkins, Hall described her "horror and despair when Cape's Counsel opened the case with a lie, with a blatant denial of the physical aspect that entered into my study of inversion!": "I can tell you that I sat there and sweated blood feeling that my work was both shamed and degraded. I had written that book for the sake of the truth, for the sake of helping these unfortunate people" (14 November 1928, Berg).

32. Ellen Bayuk Rosenman, "Sexual Identity and *A Room of One's Own*: 'Secret Economies' in Virginia Woolf's Feminist Discourse," *Signs* 14, 3 (Spring 1989): 645.

33. Hall, quoted by Dickson, *Radclyffe Hall,* pp. 209–10.

34. Ellis, quoted by Baker, *Our Three Selves*, p. 235.

35. See Jeffrey Weeks, *Sex, Politics and Society: The Regulation of Sexuality since 1800* (London: Longman, 1989), p. 142. As Weeks points out, Ellis was not the only sexologist censored in Britain. Iwan Bloch's *The Sexual Life of Our Time* was suppressed when an English translation appeared in 1908. Though granting that women's sexual pleasure could be as intense as men's (if of a different kind), Bloch stopped short of full recognition for lesbianism, claiming, "I do not know what actually occurs in practice"; *The Sexual Life of Our Time in Its Relations to Modern Civilization*, trans. M. Eden Paul (London: Rebman, 1908), p. 369.

36. Ellis deals specifically with lesbianism in "Sexual Inversion in Women," *Alienist and Neurologist* 16 (1895): 141–58.

37. See Wayne Koestenbaum, *Double Talk: The Erotics of Male Literary Collaboration* (London: Routledge, 1989), pp. 54–55.

38. Dickson, *Radclyffe Hall*, p. 161.

39. It should be said in Ellis's defense that on account of his stutter, he was equally disinclined to take the stand when *Sexual Inversion* went on trial in 1898. "I knew also," he wrote, "that those same defects which have always prevented me from attempting any kind of public speech would make me a bad witness"; *My Life: An Autobiography of Havelock Ellis* (Boston: Houghton Mifflin, 1939), p. 363.

40. Biron, quoted by Dickson, *Radclyffe Hall*, p. 165.

41. For a history of this reading of hysteria see Elaine Showalter, *The Female Malady: Women, Madness, and English Culture, 1830–1980* (New York: Pantheon Books, 1985).

42. Havelock Ellis, *Sexual Inversion* (1897); reprinted in *Studies in the Psychology of Sex*, vol. 1 (New York: Random House, 1942), p. 296.

43. Stimpson, "Zero Degree Deviancy," pp. 364–65.

44. Evelyn Irons, "Woman's Place *Is* the Home," *The Daily Mail* (20 July 1928): 4.

45. Hall, quoted by Baker, *Our Three Selves*, p. 248.

46. Ibid., p. 219. It is interesting to compare Hall's conception of lesbian relations with that of Vita Sackville-West. Sackville-West, as Suzanne Raitt stresses, was firmly committed to the institution of marriage, not for lesbians, but for heterosexuals. It was heterosexual marriage, Raitt argues, that created "a safe space" in which Sackville-West "could risk passionate, but discreet, lesbian affairs." Yet because Sackville-West's version of lesbianism, dramatized in her novels as in her life, often conformed to the aggressive/passive relation, it was just as unstable as the version promoted by Hall. See Raitt, *Vita and Virginia*, pp. 116, 95–96.

47. Jean Radford, "An Inverted Romance: *The Well of Loneliness* and Sexual Ideology," in *The Progress of Romance: The Politics of Popular Fiction*, ed. Jean Radford (London: Routledge and Kegan Paul, 1986), p. 108.

48. Radclyffe Hall, *The Unlit Lamp* (New York: Dial Press, 1981), p. 201; cited hereafter as *UL*.

49. Radclyffe Hall, Author's Forenote, *Miss Ogilvy Finds Herself* (London: Heinemann, 1934); cited hereafter as *MOFH*.

50. Hall, quoted by Dickson, *Radclyffe Hall*, p. 140. Like Stephen Gordon, Joan Ogden is described in *The Unlit Lamp* as "like a boy," a "freak," "queer," and "unnatural." Similarly, the title character of *Miss Ogilvy Finds Herself* is considered "odd" and "strange." In these earlier works, however, the question of sexual inversion is not raised explicitly.

51. Hall, quoted by Baker, *Our Three Selves*, p. 254. Colonel Barker was really Lillian Smith, who for many years masqueraded as a military hero, and even married a

woman whom she abandoned three years later, before being exposed in a bankruptcy case in the spring of 1929. On 25 April 1929, Smith was found guilty of perjury and given a nine-month prison sentence.

52. This list also might include Gian-Luca, the hero of Hall's previous novel, *Adam's Breed* (1926), and Charles Duffell, the protagonist of her short story "The Rest Cure—1932." Duffell's madness clearly resembles the hysteria of Stephen Gordon and Miss Ogilvy. Like his lesbian counterparts, Duffell is a survivor of the war. His maleness is further compromised by the fact that he plays no part in the war; he stays home and becomes a successful businessman instead. At least Gian-Luca goes to France. His survival is virtually ensured by his role as a waiter in the Officers' Mess at the British Army Base, a role which, he laments, denies him the opportunity to display his prowess on the battlefield. Even so, when the war is over he experiences a severe nervous breakdown, which compels him first to recuperate and then (like Duffell) to abandon civilization altogether. Gian-Luca and Duffell are two more of Hall's outcasts whose flight from civilization to seek transcendence anticipates (or, in Duffell's case, imitates) the dénouement of *The Well of Loneliness*. In *The Well*, however, Hall provides a sexual motive that is absent in *Adam's Breed*, as it appears to be in "The Rest Cure."

53. For discussion of the mannish lesbian in historical context, see Rosenman, "Sexual Identity," p. 645; Esther Newton, "The Mythic Mannish Lesbian: Radclyffe Hall and the New Woman," *Signs* 9, 4 (Summer 1984): 573.

54. E. M. Forster, Terminal Note, *Maurice* (New York: W. W. Norton, 1987), p. 250. This statement may also help to explain Forster's lack of enthusiasm for *The Well of Loneliness*. Though Forster himself was eager to use fiction as a vehicle for polemical purposes, perhaps Hall seemed to misuse it by insisting on the unhappy ending that homophobic readers expected of a lesbian love story.

55. Forster, *Maurice*, p. 252. Forster's gamekeeper gives an interesting twist to D. H. Lawrence's "greenwood" novel, *Lady Chatterley's Lover*. Forster claimed that Alec "is senior in date to the prickly gamekeepers of D. H. Lawrence," implying that the natural world to which Lawrence's lovers retreat in the postwar era had been rendered homosexual by his own prewar novel. Forster's claim was not strictly true, however, since Lawrence's first gamekeeper, Annable, appeared in *The White Peacock*. Forster must have known this: he wrote the terminal note to *Maurice* in September 1960 but had read Lawrence's first novel soon after its publication in 1911. In fact, Forster's attention was attracted by the homoerotic overtones of the bathing scene in *The White Peacock*. Frederick McDowell has argued, moreover, that *Lady Chatterley* may have prompted Forster to write with greater candor when he revised *Maurice* in 1931 and again in 1959; "'Moments of Emergence and of a New Splendour': D. H. Lawrence and E. M. Forster in Their Fiction," in *D. H. Lawrence's "Lady": A New Look at* Lady Chatterley's Lover, ed. Michael Squires and Dennis Jackson (Athens: University of Georgia Press, 1985), pp. 58–90.

56. Raitt, *Vita and Virginia*, p. 12.

57. Radford, "An Inverted Romance," p. 107.

58. Rosenman, "Sexual Identity," p. 643; Sherron E. Knopp, "'If I Saw You Would You Kiss Me?': Sapphism and the Subversiveness of Virginia Woolf's *Orlando*," *PMLA* 103, 1 (January 1988): 29. Knopp describes the lesbianism of *Orlando* as "one of the best-kept secrets of literary history."

59. Nigel Nicolson, *Portrait of a Marriage* (New York: Atheneum, 1973), p. 225. In the New York *Bookman* (February 1929), Raymond Mortimer wrote, "it is no secret that *Orlando* is a portrait of Mrs Harold Nicolson, who writes under her unmarried name, V. Sackville-West"; "Virginia Woolf and Lytton Strachey," in *Virginia Woolf:*

The Critical Heritage, ed. Robin Majumdar and Allen McLaurin (Boston: Routledge and Kegan Paul, 1975), p. 241. A review in *The Daily Mail* was entitled, "A Fantastic Biography: Mrs H. Nicolson and Orlando. 300 Years as Man and Woman"; see Victoria Glendinning, *Vita: The Life of V. Sackville-West* (London: Weidenfeld and Nicolson, 1983), p. 205.

60. Leonard Woolf later observed that *Orlando* marked the "turning-point in Virginia's career as a successful novelist," selling more than 8,000 copies in the first six months; *Downhill All the Way: An Autobiography of the Years 1919–1939* (New York: Harcourt Brace Jovanovich, 1975), p. 143.

61. Benstock, "Expatriate Sapphic Modernism," pp. 185–86.

62. Louise A. DeSalvo, "Lighting the Cave: The Relationship Between Vita Sackville-West and Virginia Woolf," *Signs* 8, 2 (Winter 1982): 206–7; Dickson, *Radclyffe Hall,* p. 223. While conceding that "no comparison between the two books can be made on literary grounds," Dickson contrasts Hall's "honesty" with the "tittering jokes of *Orlando* and the secret passion indulged in hotels abroad" by Woolf and Sackville-West. Jane Marcus, on the other hand, claims that Woolf affirms a lesbian identity; "Storming the Toolshed," *Signs* 7, 3 (Spring 1982): 629.

63. As noted earlier, Egan also designed a series of cartoons to accompany an anonymous poem that parodied the *Well of Loneliness* scandal, *The Sink of Solitude* (London: Hermes Press, 1928). One of the cartoons, "St. Stephen," is reproduced here as Figure 1. The poem may be found in Donald Thomas, *A Long Time Burning: The History of Literary Censorship in England* (New York: Frederick A. Praeger, 1969), pp. 516–21.

64. Virginia Woolf, *Collected Essays,* vol. 2, ed. Leonard Woolf (New York: Harcourt, Brace, and World, 1966), p. 71.

65. Virginia Woolf, *The Letters of Virginia Woolf,* vol. 4, ed. Nigel Nicolson and Joanne Trautmann (New York: Harcourt Brace Jovanovich, 1978), p. 14. Compare with *L3,* pp. 155–56.

66. Sackville-West to Woolf, [6 February] 1929, in *The Letters of Vita Sackville-West to Virginia Woolf,* ed. Louise A. DeSalvo and Mitchell A. Leaska (New York: Morrow, 1985), p. 318.

67. Virginia Woolf, *Orlando: The Holograph Draft,* transcribed and ed. Stuart Nelson Clarke (London: S. N. Clarke, 1993), pp. 12, 20, 121, 70; cited hereafter as *OHD.*

68. Hermione Lee, "Orlando and Her Biographer," *Times Literary Supplement* (18 March 1994): 5.

69. Virginia Woolf, "Friendships Gallery," ed. Ellen Hawkes, *Twentieth Century Literature* 25, 3–4 (Fall–Winter 1979): 279.

70. Virginia Woolf, Monk's House Papers (Brighton: Harvester Press Microfilms, 1985), MH/B6.e.

71. Rosenman, "Sexual Identity," pp. 636–37.

72. Virginia Woolf, *A Room of One's Own* (New York: Harcourt Brace Jovanovich, 1981), p. 83; cited hereafter as *AROO.*

73. Also remarking on the unexceptional nature of the published version of *A Room,* Alex Zwerdling attributes Woolf's coyness here to a "heightened awareness of a possibly hostile audience," that is, the men who may be standing behind the women listening to Woolf's lectures at Girton College, Cambridge; *Virginia Woolf and the Real World,* pp. 255–56.

74. Virginia Woolf, "The Censorship of Books," *The Nineteenth Century and After* (April 1929): 447.

75. Woolf to Sackville-West (9 October 1927), quoted by Sackville-West, "Virginia Woolf and *Orlando*," *The Listener* (27 January 1955): 157. It is a mark of Woolf's excitement over *Orlando* that she should have written so enthusiastically about the possibility of a revolution, since she tended to be wary of such violent ruptures. Though conceding that, "for all I know, every great book is an act of revolution," she clearly found it easier to reconcile herself to the gradual development she saw in the work of Conrad than to the upheavals occasioned by Joyce; "Modern novels (Joyce)," holograph notebook, n.d. (Berg).

76. Virginia Woolf, *Orlando: A Biography* (San Diego: Harcourt Brace Jovanovich, 1956), p. 309; cited hereafter as *O*. Woolf's subversion of traditional biography in *Orlando* is also discussed by Suzanne Raitt. Raitt's analysis, like mine, emphasizes that in *Orlando*, "it is the central ambiguity of gender which displaces all sorts of other certainties." The result, Raitt argues, is a "personal communication" to Sackville-West, "a complex manœuvre that speaks of both hate and love"; *Vita and Virginia*, pp. 23, 18, 38. Other aspects of Woolf's exploration of biographical modes are discussed by Avrom Fleischman in his chapter on *Orlando* in *Virginia Woolf: A Critical Reading* (Baltimore: Johns Hopkins University Press, 1977), pp. 135–49.

77. Bell represents Woolf's lack of children as a constant source of anxiety, of feelings of inadequacy, and of jealousy of her sister (his mother), Vanessa Bell. The production of books becomes a substitute for giving birth to children. Further, Bell ends the first volume of the biography with his aunt's acceptance of Leonard Woolf's marriage proposal, which is described as "the wisest decision of her life." That a biography should be divided along such novelistic lines underscores a major theme of *Orlando*: the fictionality of the biographical mode. Bell acknowledges, however, that a biography depends on guesswork, and that it is therefore unable to provide more than an outline of its subject; *Virginia Woolf: A Biography* (New York: Harcourt Brace Jovanovich, 1972), vol. 1, p. 187, vol. 2, p. 109.

78. Sackville-West, quoted in Virginia Woolf, "*Orlando*: An Edition of the Manuscript," ed. Madeline Moore, *Twentieth Century Literature* 25, 3–4 (Fall–Winter 1979): 349; cited hereafter as *OMS*.

79. Sackville-West told Nicolson that she felt "extraordinarily protective towards Woolf," who had "a sweet and childlike nature" (*OMS*, pp. 350–51). Woolf wrote that Sackville-West "lavishes on me the maternal protection which, for some reason, is what I have always most wished from everyone"; quoted by Bell, *Virginia Woolf*, vol. 2, p. 118. Also see Raitt, *Vita and Virginia*, pp. 62–86.

80. Following Flores Delattre, Joanne Trautmann has argued that "Woolf's Orlando is an amalgamation of Shakespeare's Orlando and Rosalind"; *The Jessamy Brides*, p. 41.

81. In a recent essay, Karen Lawrence argues that the androgynous and titillating effects of Orlando's clothes are heightened by their Turkishness. Woolf's novel, Lawrence suggests, draws on "the overdetermined figure of Eastern travel" in order to reinscribe the East "as a site of erotic freedom and liminality." Thus, it may be no accident that the sex change occurs in Turkey; in *Orlando*, as Lawrence points out, "gender crossing is imagined as a cultural border crossing as well." See "Orlando's Voyage Out," *Modern Fiction Studies* 38, 1 (1992): 259, 256.

82. D. H. Lawrence, *Phoenix: The Posthumous Papers of D. H. Lawrence*, ed. Edward D. McDonald (New York: Viking Press, 1936), pp. 710–11.

83. Virginia Woolf, *Collected Essays*, vol. 4, ed. Leonard Woolf (New York: Harcourt, Brace, and World, 1966), pp. 234, 221–28. James Naremore has taken these remarks as Woolf's final words on the relation between fact and fiction. From my

commentary it follows, however, that to read *Orlando* and *Between the Acts* as showing the "triumph of imagination over the historical process" is to oversimplify Woolf's intense grappling with this question. See Naremore, *The World Without a Self: Virginia Woolf and the Novel* (New Haven, Conn.: Yale University Press, 1973), pp. 195, 217–18.

84. Virginia Woolf, *Collected Essays*, vol. 1, ed. Leonard Woolf (New York: Harcourt, Brace, and World, 1966), p. 334.

85. Woolf, "Modern novels (Joyce)" (Berg).

86. Virginia Woolf, *The Essays of Virginia Woolf*, vol. 2, ed. Andrew McNeillie (New York: Harcourt Brace Jovanovich, 1987), p. 315.

87. Many critics have discussed the androgynous vision of *A Room* and its implications for *Orlando*, but not all have paid sufficient attention to the ways in which the novel complicates the polemic. Rachel Blau DuPlessis, for example, unwittingly reproduces the imagery of fusion and interpenetration when describing the function of androgyny in *Orlando*; *Writing Beyond the Ending: Narrative Strategies of Twentieth-Century Women Writers* (Bloomington: Indiana University Press, 1985), p. 62. The most sophisticated and convincing exploration of Woolfian androgyny may be found in Pamela L. Caughie, "Virginia Woolf's Double Discourse," in *Discontented Discourses: Feminism / Textual Intervention / Psychoanalysis,* ed. Marleen S. Barr and Richard Feldstein (Urbana: University of Illinois Press, 1989), pp. 41–53. Also see Caughie, *Virginia Woolf and Postmodernism: Literature in Quest and Question of Itself* (Urbana: University of Illinois Press, 1991), pp. 77–84.

88. Maria DiBattista, *Virginia Woolf's Major Novels: The Fables of Anon* (New Haven, Conn.: Yale University Press, 1980), p. 120.

89. Rachel Bowlby, *Virginia Woolf: Feminist Destinations* (Oxford: Basil Blackwell, 1988), p. 54. For other discussions of the uncertainty of gender in *Orlando* see M. Keith Booker, *Techniques of Subversion in Modern Literature: Transgression, Abjection, and the Carnivalesque* (Gainesville: University of Florida Press, 1991), pp. 183–85; and Makiko Minow-Pinkney, *Virginia Woolf and the Problem of the Subject* (Brighton: Harvester Press, 1987), especially pp. 121–47. Booker approaches this topic through genre and Bakhtin's theory of the carnivalesque; Minow-Pinkney's study is psychoanalytic.

90. Bowlby, *Virginia Woolf,* pp. 57, 59.

91. Ibid., p. 58.

92. Daniel Albright, *Personality and Impersonality: Lawrence, Woolf, and Mann* (Chicago: University of Chicago Press, 1978), pp. 96–97.

93. Virginia Woolf, *The Voyage Out* (New York: Harcourt, Brace, and World, 1948), p. 295.

94. For a discussion of this aspect of *Mrs. Dalloway* see Albright, *Personality and Impersonality,* especially pp. 131–35.

95. Virginia Woolf, *Mrs. Dalloway* (New York: Harcourt Brace Jovanovich, 1981), p. 186; cited hereafter as *MD.*

96. In her diary entry for 14 October 1922, Woolf wrote that *Mrs. Dalloway* shows "the world seen by the sane & the insane side by side." See Virginia Woolf, *The Diary of Virginia Woolf,* vol. 2, ed. Anne Olivier Bell with Andrew McNeillie (New York: Harcourt Brace Jovanovich, 1980), p. 207, cited hereafter as *D2*; Phyllis Rose, *Woman of Letters: A Life of Virginia Woolf* (London: Routledge and Kegan Paul, 1978), pp. 135–36. Using this quotation in her discussion of the novel, Maria DiBattista stresses that madness and sanity are "adjacent, *never identical,* aspects of the same reality"; *Virginia Woolf's Major Novels,* p. 28.

97. A similar parallel may be drawn between two of Hall's characters: the heroine of *The Unlit Lamp,* Joan Ogden, and the hero of *Adam's Breed,* Gian-Luca. The latter, as I have noted, may be counted among the damaged males of postwar fiction. And by the time the war is over, Joan, like Clarissa Dalloway, is too middle-aged to profit from social change: as we have seen, instead of becoming a doctor she settles into the orthodox "feminine" role of nurse. When in prewar years Joan announces her intention to train as a doctor, her father castigates medicine as an "unsexing, indecent profession for any woman," while her mother dismisses it as "an altogether ridiculous masculine role." In the eyes of Colonel Ogden, Joan's plan is the product of "new-fangled woman's rights ideas," which have no place either in his home or, implicitly, in England (*UL,* pp. 110–11).

98. Most of *Mrs. Dalloway*'s commentators discuss the doubling of Clarissa and Septimus, an approach encouraged by Woolf's introduction to the 1928 Modern Library edition. For some examples see Alex Page, "A Dangerous Day: Mrs. Dalloway Discovers Her Double," *Modern Fiction Studies* 7, 2 (Summer 1961): 115–24; Lee, *The Novels of Virginia Woolf,* p. 107ff; Mitchell A. Leaska, *The Novels of Virginia Woolf: From Beginning to End* (New York: John Jay Press, 1977), pp. 112–17; Michael Rosenthal, *Virginia Woolf* (New York: Columbia University Press, 1979), pp. 92–94; Louise A. Poresky, *The Elusive Self: Psyche and Spirit in Virginia Woolf's Novels* (Newark: University of Delaware Press, 1981), p. 100ff. For Avrom Fleischman, however, it is misleading to focus exclusively on this relation because it obscures juxtapositions between Clarissa and other characters; *Virginia Woolf,* p. 80. Also see Elizabeth Abel, *Virginia Woolf and the Fictions of Psychoanalysis* (Chicago: University of Chicago Press, 1989), pp. 33–34.

99. Virginia Woolf, *Three Guineas* (San Diego: Harcourt Brace Jovanovich, 1966), p. 20; cited hereafter as *TG.*

100. Rose, *Woman of Letters,* p. 182.

101. Leonard Woolf, *Beginning Again: An Autobiography of the Years 1911 to 1918* (New York: Harcourt Brace Jovanovich, 1972), p. 149.

102. E. M. Forster, *Two Cheers For Democracy* (New York: Harcourt, Brace, and World, 1951), p. 254.

103. Woolf, "The Censorship of Books," pp. 446, 447.

104. Virginia Woolf, *The Diary of Virginia Woolf,* vol. 5, ed. Anne Olivier Bell with Andrew McNeillie (New York: Harcourt Brace Jovanovich, 1984), p. 229.

105. Sandra M. Gilbert, "Costumes of the Mind: Transvestism as Metaphor in Modern Literature," in *Writing and Sexual Difference,* ed. Elizabeth Abel (Chicago: University of Chicago Press, 1982), p. 214.

106. Virginia Woolf, *Between the Acts* (San Diego: Harcourt Brace Jovanovich, 1969), p. 197; cited hereafter as *BA.*

107. Albright, *Personality and Impersonality,* p. 173.

Bibliography

Abel, Elizabeth. *Virginia Woolf and the Fictions of Psychoanalysis*. Chicago: U of Chicago P, 1989.

Adams, Robert. *Surface and Symbol: The Consistency of James Joyce's* Ulysses. New York: Oxford UP, 1962.

Adorno, Theodor W. *Aesthetic Theory*. Trans. C. Lenhardt. Ed. Gretel Adorno and Rolf Tiedemann. London: Routledge and Kegan Paul, 1984.

Albright, Daniel. *Personality and Impersonality: Lawrence, Woolf, and Mann*. Chicago: U of Chicago P, 1978.

"Alleged Obscene Novel. Proceedings at Bow-Street." *The Times* (10 November 1928): 9.

Anderson, Margaret. "Judicial Opinion (Our Suppressed October Issue)." *Little Review* 4, 8 (December 1917): 46–49.

———. "An Obvious Statement (for the Millionth Time)." *Little Review* 7, 3 (September–December 1920): 8-16.

———. "*Ulysses* in Court." *Little Review* 7, 4 (January–March 1921): 22–25.

Andrews, W. T., ed. *Critics on D. H. Lawrence: Readings in Literary Criticism*. Coral Gables, Fla.: U of Miami P, 1971.

Auden, W. H. *Forewords and Afterwords*. Selected by Edward Mendelson. New York: Random House, 1973.

Baker, Michael. *Our Three Selves: The Life of Radclyffe Hall*. New York: William Morrow, 1985.

Balbert, Peter. *D. H. Lawrence and the Phallic Imagination: Essays on Sexual Identity and Feminist Misreading*. New York: St. Martin's, 1989.

Balbert, Peter, and Marcus, Phillip L., eds. *D. H. Lawrence: A Centenary Consideration*. Ithaca, N.Y.: Cornell UP, 1985.

Baldanza, Frank. "Orlando and the Sackvilles." *PMLA* (1955): 274–79.

Barthes, Roland. *Mythologies*. Trans. Annette Lavers. New York: Noonday, 1972.

Beauvoir, Simone de. *The Second Sex*. Trans. H. M. Parshley. New York: Alfred A. Knopf, 1953.

Bell, Michael. *D. H. Lawrence: Language and Being*. Cambridge: Cambridge UP, 1992.

215

Bell, Quentin. *Virginia Woolf: A Biography*. New York: Harcourt Brace Jovanovich, 1972.

Bennett, Arnold. Editorial. *Evening Standard* (9 August 1928): 6.

Benstock, Bernard, ed. *The Seventh of Joyce*. Bloomingon: Indiana UP, 1982.

Bernheimer, Charles, and Kahane, Claire, eds. *In Dora's Case: Freud—Hysteria— Feminism*. New York: Columbia UP, 1985.

Black, Michael. *D. H. Lawrence: The Early Philosophical Works*. Cambridge: Cambridge UP, 1992.

Blanchard, Lydia. "Love and Power: A Reconsideration of Sexual Politics in D. H. Lawrence." *Modern Fiction Studies* 21, 3 (Autumn 1975): 431–43.

Bloch, Iwan. *The Sexual Life of Our Time in Its Relations to Modern Civilization*. Trans. M. Eden Paul. London: Rebman, 1908.

Bonds, Diane. *Language and the Self in D. H. Lawrence*. Ann Arbor: U of Michigan Research P, 1987.

Booker, M. Keith. *Techniques of Subversion in Modern Literature: Transgression, Abjection, and the Carnivalesque*. Gainesville: U of Florida P, 1991.

Bowlby, Rachel. *Virginia Woolf: Feminist Destinations*. Oxford: Basil Blackwell, 1988.

Box, Muriel, ed. *The Trial of Marie Stopes*. London: Femina Books, 1967.

Brett, Dorothy. *Lawrence and Brett: A Friendship*. Philadelphia: J. B. Lippincott, 1933.

Brittain, Vera. *Radclyffe Hall: A Case of Obscenity?* London: Femina Books, 1968.

Britton, Derek. *Lady Chatterley: The Making of the Novel*. London: Unwin Hyman, 1988.

Brown, Keith, ed. *Rethinking Lawrence*. Milton Keynes, England: Open UP, 1990.

Brown, Richard. *James Joyce and Sexuality*. Cambridge: Cambridge UP, 1985.

Budgen, Frank. *James Joyce and the Making of* Ulysses. Bloomington: Indiana UP, 1934.

Butler, Judith. *Gender Trouble: Feminism and the Subversion of Identity*. New York: Routledge, 1990.

———. "Performative Acts and Gender Constitution: An Essay in Phenomenology and Feminist Theory." In *Performing Feminisms: Feminist Critical Theory and Theatre*. Ed. Sue-Ellen Case. Baltimore: Johns Hopkins UP, 1990, 270–82.

Byrnes, Robert. "Bloom's Sexual Tropes: Stigmata of the 'Degenerate' Jew." *James Joyce Quarterly* 27, 2 (Winter 1990): 303–23.

Carpenter, Humphrey. *A Serious Character: The Life of Ezra Pound*. Boston: Houghton Mifflin, 1988.

Carter, John. "The *Rainbow* Prosecution." *Times Literary Supplement* (27 February 1969): 216.

Caughie, Pamela L. *Virginia Woolf and Postmodernism: Literature in Quest and Question of Itself*. Urbana: U of Illinois P, 1991.

———. "Virginia Woolf's Double Discourse." In *Discontented Discourses: Feminism / Textual Intervention / Psychoanalysis*. Ed. Marleen S. Barr and Richard Feldstein. Urbana: U of Illinois P, 1989, 41–53.

Chamberlain, John R. "D. H. Lawrence Shows Himself More Prophet than Artist." *New York Times Book Review* (3 June 1928): 2.

Chance, Roger. "Love and Mr. Lawrence." *Fortnightly Review* (October 1929): 500–511.

Cheng, Vincent S., and Martin, Timothy, eds. *Joyce in Context*. Cambridge: Cambridge UP, 1992.

Cohen, Ed. *Talk on the Wilde Side: Toward a Genealogy of a Discourse on Male Sexualities.* New York: Routledge, 1992.

Collins, Joseph. *The Doctor Looks at Literature: Psychological Studies of Life and Letters.* New York: George H. Doran, 1923.

Connolly, Cyril. "New Novels." *The New Statesman* (25 August 1928): 614–15.

Conrad, Joseph. *Heart of Darkness.* New York: Penguin Books, 1973.

Coombes, H., ed. *D. H. Lawrence: A Critical Anthology.* Harmondsworth, England: Penguin Books, 1973.

Cowan, James C. *D. H. Lawrence and the Trembling Balance.* University Park: Pennsylvania State UP, 1986.

Cox, Marian. "Music and War-Kultur." *English Review* 21 (October 1915): 301–11.

Craft, Christopher. "Alias Bunbury: Desire and Termination in *The Importance of Being Earnest.*" *Representations* 31 (Summer 1990): 19–46.

Daleski, H. M. *The Forked Flame: A Study of D. H. Lawrence.* Madison: U of Wisconsin P, 1987.

Davies, Alistair. "Contexts of Reading: The Reception of D. H. Lawrence's *The Rainbow* and *Women in Love.*" In *The Theory of Reading.* Ed. Frank Gloversmith. Totowa, N.J.: Barnes and Noble, 1984, 199–222.

Davies, Rosemary Reeves. "The Eighth Love Scene: The Real Climax of *Lady Chatterley's Lover.*" *D. H. Lawrence Review* 15, 1–2 (Spring–Summer 1982): 167–76.

Dawson, Arnold. "The Stunters and the Stunted." *Daily Herald* (20 August 1928): 4.

———. "Novel Sent to 'Jix' for Judgment." *Daily Herald* (21 August 1928): 1.

———. "The Battle of a Book." *Daily Herald* (22 August 1928): 5.

———. "Should the Bible Be Banned?" *Daily Herald* (22 August 1928): 7.

———. "Shaw and Wells in Banned Book Battle." *Daily Herald* (6 October 1928): 1.

De Grazia, Edward. *Girls Lean Back Everywhere: The Law of Obscenity and the Assault on Genius.* New York: Random House, 1992.

Delany, Paul. *D. H. Lawrence's Nightmare: The Writer and His Circle in the Years of the Great War.* New York: Basic Books, 1978.

Delavenay, Emile. *D. H. Lawrence: The Man and His Work. The Formative Years: 1885–1919.* Trans. Katharine M. Delavenay. London: Heinemann, 1972.

Dellamora, Richard. *Masculine Desire: The Sexual Politics of Victorian Aestheticism.* Chapel Hill: U of North Carolina P, 1990.

Deming, Robert H., ed. *James Joyce: The Critical Heritage.* 2 vols. London: Routledge and Kegan Paul, 1970.

DeSalvo, Louise A. "Lighting the Cave: The Relationship Between Vita Sackville-West and Virginia Woolf." *Signs* 8, 2 (Winter 1982): 195–214.

Devlin, Kimberly J. "The Romance Heroine Exposed: 'Nausicaa' and *The Lamplighter.*" *James Joyce Quarterly* 22, 4 (1985): 383–96.

———. "The Female Eye: Joyce's Voyeuristic Narcissists." In *New Alliances in Joyce Studies.* Ed. Bonnie Kime Scott. Newark: U of Delaware P, 1988, 135–43.

"The D. H. Lawrence Paintings." *The Daily Telegraph* (9 August 1929): 5.

DiBattista, Maria. *Virginia Woolf's Major Novels: The Fables of Anon.* New Haven, Conn.: Yale UP, 1980.

Dickson, Lovat. *Radclyffe Hall at the Well of Loneliness: A Sapphic Chronicle.* London: Collins, 1975.

Doherty, Gerald. "One Vast Hermeneutic Sentence: The Total Lawrentian Text." *PMLA* 106, 5 (October 1991): 1134–45.

Draper, R. P., ed. *D. H. Lawrence: The Critical Heritage*. New York: Barnes and Noble, 1970.

DuPlessis, Rachel Blau. *Writing Beyond the Ending: Narrative Strategies of Twentieth-Century Women Writers*. Bloomington: Indiana UP, 1985.

Eksteins, Modris. *Rites of Spring: The Great War and the Birth of the Modern Age*. Boston: Houghton Mifflin, 1989.

Eliot, T. S. *After Strange Gods: A Primer of Modern Heresy*. London: Faber and Faber, 1934.

Ellis, Havelock. *More Essays of Love and Virtue*. Garden City, N.Y.: Doubleday, Doran, 1931.

———. *Studies in the Psychology of Sex*. 2 vols. New York: Random House, 1942.

———. "Sexual Inversion in Women." *Alienist and Neurologist* 16 (1895): 141–58.

Ellmann, Richard. *James Joyce*. New York: Oxford UP, 1965.

———. Ulysses *on the Liffey*. New York: Oxford UP, 1972.

———. *Oscar Wilde*. New York: Alfred A. Knopf, 1988.

Ernst, Morris, and Schwartz, Alan U. *Censorship: The Search for the Obscene*. New York: Macmillan, 1964.

Fernihough, Anne. *D. H. Lawrence: Aesthetics and Ideology*. Oxford: Clarendon P, 1993.

Finot, Jean. "La Solidarité Franco-Anglo-Italienne: Essai de réalisation d'un programme intellectuel de demain. *The Athenæum* (27 November 1915): 388–90.

Flaubert, Gustave. *The Letters of Gustave Flaubert, 1830–1857*. Selected, ed., and trans. Francis Steegmuller. Cambridge, Mass.: Belknap P of Harvard UP, 1980.

———. *Madame Bovary*. Trans. Alan Russell. New York: Penguin Books, 1950.

Fleischman, Avrom. *Virginia Woolf: A Critical Reading*. Baltimore: Johns Hopkins UP, 1977.

Fletcher, John Gould. "Night-Haunted Lover." *New York Herald Tribune Books* (14 July 1929): 1, 6.

Ford (Hueffer), Ford Madox. *Parade's End*. New York: Vintage Books, 1979.

———. *When Blood Is Their Argument*. London: Hodder and Stoughton, 1915.

———. "Women and Men." *Little Review* 4, 9 (January 1918): 17–31.

Ford, George H. *Double Measure: A Study of the Novels and Stories of D. H. Lawrence*. New York: Holt, Rinehart, and Winston, 1965.

Ford, George H., Kermode, Frank, Clarke, Colin, and Spilka, Mark. "Critical Exchange." *Novel* 5, 1 (Fall 1971): 54–70.

Forster, E. M. *Aspects of the Novel*. San Diego: Harcourt Brace Jovanovich, 1955.

———. *The Life to Come*. New York: W. W. Norton, 1987.

———. *Maurice*. New York: W. W. Norton, 1971.

———. "The New Censorship." *The Nation and Athenæum* (1 September 1928): 696.

———. *Two Cheers For Democracy*. New York: Harcourt, Brace, 1951.

Forster, E. M., and Woolf, Virginia. "The New Censorship." *The Nation and Athenæum* (8 September 1928): 726.

Foucault, Michel. *The History of Sexuality*. Vol. 1: *An Introduction*. Trans. Robert Hurley. New York: Vintage Books, 1990.

———. *The History of Sexuality*. vol. 2: *The Use of Pleasure*. Trans. Robert Hurley. New York: Pantheon Books, 1985.

Fowell, Frank, and Palmer, Frank. *Censorship in England*. New York: Benjamin Blom, 1969.

French, Marilyn. *The Book as World: James Joyce's* Ulysses. Cambridge, Mass.: Harvard UP, 1976.

French, Susan. "Lawrence's Women." *Times Literary Supplement* (5 February 1993): 15.

Freud, Sigmund. *Dora: An Analysis of a Case of Hysteria.* New York: Collier Books, 1963.

———. *The Interpretation of Dreams.* Trans. and ed. James Strachey. New York: Avon Books, 1965.

———. *Three Essays on the Theory of Sexuality.* Trans. and ed. James Strachey. New York: Basic Books, 1975.

Freud, Sigmund, and Breuer, Josef. *Studies on Hysteria.* Trans. and ed. James Strachey. New York: Basic Books, 1957.

Fussell, Paul. *The Great War and Modern Memory.* New York: Oxford UP, 1975.

Gadamer, Hans-Georg. *Truth and Method.* Trans. revised by Joel Weinsheimer and Donald G. Marshall. New York: Crossroad, 1989.

Gagnier, Regenia. *Idylls of the Marketplace: Oscar Wilde and the Victorian Public.* Stanford, Calif.: Stanford UP, 1986.

———, ed. *Critical Essays on Oscar Wilde.* New York: G. K. Hall, 1991.

Garnett, Edward. *The Trial of Jeanne D'Arc and Other Plays.* London: Jonathan Cape, 1931.

Gertzman, Jay A. "The Piracies of *Lady Chatterley's Lover*: 1928–1950." *D. H. Lawrence Review* 19, 3 (Fall 1987): 267–99.

Gide, André. *Oscar Wilde: In Memoriam (Reminiscences).* Trans. Bernard Frechtman. New York: Philosophical Library, 1949.

Gifford, Don, with Seidman, Robert J. Ulysses *Annotated: Notes for James Joyce's* Ulysses. Berkeley: U of California P, 1988.

Gilbert, Sandra M. "Costumes of the Mind: Transvestism as Metaphor in Modern Literature." In *Writing and Sexual Difference.* Ed. Elizabeth Abel. Chicago: U of Chicago P, 1982, 193–219.

Gilbert, Sandra M., and Gubar, Susan. *No Man's Land: The Place of the Woman Writer in the Twentieth Century.* Vol. 1: *The War of the Words.* New Haven, Conn.: Yale UP, 1987.

———. *No Man's Land: The Place of the Woman Writer in the Twentieth Century.* Vol. 2: *Sexchanges.* New Haven, Conn.: Yale UP, 1989.

Gilbert, Stuart. *James Joyce's* Ulysses: *A Study.* New York: Vintage Books, 1955.

Glendinning, Victoria. *Vita: The Life of V. Sackville-West.* London: Weidenfeld and Nicolson, 1983.

Goodheart, Eugene. "Censorship and Self-Censorship in the Fiction of D. H. Lawrence." In *Representing Modernist Texts: Editing as Interpretation.* Ed. George Bornstein. Ann Arbor: U of Michigan P, 1991, 223–40.

Green, William. "Oscar Wilde and the Bunburys." *Modern Drama* 21, 1 (1978): 67–80.

Hall, Radclyffe. *Adam's Breed.* London: Virago P, 1985.

———. *Miss Ogilvy Finds Herself.* London: Heinemann, 1934.

———. *The Unlit Lamp.* New York: Dial P, 1981.

———. *The Well of Loneliness.* New York: Anchor Books, 1990.

Harper, Howard. *Between Language and Silence: The Novels of Virginia Woolf.* Baton Rouge: Louisiana State UP, 1982.

Harris, Janice. "Lawrence and the Edwardian Feminists." In *The Challenge of D. H. Lawrence.* Ed. Michael Squires and Keith Cushman. Madison: U of Wisconsin P, 1990, 62–76.

Hart, Clive, and Hayman, David, eds. *James Joyce's* Ulysses: *Critical Essays*. Berkeley: U of California P, 1974.

Hartley, L. P. "New Fiction." *Saturday Review* (28 July 1928): 126–27.

Hayman, David. "The Empirical Molly." In *Approaches to* Ulysses. Ed. Thomas F. Staley and Bernard Benstock. Pittsburgh: U of Pittsburgh P, 1970, 103–35.

Heap, Jane. "Art and the Law." *Little Review* 7, 3 (September–December 1920): 5–7.

Heilbrun, Carolyn. *Toward a Recognition of Androgyny*. New York: Alfred A. Knopf, 1973.

Henke, Suzette. "Joyce and Krafft-Ebing." *James Joyce Quarterly* 17, 1 (Fall 1979): 84–86.

Henke, Suzette, and Unkeless, Elaine, eds. *Women in Joyce*. Urbana: U of Illinois P, 1982.

Herr, Cheryl. *Joyce's Anatomy of Culture*. Urbana: U of Illinois P, 1986.

———. "'One Good Turn Deserves Another': Theatrical Cross-Dressing in Joyce's 'Circe' Episode." *Journal of Modern Literature* 11, 2 (July 1984): 263–76.

———. "'Penelope' as Period Piece." *Novel* 22, 2 (Winter 1989): 130–42.

Huysmans, J. K. *Against the Grain (A Rebours)*. New York: Dover Publications, 1969.

Hyde, H. Montgomery. *The Love That Dared Not Speak Its Name: A Candid History of Homosexuality in Britain*. Boston: Little, Brown, 1970.

———, ed. *The Trials of Oscar Wilde*. New York: Dover Publications, 1973.

Hyde, Virginia. *The Risen Adam: D. H. Lawrence's Revisionist Typology*. University Park: Pennsylvania State UP, 1992.

Hyland, Paul, and Sammells, Neil, eds. *Writing and Censorship in Britain*. New York: Routledge, 1992.

Hynes, Samuel. *A War Imagined: The First World War and English Culture*. New York: Atheneum, 1991.

"Improper Novel Costs Women $100." *New York Times* (22 February 1921): 13.

"Indecent Books." *The Times* (6 March 1929): 11.

Ingersoll, Earl. "*The Rainbow*'s Winifred Inger." *D. H. Lawrence Review* 17, 1 (Spring 1984): 67–69.

Irons, Evelyn. "Woman's Place *Is* the Home." *The Daily Mail* (20 July 1928): 4.

Iser, Wolfgang. *The Implied Reader: Patterns of Communication in Prose Fiction from Bunyan to Beckett*. Baltimore: Johns Hopkins UP, 1974.

Jackson, Dennis. "*Lady Chatterley's Lover*: Lawrence's Response to *Ulysses?*" *Philological Quarterly* 66, 3 (Summer 1987): 410–16.

Jackson, Tony E. "'Cyclops,' 'Nausicaa,' and Joyce's Imaginary Couple." *James Joyce Quarterly* 29, 1 (Fall 1991): 63–83.

James, Norah C. *Sleeveless Errand*. Paris: Henry Babou and Jack Kahane, 1929.

Jauss, Hans Robert. *Toward an Aesthetic of Reception*. Trans. Timothy Bahti. Minneapolis: U of Minnesota P, 1982.

Jay, Karla, and Glasgow, Joanne, eds. *Lesbian Texts and Contexts*. New York: New York UP, 1990.

J. F. H. "Mr. Lawrence's Criticism." *The New Statesman* (2 August 1924): 498.

Joyce, James. *Exiles*. Harmondsworth, England: Penguin Books, 1973.

———. *Letters of James Joyce*. Vol. I. Ed. Stuart Gilbert. New York: Viking, 1957.

———. *Letters of James Joyce*. Vols. 2–3. Ed. Richard Ellmann. New York: Viking, 1966.

———. *A Portrait of the Artist as a Young Man*. London: Penguin Books, 1976.

———. *Selected Letters of James Joyce*. Ed. Richard Ellmann. New York: Viking, 1975.

——. *Ulysses: The Corrected Text*. Ed. Hans Walter Gabler. New York: Vintage Books, 1986.

Joynson-Hicks, Sir William (Viscount Bedford). *Do We Need a Censor?* London: Faber and Faber, 1929.

Kalnins, Mara, ed. *D. H. Lawrence: Centenary Essays*. Bristol: Bristol Classical P, 1986.

Kelsey, Nigel. *D. H. Lawrence: Sexual Crisis*. New York: St. Martin's, 1991.

Kenner, Hugh. "Molly's Masterstroke." In Ulysses: *Fifty Years*. Ed. Thomas F. Staley. Bloomington: Indiana UP, 1974: 19–28.

——. *Ulysses*. Baltimore: Johns Hopkins UP, 1987.

Kent, Susan Kingsley. *Sex and Suffrage in Britain, 1860–1914*. Princeton, N.J.: Princeton UP, 1987.

Kermode, Frank. "Lawrence and the Apocalyptic Types." *Critical Quarterly* 10 (1968): 14–38.

Kiely, Robert. *Beyond Egotism: The Fiction of James Joyce, Virginia Woolf, and D. H. Lawrence*. Cambridge, Mass.: Harvard UP, 1980.

Kinkead-Weekes, Mark. "The Marble and the Statue: The Exploratory Imagination of D. H. Lawrence." In *Imagined Worlds: Essays in Honor of John Butt*. Ed. Ian Gregor and Maynard Mack. London: Methuen, 1968, 371–418.

Knight, G. Wilson. "Lawrence, Joyce and Powys." *Essays in Criticism* 11, 4 (1961): 403–41.

Knopp, Sherron E. "'If I Saw You Would You Kiss Me?': Sapphism and the Subversiveness of Virginia Woolf's *Orlando*." *PMLA* 103, 1 (January 1988): 24–34.

Koestenbaum, Wayne. *Double Talk: The Erotics of Male Literary Collaboration*. New York: Routledge, 1989.

LaCapra, Dominick. *Madame Bovary on Trial*. Ithaca, N.Y.: Cornell UP, 1982.

Landow, George P. *Images of Crisis: Literary Iconology, 1750 to the Present*. Boston: Routledge and Kegan Paul, 1982.

——. "The Rainbow: A Problematic Image." In *Nature and the Victorian Imagination*. Ed. U. C. Knoepflmacher and G. B. Tennyson. Berkeley: U of California P, 1977, 341–69.

Law, Jules David. "'Pity They Can't See Themselves': Assessing the 'Subject' of Pornography in 'Nausicaa.'" *James Joyce Quarterly* 27, 2 (1990): 219–39.

Lawrence, D. H. *Aaron's Rod*. Ed. Mara Kalnins. Cambridge: Cambridge UP, 1988.

——. *The Complete Poems of D. H. Lawrence*. Ed. Vivian de Sola Pinto and Warren Roberts. New York: Viking, 1964.

——. *The Complete Stories*. 3 vols. London: Penguin Books, 1977.

——. *The First Lady Chatterley*. London: Penguin Books, 1973.

——. "Italian Studies: By the Lago di Garda." *English Review* 15 (September 1913): 202–34.

——. *John Thomas and Lady Jane*. New York: Penguin Books, 1977.

——. *Kangaroo*. London: Penguin Books, 1950.

——. *Lady Chatterley's Lover; A Propos of* Lady Chatterley's Lover. Ed. Michael Squires. Cambridge: Cambridge UP, 1993.

——. *The Letters of D. H. Lawrence*. 7 vols. Ed. James T. Boulton et al. Cambridge: Cambridge UP, 1979–1993.

——. *The Lost Girl*. Ed. John Worthen. Cambridge: Cambridge UP, 1981.

——. *The Paintings of D. H. Lawrence*. London: Mandrake, 1929.

——. *Phoenix: The Posthumous Papers of D. H. Lawrence*. Ed. Edward D. McDonald. New York: Viking, 1936.

————. *Phoenix II: Uncollected, Unpublished, and Other Prose Works.* Ed. Warren Roberts and Harry T. Moore. Harmondsworth, England: Penguin Books, 1978.

————. *The Plumed Serpent (Quetzalcoatl).* Ed. L. D. Clark. Cambridge: Cambridge UP, 1987.

————. *The Rainbow.* Ed. Mark Kinkead-Weekes. Cambridge: Cambridge UP, 1989.

————. *Reflections on the Death of a Porcupine and Other Essays.* Ed. Michael Herbert. Cambridge: Cambridge UP, 1988.

————. "Samson and Delilah." *English Review* 24 (March 1917): 209–24.

————. *Sons and Lovers.* Cambridge: Cambridge UP, 1992.

————. *St. Mawr and the Man Who Died.* New York: Vintage Books, 1953.

————. *Studies in Classic American Literature.* New York: Doubleday, 1951.

————. *Study of Thomas Hardy and Other Essays.* Ed. Bruce Steele. Cambridge: Cambridge UP, 1983.

————. *The Symbolic Meaning: The Uncollected Versions of* Studies in Classic American Literature. Ed. Armin Arnold. Arundel, England: Centaur Press, 1962.

————. *Twilight in Italy.* New York: Viking, 1958.

————. "Two Hitherto Unknown Pieces by D. H. Lawrence." Ed. Carl Baron. *Encounter* 33, 2 (August 1969): 3–6.

————. *The Virgin and the Gipsy.* New York: Vintage Books, 1984.

————. *The White Peacock.* Ed. Andrew Robertson. Cambridge: Cambridge UP, 1983.

————. *Women in Love.* Ed. David Farmer, Lindeth Vasey, and John Worthen. Cambridge: Cambridge UP, 1987.

Lawrence, Karen. *The Odyssey of Style in* Ulysses. Princeton, N.J.: Princeton UP, 1981.

————. "Orlando's Voyage Out." *Modern Fiction Studies* 38, 1 (1992): 253–77.

Leaska, Mitchell A. *The Novels of Virginia Woolf: From Beginning to End.* New York: John Jay, 1977.

Leavis, F. R. *D. H. Lawrence: Novelist.* New York: Simon and Schuster, 1969.

Lee, Hermione. *The Novels of Virginia Woolf.* New York: Holmes and Meier, 1977.

————. "Orlando and her Biographer." *Times Literary Supplement* (18 March 1994): 5–6.

Leed, Eric. *No Man's Land: Combat and Identity in World War I.* Cambridge: Cambridge UP, 1979.

Leonard, Garry. "The Virgin Mary and the Urge in Gerty: The Packaging of Desire in the 'Nausicaa' Chapter of *Ulysses.*" *University of Hartford Studies in Literature* 23, 1 (1991): 3–23.

————. "Women on the Market: Commodity Culture, 'Femininity,' and 'Those Lovely Seaside Girls' in Joyce's *Ulysses.*" *Joyce Studies Annual* 2 (1991): 27–68.

Levenson, Michael. *A Genealogy of Modernism: A Study of English Literary Doctrine, 1908–1922.* Cambridge: Cambridge UP, 1984.

————. *Modernism and the Fate of Individuality: Character and Novelistic Form from Conrad to Woolf.* Cambridge: Cambridge UP, 1991.

Lewiecki-Wilson, Cynthia. *Writing Against the Family: Gender in Lawrence and Joyce.* Carbondale: Southern Illinois UP, 1994.

Lewis, Wyndham. *The Apes of God.* London: Penguin Books, 1965.

————. "Cantleman's Spring Mate." *Little Review* 4, 6 (October 1917): 8–14.

————. *The Roaring Queen.* London: Secker and Warburg, 1973.

————. "The Son of Woman." *Time and Tide* (18 April 1931): 470–72.

Litvak, Joseph. *Caught in the Act: Theatricality in the Nineteenth-Century English Novel.* Berkeley: U of California P, 1992.

Litz, A. Walton. "Lawrence, Pound, and Early Modernism." In Balbert and Marcus, *D. H. Lawrence: A Centenary Consideration*, pp. 15–28.

Lombroso, Cesare. *The Man of Genius*. New York: Garland, 1984.

Longenbach, James. *Modernist Poetics of History: Pound, Eliot, and the Sense of the Past*. Princeton, N.J.: Princeton UP, 1987.

———. "Pound among the Women." *Review* 12 (1990): 135–58.

Lowe-Evans, Mary. *Crimes Against Fecundity: Joyce and Population Control*. Syracuse, N.Y.: Syracuse UP, 1989.

———. "Sex and Confession in the Joyce Canon: Some Historical Parallels." *Journal of Modern Literature* 16, 4 (Spring 1990): 563–76.

Lynd, Robert. *The Art of Letters*. Freeport, N.Y.: Books for Libraries, 1971.

———. *Books and Writers*. Freeport, N.Y.: Books for Libraries, 1970.

Mackenzie, Compton. *Extraordinary Women*. London: Hogarth, 1986.

———. *My Life and Times: Octave Five, 1915–1923*. London: Chatto and Windus, 1966.

Maddox, Brenda. *Nora: The Real Life of Molly Bloom*. Boston: Houghton Mifflin, 1988.

———. "Reluctant to Kiss." *Times Literary Supplement* (15 January 1993): 5.

Mahaffey, Vicki. *Reauthorizing Joyce*. Cambridge: Cambridge UP, 1988.

Mailer, Norman. *The Prisoner of Sex*. Boston: Little, Brown, 1971.

Majumdar, Robin, and McLaurin, Allen, eds. *Virginia Woolf: The Critical Heritage*. Boston: Routledge and Kegan Paul, 1975.

Marcus, Jane. "Storming the Toolshed." *Signs* 7, 3 (Spring 1982): 622–40.

———. *Virginia Woolf and the Languages of Patriarchy*. Bloomington: Indiana UP, 1987.

Marshall, David. *The Figure of the Theater: Shaftesbury, Defoe, Adam Smith and George Eliot*. New York: Columbia UP, 1986.

———. *The Surprising Effects of Sympathy: Marivaux, Diderot, Rousseau and Mary Shelley*. Chicago: U of Chicago P, 1988.

McFee, William. "Novels to the Fore." *Bookman* (July 1928): 568–72.

McGee, Patrick. *Paperspace: Style as Ideology in Joyce's* Ulysses. Lincoln: U of Nebraska P, 1988.

McLaughlin, Ann. "The Clenched and Knotted Horses in *The Rainbow*." *D. H. Lawrence Review* 13, 2 (1980): 176–86.

Meyers, Jeffrey. *D. H. Lawrence: A Biography*. New York: Alfred A. Knopf, 1990.

———. *The Enemy: A Biography of Wyndham Lewis*. London: Routledge and Kegan Paul, 1980.

———. *Painting and the Novel*. Manchester: Manchester UP, 1975.

Millett, Kate. *Sexual Politics*. New York: Ballantine Books, 1978.

Minow-Pinkney, Makiko. *Virginia Woolf and the Problem of the Subject*. Brighton: Harvester, 1987.

Moore, Harry T. *The Intelligent Heart: The Life of D. H. Lawrence*. New York: Grove, 1962.

———. *The Priest of Love: A Life of D. H. Lawrence*. New York: Farrar, Straus, and Giroux, 1974.

Mortimer, Raymond. "New Novels." *The Nation and Athenæum* (9 June 1928): 332.

Moynahan, Julian. *The Deed of Life: The Novels and Tales of D. H. Lawrence*. Princeton, N.J.: Princeton UP, 1963.

"Mr. Lawrence's Pansies." *The New Statesman* (27 July 1929): 501–2.

Murry, John Middleton. "The Poems of D. H. Lawrence." *The New Adelphi* (December 1928): 165–67.

———. *Son of Woman: The Story of D. H. Lawrence.* London: Jonathan Cape, 1931.

Myers, Neil. "Lawrence and the War." *Criticism* 4, 1 (1962): 44–58.

Naremore, James. *The World Without a Self: Virginia Woolf and the Novel.* New Haven, Conn.: Yale UP, 1973.

Nehls, Edward. *D. H. Lawrence: A Composite Biography.* 3 vols. Madison: U of Wisconsin P, 1957–1959.

Newton, Esther. "The Mythic Mannish Lesbian: Radclyffe Hall and the New Woman." *Signs* 9, 4 (Summer 1984): 557–75.

Nicolson, Nigel. *Portrait of a Marriage.* London: Weidenfeld and Nicolson, 1973.

Nin, Anaïs. *D. H. Lawrence: An Unprofessional Study.* London: Black Spring, 1985.

Nixon, Cornelia. *Lawrence's Leadership Politics and the Turn Against Women.* Berkeley: U of California P, 1986.

Nordau, Max. *Degeneration.* New York: D. Appleton, 1895.

"Novel Condemned as Obscene." *The Times* (17 November 1928): 5.

Page, Alex. "A Dangerous Day: Mrs. Dalloway Discovers Her Double." *Modern Fiction Studies* 7, 2 (Summer 1961): 115–24.

Peake, Charles. *James Joyce: The Citizen and the Artist.* Stanford, Calif.: Stanford UP, 1977.

Pearson, Hesketh. *Oscar Wilde: His Life and Wit.* New York: Harper and Brothers, 1946.

Poresky, Louise A. *The Elusive Self: Psyche and Spirit in Virginia Woolf's Novels.* Newark: U of Delaware P, 1981.

Pound, Ezra. "The Classics Escape." *Little Review* 7, 11 (March 1918): 32–34.

———. "James Joyce. At Last the Novel Appears." *The Egoist* 4, 2 (February 1917): 22.

———. *Letters of Ezra Pound, 1907–1941.* Ed. D. D. Paige. New York: Harcourt, Brace, 1950.

———. *Literary Essays of Ezra Pound.* Ed. T. S. Eliot. New York: New Directions, 1968.

———. *Personae: The Shorter Poems of Ezra Pound.* Ed. Lea Baechler and A. Walton Litz. New York: New Directions, 1990.

———. *Pound/Joyce: The Letters of Ezra Pound to James Joyce, with Pound's Essays on Joyce.* Ed. Forrest Reed. New York: New Directions, 1967.

———. *Selected Letters of Ezra Pound to John Quinn, 1915–1924.* Ed. Timothy Materer. Durham, N.C.: Duke UP, 1991.

———. *Selected Prose, 1909–1965.* Ed. William Cookson. London: Faber and Faber, 1973.

———. "*Tarr,* by Wyndham Lewis." *Little Review* 4, 11 (March 1918): 35.

Powell, Kerry. *Oscar Wilde and the Theatre of the 1890s.* Cambridge: Cambridge UP, 1990.

Preston, Harold P. "*Ulysses.*" *Modern Review* 1, 1 (Autumn 1922): 40–42.

Quennell, Peter. "The Later Period of D. H. Lawrence." In *Scrutinies,* vol. 2. Ed. Edgell Rickwood. London: Wishart, 1931, 124–37.

Radford, Jean, ed. *The Progress of Romance: The Politics of Popular Fiction.* London: Routledge and Kegan Paul, 1986.

Raitt, Suzanne. *Vita and Virginia: The Work and Friendship of V. Sackville-West and Virginia Woolf.* Oxford: Clarendon Press, 1993.

Reid, B. L. *The Man from New York: John Quinn and His Friends*. New York: Oxford UP, 1968.

Richards, Thomas. *The Commodity Culture of Victorian England: Advertising and Spectacle, 1851–1914*. Stanford, Calif.: Stanford UP, 1990.

Ricks, Christopher. *T. S. Eliot and Prejudice*. Berkeley: U of California P, 1988.

Riquelme, John Paul. *Teller and Tale in Joyce's Fiction: Oscillating Perspectives*. Baltimore: Johns Hopkins UP, 1983.

Roberts, Warren. *A Bibliography of D. H. Lawrence*. Cambridge: Cambridge UP, 1982.

Roberts, W. H. "D. H. Lawrence: Study of a Free Spirit in Literature." *Renaissance Studies* 18 (1974): 5–16.

Rolph, C. H., ed. *The Trial of Lady Chatterley*. Harmondsworth, England: Penguin Books, 1961.

Rose, Phyllis. *Woman of Letters: A Life of Virginia Woolf*. London: Routledge and Kegan Paul, 1978.

Rosenman, Ellen Bayuk. "Sexual Identity and *A Room of One's Own*: 'Secret Economies' in Virginia Woolf's Feminist Discourse." *Signs* 14, 3 (1989): 634–50.

Rosenthal, Michael. *Virginia Woolf*. New York: Columbia UP, 1979.

Rosenzweig, Paul. "A Defense of the Second Half of *The Rainbow*: Its Structure and Characterization." *D. H. Lawrence Review* 13, 2 (1980): 150–60.

Ross, Charles L. *The Composition of* The Rainbow *and* Women in Love: *A History*. Charlottesville: UP of Virginia, 1979.

Roth, Samuel. "An Offer to James Joyce." *Two Worlds Monthly* 3, 3 (September 1927): 181–82.

Ruderman, Judith. *D. H. Lawrence and the Devouring Mother: The Search for a Patriarchal Ideal of Leadership*. Durham, N.C.: Duke UP, 1984.

Sackville-West, Vita. *The Letters of Vita Sackville-West to Virginia Woolf*. Ed. Louise A. DeSalvo and Mitchell A. Leaska. London: Hutchinson, 1984.

———. "Virginia Woolf and *Orlando*." *The Listener* (27 January 1955): 157–58.

Saunders, David. "The Trial of *Lady Chatterley's Lover*: Limiting Cases and Literary Canons." *Southern Review* 15, 2 (July 1982): 161–77.

Schleifer, Ronald. "Lawrence's Rhetoric of Vision: The Ending of *The Rainbow*." *D. H. Lawrence Review* 13, 2 (1980): 161–75.

Scott, Bonnie Kime. *Joyce and Feminism*. Bloomington: Indiana UP, 1984.

Sedgwick, Eve Kosofsky. *Between Men: English Literature and Male Homosocial Desire*. New York: Columbia UP, 1985.

Segall, Jeffrey. *Joyce in America: Cultural Politics and the Trials of* Ulysses. Berkeley: U of California P, 1993.

"Seized Novel Condemned." *The Times* (5 March 1929): 13.

"Seized Pictures Case." *The Times* (9 August 1929): 9.

Shonfield, Andrew. "Lawrence's Other Censor." *Encounter* 17, 3 (September 1961): 63–64.

Showalter, Elaine. *The Female Malady: Women, Madness, and English Culture, 1830–1980*. New York: Pantheon Books, 1985.

Siegel, Carol. *Lawrence among the Women: Wavering Boundaries in Women's Literary Traditions*. Charlottesville: UP of Virginia, 1991.

Simpson, Hilary. *D. H. Lawrence and Feminism*. London: Croom Helm, 1982.

Smith, Anne, ed. *Lawrence and Women*. London: Vision, 1977.

Smith, Timothy D'Arch. *Love in Earnest: Some Notes on the Lives and Writings of English "Uranian" Poets from 1889 to 1930*. London: Routledge and Kegan Paul, 1970.

Sparrow, John. "Regina v. Penguin Books Ltd.: An Undisclosed Element of the Case." *Encounter* 18, 101 (February 1962): 35–43.

Spilka, Mark. "Lawrence Up-Tight, or the Anal Phase Once Over." *Novel* 4, 3 (Spring 1971): 252–67.

———. *The Love Ethic of D. H. Lawrence*. Bloomington: Indiana UP, 1955.

Squires, Michael. *The Creation of* Lady Chatterley's Lover. Baltimore: Johns Hopkins UP, 1983.

Squires, Michael, and Jackson, Dennis, eds. *D. H. Lawrence's "Lady": A New Look at* Lady Chatterley's Lover. Athens: U of Georgia P, 1985.

Stephens, John Russell. *The Censorship of English Drama, 1824–1901*. Cambridge: Cambridge UP, 1980.

Stimpson, Catharine R. "Zero Degree Deviancy: The Lesbian Novel in English." *Critical Inquiry* 8, 2 (Winter 1981): 363–79.

Stoehr, Taylor. "'Mentalized Sex' in D. H. Lawrence." *Novel* 8, 2 (Winter 1975): 101–22.

Stopes, Marie. *Contraception*. London: J. Bale, Sons, and Davidson, 1928.

———. *Married Love*. London: Fifield, 1918.

Suckow, Ruth. "Two Temperaments." *The Outlook* (29 August 1929): 713–14.

Sultan, Stanley. *The Argument of* Ulysses. Columbus: Ohio State UP, 1964.

Swift, Jennifer. "The Body and Transcendence of Two Wastelands: *Lady Chatterley's Lover* and *The Waste Land*." *Paunch* 63–64 (December 1990): 141–71.

Taylor, Rachel Annand. "In Three Continents." *Spectator* (2 June 1928): 844–47.

Thomas, Brook. "*Ulysses* on Trial: Some Supplementary Reading." *Criticism* 33, 3 (Summer 1991): 371–93.

Trautmann, Joanne. *The Jessamy Brides: The Friendship of Virginia Woolf and Vita Sackville-West*. Pennsylvania State Studies #36. University Park: Pennsylvania State UP, 1973.

Trilling, Lionel. *Sincerity and Authenticity*. New York: Harcourt Brace Jovanovich, 1973.

"*Ulysses* Adjudged Indecent; Review Editors Are Fined." *New York Tribune* (22 February 1921): 13.

Walkley, R. Barrie. "The Bloom of Motherhood: Couvade as a Structural Device in *Ulysses*." *James Joyce Quarterly* 18, 1 (Fall 1980): 55–67.

Waugh, Evelyn. *Vile Bodies*. Boston: Little, Brown, 1958.

Weeks, Jeffrey. *Sex, Politics and Society: The Regulation of Sexuality since 1800*. London: Longman, 1981.

Weininger, Otto. *Sex and Character*. New York: G. P. Putnam's Sons, 1906.

"*The Well of Loneliness* in Court." *Daily Express* (10 November 1928): 2.

West, Rebecca. *The Return of the Soldier*. New York: Dial, 1980.

Whelan, P. T. *D. H. Lawrence: Myth and Metaphysic in* The Rainbow *and* Women in Love. Ann Arbor: U of Michigan Research P, 1988.

White, Allon. *The Uses of Obscurity*. London: Routledge and Kegan Paul, 1981.

Widmer, Kingsley. *Defiant Desire: Some Dialectical Legacies of D. H. Lawrence*. Carbondale: Southern Illinois UP, 1992.

Wilde, Oscar. *The Complete Works of Oscar Wilde*. New York: Harper and Row, 1989.

———. *The Letters of Oscar Wilde*. Ed. Rupert Hart-Davis. New York: Harcourt, Brace, and World, 1962.

Wohl, Robert. *The Generation of 1914*. Cambridge, Mass.: Harvard UP, 1979.

Woolf, Leonard. *Beginning Again: An Autobiography of the Years 1911–1918*. New York: Harcourt Brace Jovanovich, 1972.

———. *Downhill All the Way: An Autobiography of the Years 1919–1939*. New York: Harcourt Brace Jovanovich, 1975.

———. "The World of Books. *The Well of Loneliness*." *The Nation and Athenæum* (4 August 1928): 593.

Woolf, Virginia. *Between the Acts*. San Diego: Harcourt Brace Jovanovich, 1969.

———. "The Censorship of Books." *The Nineteenth Century and After* (April 1929): 446–47.

———. *Collected Essays*. 4 vols. Ed. Leonard Woolf. New York: Harcourt, Brace, and World, 1966.

———. *The Diary of Virginia Woolf*. 6 vols. Ed. Anne Olivier Bell with Andrew McNeillie. New York: Harcourt Brace Jovanovich, 1977–1984.

———. *The Essays of Virginia Woolf*. 3 vols. Ed. Andrew McNeillie. New York: Harcourt Brace Jovanovich, 1986–1993.

———. "Friendships Gallery." Ed. Ellen Hawkes. *Twentieth Century Literature* 25, 3–4 (Fall–Winter 1979): 270–302.

———. *The Letters of Virginia Woolf*. 6 vols. Ed. Nigel Nicolson and Joanne Trautmann. New York: Harcourt Brace Jovanovich, 1975–1980.

———. *Mrs. Dalloway*. New York: Harcourt Brace Jovanovich, 1953.

———. *Orlando: A Biography*. New York: Harcourt Brace Jovanovich, 1956.

———. "*Orlando*: An Edition of the Manuscript." Ed. Madeline Moore. *Twentieth Century Literature* 25, 3–4 (Fall–Winter 1979): 303–55.

———. *Orlando: The Holograph Draft*. Transcribed and ed. Stuart Nelson Clarke. London: S. N. Clarke, 1993.

———. *Roger Fry: A Biography*. New York: Harcourt Brace Jovanovich, 1976.

———. *A Room of One's Own*. New York: Harcourt Brace Jovanovich, 1957.

———. *Three Guineas*. San Diego: Harcourt Brace Jovanovich, 1966.

———. *The Voyage Out*. New York: Harcourt, Brace, and World, 1948.

Worthen, John. *D. H. Lawrence*. Cambridge: Cambridge UP, 1991.

"The Year's Harvest of Noteworthy Poetry." *New York Times Book Review* (26 November 1916): 508.

Yeats, W. B. *The Autobiography of William Butler Yeats*. New York: Collier Books, 1965.

———. *The Letters of W. B. Yeats*. Ed. Allan Wade. New York: Macmillan, 1955.

Zwerdling, Alex. *Virginia Woolf and the Real World*. Berkeley: U of California P, 1986.

Index

Lawrence, 24, 26, 27, 38–39, 42, 55, 112; and *Little Review,* 72; Nordau on, 29; and sexual deviance, 7–8, 10; and Wilde, 7–10, 27, 72, 148. *See also* Aestheticism; Degeneracy and Degeneration
Defence of the Realm Act, 3
Degeneracy and degeneration: and Britain, 72, 110; and the Continent, 112; and democracy, 60; and Germany, 6, 27–29; and Hall, 147–48; and homosexuality, 8, 13–14; and Lawrence, 28–29, 60, 110, 112, 121; Lombroso on, 13–14; and modernism, 27, 72; Nordau on, 13–14, 29–30, 188 nn.26–27; and Wilde, 8, 13–14, 72. *See also* Decadence
Delany, Paul, 31, 39
Delattre, Flores, 212 n.80
Delavenay, Emile, 31, 188 n.31
Dellamora, Richard, 182 n.10, 183 n.18, 185 n.47
Derby, Lord, 27
DeSalvo, Louise A., 211 n.62
Devlin, Kimberly J., 78, 196 n.54, 196–97 n.61
DiBattista, Maria, 170, 213 n.96
Dickens, Charles, viii, x, 183 n.24
Dickinson, Sir John, 21, 26, 144, 187 n.17
Dickinson, Violet, 164
Dickson, Lovat, 154, 211 n.62
Doherty, Gerald, 206 n.80
Dostoyevsky, Fyodor, 33
Douglas, James: on Hall, 147–49, 158; as hysterical, 149; on Joyce, 77–78, 195 n.45; on Lawrence, 25–26, 29, 44, 48, 58, 63, 77
Douglas, Lord Alfred: "In Praise of Shame," 9–10; sued by Robert Ross, 8, 27; "Two Loves," 9, 10; and Wilde, 8, 12
Duckworth, George, 37–38, 188 n.35
DuPlessis, Rachel Blau, 213 n.87

Earnestness, 15–17, 137, 146. *See also* Sincerity
Earp, Thomas, 113, 138
Egan, Beresford, viii, x, 162, 211 n.63
Egoist, The, 75, 195 nn.38,45

Eksteins, Modris, 187 n.19
Eliot, T. S.: *After Strange Gods,* 200 n.11, 201 n.26; and 1890s, 194 n.32; and Faber and Faber, viii; on Lawrence, 109, 201 n.26; and Roth petition, 200 n.9; *The Waste Land,* 75, 205 n.65
Ellis, Havelock: on bisexuality, 97; on censorship, 177; on courtship, 156; and Hall trial, 152, 153–54, 208 n.21; and hysteria, 115, 154–55; on obscenity, 83; and preface to *The Well of Loneliness,* 146, 152–55; and Roth petition, 200 n.9; on sexual inversion, 146, 152–55, 156, 209 n.36; *Sexual Inversion,* 14, 115, 116, 153–55; —, suppression of, 14, 115, 153, 185 n.40, 209 nn.35,39
Ellmann, Richard, 94, 97, 102, 182 n.14, 197 nn.67,71, 198 n.74
English Review, 27–28, 35, 41
Ernst, Morris L., 181 n.3, 182 n.10

Faber and Faber, viii
Fanny (Feydeau), 6
Faust (Goethe), 102
Feminism: and essentialism, 18, 120, 121; Forster on, 177; and Hall, 155–56; and hysteria, 111, 119–20; and Joyce, 91–94, 197 n.70; and Lawrence, 41–44, 56, 57–58, 62–64, 114, 119–21, 122, 189 nn.45–46, 192 n.81, 202 nn.32,34, 203–4 n.55; and lesbianism, 57–58, 155–56; and postwar antifeminism, 114, 120; and sex war, 19, 41–44, 114, 119–20; and theory of self, 18–19; and Wilde, 18; and Woolf, 165, 177; and World War I, 19, 42–43, 114. *See also* Suffragism
Fernihough, Anne, 111, 203 n.52
Fineman, Joel, 184 n.30
Finot, Jean, 27
Flaubert, Gustave: *Bouvard et Pécuchet,* 5; and impersonal narration, 5, 130; and *Madame Bovary* trial, 5–6, 151–52, 208 n.27; Pound on, 69; and Salome theme, 7
Fleischman, Avrom, 212 n.76, 214 n.98
Fleischmann, Martha, 95, 197 n.71